Maria Montessori

DOROTHY DAY
A Radical Devotion
Robert Coles

SIMONE WEIL
A Modern Pilgrimage
Robert Coles

MARGARET BOURKE-WHITE
A Biography
Vicki Goldberg
Foreword by Phyllis Rose

MARY CASSATT
Nancy Hale
Foreword by Eleanor Munro

THE THIRD ROSE
Gertrude Stein and Her World
John Malcolm Brinnin
Foreword by John Ashbery

MARGARET FULLER
From Transcendentalism to Revolution
Paula Blanchard
Foreword by Carolyn Heilbrun

CHARLOTTE MEW AND HER FRIENDS
Penelope Fitzgerald
Foreword by Brad Leithauser

THE ALCHEMY OF SURVIVAL
One Woman's Journey
John E. Mack, M.D.
with Rita S. Rogers, M.D.

EMILY DICKINSON
Cynthia Griffin Wolff
Foreword by R. W. B. Lewis

BALM IN GILEAD
Journey of a Healer
Sara Lawrence Lightfoot

MARIA MONTESSORI
A Biography
Rita Kramer

Published by Delacorte Press

HELEN AND TEACHER
The Story of Helen Keller and Anne Sullivan Macy
Joseph P. Lash

WOMEN OF CRISIS
Lives of Struggle and Hope
Robert Coles and Jane Hallowell Coles

WOMEN OF CRISIS II
Lives of Work and Dreams
Robert Coles and Jane Hallowell Coles

BUYING THE NIGHT FLIGHT
Georgie Anne Geyer

RADCLIFFE BIOGRAPHY SERIES

Maria Montessori
A Biography

Rita Kramer

Foreword by Anna Freud

A Merloyd Lawrence Book

ADDISON-WESLEY PUBLISHING COMPANY, INC.
Reading, Massachusetts   Menlo Park, California   New York
Don Mills, Ontario   Wokingham, England   Amsterdam   Bonn
Sydney   Singapore   Tokyo   Madrid   San Juan

Photographs dated 1913, 1919, 1949, circa 1950, and circa 1951 are reproduced with the kind permission of the American Montessori Society.

Library of Congress Cataloging-in-Publication Data

Kramer, Rita.
  Maria Montessori : a biography / Rita Kramer ; Foreword by Anna
Freud.
      p.   cm. — (Radcliffe biography series)
  Reprint. Originally published: Chicago: University of Chicago
Press, 1983, c1976.
  "Merloyd Lawrence book."
  Includes bibliographical references and index.
  ISBN 0-201-09227-1
  1. Montessori, Maria, 1870–1952.   2. Educators—Italy—Biography.
I. Title.   II. Series.
LB775.M8K7   1988
370'.92'4—dc19   88-22287
[B]

Cover design by Copenhaver Cumpston

ABCDEFGHIJ-HA-898

First printing, August 1988

For W.A.S.

Radcliffe Biography Series

Radcliffe College is pleased and proud to sponsor the Radcliffe Biography Series depicting the lives of extraordinary women.

Each volume of the series serves to remind us of two of the values of biographical writing. A fine biography is first of all a work of scholarship, grounded in the virtues of diligent and scrupulous research, judicious evaluation of information, and a fresh vision of the connections between persons, places, and events. Beyond this, fine biographies give us both a glimpse of ourselves and a reflection of the human spirit. Biography illuminates history, inspires by example, and fires the imagination to life's possibilities. Good biography can create lifelong models for us. Reading about other people's experiences encourages us to persist, to face hardship, and to feel less alone. Biography tells us about choice, the power of a personal vision, and the interdependence of human life.

The timeless women whose lives are portrayed in the Radcliffe Biography Series have been teachers, reformers, adventurers, writers, leaders, and scholars. The lives of some of them were hard pressed by poverty, cultural heritage, or physical handicap. Some of the women achieved fame; the victories and defeats of others have been unsung. We can learn from all of them something of ourselves. In sponsoring this series, Radcliffe College is responding to the continuing interest of our society in exploring and understanding the experience of women.

The Radcliffe Biography project found its inspiration in the publication in 1971 of *Notable American Women*, a scholarly encyclopedia sponsored by Radcliffe's Schlesinger Library on the history of women in America. We become convinced that some of the encyclopedia's essays should be expanded into full-length biographies, so that a wider audience could grasp the many contributions women have made to American life—an awareness of which is as yet by no means universal. Since then the concept of the series has expanded to include women of our own times and in other countries. As well as commissioning new biographies, we are also adding reprints of distinguished books already published, with forewords written for the series.

It seems appropriate that an institution dedicated to the higher education of women should sponsor such a project, to hold a mirror up

RADCLIFFE BIOGRAPHY SERIES

to the lives of particular women, to pay tribute to them, and so to deepen our understanding of them and of ourselves.

We have been joined in this project by a remarkable group of writers. I am grateful to them and to the editorial board—particularly to Deane Lord, who first proposed the series, both in concept and in detail. Finally, I am happy to present this volume in the Radcliffe Biography Series.

Matina S. Horner
President
Radcliffe College
Cambridge, Massachusetts

CONTENTS

Maria Montessori

Foreword by Anna Freud

Maria Montessori's personality and the value of her contributions justify the thorough, scrupulous description that is allotted to them in this book. Those who were aware only of the later effects of her work will now see her endeavours arranged in the historical context to which they owe their origin, and can follow the bitter struggle for social progress of which only a strong will like hers could be capable. Guided by the author in an enthralling manner, the reader will see develop before him the picture of Maria Montessori, who in 1896 was the first woman to become a physician in Italy. She was fascinated by the goal of improving the lot of poor, subnormal children who were disadvantaged both by physical constitution and circumstances. What followed, and is here made completely comprehensible for the first time, is her turning away from medicine to pedagogy, and the broadening of her circle of influence beyond her native Italy to all the countries of the world—an inevitable step of momentous importance for entire generations of normal children.

As a contemporary of Maria Montessori and her co-workers, I can attest from my own experience to the grateful enthusiasm which is described in this book, the enthusiasm with which her teachings were received and applied in many places and under many titles. Social workers, kindergarten teachers, child psychologists, and child psychoanalysts agreed in the conviction that the Montessori method in important aspects surpassed everything that had been offered to the educator up to then. In a 'Montessori Children's House' (like the one in Vienna) the child was master in his own house. For the first time his interest in the material on hand could develop freely, instead of being arranged as in the usual kindergarten in a prescribed group activity. For the first time not the praise and disapproval of adults, but joy in the success of one's own work came into its own as a suitable impetus. Above all, not authoritarian discipline, but freedom within carefully placed limits was the principle of education.

Today, twenty-five years after Maria Montessori's death, her teachings share the fate of other innovations that were pioneering in their time; they are not always applied in the pure form sanctioned by their originators, but have had to submit to amplifications and changes.

Furthermore, only a few of those who are active today along the lines of Maria Montessori share her own religious and sense-perception/psychological background. That, however, does not alter the fact that the most important elements of the Montessori method have entered into modern pedagogy in one form or another and have become indispensable components of the education of small children, components that cannot be ignored.

Preface

This book is an attempt to look at Maria Montessori's life and work in order to see who she was, where she came from, and what happened to her: to identify the intellectual influences on her thought and suggest the role of her personality in her work, not in order to diminish but to explain it—to show in just what her originality consisted. All ideas build on other ideas. The interesting thing is not that mere fact but which ones they were and how they were made use of and changed, combined and refined into something new.

Maria Montessori is much more complicated and interesting than the plaster saint her devoted followers have made her into. Under all the quasi-mystical reverence, the hagiography that has passed for biography, is a tough, intelligent woman who, at least in her youth, thought and did things no one had ever done before.

It is the search for that woman which motivated this attempt to go beyond a narrow cultist view of her self and her achievements, to introduce Maria Montessori to those to whom she remains unknown or misunderstood.

It is a search that led across several continents, into forgotten archives and into the memories of men and women whose lives she touched and often changed. What it revealed was a new woman—both in the sense in which Montessori herself used the term and in the biographer's sense.

Biographies of famous men and women go through stages which seem to obey a set of laws applying to all ideas. Every generation consists of revisionists. Early attempts to gather facts and interpret them are inevitably superseded by views based on new discoveries, new outlooks.

If this history of Montessori's life and work serves to stimulate further research into her achievements and new ways of looking at them, it will have accomplished its purpose—to reintroduce her to new generations as a teacher from whom they have learned much of what they know and from whom they may still learn—about children, about her, about themselves.

Acknowledgments

The success of a work like this, for which the sources are in large part materials which have not been previously collected or published, depends greatly on the cooperation of others. Foremost among those who helped make it possible for me to learn what I had to know in order to write this account of Maria Montessori's life and work were her son, Mario Montessori, and his wife, Ada Montessori-Pierson, whose generosity in providing documents and sharing their memories was equaled only by the freedom they allowed me to use what they made available in my own way, interpreting it according to my own point of view as it evolved in the course of research and writing. During the years that I worked on this book they repeatedly made time to talk with me at their home in Holland, where they received me with cordial hospitality and never made me feel that my questions were impertinent. Mario Montessori talked with me freely about the many years he spent assisting his mother in her work and her travels as well as about his own early childhood experiences and what he had been told about his mother's early life. Without his confidences it would have been impossible to see the story of her life in any wholeness.

Dr. Mario M. Montessori, Jr., Maria Montessori's grandson, shared with me his memories of his grandmother and his own view of her work as a psychoanalyst interested in child development.

Between visits, Mario and Ada Montessori answered numerous letters full of queries with detailed information gathered from letters and documents in their personal possession and in the offices of the Association Montessori Internationale in Amsterdam. I am particularly indebted to them for preparing from documents in their possession a detailed chronology of events in the lives of Maria Montessori's parents and of her early school years and for making available to me the contents of a book of press clippings put together by Alessandro Montessori in the first year of this century, a unique record of the public events in Maria Montessori's life in the years from 1892 to 1900. In addition, they gave me free access to the clippings and other materials in the AMI offices in Amsterdam, where I was helped in countless ways by its executive secretary Nicolette VanderHeide-Verschuur.

The contributions of the Montessori family extended to making no conditions as to my use of the material they provided. Much of the credit for the depth and breadth of the story told in the early pages of this book belongs to them; any limitations it has are my own. Although I had the unflagging cooperation of the Montessori family in the research on which this book is based, it is in no sense an "authorized" biography.

Many others made valuable contributions over the years:

Cleo Monson of the American Montessori Society opened her files and gave generously of her time and interest, and her assistant Judith Delman helped me locate many of Montessori's former pupils all over the world.

Many old friends and former students of Maria Montessori's shared their experiences and their impressions of her in letters and interviews. They are mentioned in the notes to the chapters in which their memories appear, but I would like to acknowledge in particular the interest shown by Elise Braun Barnett, Catherine Pomeroy Collins, Maria H. Mills, and Emma N. Plank, all of whom made singular contributions to the portrait of Montessori that emerges in these pages.

The first reader of early sections of the manuscript was my friend Diane Ravitch, whose own work in educational history suggested many ideas I applied in writing about the vicissitudes of the Montessori movement and whose encouragement was supplemented by the most practical kinds of help, not the least of which was inviting me to come with her to hear Lawrence A. Cremin lecture at Teachers College on the history of American education. Professor Cremin's lectures, and his book *The Transformation of the School: Progressivism in American Education, 1876–1957* (New York, 1961), illuminated the dominant social and intellectual trends of the time of Maria Montessori's confrontation with the American teaching establishment and suggested numerous fruitful ways of thinking about the nature of education and the role of the educator. I am indebted to him for suggesting many kinds of questions the biographer can ask of the historical data in order to arrive at what he calls "the imaginative reconstruction of the past."

Professor Salvatore Saladino of the Department of History of Queens College of the City University of New York generously supplemented what I learned from his *Italy from Unification to 1919* (New York, 1970) in conversations which furthered my understanding of the periods in Italian history in which Montessori grew up and attended school and in which she returned to work there during the Fascist regime.

Acknowledgments

Dr. Bernard C. Meyer and the other members of the study group on biography and psychoanalysis held under the auspices of the New York Psychoanalytic Institute shared their ideas about character and creativity and listened to portions of the work in progress with the interest in "what happened next" that is a writer's greatest encouragement.

I am grateful to my scholar-friends Perle Epstein, who read sections of the manuscript and made a number of ruthless and therefore useful suggestions, and Louise J. Kaplan, Professor of Psychology at New York University, whose knowledge of early childhood education and passionate interest in how women live their professional lives made her a stimulating critic of an early draft of the chapters on Montessori's youth and early career.

Margherita Repetto did much valuable research for me in Italian archives.

More personal kinds of thanks remain to be recorded:

To my husband Yale, who supported this project in every way from making it possible for me to give it my full time through three years of research and writing to taking an unflagging interest in its progress; my daughter Mimi, who acted on her belief that mothers should be encouraged to leave home and strike out on their own; and my old friend architect Lewis Davis and his partners at Davis, Brody & Associates, who provided me with a room of my own where I could build my book. And to my editor, Walter Betkowski, whose idea it was to begin with.

New York
August, 1975

Introduction

When the Hamburg-America Line's *Cincinnati* steamed into New York harbor on a cool December morning in 1913, a stout, smiling woman in black, wrapped in furs, her thick chestnut hair piled under a large black hat and veil, stood at the railing. She stood there quietly from the moment the New York skyline became visible until the liner had docked. "I must see everything," she said to a companion. She had begun as an observer, and the habit of observation had led her to this moment. The ship docked and she came down the gangplank with regal self-assurance, a motherly smile for the disciples and dignitaries who surrounded her six-deep, embracing, gesturing, speaking at once in excited Italian. It was a royal welcome.[1]

When Maria Montessori arrived in America at the end of 1913 she was at the height of her fame—indeed, one of the most famous women in the world. Newspapers, among them the august *New York Times,* devoted whole pages to interviews with her, and controversy about her ideas raged on the editorial pages and in letters-to-the-editors columns of all the major newspapers. The *New York Tribune* called her the most interesting woman in Europe. The *Brooklyn Daily Eagle* described her as "a woman who revolutionized the eduational system of the world . . . the woman who taught the idiot and the insane to read and write—whose success has been so wonderful that the Montessori method has spread into nation after nation as far east as Korea, as far west as Honolulu and south to the Argentine Republic." Even the conservative *New York Sun* noted her arrival in headlines, along with the fact that she brought with her "a new race plan."

An eager public was waiting for Montessori in America.

Her arrival shared front-page space with the activities of Pancho Villa in Mexico, the arrest ofthe militant suffragist Mrs. Pankhurst in England and President Wilson's refusal in Washington to make a public statement on the question of women's suffrage, and the recovery in Italy of the stolen "Mona Lisa" of Da Vinci. For many, although they didn't know it, it was the last good year, the year before the first of the world wars that would devastate Europe and change the world forever. Women still hobbled in long skirts, the construction of the Panama Canal was under way, and the help-wanted columns were full of ads for valets and ladies'

15

maids. Life was comfortable for an unprecedented number of Americans, and if there were also unprecedented numbers of immigrant poor, noblesse oblige still went along with privilege. The middle classes and the wealthy thought about education—to enrich the lives of their own children and to help civilize and Americanize the newly arrived urban hordes. The miracle-working woman doctor from Italy seemed to be bringing an answer to both needs.

Everywhere she went she was hailed as a prophet of pedagogy and a major force for wide social reforms, and by the time she sailed for home on Christmas Eve it seemed reasonable to suppose that American schools would never be the same again—at the very least, that Montessori would leave some lasting effect on education here.

History has a way of confounding expectation. Within five years Montessori was all but forgotten by the American public. Ten years later hardly anyone but a few professors of education knew her name.

And while many of her ideas took root in England, in Europe, and in Asia, they became enshrined in a movement that took on more and more of the character of a special cult rather than becoming part of the mainstream of educational theory and practice. She continued to work indefatigably, traveling throughout Europe and Asia, lecturing and writing, founding schools and teaching, until her death in Holland at the age of almost eighty-two. She had become a grande dame, a symbol to her devoted followers, little known to the rest of the world, no longer considered a major influence in educational thought but a historical relic. At the time of her death in 1952 many readers of her obituaries either did not know who she was or were surprised that she had still been alive and active in the postwar years. She seemed to belong to another time.

A decade after her death, half a century after her triumphant first visit to the United States, Montessori was rediscovered as the pendulum of school reform swung back to her view of the nature and aims of the educational process.

With the perspective of time, her genius becomes clearer. She remains one of the true originals of educational theory and practice.

PART I
The Early Struggles

1

For more than a century before it became a single unified nation in 1870, Italy had been a backwater of Western Europe. Most of the population of the various kingdoms, principalities, and duchies of the peninsula, particularly in the agrarian south, lived in miserable poverty, with an illiteracy rate second only to that of Portugal. New developments in European thought and politics were imported, usually some years late and in distorted form, and often the best of them failed to take root. Social reforms undertaken in other countries were untried if not unheard of in the Italian states. In the early nineteenth century the French, and after 1848 the Austrians, dominated the peninsula. A political bureaucracy endlessly fouled in red tape made it impossible'to get anything done. The absence of civil liberties and a free press, a school system a hundred years behind the times and attended by only a small fraction of the population, a superstitious and starving peasantry—all seemed like anachronisms in late-nineteenth-century Europe. Intellectuals and entrepreneurs alike wanted to bring Italy into the modern world but to do so it would be necessary to drive out foreign interests and subdue the power of the Catholic Church.

If the key to Italy's economic and social retardation was her division and subjection to foreign powers, then reform could be achieved only if Piedmont and Tuscany, Parma and Romagna, Umbria and the Marches, the Two Sicilies and all of the other separate states united to gain their independence and form one nation.

The Risorgimento was the liberal movement that expressed the awakening Italian national consciousness and sounded the call for freedom and unity. It began with the ideas of Mazzini and the arms of Garibaldi in the 1830s and 1840s. During the 1860s the king of Sardinia, Victor Emmanuel, and his minister the Count of Cavour succeeded in driving out the Austrians and united the peninsula with the annexation of the last of the Papal States in 1870. Italy was now one territorial entity. It remained to make it one nation.

Unification had changed the political format but hardly altered the social fabric in any radical way. The electorate consisted of a tiny minority—less than five percent of the male population—local bureaucracy was only reinforced by a new superstructure of central regulations, and an essentially conservative monarchy was in power.

19

The citizens of the new country remained deeply divided. The wealthy and well educated enjoyed power and privileges while the workers and the huge peasant population were no better off than they had been before. Unification had brought about neither political democracy nor social revolution. In fact, equality had never been an issue. Class differences were rigidly stratified and lines were drawn between north and south, urban businessmen and rural landowners, monarchists and republicans, those who favored loose federation and those who wanted a strong central government—and there was the perpetual church-state conflict between Catholics and atheistic liberals over who would control the education and therefore the minds of the young.

The papacy struck against the secular power that had annexed its territories by prohibiting the faithful to vote in the national elections, and a large segment of the population did not participate in politics on a national level until well into the twentieth century.

In the mid-1870s the government passed from the hands of the right to the left and a new collaboration of liberals and conservatives resulted in a middle-of-the-road program known as *transformismo,* dedicated to such basic reforms as extension of voting rights, civil liberties, greater equalization of the tax system, and the development and support of public education.

Even moderate reformers saw that education was the key to effective change. As prime minister, Cavour began to build schools that would be under state control, disestablished from the Church, which meanwhile maintained its own separate, parallel system of schools. Universal compulsory education on the elementary level—up to the third grade and between the ages of six and ten—had been on the books as early as 1859, but little effort had been made at enforcement. In 1860 three quarters of the population over ten could neither read nor write, with illiteracy highest in the south, where if parents decided they needed their children to work in the fields, no one would or could insist that they send them to school instead. Textile factories could legally employ nine-year-olds and many children were sent to work by families whose grinding poverty made eating more important than reading.

In 1877 a new law was passed to establish compulsory primary education for males and females in all eight thousand communes of the Italian kingdom in free nondenominational schools, but enforcement was still sporadic.

The new public educational system consisted of four years of primary school followed, from the age of ten, by either of two branches of secondary education. The classical program consisted of five years of *gin-*

nasio (junior high school) followed by three years of *liceo* (high school) and prepared for university entrance. The other alternative was seven years of scientific and technical education, "modern" as opposed to classical.

Female education had traditionally been private, the business of the family and the Church. Now public girls' schools were founded along with normal schools to train secular teachers for the new system of public instruction. But public schools continued to be primarily attended by boys, while girls predominated in the private Catholic schools.

The high hopes of the seventies and eighties turned to gradual disappointment by the end of the century. The bulk of the population remained destitute and illiterate. Workers put in an average of twelve hours a day in the fields and mines, and child labor was common in both.

There were repeated violations of freedoms of press and assembly by the federal government, strikes were illegal, and administrative corruption was rife. The enthusiasm of 1870 was overtaken by a creeping apathy, a dwindling belief in the possibility of any real reform in the face of the strangling regulations of rigid bureaucracy and the lack of concern for the education of the poor on the part of the monied and powered classes. Both the early hopes of reformers and their later disillusionment had their effect on Maria Montessori's education as a female and her career as a social reformer.

Maria Montessori was born in the town of Chiaravalle in the province of Ancona on August 31, 1870, in the very year that the new nation came into being. In the seaport of Ancona women still carried jars of water home from the ancient fountain on the hill overlooking the Adriatic. Below them was the modern town, noisy and crowded, with its wharves and sheds, its sprawling tenements. Here were the two worlds of Italy, the old and the new. Maria Montessori belonged to both; disciplined by the past, she set herself the task of helping to shape the future.

The spirit of the Risorgimento, and of the upper classes in the years that followed unification, was essentially anticlerical and strongly pro-science. The spirit of the enlightenment, like everything else, was late in coming to Italy. The newly united Italy of Maria Montessori's childhood was characterized by a mood and a reality. The initial impulse was post-revolutionary optimism and a new sense of hope for the oppressed—the poor and the female. However, the gradually emerging reality was that the working and living conditions of the agricultural workers in the south as well as those of the new class of urban industrial poor, the emigrants flocking to the cities from the fields, were still abysmal. The new awareness among the working classes found sympathy among a few, but most of the middle and upper classes saw it as a threat to the social fabric.

As a young girl Maria Montessori found it possible to bend the rules of the world she moved in to effect change for herself. She began by breaking the traditional barriers between males and females in education, as she would later break those between teacher and pupil, and in the process redefine the role of each. She managed her career and her own education with the attitude that change was possible and with the conviction that she could effect it. And she brought that general attitude and that personal conviction to bear on the social problems she saw around her.

Maria's father, Alessandro Montessori, was an old-fashioned gentleman of conservative temper and military habits. He had been a soldier in his youth, became a civil servant later in life, and belonged to a generation that welcomed the creation of the New Italy but found itself bewildered by many of the changes that came with it. He wore his decorations, including the ribbon of a Cavaliere, proudly, and was equally proud of his handsome wife and her impressive lineage.

He was born in August 1832 in Ferrara, the son of Nicola Montessori, who had come from Bologna, where he had been employed, probably in a middle-managerial capacity, at a tobacco warehouse. Alessandro studied rhetoric and arithmetic, wrote with a fine hand, and spoke only Italian.[1]

In the fervor of revolution that swept Europe in 1848 Italians from the various kingdoms and principalities that made up the still-to-be-unified country joined forces in an abortive attempt to liberate the country from Austrian rule. Young Alessandro Montessori took part in one of the early battles for liberation that eventually led to unification and was decorated in 1849. The following year he went to work for the papal state as a clerk in the finance department, a post from which he asked to be dismissed in 1853. For the next five years he was employed at the salt factories of Comacchio and Cervia and then as an inspector in the salt and tobacco industries of Bologna and Faenza, becoming an inspector for the ministry of finance in 1859 and an accountant in its departments of salt and tobacco manufacture in 1863. In 1865 he was sent to Chiaravalle, a town in the fertile valley of the Esino River where tobacco was grown and processed. Grain, wine grapes, and olives were also grown in the surrounding countryside, and small glass, ceramic, and leather factories in the town itself added a population of manual workers and middle-class managers to the landowners and farmers. Chiaravalle was a typical provincial town in an agricultural area, and probably stifling to anyone with unconventional interests or aspirations.

When Alessandro Montessori went there he was thirty-three, a successful government official involved in the financial management of the state-run tobacco industry. Whatever his revolutionary dreams or memories, he had become a respectable member of the bourgeois civil service.

It was then that he met Renilde Stoppani, a member of a landed family and eight years his junior. She was unusually well educated for the time, a girl who devoured books in a town in which it was a matter of pride to be able to write one's name. She was also fiercely patriotic, devoted to the ideals of liberation and union for Italy, and in Alessandro she met a man who, unlike many Catholic provincials, shared her ideals.

They were married in the spring of 1866 and the following year his work took them to Venice. In 1869 they returned to Chiaravalle, and Maria was born the following year. The existence of a finance official of Alessandro's level was a mobile one, the government transferring him from factory to factory in various regions, and when Maria was three, the Montessoris moved to Florence.

They were an attractive couple: he with curly dark hair and a drooping moustache; she fashionably plump, dark-eyed, and soft-featured. When they walked in the town, Alessandro in a business suit adorned with a dangling watch chain and Renilde in matronly black, her lace collar set off by a small gold cross and a single rose in the dark curls piled atop her head, they seemed the very image of respectability and prosperity.

In 1875, when Maria was five, Alessandro was transferred again, this time to Rome, as an accountant first-class. It was their last move. The Montessoris remained in Rome, Alessandro continuing to advance by stages and being rewarded for his long years of loyal and efficient service with the title of Cavaliere in the Order of the Corona d'Italia in 1880, when Maria was ten, and the Order of St. Maurizio e Lazzaro in 1890, the year before his retirement. In the late nineteenth century the title of *cavaliere*—originally the equivalent of an English knighthood—was bestowed by the government for many kinds of small services on the part of businessmen as well as politicians. One premier remarked that "Italy is governed by decorations," and Victor Emmanuel II used to say, "A cavalier's cross or a cigar is a thing one can refuse to no one."[2] The right to use the title did bestow a certain social distinction; at the very least it separated one from the common horde.

MARIA MONTESSORI: A BIOGRAPHY

In the beginning it was not always easy for Alessandro Montessori to accept the pace at which his world was changing or to adjust to it. His wife, however, was more receptive to the promise of change. In fact, she welcomed it, particularly for her only child.

Renilde Stoppani was a niece of Antonio Stoppani, a distinguished scholar-priest to whom the University of Milan erected a monument when death ended his tenure there in 1891. A professor of geology, he was well known not only as a naturalist, but as a liberal cleric who argued for a rapprochement between church and state under the new regime to which so many orthodox members of the Catholic hierarchy remained bitterly opposed in the two decades following unification.

Stoppani was a poet as well as the author of numerous scientific works, the founder of a liberal journal in which he sought to reconcile the spirit of the natural sciences with that of religion. *Il dogma e le scienze positive* was published when his great-niece Maria was sixteen. A dozen years later she was urging the application of that same scientific positivism to social problems in Italy.

Stoppani's outlook and achievements were part of Maria's legacy from her mother. Another was a childhood which made her strong enough and sure enough of herself to pattern her life on his kind of achievement rather than on the traditional woman's role.

The facts about Montessori's childhood are scanty. Most of what has been recorded about her early years is anecdote, stories retold years later by devoted followers remembering events she had described to them, her memories and theirs colored by the passage of years in which she had become famous, and creating—whether consciously or unconsciously—a legend that is effective, like all stories of a hero's childhood, because of historical irony: what we are told about the past takes on its significance only in the light of what we know was to come.

Her lifelong collaborators Anna Maccheroni and E. M. Standing[3] have told about her childhood in memoirs that contain many contradictions, omissions, and mistaken dates. Yet a portrait does emerge—a sketch and not a photograph, but a recognizable individual.

Renilde Montessori believed in God, for all her liberal ideas. It was possible to be anticlerical without being irreligious. She also believed in disciplining children firmly. Once, when the family returned from a month's vacation to a house that needed to be put in order again, little Maria complained she was hungry and demanded something to eat. Renilde said she would have to wait a while, but Maria insisted on being fed right away. Renilde found a piece of month-old bread in a cupboard and said, "If you can't wait, take this." Indulgence was not part of Maria's upbringing.

She was expected to help her less fortunate neighbors, and had a daily quota of knitting to do for the poor. She took an interest in a hunchbacked girl who lived nearby and took her out for frequent walks until it occurred to Renilde that the striking contrast between the two girls probably made these public excursions more of a pain than a pleasure for Maria's companion and that it might be preferable to find other ways of helping her.

Little Maria assigned herself the job of washing a certain number of squares whenever the tile floor had to be cleaned, an experience she must have enjoyed and which sounds strikingly like what later came to be known as "exercises of practical life" in the Montessori school.

Another early childhood memory involved Maria's role as peacemaker between her parents. She heard them quarreling, dragged a chair over to where they stood, and climbed up on it, taking both their hands and clasping them together in hers and thus, we are led to believe, reconciling the family.

The Montessoris did not move to Rome when Maria was twelve "so as to be able to give their only child a better education than Ancona could offer,"[4] as Standing later wrote, but because Alessandro Montessori's work brought them there when she was, in fact, five. Even today it would be unusual for a family to uproot itself and move to another city so that a five-year-old girl could have a better education. In those days, in that society, to a man of Cavaliere Montessori's temperament and views, it would have seemed absurd. But they probably did welcome, may even have sought the transfer from a provincial to a more sophisticated environment. It is certain that Renilde Montessori would not have been unaware of the advantages Rome would afford her only child.

At the time it was joined to the rest of Italy by plebiscite in 1870, Rome was an isolated city, an urban island in the sea of untouched countryside known as the Roman Campagna—eight hundred square miles, half a million acres of untilled grazing land. Sheep and cattle still roamed the vast rolling prairie, the land was uncultivated, the malarial swamps undrained. The next decade saw dramatic growth. By the time the Montessoris came there in 1875, they joined a growing urban middle class formed by nobles and landowners, many of whom had lost their money and their property and come to the towns to marry and settle down, while at the same time peasants flocked to the cities in search of something better than the bare subsistence they could scrape out of the impoverished countryside.

25

MARIA MONTESSORI: A BIOGRAPHY

The city has always been a teacher, and if the Montessoris did not move to Rome primarily for the sake of their young daughter, the fact remains that she would benefit from the move. She would grow up in the capital, a cultural center where there were a number and variety of institutions—a university, libraries, museums—not available in Ancona. In addition there was the lively atmosphere created by the presence of theaters, opera, the cafés that were gathering places of intellectuals, journalists, artists. There were more newspapers to read, more kinds of people to meet.

Like most Roman families the Montessoris lived in an apartment rather than a private house, another circumstance which meant freer contact for a child with other people, the neighboring families and their children.

When Maria was six she was enrolled in the first grade of the public school on the Via di San Nicolo da Tolentino. While she undoubtedly had better teachers, more stimulating companions, and attended a more modern school building in Rome than if she had gone to school in the provinces, the entire educational system of the country, including that of the capital, left much to be desired.

At the turn of the century an English historian of modern Italy could still write, "Education is the gloomiest chapter in Italian social history."[5] The new kingdom had set about the job of reforming the backward school system with zeal and good intentions, but was defeated by a system in which "laws and codes and ministerial circulars hurtle against each other, confusing all stability with their ill-ordered contradictions."[6] Between 1860 and 1900 there were thirty-three ministers of education, each with his own policies and none with enough government funds to accomplish anything at all. What they succeeded in producing was a seeming infinity of laws, codes, circulars—many of them contradictory— in what one writer of the time described as "self-destructive profusion."

In Montessori's childhood, elementary education was a local affair, in the hands of the individual communes. Most provincial administrative officials were men whose own education was impressive only in a community in which half the population could neither read nor write. Those who made official decisions about the schools were usually innocent of any ideas about education, having had little or none themselves, and their ignorance was matched only by their prejudice. They housed their schools in stables and kept their teachers waiting for months for their inadequate salaries. Some fired their teachers at the end of two years rather than provide the automatic raise in salary the law demanded. Often, they would then reappoint them at the old salary.

* * *

The Early Struggles

The typical Italian elementary school of the time was crowded and dirty, presided over by a schoolmaster or mistress who earned as little as the equivalent of $120 a year—less for women than for men. Most of them were men and women struggling to make their way out of the peasantry and gain a precarious footing in the lower middle classes. Not only were they miserably paid, but they garnered little prestige in the community to compensate for the lack of its material rewards. Often required to teach three grades of boys and girls, their own education seldom went much beyond a competence in the three Rs. The two methods of learning most employed were drill and more drill. Their work consisted primarily of seeing that the required exercises were performed by the students; they did not impart knowledge themselves about the ideas of the past or the world of the present.

In the schools of the smaller communes, which stopped at the third-grade level, the children, who often spoke only their native dialect, were taught Italian, the rudiments of reading and writing, a fair amount of arithmetic, and a smattering of natural science. In larger towns like Rome, where Maria went to school and where the schools went beyond third grade, pupils learned some history and geography, more elementary science and some geometry. In those schools that went beyond third grade, boys and girls were required to be separated.

There were seldom enough books, sometimes not even a map of Italy, often no ink or pens or other kinds of teaching materials. Religious instruction was not required by law but was often provided by the commune, particularly in the small towns where parents of the community were likely to demand it.

Even in the schools of a city like Rome, it was not a system that did much to develop young minds or encourage imagination.

Maria was not a precocious child. According to her grandson, she was considered a sweet, not especially bright little girl, and that was how she thought of herself. Her mother saw special qualities in her, but she did not stand out in her first years in school. In first grade, she was awarded her first distinction, a certificate for good behavior, and in second grade she received another award for *lavori donneschi*, "women's work," which meant sewing and other kinds of needlework. She seems to have been uncompetitive academically. When she saw a classmate crying because she hadn't been promoted to another class, Maria couldn't understand her emotion. One room, she told the other girl, seemed just as good to her as another.

For a time, like many young girls, she wanted to become an actress. She did not even think of an academic career. But when she found that she learned easily and did well on her exams she concluded that "it

27

would be nonsense not to do so." She began to study with such single-mindedness that once when she was taken to the theater she took her math book along and studied in the semidarkness during the performance.[7]

There was a certain note of authority to her personality. In games with other children she was usually the leader. Playmates sometimes objected to the contemptuous way she could treat them. She had a strong, sometimes flippant way about her. Those she disapproved of she dismissed with a phrase like "You! You aren't even *born* yet," or "Please remind me that I've made up my mind never to speak to you again." She held her own with adults too. When a teacher objected to the expression in "those eyes," Maria responded by never raising her eyes in that teacher's presence again.

Looking back on her school days years later, Maria Montessori remembered a teacher who made her pupils memorize the stories of the lives of great women of the past, urging them to follow in their footsteps and become famous themselves someday. Young Maria's response to this exhortation was that she cared too much for the children of the future to add another biography to the list.

One of the stories about Montessori's childhood recounted by Anna Maccheroni, who was herself a very old woman when she told it, is of the ten-year-old Maria, seriously ill, telling her anxious mother, "Do not worry, Mother, I cannot die; I have too much to do."

These events may or may not have happened in just the way they were remembered by Montessori and repeated by her devotees. But at the very least they tell us how Montessori thought of herself as a child and probably something of how she appeared to others. The girl that comes through these stories is self-confident, strong-willed, a little smug. She has the sense of duty that sometimes makes for intolerance of others. In short, a born social reformer. Certainly a striking maverick in that time and place.

With an irrepressible enthusiasm that probably owed more to Renilde's stimulation and encouragement than to anything that happened in school, young Maria read books, asked questions, and began to think of going on with her education. By this time, possibly influenced by exposure to her father's work as an accountant, she had developed a passionate interest in mathematics, and some ideas of her own about her future. Most of the relatively small number of girls who then went beyond elementary school in the public educational system pursued the classical course. At twelve, Maria had decided that she wanted to go on to a technical school and, as usual, she had her way.

The choice seems a strange one, and suggests a number of questions about the character of this strong-willed twelve-year-old, although it raises more questions than can be answered with any certainty. Was she fulfilling the fantasies of a mother who identified with her own scholar-uncle and felt her own life had been unfulfilled? Was she rebelling against a father who tried to impose too narrow a set of conditions on her for winning his love and approval—that she be a model young lady of the time rather than a "masculine" achiever? Surely she was less singular in possessing strengths and abilities not encouraged in females of her world than in her determination to pursue them, to make her way in a man's world on what were then a man's terms. As a young child she had been bossy; now she had become competitive. She knew what she was good at, she welcomed challenge, she chose the more difficult course rather than avoiding it. And she chose it to please herself. The choice would certainly not please anyone else—with the single and important exception of her mother.

It must be added that while she was not born into a world that expected her to assert herself, to strive to fulfill herself in ways that were not considered appropriate for females, it was a world that no longer made it impossible to do so.

Montessori belonged to the first generation to grow up in the years following unification. She was a child while the bloom was still on the hopes of the Risorgimento, and her character and outlook on life were already formed by the time disillusionment had set in. Her self-confidence, her optimism, her interest in change, and her belief in the possibility of effecting it were certainly formed by the interaction of her robust, aggressive constitution and the child-rearing practices of her mother. But if her basic outlook on life was defined in that earliest relationship, it could only have been reinforced by the cultural climate of the years in which she first became aware of the world, went to school, listened to the talk of grown-ups, found role models among them. It was a time in which people liked to quote the statesman Massimo d'Azeglio: "Italy is made; we must now make the Italians." One observer wrote, "There is a widespread conviction among the present generation of Italians that all of them have more or less borne a hand in 'making' their country."[8] And an American visitor noted that "there is a rage for education in new Italy."[9] This was the dominant mood of the country in the years following unification, the years in which Montessori was growing up.

With the general trend toward liberalization of social institutions, the role of women was beginning to change. One observer wrote in the

1880s, when Maria Montessori was a teenager: "The practice of immuring tender girls into a nunnery till the time comes to give them up to a husband they have never seen or heard of is being rapidly discontinued; and very creditable free lay institutions for the instruction of girls of every rank and condition of life are rising in almost every important town in the Peninsula. . . . Still, the notion that the mother's home is the best school for a girl to be reared in is almost universally prevalent . . . a girl in Italy is too generally looked upon as the most brittle piece of china, which the least touch can crack."[10]

Well into the 1890s it was not considered proper for women—even married women, even the middle-aged—to venture out on the streets alone, and young girls never went out unaccompanied. Legally the position of women was still so primitive that no married woman could write a check on her own account; whatever money she had was the property of her husband. She could not give evidence in a court of law without his presence. For most middle-class women, it was a dull, empty life. An Englishwoman who married an Italian nobleman and went to live in a village on the Adriatic coast, not far from Maria Montessori's birthplace, wrote of provincial bourgeois Italian women: "One favourite amusement was to light box after box of Lucifer matches, which was acknowledged to be wasteful, but it made the time pass."[11]

It was a culture in which women could be saints but not senators. But there were, in the somewhat more permissive climate of the years after unification, some women who cracked the mold. Renilde Stoppani Montessori was a woman in transition. Her own life was conventional, but she encouraged her daughter to break the stereotyped role. From the little we know about her, there emerges an impression of strength and discipline. Not a woman to sit around lighting matches, she must have been a trial if not a tribulation to the more conventional Cavaliere. The story Montessori told years later of climbing up on a chair as a small child to join her parents' hands and restore peace when they had quarreled does establish the fact that they sometimes quarreled. One wonders about what. About her? It is clear that the two Montessori parents did not see eye-to-eye on what was desirable for their talented, headstrong daughter. And while she remained close to her father until his death, she never made a secret of the fact that it was her mother who had encouraged all her early dreams and ambitions, sat up late with her talking over her work and her plans, and—we would guess—took a vicarious pleasure in her maverick daughter's efforts and successes.

Those early efforts—even the successes—must have seemed outrageous to her father. What a nineteenth-century Roman civil servant and cavaliere wanted—expected—of a daughter was that she possess the social graces admired by the community. Intelligence and wit were admirable qualities—in their place. And that place was in the family—first her father's, then her husband's. Maria's interests and ambitions must have appalled him at the same time that they gratified Renilde.

Maria was persistent. Her mother was sympathetic, and just as stubborn. Together, they prevailed.

Maria entered the Regia Scuola Tecnica Michelangelo Buonarroti in the fall of 1883, just turned thirteen.

It was the next step on in an educational world from which she would both take what she could and find much to rebel against later.

The technical school Maria entered was no more liberating than her earlier schooling had been. If the Italian elementary system suffered from the lack of imaginative policy or competent leadership that resulted from local control, the secondary and higher education systems, which were run by the national government, suffered as much from the opposite situation—overcentralization.

After unification the Italian government had adopted the French system of political administration, its separate districts organized under a highly centralized government. The secondary schools and universities, like everything else run by the government, were all but strangled by a ubiquitous and top-heavy bureaucracy and its endless red tape.

Regulations ruled supreme in the secondary schools of Montessori's time. One uniform curriculum was imposed by the central Ministry of Education in all schools from one end of Italy to the other.

The ministry determined what would be taught, hired (it seldom found cause to fire) teachers, and made up all examinations. The examinations alone determined a student's progress—whether he was to go on, be left back, or—in extreme cases—be expelled. They were the single deciding factor in whether a student went on to the university and therefore controlled his entire future.

At the end of the year a student in the urban north and one in the agrarian south would both sit down at the same moment to answer the same questions made up by a civil servant totally unacquainted with the school or the larger community of either one. A contemporary account of the results tells us that "the ministry is so overwhelmed with petty details as to the state of the desks in the lyceum at Foggia, or the unsuitable accommodations for the porter at the technical school in Udine, that he has little time to think of wide schemes of reform. With every new Minister of Education a change of regulations and the course of study takes place. There is no time for real reforms, but one subject is substituted for another, written papers are introduced for mathematics and suppressed in Greek, the standard of marks is changed—for six months. Then comes a cabinet crisis and the new minister reverts to the old plan or introduces some fresh novelty, to be rescinded in its turn by his successor."[12]

It was a system that could not have been better designed to quash individuality, but it failed to quash Maria's. And when she eventually turned her attention to education per se, it gave her a clear model of what a school should *not* be.

The secondary schools were divided into the classical and the technical systems. The classical consisted of five years of the *ginnasio*, from age ten or eleven to fifteen or sixteen, followed by three years of the *liceo*, and stressed literature and the classics. In the typical classroom students sat immobile for hours learning their hated Latin and Greek by rote under the supervision of tyrannical pedants, bitter and underpaid, all for the sake of a diploma that was a necessary passport to any further education, any future career.

The technical system provided seven years of a modern curriculum. These schools offered a three-year course including French, arithmetic and bookkeeping, algebra and geometry, history, geography, and a smattering of science. This was followed by the four-year course at the technical institute which offered modern languages—French, German, English—and mathematics, in addition to commercial subjects. Physics and chemistry were included but occupied a less important place in the curriculum.

There was a syllabus to be taught in every subject, and most teaching was by means of this printed text only, which pupils were required to memorize and repeat. It was heresy to dissent in any way from the ideas as presented in the syllabus. Even a subject like botany was learned from a textbook; pupils sat at their desks and studied a diagram of a leaf; they did not observe nature, were not given a real leaf to hold, look at, take apart.

The school term lasted from mid-October to mid-June. Pupils usually came to school for three hours in the morning, went home for the midday meal, and returned for two hours in the afternoon. They listened to lectures, repeated their lessons, and submitted the written exercises they did at home or in the library. No actual work was done in class.

As might be expected, "cribbing" was common in a system in which work was done outside of school and passing exams was almost literally a matter of life or death.

Regular attendance was insisted on, physical immobility was enforced, everyone moved at the same pace over the same material at the same time, and knowledge was something to be passively ingested, not a matter of ideas to be questioned or discussed. The school taught a body of facts, certain techniques and skills, and taught them in a punitive atmosphere. It did not teach love of learning or how to think independently.

It was a system that from first grade through the university required of the student only that he obediently receive information from an authority and then prove his ability to repeat it back in the same form on command. In primary and secondary school one acquired a set of skills by means of tightly supervised day-by-day drill. In the university one used those skills to ingest a rigidly defined body of knowledge on one's own. As a girl, Maria must have had an unusual capacity to resist conformity, to form her own judgments, and to retain confidence in her own way of perceiving the world and her place in it. Only a certain eccentricity of mind and a forceful character could survive such a system with the ability to see things freshly and reassemble the elements of experience in novel ways. It is usually called genius, and it is what Montessori had. What she used it for was to show how that system, which taught, but did not educate, could be radically changed.

At the technical school no one knew what to do about the girl students at recess time—they couldn't mix with the boys and had to be protected from teasing—and so they spent the period shut off in a room by themselves. Maria took Italian literature, history and geography, mathematics, drawing and calligraphy in her first year and did well in all her subjects although her highest marks were for conduct—she did rather poorly in drawing, in which she evidently found it more difficult to be attentive than in her academic subjects.

She graduated from the technical school in the spring of 1886 with high marks in all of her subjects and a final grade of 137 out of a possible 150, a very creditable showing. She continued to do well in the technical institute, the Regio Istituto Tecnico Leonardo da Vinci, which she attended from 1886 to 1890. She studied modern languages and natural science, but her favorite subject, and the one in which she excelled, was mathematics. To the disbelief of her father, who was prepared to concede that a modern woman might become a teacher but could think of no other acceptable role besides that of wife and mother, it occurred to Maria that she wanted to do what so many of her fellow students in the technical institute were planning to do—become an engineer.

There is a splendid irony in the adolescent Maria's adamant refusal even to consider teaching as her future career.

By the time she was ready to graduate from the technical institute, she had changed her mind about engineering, but any relief her father might have felt at her abandonment of this inappropriate career choice was short-lived. She had become increasingly interested in the biological sciences. Now she gave up the idea of becoming an engineer for that of studying medicine—something no woman in Italy had ever done.

What changed her mind, her old friend Anna Maccheroni reported years later, was a kind of mystical experience: "She herself cannot explain how it came about. It happened all in a moment. She was walking in a street when she passed a woman with a baby holding a long, narrow, red strip of paper. I have heard Dr. Montessori describe this little street scene and the decision that then came to her. At such times there was in her eyes a long deep look, as if she were searching out things which were far beyond words. Then she would say, 'Why?' and with a little expressive movement of her hand indicate that there are strange things happening within us guiding us toward an end we do not know."[13]

The significance of the experience is hard to explain. We can only wonder what thoughts or what fantasies in Montessori's mind at the time came to be represented by the image of what she had actually beheld at the moment she remembered as so decisive for her future life, the image of a child holding a red paper.

In any case, it was not the last time Montessori would explain a crucial life decision in terms of an intuitive rather than a rational process.

Relatives and friends of the family were shocked and disapproving, especially her father. He stopped short of actually forbidding her, however, and she managed to make an appointment to see Guido Baccelli, the professor of clinical medicine at the University of Rome. Baccelli not only headed the medical faculty but was a member of the Chamber of Deputies, where in an elegant classical rhetorical style he had introduced legislation for the reform of the entire school system through the university level. But innovation obviously had its limits, and they did not extend to admitting a woman to the school of medicine. Baccelli served as minister of public instruction in several cabinets in the eighties and nineties and their paths would cross again, but on this occasion their interview consisted of his firm refusal to encourage her plan to apply for admission to the medical school. She remembered later that they had a pleasant talk and that when they shook hands as she was leaving she said, "I *know* I shall become a doctor." What he thought of her persistence we can only guess.

Maria enrolled in the University of Rome in the fall of 1890 as a student of physics, mathematics, and natural sciences. She devoted herself single-mindedly to her studies, poring over thick volumes of zoology and botany, physics and chemistry, late into the nights while the other young women she knew were reading romances and dreaming of homes and husbands. When she passed her examinations, including Italian and Latin, in the spring of 1892, with a final grade of 8 out of a possible 10 points, she received the Diploma di licenza that made her eligible—except for the fact that she was a woman—to begin the actual study of medicine, the four years of courses in anatomy and pathology and clinical work which followed the two years of premedical scientific study and led to the medical degree.

For the capable young woman student of the sciences to go on into the department of clinical medicine was not only unprecedented, it was unthinkable. However, unperturbed by the general disapproval she met with, and supported in her ambitions by her mother, Maria persisted until she was accepted. There is no record of how she managed it, what strings were pulled, what officials appealed to until the rules were relaxed for her. All we know is that, with a perseverance that was characteristic of her, she did manage it.

Montessori herself was quoted as saying, in interviews she gave some twenty years later, that she had appealed to the Pope and that it was due to his intervention on her behalf that she was allowed to study medicine. An article published at the time of her first American visit says that "it was due to the late Pope Leo XIII that she was able to be the first woman to enter the Medical College in Rome" and quotes her as saying, "There was much opposition. Leo told me he believed medicine was a noble profession for a woman."[14] And, according to a similar report in another newspaper of the day, "In the end Pope Leo XIII issued a statement in which he said the best profession a woman could enter was medicine and this put a stop to the protest."[15]

However, both articles are rather careless in dealing with other facts that can be checked and it is hard to know what the reporters' fancy made of remarks translated from Montessori's Italian. Still another newspaper account gives the impression that the Pope made his statement later, quoting Montessori as having said, "The fact that a woman was studying medicine caused such a furore in Rome that at last Pope Leo XIII came to my rescue. The Holy Father gave it as his opinion that medicine was a profession pre-eminently suited for women, and one which they should take up. That changed matters considerably."[16] Whether the Pope was actually instrumental in the decision that was made to admit her to medical school or supported that decision in a statement made afterward is a question shrouded in a journalistic mist.

35

2

Some idea of what a radical event Maria's presence in the medical school was, and how shocking it was that a woman should work side by side with men examining a patient or studying the human body, can be gathered from the fact that in 1912, when Abraham Flexner wrote his influential report on medical education in Europe, women medical students in Berlin had a dissecting room of their own. In the sciences Germany was a leader of modern Europe; its educational institutions were models. Yet the status of women in those institutions up to World War I had reached no further than separate but equal. Flexner considered it noteworthy enough to point out that there were some places where "men and women attend the same classes and demonstrations and dissect at the same tables." And this was twenty years after Maria Montessori made her first appearance at a class in the medical school of the University of Rome.

When Montessori was a student at the university it was an institution that, like the city itself, reflected the restlessness of Italy.

In 1892–93 riots by peasants and socialists were suppressed by the military under the Crispi government but had an effect nevertheless. If they achieved nothing else they called widespread public attention to increasingly intolerable social conditions.

During the nineties the University of Rome was considered by many to be a seedbed of Marxist thought. Socialist philosopher-statesman Antonio Labriola was one of those who lectured there. A growing number of radical socialist periodicals appeared, and a survey of two hundred leading intellectuals in 1895 found that two thirds favored socialism to some degree—more than three quarters of the scientists among them expressing complete support. Among socialist deputies there was a high proportion of physicians and university professors, including a professor of anthropology. According to philosopher Benedetto Croce, to have been indifferent to socialism at the time was a sure mark of intellectual inferiority.

In such an atmosphere Montessori was bound to think in terms of social reform, not just of how to use her newly acquired status and skills to organize her own life but to make a contribution to society.

Despite the climate of radical thought among the more politically aware faculty and students, the university in which Montessori studied

36

medicine and later taught was a peculiar institution which has to be understood in the context of the society of which it was an arm—highly bureaucratized and rigidly stratified. As a degree-granting institution it existed to confer status, to define social place, more than it did to educate in the real sense of the word. The fact that in such an institution Montessori was able to educate herself in a way that went beyond the requirements for certification was remarkable—and doubly so for a woman.

The University of Rome was a state institution, supported by the government. There were four faculties—classics and philosophy, mathematics and science, medicine, and law—with a combined student body of about fifteen hundred and a teaching staff of around a hundred. There was one full professor in every subject. All of the stress was on acquiring the diploma that automatically conferred social prestige in a society in which anyone engaged in business, manufacturing, or agriculture was considered inferior to anyone with the title of doctor, professor, or lawyer, whether or not he practiced his profession.

Italian universities of the time, like so many other government-run institutions, were a maze of red tape. Regulations took precedence over learning. It was a system in which all funds had to be allocated by the central government—not one lira could be spent without being approved. As one member of the faculty described the situation, "If a retort is broken in a chemistry laboratory, the affair must go and come from the laboratory to the Ministry of Public Instruction."[1] The curriculum, the examinations—their dates and every detail of their contents—were all fixed by official regulations from above and all questions of change of any kind had to be decided by the ministry.

The faculty in such a situation was forced to be more concerned with ministerial requirements than with effective teaching and learning. "There is no question of doing well or ill," a faculty member complained. "The whole concern is that the Regulations should not be contravened."[2]

The professor was there not primarily to teach but to oversee the teaching of his subject, often by assistants. The professor himself was the undisputed authority in his field and therefore enjoyed immense prestige.

The university existed primarily to administer examinations, a highly ritualized set of hurdles marking the progress of the student toward his diploma, and he could prepare himself for them as he saw fit as long as he produced the required answers—all of which could be found in his lecture notes. Sometimes these would be given out by the faculty; at other times students would exchange and circulate lecture notes among themselves.

The student registered for a certain number of courses, prepared himself for examinations while living at home, and often found it possible to present himself for examinations and even to pass them without having attended more than a sufficient number of lectures to be recognizable to the instructor as someone he had seen before.

The faculty at the university did include many professors with European reputations as well as some politicians of note, intellectuals taking a significant part in the governments that came into power, fell, and returned again in the game of musical chairs that was Italian politics. A professor's salary was small, but his duties were minimal. The university was in session only six months of the year, during which time he was usually required to give no more than three lectures a week, and these could be repeated to one group of students after another. Little more was required beyond the occasional conferences requested by the more diligent students, of whom Montessori was always one. Members of the medical faculty usually carried on a private practice as well.

Classes began in November, when, according to a writer of the time, the student "attends the lectures—or he does not."[3] The accepted system was to take notes on the lectures or borrow someone else's and read them during the last weeks before the final examination at the end of the year. A certificate of attendance had to be signed by the professor, but his signature was seldom refused unless the student had *never* been seen at his lectures.

The examinations lasted half an hour, were oral, and were strictly limited to what was covered in the lectures. No extra reading was necessary or expected; a student who memorized his lecture notes were was sure to pass with high marks. In such a system few students ever failed to pass their university exams. The medical faculty was stricter than those of law or philosophy—there was always the chance that the student might wind up practicing on patients—but in general a few weeks' cramming at the end of the term could produce good enough results to satisfy the examiners—the professor of the subject, another professor, and one outsider.

In this diploma mill Montessori stood out not only by virtue of her sex but—what her fellow students must have resented even more—because of her attitude that she was there to learn. She attended all of the lectures and inevitably attracted the attention of the leading lights of the faculty—those men of some professional distinction who cared about their subject and appreciated a student who took a genuine interest in it.

During her years as a medical student Montessori, like all students at the university, lived at home with her family. There was little real university life. She attended lectures and went home to go over her notes and read. There was no supervision over one's study during the year and little contact outside of the lectures between faculty and students. What contact she had with professors—and she made herself known to those whose work especially interested her—was undertaken at her own initiative. As the first woman in the student body she would have stood out in any case, but as the years went on she began to attract attention for the quality of her work and the extent of her interest and initiative.

What student life there was centered on occasional festivals and charity entertainments. The chief occupations of university students of the time, as described by a contemporary observer, were "walking about the town, dropping into the cafés, and rioting."[4]

Official discipline was as lax as official rules and regulations were numerous. One of the rules was that examinations could be given only in courses in which the entire series of lectures had been completed, and students who wanted to cut down the number of examinations they had to take in a given year staged frequent riots, which would result in the closing down of classes before the end of the term and thus in fewer courses to be examined on that year. The head of the university was powerless in the face of these riots. If he called in the police, the press and politicians in the Chamber of Deputies would condemn his attack on academic freedom and the minister of education, to whom he owed his appointment, could very well be ousted in a cabinet crisis.

Here is one particularly enraged contemporary commenting on the state of the universities in the late 1880s:

> The Italian student has his university almost in his own street, next door to his father's house. He studies in his class, but lives with his family. For a few hours of the morning or afternoon he may have college duties, but the remainder of the day is at his own disposal, and nothing interferes with his domestic habits or social engagements. He can freely frequent his café, his theater, dividing his time between duty and pleasure like any other grown-up idle individual. . . . The whole class he belongs to is a loose mob, frittering away their best years, reading bad novels, writing for worse newspapers, dabbling in politics, attending public meetings, holding meetings of their own, passing resolutions, getting up petitions and deputations.[5]

Allowing for some exaggeration and for the fact that the situation had improved somewhat over the next few years, the picture this gives of the Italian university students of the time suggests how with her character and seriousness of purpose Montessori must have stood out, and why even traditionally antifeminist faculty members responded by taking an interest in their girl student.

She was a good student, more intelligent, more interested in learning than many of the young gentlemen who were there to pass examinations for the sake of a degree they would never use. They were interested in the prestige of a medical degree; she was interested in the practice of medicine.

She had impressed the faculty with her seriousness and ability, and in June 1894, at the end of her fourth year at the university, her second in medicine and surgery, she won the coveted Rolli Prize and the scholarship that went with it. Adding to the scholarships she continued to win each year by doing private tutoring, she was able to pay most of her own way through medical school. Maria's relative economic independence made it even harder for her father to justify his disapproval of what she was doing, but his resentment persisted, expressed in a coldness of manner toward her despite the fact that he often walked her to classes. She had broken a traditional sex barrier in one of the major professions but it was still not considered proper for her to walk outdoors alone.

Not only did she have to be escorted to and from the university but she was not allowed to enter the lecture hall until the other students had taken their seats. It would not do for a young woman to move freely in close contact with men.

Her fellow students resented her at first and in the beginning did what they could to make her life miserable. She was a woman invading a hitherto exclusively male professional domain, she was doing better at it than most of them, and she was doing so with apparent ease. Not only was their masculine pride threatened by her success but her self-assuredness and competence were annoying to a society of men who were used to flatteringly helpless women.

They treated her accordingly. They shunned her, made contemptuous noises when they passed her in the corridors, talked about her with open hostility, arranged it so there would be no seat left for her in the small amphitheater where clinical demonstrations were held. Unprovoked, she went her way, trying to respond with good humor or at least with equanimity. Her response to her fellow students was that with which she met all problems—as challenges to be overcome through patient and persistent effort. She must have seemed imperturbable as she calmly went her way.

But she was not without feelings. It was unthinkable that men and women should confront a naked body—even a dead one—together, and so she was not allowed to attend dissecting classes along with the other students. Instead, arrangements were made for her to come to the anatomy building after hours, where she could work alone in the evening among the cadavers. In addition to the isolation, she found she had another problem. She was repelled by the smell of the anatomy hall. She hired a man to stand by her side and smoke while she dissected. When this became too complicated she tried smoking herself.

Accounts of those years have tended to stress the external obstacles Montessori had to overcome in studying medicine but say little about the internal ones she also faced. She later described what she experienced on her first day in the anatomy hall in a letter[6]—one of the few descriptions we have of her personal feelings in her own voice—that gives a dramatic glimpse of what the struggle was like for her:

> The first lesson . . . was at the Institute of Anatomy. I went a quarter of an hour earlier and they showed me into a hall.
> It was dark, and they opened a window. I saw that it was very long, divided in two by an arcade. It had six windows. That one window let in only a little light and turning around in the semidarkness I saw an enormous skeleton, standing upright. I looked at it for a long time and then I turned. In a cupboard there were jars with intestines and other internal organs immersed in alcohol. That skeleton oppressed me. I passed through the arch and found myself in the other half of the room. It was almost dark there. In a cupboard I saw a row of skulls: on their foreheads words were written with black ink. I went nearer and read "murderer," "thief," "patricide." Next to each was the respective brain. I went back to the skeleton. As I stared at it, it seemed to move. I turned my eyes away and began to walk back and forth, repelled by everything I saw.
> While walking I was not thinking, I was feeling: those internal organs seemed to me instruments of torture that had inflicted terrible pain on someone. Those skulls were novels of infinite suffering: gruesome grinning mouths, toothless, old; those foreheads were marked with infamy for all time. In the circumvolutions of the brains I found something to distract me. I counted them, thinking, "What a difficult study," and tried to think of nothing else, but little by little an invincible force urged me to think of my own brain which was made in the same way so as to make me find with my thoughts my own circumvolutions. I felt as if my brain were growing into many protuberances. . . . I told myself, "Come on, get away from here." There, on the other side, the skeleton—ever more enormous—seemed to move. "My God, what have I done to suffer in this way? Why me all alone in the midst of all this death?" . . . "Come, come! These are only feelings. Sensations must be overcome. . . . This skeleton does not budge. And what is a skeleton, after all? And if I were to touch it?" A shiver ran through my bones. I felt as if my skeleton were separated from the rest, to be reduced like the one that stood in front of me. "Curse this madness," I mumbled and went over to the window. . . .
> There was light out there; people passed by, the women dressed in vivid colors. Everything looked beautiful to me. In the entrance of a shop across the way a young milliner stood on the threshhold. I looked

at her with intense jealousy. She was outside, she was free, everything was alive around her. Her thoughts went no further than her little hats. She found her satisfaction in a good sale. She partook of that immense happiness without noticing it. She was feeling and enjoying the sunshine without thinking about it. . . . While I was looking out at the sun and at life, a great load was oppressing me. That skeleton, those skulls and those organs: they drew me. My thoughts had not left them for a moment.

I went back feeling a void in my heart, with trembling knees, and my heart suffused with blood. . . . I stood leaning against the wall with my eyes glued to that gleam of light. I felt that I loved everything which was outside of that room. I felt an extreme weakness and then a feeling of anxiety as if little by little my body were dying. I was leaning against that wall, beside myself, suffering tortures. . . .

Then the attendant came to call me to the lesson. . . .

In the class there was a lot of life around me. The little death that was on a table was bearable. I looked at it. It was something dark, misshapen, softish that little by little made me aware of a horrible smell. Then they brought in some bones in a basin. These were very fresh and equipped with pinkish flesh. To my excited mind that flesh took on gigantic proportions. I felt as if a very thin thread were connecting my flesh to it.

"They are the bones of a person who has thought," and my fixed stare did not move from the spot. It was the moral life that had animated those miserable remains, it was his thought, his suffering that were killing me.

Suddenly I heard the professor say, "In man the reproduction is internal." I felt as if my heart had been stabbed—and because of this blow the blood flocked slowly to my head in continuous waves. I wanted to perk up and I was not able to. The blood surged and surged and already my ears were whistling so much that I was unable to hear any other sound. A sharp pain was stabbing my temples and I felt such a weight in my head that I had to lean. When the lesson ended, the blood still oppressed my brain.

That evening at home I tried to pluck up some courage. They noticed at once that I was upset. I forced myself to eat and I did. Then we talked. My father said, "It is useless for you to force youself, you can't." And my mother: "It is bad for you, my child, don't go back." "But it is the first time," I said, "don't forget, it is the first time. . . . At least I did not faint." . . . I got up and went to my room. . . . I took my head in my hands in desperation.

I was sick. . . .

In bed I did not find peace: I kept thinking of the horror I had felt of a skeleton. What will it be with a corpse? . . . I had never seen death. Till then life and its sweet affections had surrounded me with happiness and I had lived in the innocent ignorance of children. My mother had brought me up this way. My ignorance had made me so delicately pure. How would I react at certain explanations? If an allusion, a mere allusion had affected me that way . . . a detailed description would bring so much blood to my head that I would die of a stroke. Not faint, no—die. How easy it is to die.

How had it even occurred to me to study anatomy? But then, oh come on now, what about the future? The goal, what a splendid goal!

It seemed to me that up on top, the goal was luminous. But the road leading to it! No, the road was too awful. . . . I was perspiring all over, panting. The desired object of my life was eluding me. I who believed in life saw its uselessness. I won't be able to do anybody any good, I will be a useless thing, like so many others! I will work hard to earn a pittance like so many teachers. But it does not matter. Better to be a dressmaker, a servant. . . . But not that, not that.

At last I came to a decision: to write to the professor, to thank him for his thoughtfulness on that first day, asking to be excused for having inconvenienced him uselessly and confessing that for me the study of the human anatomy would be absolutely impossible. . . .

It seemed to me the wisest decision and so, almost quieted down, I fell asleep. It was a short sleep, but nevertheless I felt immediately better. Again and again I emphatically approved my new resolution. All the admonitions I had received before I decided to study anatomy came back to my mind: Women doctors have nothing to do, nobody calls them, the only thing they earn is universal dislike. Women or at least the greater number of them prefer to be treated by men. And besides, the purity of a girl rebels against certain studies. . . . Apart from purity, the horror . . . the loathesomeness . . . a young girl at the dissection of a corpse that emanates an impossible stench. All this was turning around in my mind. . . .

But who knows? . . . It was like a deep inner faith: Who knows?

And I drank the bitter cup down to the dregs.

It is hardly surprising that a young woman of the late nineteenth century, brought face to face with naked bodies and human organs, should react with shock and anxiety. What is surprising is that she was able to master her feelings of repugnance in order to accomplish the goal she had set for herself.

Her aversion for the smells and sights of the anatomy room remained with her—one of her rather charmingly anachronistic "feminine" characteristics—to the end of her life. She was extremely modest about exposure of herself—her pupils noted with amusement that she never allowed anyone to walk up stairs behind her; they always had to go ahead and she would follow—and admitted to having "a distaste for all that nature has covered up with skin." As an old woman, having taught and lectured for half a century, she turned to her audience before showing an anatomical drawing to illustrate a lecture and said, "Excuse me if I show you this."[7]

Despite her distaste for viewing or handling flesh and organs, once she had made up her mind to stick at medical school she kept her feelings under control and managed to do well in both anatomy and surgery. It was an exercise in self-discipline, like the little girl's washing the floor tiles and knitting.

Most of the students welcomed any excuse to avoid attending classes. But even in a snowstorm she came—to find herself the only student in the lecture hall. Such an attitude could only annoy the members of a student body devoted primarily to passing exams with as little effort as possible.

She later remembered another moment when it all seemed too much to struggle against—her father's persistent opposition and his emotional withdrawal from her, the hostility of her fellow students and even some of the faculty, the special arrangements which made everything just a little more difficult for her. She left the dissecting room that evening depressed and thinking about never coming back—leaving medical school and finding something else to do.

Her first biographer described what happened next—a chance encounter and a kind of mystical revelation of purpose. Walking through the nearly deserted Pincio Park on her way home and thinking about what to do, she was approached by a beggar, a dirty woman dresed in rags with a child of about two who was playing with a small piece of colored paper. What Montessori remembered about them later was the child's expression of happiness, its total absorption in the little scrap it was playing with. And she told Standing how, "moved by emotions she could not herself explain, she turned round, and went straight back to the dissecting room," where she found that "from that moment her revulsion to the work in those uncongenial surroundings left her, never to return." After that, Standing remembers Montessori telling him, she never had another moment's doubt about the course she was pursuing. "She had a vocation."[8]

Now it strikes a reader of Maccheroni's and Standing's memoirs that both are telling the same story—a life decision is recalled later in terms of an epiphany, a moment in which something is made manifest. Both the Feast of the Epiphany and the image of the child absorbed in its work/play take on a special meaning in terms of the later events of Montessori's life as it turned out. One of the tellers places the experience in Montessori's early adolescence and relates it to her decision to study medicine instead of engineering, while the other places it later, when she was already a medical student, and relates it to her decision to go on rather than dropping out of the course. There is no way of knowing what she actually told either of them—just that in some way she herself believed in some kind of mystic purpose, that she came to feel she had a destiny to fulfill.

Maccheroni remembered Montessori saying of the child-with-the-red-paper incident, "We are not born simply to enjoy ourselves," and added, "She does feel that there are results from what we are and what we do which are not chosen by us as we choose so many things on the surface of our lives. . . .

"In one of her recent lectures she spoke of man's superior mission of which he is not aware. She instanced the corals. They, tiny as they are, can have no outlook beyond their own life. Yet, as a result of their living, new islands and even new continents are born.

"'We human beings,' she said, 'we must have a mission, too, of which we are not aware.'

"When she spoke of the sudden change in her life plans I could feel the inner certitude which made her persevere against her father's strong opposition and all the other difficulties that beset her path."[9]

Standing also told how Montessori described the incident to him. In his version, Montessori went on to say, "I cannot explain it. It just happened like that. You will probably think it a very silly story: and if you told it to others they would probably just laugh at it," and Standing goes on to speak of "that mysterious affinity which exists, deep down in the soul of the genius, towards that work which he is destined to perform" and his belief that she was "sent into the world to shed new light on the unfathomed depths of the child's soul . . . her life's mission."[10]

All of this tells us much more about the thinking of Montessori's followers later in life, as well as about her own gradually deepening mysticism as she grew older, than it does about the actual events in the years when she was a young student of medicine and the positive sciences. And it indicates the difficulty of separating fact from myth in those accounts of her life which were written by her devotees. But there must have been some relationship between what she actually experienced and what she later remembered and the way she spoke about it to her friends, some definition of purpose that she later came to see almost as a calling, a conversion experience, resulting in a sense of mission. What seems clear is her sureness of herself and of her ability to accomplish what she set out to do and the fact that she decided what that would be intuitively and trusted her intuitions enough to act on them. She was tough, independent, and not inclined to surrender to self-doubts. Self-direction, stubbornness, and intuitions that proved valid as well as original were characteristics that appeared early in her life and shaped her career.

Gradually the other students began to accept her. She interpreted this later as grudging admiration for the way she stood up to them. She told how she had responded to the whistles with wh ch they greeted her in the corridors with a little rhyme: "The harder you blow, the higher I'll go." When she turned a defiant look on a fellow student who was kicking the back of her chair during a lecture, she remembered him saying, "I must be immortal or a look like that would have killed me." "In those days," she once told Standing, "I felt as if I could have done anything."[11]

The estrangement between father and daughter continued through her years at medical school and must have imposed a considerable strain in the Montessori home, where her mother continued to actively support and encourage her. In the evenings she listened as Maria read the interesting parts of the day's lectures and helped her study her notes. She found little ways of making life easier, like separating the sections of the heavy medical textbooks so Maria carried around only those portions she was actually studying at the time, and then having the books bound for her again at the end of the year. Renilde Stoppani had capacities she had not been able to make use of in her own life. Marriage had been her only career, but with a persistence she passed on to her daughter, and in the face of considerable opposition from her husband, she devoted her capabilities to her only child.

During these years Maria was developing a sense of her own possibilities as an individual and as a woman. She felt no rivalry with men; she continued to dress attractively in the conventional feminine way, to wear her hair nicely arranged, and to behave socially in the manner of young ladies of the time. She had seen as a young schoolgirl that there were many things she was capable of learning and doing even though she was a woman. And she had begun to do them.

Life in medical school was not all work and study. In the spring of 1892 students of the University of Rome, with the enthusiastic participation of members of some of the city's wealthy titled families, organized a festival of flowers at the Villa Borghese gardens.[12] The guests came in elaborate costumes, riding in carriages decorated with blossoms of all kinds. The most impressive of all was that of Queen Margherita, which was awarded first prize. The honor of presenting the award of a hand-painted banner and a bouquet to her majesty was given to the attractive young female student of medicine, Maria Montessori. In her first recorded public appearance, Montessori exhibited both tact and persistence. The queen demurred; she did not wish to accept the prize, she asked that it be given to someone else. Montessori found the right words to convince the queen who, at Maria's gentle insistence, found herself graciously accepting the prize from the hands of the young student. Fifteen years later, Montessori would receive the queen as a frequent visitor to her school and a guest in her own house.

In her unique position as a woman in the medical school, everything she did was bound to be noticed. When one of her professors died in the spring of 1893, the papers noted the presence of the young woman medical student in the funeral procession.

Before long, however, she was being noticed not for the anomaly of her sex but for her achievements. After having won the prize of a thousand lire—at that time a considerable sum—given annually to a student in the department of medicine and surgery by the Rolli Foundation for work in general pathology, in the following year, 1895, she won a competition for a coveted position as assistant in the hospital, making it possible for her to gain some clinical experience a year before her graduation from medical school, at which time she would normally have been invited to join a hospital staff.

In her last two years she studied pediatrics at the Children's Hospital as well as serving as adjunct or assistant doctor *(aggiunto di medicina)* at the women's hospital of S. Salvatore al Laterano and at the Ospedale Santo Spirito for men in Sassia. She also attended the psychiatric clinic, the Regia Clinica Psichiatrica, studying the material on which she would write her thesis.

At the Ambulatorio Infantile, the out-patient clinic of the children's hospital, she worked in the consulting room, where she made diagnoses and prescribed treatment, and on the emergency service, where she assisted at surgery in the accident ward during her last year before graduation and the year that followed. She was becoming an expert in the illnesses of young children.

In the final year each medical student was asked to give a lecture to the assembled class. Montessori later told Standing that she had expected her fellow students to be highly critical—had, in fact, anticipated some kind of disturbance. The young men might be expected to jeer, even riot. "I felt like a lion tamer that day," she recalled.[13]

As it turned out, the lecture was a double triumph for her. Not only were her listeners quiet and attentive, impressed by both the quality of her lecture and the compelling style of her delivery, but her father was in the audience to witness her success. Family legend has it that Alessandro Montessori was approached by a friend who saw him on the street on the morning of the lecture and asked, "Aren't you coming to your daughter's lecture?" He either had not known about it or had not planned to come, but the friend persuaded him and, rather reluctantly, he attended. Maria received an ovation, Alessandro found himself being congratulated on all sides by her admirers, and the story has it that the pride he felt in her achievement ended the estrangement between father and daughter which had persisted since her defiance of his wishes in entering medical school.

In the spring of 1896, at the end of her final year as a medical student, Montessori handed in her written thesis. The requirement was that it be an essay on some topic directly connected with the course of studies, preferably of a controversial character. Having taken a particular interest in the nervous diseases, she wrote her thesis on a psychiatric subject. The manuscript of ninety-six carefully handwritten pages was entitled "Contributo clinico allo studio delle Allucinazioni a contenuto antagonistico" ("A Clinical Contribution to the Study of Delusions of Persecution" would be a rough translation, the term "antagonistico" referring to what would today be called "paranoid").

Then, with the formal examinations completed, she was told to present herself on July 10 to discuss her thesis. Formal dress was required on the occasion—which up to now had meant young men in frock coats. On this occasion the eleven solemn men seated in the main lecture hall were treated to the sight of a very handsome young woman elegantly dressed, wearing gloves and carefully coifed for the occasion. She looked as demure as any of their wives or daughters and was prepared to defend her thesis with a lilting voice and graceful gestures but with as much toughness of mind as any of their male students. For an hour she discussed her work and answered whatever criticisms they could think of putting to her. Then she was asked to withdraw while the professors discussed her case and decided what marks to give her.

She waited on the other side of the door until, having formally approved her thesis, the examiners summoned her back into their presence and conferred the degree of doctor—*laurea*—of medicine, making her the first woman to graduate from a medical school in Italy.

Outside, her family and friends waited for the results. When she came out, smiling, an official presented her with a bouquet and the new doctor went home to celebrate and send visiting cards to friends and acquaintances announcing her new status.

She had graduated with an impressive record. Each of the eleven examining professors could contribute as many as ten points to the candidate's final grade. Anything over 100 was considered a brilliant showing. Montessori scored 105.

Professors, classmates, friends, and relatives crowded into the Montessoris' modest apartment for a celebration later that week. It was hard to tell whether it was a family party or a scientific gathering. For Maria, it was a victory celebration, crowning years of effort, and she sailed through the evening with a kind of serene modesty, accepting congratulations and embraces, enjoying her parents' pride and presenting the honors of the house like any well-bred young hostess. An elderly journalist who was among the guests was pleased to note that a woman did not have to lose her femininity if she studied hard or pursued a serious occupation.

Her ordeal over, Maria wrote to a friend:

> Now everything is finished. All emotions have come to an end. In this last examination, a public one, a Senator of the Kingdom congratulated me heartily and then got up to shake my hand. That was my humble fringe of the laurel crown. But I must tell you that I make a very odd impression. Let me explain: In the morning I go to the Pincio. Every-. body looks at me and follows me as if I were a famous personality: some old ladies address my mother to ask her if I am the only medical student in Rome. My celebrity derives from this fact: I look delicate and rather shy, and it is known that I look at corpses and touch them, that I bear their smell with indifference, that I look at naked bodies (I—a girl alone among so many men!) without fainting. That nothing shakes me, nothing; not even a public examination; that I speak aloud of difficult things with such indifference and so coldbloodedly that the very examiners are disconcerted; that I possess the moral force one could expect in a very elderly and sturdy woman; that I touch a putrified corpse and listen to public praise by a scientific celebrity with the same impassiveness.
>
> So here I am: famous! On the other hand, my dear, it is not very difficult, as you see. I am not famous because of my skill or my intelligence, but for my courage and indifference towards everything. This is something which, if one wishes, one can always achieve, but it takes tremendous efforts.[14]

When Maria Montessori was given her diploma as a doctor of medicine and surgery, many of the words printed on the document had to be changed in pen and ink from the masculine to the feminine (for example, *"gli esami sostenuti dal Signor———"* to *"dalla Signora"*). The impressively elaborate document had not been designed with the idea in mind that it might be intended for anyone not of the masculine sex.

Since so many young men attended the faculties of law and medicine primarily to qualify as professional gentlemen, the universities graduated a good number of professionals who never practiced their professions. There were too many doctors, and not enough good ones. Cheap and easily available professional education meant a flood of graduates each year for whom there were no jobs and created what one contemporary writer described as an "army of educated unemployed," adding, "Every year a large number of graduates in medicine are turned out into the world to enter a profession in which there is no room for them."[15]

In this buyer's market, Montessori was offered a professional position as soon as she had graduated. Being a woman would not have been enough—she was also good at her work, and that fact had been made clear to her teachers, who were now her colleagues. She was given a job as an assistant at the San Giovanni Hospital attached to the university, and also succeeded in starting a private practice with the help of these same colleagues, who referred patients to her.

She had already done original research considered significant enough to be published in a scientific journal—a paper on "The Significance of the Crystals of Leyden in Bronchial Asthma."[16]

3

Montessori graduated from medical school in the year that the Crispi government fell, its policy of African conquest and colonization repudiated by many Italian intellectuals in a mood not unlike that of Americans toward their government's Vietnam adventure in the late 1960s. "Out of Africa" was the watchword, along with a demand for more attention to solving social and economic problems at home.

The daily wage of an experienced workman in a candle factory in Turin was the equivalent of sixty-five cents; for a woman, twenty cents. Mill workers earned as little as twenty-eight cents a day and women in those same mills were paid as little as twelve cents. In the poorest regions of the country women worked bent over in ankle-deep water all day in the rice fields and children worked a twelve-hour day in the sulfur mines.

Rome, where Montessori lived and studied, was a city of almost half a million and newcomers were arriving from other parts of Italy every day. Half the population came from somewhere else. The population was overflowing the city walls and new buildings were going up outside the city gates. Among the ancient ruins and monuments a modern city was developing. Princely villas were being subdivided into lots for building.

The city had its bohemian element, including many American art students, who frequented the cafés. There were the urban poor, increasing every day as newcomers arrived from the starving countryside looking for the better life they hoped to find in the capital. And there were the comfortable upper classes, including among them a sizable contingent of English and American women married to Italian nobility and professional men. They were far more emancipated than Italian wives, and tended to take an active interest in those areas of private charity and public good works which had already become accepted as appropriate for women in Anglo-Saxon countries. With leisure and money and a tradition behind them that encouraged them to make at least some good use of both, a number of them naturally took an interest in projects relating to children. They were interested in the education of the children of the poor as well as of their own.

Montessori met many of these women as she increasingly began to move in wider circles of academic and social life in Rome. It began to occur to her that since they shared her growing interest in the problems of deprived children they might be stimulated to support social programs to deal with those problems in a country where private philanthropy was still more significant than anything undertaken by the state. The question was how to utilize their interest and their means.

In August 1896, only a month after her graduation from medical school, Montessori was chosen as one of the delegates to represent Italy at an international women's congress to be held in Berlin that fall. The news reached Ancona, the province where the Montessoris had lived during the early years of their marriage and where she had been born, and where the family still had many friends. On her twenty-sixth birthday, in a gesture of home-town pride, a committee of women from Chiaravalle announced that they had raised fifty lire as a contribution to be made through the local council toward her expenses at the congress. It was a modest sum, but it was a poor town, and the members of the committee said their main purpose was to show how honored her birthplace was by her distinction.

A reporter who came to the Montessoris' apartment in Rome to interview her before she left for Berlin wrote a rhapsodic account of the young doctor's charms. Expecting to find a stereotype of the militant feminist scholar—bony figure, stern visage, masculine attire, lorgnette perched on aquiline nose—the reporter was met by a pleasant young women with large bright eyes and a warm smile, her attractive figure showing to good advantage in a simple summer dress, and who immediately put her visitor at ease.

They talked about her career, her interest in the diseases of children, her work as an adjunct in the hospital for the past year and about the suffering she saw there. The reporter asked how the patients reacted—did they trust such a young woman as their doctor? Montessori replied that she had been assigned to the women's wards, "And I assure you that they ask for me, they want me. They are like children—they know intuitively when someone really cares about them. And those who work and suffer prefer those who also have their daily work and can understand the suffering of others. It is only the upper classes that have a prejudice against women leading a useful existence."

Asked about the attitude of her fellow students toward her invasion of a profession that up to then had been their exclusively male province she gallantly maintained that they had always treated her with respect, although she admitted they had been a bit sulky when she won the competition for the thousand-lire Rolli prize. "But," she added, "it's natural for them to have preferred the winner to be one of their own sex."

"I've lived a good deal among men," she told her visitor, "and observed the way they relate to women, and I think our aim should be to befriend them, not to alienate them from us."

The reporter wondered whether as a woman the young physician took any interest in domestic work. Did she like to plan menus, cook, do needlework? Yes, she found time for everything. She showed her embroidery, the linens she had initialed in skillful featherstitch, and the reporter noted such "feminine touches" as the arrangements of fresh flowers beside the apparatus of her chemistry experiments and the musical scores standing open on the piano.

The reporter confessed to being highly impressed with the representative the Italian women were sending to Berlin: "Well chosen. The delicacy of a talented young woman combined with the strength of a man—an ideal one doesn't meet with every day."[1]

The combination of her youthful feminine charm and tact with her professional accomplishments and intellectual ability proved equally irresistible to the press reporting on the congress from Berlin the following month.

The congress opened on September 20 in Berlin's municipal hall with five hundred women of all ages present. Most of them were German, but there were delegates from America, Denmark, England, Finland, Holland, Italy, Austria, Persia, Portugal, Armenia, India, Spain, and Switzerland. Some, like the Armenian representative, who was also a medical doctor, appeared in their national costumes. Some wore the typical bluestocking uniform of man-tailored suit and tie. Some were dressed elegantly, like the Frenchwoman in a lace-trimmed gown, others in bizarre fashion like the American student in an outfit resembling that of Pope Leo XIII.

Young and old, dour or dramatic, they were all serious about the purpose for which they had met—to call attention to the condition of women and to press for reforms. They proceeded in highly organized fashion, speakers following each other in orderly progress, beginning when a bell rang, stopping when it rang again.

Despite the businesslike nature of the proceedings, some male members of the press could not refrain from a smirking tone and such patronizing remarks as one reporter's comment that he would rather have danced with the delegates than listened to them.

Surely he would not have wanted to dance with Lina Morgenstern, the organizer of the congress, a stern-visaged, stout German of middle age with a severely pulled-back hairdo and rimless glasses, whose cause was home economics and what today we would call consumer education and

53

who spoke about the importance of teaching working-class women how to spend their money wisely for nutritional value. When she bought an egg, she made it clear, she knew exactly how much albumen she was getting for her money.

On the opening day of the congress a group of socialist women bearing a petition signed by three thousand of their number gathered to stage a counterdemonstration in protest against what they called the congress of bourgeois women. Their objection was that the bourgeois women were contented with mere reforms while they—the socialist women—demanded revolution. Montessori agreed to address them. She said that to the women of Italy class differences did not exist—the struggle for the rights of all women was what mattered—and she brought greetings from all of the women of Italy to all of those engaged in that struggle and to the socialist women in particular. The assembly broke into wild applause and the meeting broke up with cries of *"Viva l'agitazione femminile!"*

The next day Montessori addressed the congress.

She wrote to her parents afterward: "So ended the day of my great speech. Then *l'enfant gâté* of the Congress became *l'enfant terrible.* . . . Yesterday, I continued, I brought the greetings of the Italian proletariat to the Socialist Society, and today I speak to you of the capitalist women, because what concerns me is injustice against women, and not their political party. . . ."[2]

She spoke as the representative of a broad federation of groups concerned with women's interests in every region of Italy, and in her first speech she reported on the activities of various feminist associations—in Rome, Milan, Trieste—and on the progress of women's education throughout the country. She spoke of the problems faced by the Italian women during the African war, the efforts of Roman feminists to overcome the widespread illiteracy among the poor, and described the young girls now studying at the University of Rome, assuring her listeners that they were the most diligent of students and at the same time managed to remain ladies.

All of the previous speakers, including the Milanese delegate, who had also spoken of the difficulties facing the women of Italy, had received perfunctory applause. The enthusiastic ovation that followed Montessori's talk, coming after her diplomatic triumph of the previous day, made her the press's heroine of the hour.

"The little speech of Signorina Montessori," read one account, "with its musical cadence and the graceful gestures of her elegantly gloved hands, would have been a triumph even without her medical degree or her timely spirit of emancipation—a triumph of Italian feminine grace."[3] The journalists of half a dozen European countries reported that the other delegates had called her a ray of sunshine, *ein Sonnenstrahl, un rayon de soleil,* and the journalists themselves quoted verses of romantic poetry in describing her.

When a reporter asked to see a copy of her lecture, she told him she had none. Amazed that she could have spoken so eloquently without reading from a prepared speech, he asked to see her notes. She had none. What about the papers she held? Smiling, she showed them to him. They were blank papers, a prop to hold.

When she appeared on the podium on September 23 to give her second address, on the conditions of working women in Italy, the hall was packed. Young, beautiful, and eloquent, she stood before a rapt audience and told them, "I speak for the six million Italian women who work in factories and on farms as long as eighteen hours a day for pay that is often half of what men earn for the same work and sometimes even less."[4] When she asked that the delegates approve a proposal in support of efforts by all their countries to obtain equal pay for equal work by women, starting with those employed in state-owned factories, it was enthusiastically and unanimously adopted.

For four days the congress had heard speaker after speaker discuss its main themes: social reforms, peace, equal educational opportunities, especially in higher learning and the professions. Speakers noted that among academics, those professors most favorable to opening their faculties to women were theologians; those most opposed were doctors, who welcomed women as nurses and assistants but were appalled at the thought of women as colleagues. Delegates informed each other about children's-aid organizations, institutions for the orphaned and the poor, health legislation, the position of women in teaching and their role in science.

Hardly any of their data and few of their proposals were reported in the press, but there was column after column about the young Italian delegate. She was a striking contrast to Frau Morgenstern and the other delegates, and journalists reporting on the congress were fascinated. Here was good copy, and numerous stories were written about "her elegant and genial appearance, her lady-like bearing, her charm and beauty. . . . It astounds one to read on her card *Medico-Chirurgo!* This physician-surgeon graces the speaker's podium as if it were a box at the theater, and all the large questions she talks about—the emancipation of the peasant and factory women, the economic and legal rights of married women are discussed in a Roman accent that sounds like music. Suddenly one wishes there were a hundred thousand such physician-surgeons."[5] In Montessori the journalists had found a subject and a story, and articles about her appeared in the press of Germany and France as well as all the large cities of Italy.

All of them make clear that she stood out like "a beacon, a shining light" among the other women, by whom she was also much admired. She stood out not only by virtue of her feminine attractions, so incongruous to the masculine press in one of such serious accomplishments, but by showing a sense of humor. She got the only laugh at the entire congress when her reading of a newspaper article she was quoting in the course of her speech brought shouts of "Slower, slower!" and she responded with a characteristically Latin gesture of her hands and a warm smile that proved infectious.

The Italians referred to her as *"la giovane dottoressa Montessori."* She was, after all, only two months out of medical school. The Germans called her an adorable vision, the evocation of a Titianesque dream. The Berlin correspondent of *Il Corriere della Sera* of Milan wrote that "the appearance of the dottoressa Montessori overcame the sarcasm of the gentlemen present and caused them to smile with pleasure. With such a delegate the success of the Congress was assured. The eternally feminine was splendidly incarnated in the graceful Roman. What a lovely emancipated woman! It seemed that everyone wanted to embrace her. Even those who could not understand what she was saying were enchanted by her musical voice and her expression." His colleague on *L'Illustrazione Popolare* wrote, "Her grace conquered all the pens—we might say all the hearts—of the journalists. One newspaperman in Berlin has asked us for a photograph of the charming physician-surgeon to decorate his own album, but we don't think it right to gratify only his individual interest; we wish all our readers to see the portrait of this distinguished lady and therefore are reproducing it herewith." The distinguished lady in the accompanying photograph *is* lovely looking—dark eyes, a Mona Lisa smile, a frilled collar, and a strand of pearls setting off the face framed with soft curls.

On the way home from the congress Montessori wrote to her parents from Bologna: "I see that many newspapers mention me—and who knows how many that I don't even know about—I have good reasons to believe it. Good and—not good—that's not important—I will make it all forgotten! My face will not appear in the newspapers any more and no one will dare to sing of my so-called charms again. I shall do serious work!"[6]

The serious work began as soon as she returned to Rome. In November 1896 she was appointed to replace the surgical assistant at Santo Spirito, where she had been medical assistant the previous year. She was still spending some time working at the women's and children's hospitals, and now she had her assistantship at San Giovanni as well. And, in addition to her work in the hospitals, there was her private practice.

The care she gave many of her poor patients went far beyond what was expected of a physician. "She finds it difficult," said one of her friends, "to separate the nurse's duty from the doctor's."

Young Dr. Montessori came from a nineteenth-century tradition that taught responsibility for the poor; her mother had trained her early to do her part for those less fortunate than she was, and she was no blue-stocking. Emancipation pertained to the mind, and a woman should be no less free than a man to work in the world. But she never felt that *lavori donneschi*—the "women's work" for which she had been given an award as a little schoolgirl—was demeaning. Not only were household tasks, preparing meals, nursing the sick, not beneath women, but boys too should perform what she came to call "the exercises of practical life." Montessori found satisfaction throughout her life in such tasks as preparing meals, making her bed, even occasionally scrubbing the tile floors of her apartment overlooking the Pincio. As a young doctor she not only consulted and prescribed but nursed her patients and even, if necessary, cleaned things up and cooked a good nourishing soup for them. The lace on the richly embroidered dress with butterfly sleeves she wears in the dreamily beautiful 1898 portrait photograph of her as a young doctor in Rome was a gift from a dressmaker she had nursed in the course of doctoring her.

Renilde Montessori kept in a drawer of her home a packet of letters written over the years by grateful relatives of patients her daughter had treated. One was from the mother of a little girl Dr. Montessori had been called to treat for pneumonia. She had spent nearly the whole day in the home, prepared a bath, arranged the bed, made some soup and fed the child herself. The grateful mother felt the young doctor's care had saved her child's life. Another was from the mother of newborn twins who were not expected to survive. Dr. Montessori was sent for, and Standing later described what followed:

> The parents were very poor and unable to afford either household help or nursing. On her arrival the young lady doctor took in the whole situation at a glance. Taking off her coat, she lit the fire, sent the mother to bed, heated some water, bathed the two babies, "holding them in a special way," prepared their food, and thus little by little, hour by hour, brought them back to life—servant, cook, nurse and doctor in one.[7]

These parents, too, felt they owed their children's lives to her skill and attention.

After her graduation and on into the following year, although she had long since finished the thesis she had originally gone there to work on, Montessori continued to do research work at the psychiatric clinic of the University of Rome. In 1897 she joined the staff as a voluntary assistant. She was now involved in patient care and spent part of her time in the clinic consulting room, where nervous diseases and mental illnesses were diagnosed and therapy—including some form of electric shock treatments—was prescribed.

One of the responsibilities she was given was to visit the Rome asylums for the insane in order to select suitable subjects for treatment at the clinic. In the asylums she saw feebleminded children who, unable to function at school or in their families, and with no other public provisions existing for them, were tossed into the asylums, locked up beside the stony catatonics, the raging criminally insane, and every variation of human misery between. She was a physician, oriented toward the relief of human suffering; she had taken a special interest in the diseases of children; she had a passionate commitment to social reform. Everything in her life to this point had sensitized her to this encounter with what were called "the idiot children."

Years later she told about an experience she had that year while visiting one of the asylums, already troubled by these children but not yet sure of the direction her interest should take. She had been shown into a room where a group of feebleminded children were kept like prisoners, seeing no one but each other, doing nothing but staring, sleeping, and eating the food brought them by their caretaker, who told Dr. Montessori with disgust how, after their meals, they would throw themselves on the floor to grab for dirty crumbs of bread. Montessori listened, thought about the children reaching for the crumbs, fondling them, mouthing them. She looked around the bare, blank room. And it occurred to her—not as a mystical revelation but in an act of problem-solving intelligence made possible by her understanding of children, a fortuitous intersecting of reason and intuition—that the children were starved not for food but for experience. There was nothing in their environment to touch, feel, exercise their hands or eyes on. They had nothing to play with, nothing to do. They were grabbing for the only toys that came their way, the only means of relieving the awful boredom.

She was a woman interested in solving problems—she thought of herself as a scientist as well as a practitioner of medicine. And the question of the idiot children fascinated her. They seemed to be indicating a need those in charge of their care had never suspected. Their minds were not totally useless, just unused. When they found stimulation they responded.

The Early Struggles

There is no way of knowing just how these "feebleminded" children of the Rome asylum would be diagnosed today—the degree to which their retardation involved organic impairment or was merely functional. Perhaps they were "idiots" only because their senses had never been stimulated enough for learning to take place.

In between visits to her private patients and her work at the hospitals and the psychiatric clinic, she continued to think about the children, some of whom she brought to the clinic for treatment. She observed them, she found glimmers of response to her various tentative efforts to focus their attention, direct their activity. She began to read everything she could find on mentally defective children and she soon discovered the works of Jean-Marc-Gaspard Itard and his disciple Edouard Seguin.

What she found in the writings of these two men was a revelation that gave a new direction to her thinking and set the future course of her entire life's work. What they had thought and tried she would adapt as elements in a synthesis of her own.

Jean-Marc-Gaspard Itard became physician to the institution for deaf-mutes in Paris in 1800, at the age of twenty-five. That year a boy of eleven or twelve who had been found running wild in the woods around Aveyron was brought to the institution. The boy was an object of great scientific as well as public curiosity. After his capture scientists came from all over the world to see the "natural man." What they saw was a creature more like an animal than a man, expressionless, rocking back and forth, locked in his own world, unable to do anything for himself, helpless, uncommunicative. There seemed to be no way to reach him, no way for him to learn. After the initial surge of interest died down, the boy was left in the institution for deaf-mutes. Dr. Philippe Pinel, the famous authority on the insane, stated to the Academy of Sciences his opinion that the boy was uneducable.

Itard disagreed. It seemed to him that the boy's savagery and animal nature was not the result of congenital idiocy but of lack of training. It was a case of utter lack of development of potential capacities. Itard set about trying to civilize the boy, to stimulate and channel his senses, hoping eventually to teach him the uses of language.

When he found the existing methods used to teach deaf-mutes to connect words with objects did not work with the wild boy, Itard invented a method of his own. He pasted a red circle, a blue triangle, and a black square on a board, and gave the boy three pieces of cardboard of the same size, shape, and color to place on them. He went from this to more complicated exercises and eventually to a set of cardboard letters to match with a set of metal ones. The sorting and matching activities eventually resulted in the boy's learning to pick out the letters LAIT when he wanted milk.

Unfortunately, pupil and teacher were never able to go beyond this simple accomplishment. Whether the boy suffered from congenital defects cannot be known; even if the cause was the lack of appropriate stimulation in the early stages of development, the effect was irreversible beyond a certain level.

Itard then shifted the focus of his experiments to the methods suitable for the education of the mentally defective. But still his focus was on developing the mind through the action of the senses, what he called a "medical education." The method was still, as in the experiment with the letters, to move from the simplest kind of sensory discrimination to the more complex, in sounds, temperatures, sight. But the boy was never able to progress beyond mere matching to an understanding of the meaning of the sounds and words. Eventually, Itard had to admit failure. The boy could not be taught language. And when he reached puberty, his behavior became so violent and erratic that all attempts to educate him had to be abandoned. Although the experiment in one sense had been a failure, the limited success did establish the possibility of training mentally defective children by a system of medical pedagogy which in time led to reforms in the treatment of such children. Itard used what he had learned from his work with the wild boy to arrive at methods of education for deaf-mutes. It was left to his pupil Seguin to continue the application of his work.

Edouard Seguin was born 1812 and came to study medicine under Itard. Seguin was drawn to the mystical socialism of Saint-Simon and his followers and dreamed of drawing on the human potential of the masses through education. He was especially interested in penetrating the darkness of the world of the idiot children and had an early success in an eighteen-month experiment in which he was able to train an idiot boy through the use of his senses to the point where he could speak, write, and count.

He went on to found a school for idiots where he continued this work with impressive results and in 1846 published a landmark work, *Traitement moral, Hygiène, et Education des Idiots et des autres Enfants arrières (The Moral Treatment, Hygiene, and Education of Idiots and Other Backward Children)*, which attracted the attention of educators working with mental defectives all over the world and brought psychiatrists—who were then known as alienists—from many countries to observe his work at the Hospice de Bicêtre, the famous asylum in Paris which became a model for similar institutions throughout the world. Seguin eventually moved to the United States, worked in Ohio and Massachusetts, headed the Pennsylvania Training School for Idiots, and later established a school in New York "for weak-minded and weak-bodied children" to apply the knowledge of physiology to education.

What Seguin tried to do was to adapt the ideal methods of ordinary education to the special case of the mentally deficient. He felt that ordinary education was stultifying in its regimentation, that it stressed rote memory at the expense of all other faculties of the mind, and he aimed for an education that would emphasize the potential aptitudes of the individual. "Respect for individuality," he wrote, "is the first test of a teacher," and he contrasted it with "the violent sameness of most of education."[8]

Seguin divided the education of the child into a sequence of stages of development from physical movement to intellect, beginning with "the education of activity." He developed a series of graduated exercises in motor education and used simple gymnastic apparatus like ladders and swings as well as tools used in daily life—the spade, wheelbarrow, hammer—to stimulate the sense perceptions and motor powers of the child. He used different-sized nails placed into corresponding-sized holes in a board, geometrical figures to be inserted into corresponding spaces of the same shape, beads to be threaded, pieces of cloth to be buttoned and laced, to train the children's senses and teach them the skills of everyday life. He developed the child's sense of touch by providing objects of different texture, his sense of sight by the use of colored balls to be placed in holders of the same color and sticks of graduated length to be arranged in series from longest to shortest. His children progressed from drawing lines to copying letters, a method which—contrary to what was done in the schools—led to writing before reading.

In 1866 his other major work, *Idiocy and Its Treatment by the Physiological Method,* was published in the United States.

In the light of her own observations, Seguin's work seemed to suggest the answer Montessori was looking for. "I felt that mental deficiency presented chiefly a pedagogical, rather than mainly a medical, problem."[9] These children could be helped by special methods of education. They would not be cured in hospitals; they needed to be trained in schools.

At this moment Montessori turned her attention for the first time to the study of education. During the 1897–98 university term she attended the courses in pedagogy as an auditor and read all of the major works on educational theory of the past two hundred years. Little by little, many of the ideas she found in these works would come together in her mind in a theory of her own.

Throughout the eighteenth and nineteenth centuries European

thinkers had been providing the intellectual groundwork for the movement toward universal early elementary education and the reform of the schools through changes in teaching practices. In Switzerland, Pestalozzi experimented in the education of culturally retarded children. In England, the effects of the industrial revolution, including such horrors as child factory labor, led the reform-minded to focus on the fate of children. Robert Owen established a school for the employees of his cotton mills in 1816 which eventually became the basis for the British infant schools. In the gradual evolution of the modern idea of the school as an institution for educating young children outside the home a number of theories grew out of the seeds of earlier theories and, modified by the practice of numerous educators, were grafted onto the infant school: Pestalozzi's attempts to create a freer school, Froebel's kindergarten for the very young, Seguin's and Itard's methods for educating those who had been considered uneducable, all of them to be synthesized in the work of Montessori.

If one of the roots of her thinking was the work done by the physicians Itard and Seguin on the training of mentally defective children, another consisted of the ideas about the education of all children which went back through the educators Froebel and Pestalozzi to Rousseau. Both roots meet in Rousseau's mid-eighteenth-century contemporary Jacob Rodriguez Pereira.

Pereira was a Sephardic Jew who moved to France, where he met a young woman who had been mute from birth. His interest in her led him to devote his life to the education of deaf-mutes. He studied medicine and after successfully teaching some deaf-mutes to speak founded a free school in Bordeaux in 1750, to which deaf-mutes came from all over Europe. Seguin later found in Pereira's work the idea of education based on sense-training, particularly the discovery of how much can be done to train the sense of touch as an instrument in more general learning. Pereira was a neighbor and friend of Jean Jacques Rousseau, who was a frequent visitor at his little school. When Rousseau came to work out his own educational theories in *Émile*, he extended Pereira's idea of training the sense of touch in the deaf-mutes to the training of all of the senses in the education of normal children.

For Rousseau, sense experience was the basis of all knowledge, but he placed a new emphasis on the characteristics of the individual knower—the process of learning rather than what is learned. The job of the educator, he said, is to assist in a process which is latent within the learner's mind. The educator must begin by understanding the nature of the child he wants to teach, in order to develop the innate possibilities of human nature, which he saw as apt to be distorted or even destroyed by social institutions. In *Émile* he worked out his scheme for a "natural" education, beginning with early training in sense experience. It was this emphasis on beginning the child's education with the concrete rather than the abstract that found its way into Montessori's system. It would be hard to tell, without knowing, which of them—the eighteenth-century Frenchman or the twentieth-century Italian—was the author of the following passage from *Émile:*

> In the dawn of life, when memory and imagination have not begun to function, the child only attends to what affects its senses. . . . He wants to touch and handle everything; do not check these movements which teach him invaluable lessons. Thus he learns to perceive the heat, cold, hardness, softness, weight, or lightness of bodies, to judge their size and shape and all their physical properties, by looking, feeling, listening, and, above all, by comparing sight and touch, by judging with the eye what sensation they would cause to his hand.[10]

What Rousseau proposed was to remove the artificial restraints of the schoolroom and leave the child in touch with the immediate physical world, free to learn from his own experience rather than having knowledge imposed from without by a teacher. Train the body and the senses in childhood, he believed, and the intellect would develop as a matter of course.

Montessori never believed, like Rousseau, that all civilization corrupted the child. On the contrary, she believed that work, the systematic mastery of the environment, met an innate need of the developing human being from the earliest age and was the key to both individual development and the progress of civilization. She had no desire to turn the young child out of school into the world of nature; what she wanted was to make use of nature to perfect the school, making it a place that met the real needs of children. What did come down to her through the tradition of educators who followed Rousseau was not the destructuring of education but the idea of developing the senses as a prior basis for abstract learning in a school that was structured the right way.

Rousseau's ideas were brought ito the practical world of the schoolroom by two men whose work Montessori became familiar with in the late 1890s as she educated herself in the field of education. They were Pestalozzi and Froebel, a pair of schoolmasters whose classroom practices changed the educational thinking of their time.

Johann Pestalozzi was a Swiss educational reformer born in 1746, who believed that social progress could be achieved through a new method of teaching which he expounded in his writings and demonstrated in his own school, both of which had enormous influence on nineteenth-century educational thought.

As a young man, Pestalozzi had read Rousseau and was so impressed that he left upper-class life and law school for farming and the "natural life," but like so many idealists who turn to the land for the good life, he found it rougher going than he had imagined. He then started a school with the idea of training some of the many impoverished and neglected children of the countryside, for whom no public agencies were then responsible, to earn a living as spinners or weavers so they could become self-reliant. While the youngsters worked, they learned arithmetic; in their free time they were taught reading and writing. He was impressed with their progress as he worked "in the midst of fifty little beggars, sharing in my poverty my bread with them, living like a beggar myself in order to teach beggars to live like men."[11] It was one of the first attempts to provide remedial education for the children we now call culturally deprived.

Brimming over with ideas for social reforms, he turned to the writing of long didactic novels to expound the idea that the lot of the poor could be improved through education. Practically unreadable today, these books were immensely popular at the time. Many a sentimental upper-class reader shed tears over Pestalozzi's descriptions of the poor, but no one thought seriously of putting his ideas for ameliorating their condition into practice until Napoleon invaded Switzerland in 1798. The French campaign led the Swiss government to found a school for orphans, and Pestalozzi was put in charge. It was the first of several experiments he headed, trying to translate his theories into practice. Eventually the government provided him with a castle for a school building and operating expenses for a school which turned out to be primarily for middle-class children, although a few poor students also attended. His first published report on this endeavor, a century before Montessori was to publish her *Il Metodo,* was called *Die Methode.* It begins, *"Ich suche den menschlichen Unterricht zu psychologisiren* (I seek to psychologize human education)."

Pestalozzi's main educational principle was the importance of training the senses, based on his belief that all thinking began with accurate observation of concrete objects. The curriculum he devised centered on the child's direct experience of things; it included physical activities, the making of collections, and going on field trips. Instruction was graded, and ability groupings were an attempt to allow for individual differences.

The Early Struggles

For each successive stage of learning, formal exercises were provided, moving from the simple to the complex, from the concrete to the abstract, in both mathematical symbols and language. This idea, refined and developed by so many other minds and hands in the intervening century and a half, sounds commonplace now. It was a revolutionary concept in education at the time. Montessori, more than anyone else, would see its implication and refine its uses.

For twenty years Pestalozzi's influential school at Yverdon trained teachers as well as educating children. Distinguished visitors came from all over Europe to study "the method" and returned to their countries to found scores of Pestalozzi schools.

By the time of his death in 1827, Pestalozzi was a formidable influence in European and American schools. One of the young teachers who came under his sway was Friedrich Froebel, the German schoolmaster who gave the world the kindergarten.

Froebel was thirty-six years Pestalozzi's junior and died eighteen years before Montessori was born. Applying Pestalozzi's emphasis on nature and the senses in his own peculiar way to the education of very young children, Froebel's work is a bridge between that of the Swiss schoolmaster and the Italian physician.

He was for a time employed by a follower of Pestalozzi who headed a model school in Frankfurt am Main, and then went to Pestalozzi's school at Yverdon. He found the older man's ideas inspiring but rejected some of what he saw there in the actual operation of the school, which he felt had become too rigidly routinized. He decided he could do better, and with the help of some followers of his own opened a school in Thuringia in 1816 where he and his friends formed an educational commune to put his theories into practice. They began with a formidable name—Allgemeine deutsche Erziehungsanstalt (Universal German Educational Institute)—but only five students. From this immodestly named beginning he moved ahead in his profession, as a teacher of elementary school teachers for the Swiss government and then head of an orphan asylum where, impressed with the importance of early training, he became fascinated with the possibilities of the preschool years.

In 1837 he returned to Thuringia and established a school for very young children, a radical innovation at the time. He called it, with his characteristic gift for nomenclature, a *Kleinkinderbeschäftigungsanstalt* (an "institute where small children are occupied") until he thought of a better word—*Kindergarten*, a garden where children grow like flowers unfolding. The kindergarten attracted widespread interest, including that of a wealthy patroness, the Baroness Von Marenholtz-Bülow, who de-

65

voted the rest of her life to spreading Froebel's work all over the world. As with Montessori later, early success was facilitated by the tendency of wealthy do-gooders to take up the cause of early childhood education, a promising avenue of reform which was not yet institutionalized.

Froebel's kindergartens were eventually closed down by the Prussian government as too revolutionary, but the idea had taken hold, and moved on to other ground.

The first kindergarten in London was opened in 1851 by the Baroness, who went there after the closing of the German schools to lecture on Froebel's work and found kindergartens among the poor. Dickens visited and wrote an enthusiastic account of the kindergarten in *Household Words*. The growing popular press was already emerging as an influential force in the spread of new ideas about education as about so many social questions.

The first kindergarten in the United States was founded in 1855 and by 1873 the kindergarten became part of the public school system. The idea was taken up by the influential John Dewey and put into practice in his Laboratory School at the University of Chicago. Kindergarten associations sprang up everywhere; philanthropists established kindergartens in the urban slums; and the Froebel society, founded in 1875, spread the kindergarten philosophy. In a context of romantic mysticism in which growing children were described as flowers unfolding Froebel presented his contributions to ed cational thought. He saw all education as basically a process of self-activity, the natural endowments of the individual unfolding according to the universal laws of organic development. Convinced of the value of play in early childhood learning, he introduced a series of toys or apparatus he called the "gifts," to stimulate learning through play. The gifts—balls, cubes, cylinders, blocks—were to be used to heighten the awareness of relationships between things. The teacher was told how they should be used and, in fact, every moment's activity in the kindergarten was prescribed. The Froebel materials were eventually packaged and distributed throughout Germany and in many other countries, anticipating the later marketing of the Montessori didactic apparatus.

From 1826 on Froebel published a steady stream of works which attracted many readers despite their style—involuted, repetitious, mystical, ecstatic. Buried in his turgid prose were the suggestions of ideas which Montessori would later develop in her own way. Froebel's stated aim as an educator was to discover universal principles of life and apply them scientifically so as to fully develop man's divine spiritual nature. He focused on the child's experience of the real world, the unfolding of his natural capacities, on learning as a process of self-discovery as the child passes through successive stages of development. And he saw this process of self-fulfillment through self-activity as possible only where the adult does not interfere with the child's spontaneous activity, providing guidance rather than coercion. But the kindergarten did not practice what Froebel preached. It made use of his stories and songs, his toys and blocks, it brought nature into the life of the city child and made a classroom for very young children a pleasant, pretty place. But in following the letter it missed what should have been the spirit. At the center of the kindergarten was the teacher, scheduling activities for the entire group, rewarding accomplishment with praise, and very much running the show.

The International Kindergarteners Association was founded in 1892, while Maria Montessori was a young medical student and still far from considering education as her vocation. In the ensuing years the association presided over the increasing institutionalization of the kindergarten idea, prescribing rigidly the way in which the Froebel materials were to be used, fostering a quasi-religious reverence for procedures. In effect, the church had been founded, the master canonized, the liturgy established and the rituals laid down for all time. Stagnation was the ultimate consequence, reformation the inevitable response.

A closed system, admitting of no change from within, necessarily remains a separatist, insulated institution. When change does come, it comes from without, revolutionary rather than evolutionary, a by-product of the search for effective answers to new problems, or to new ways of seeing the old ones in a changing world.

In this process, Froebelian would give way to Montessorian until, inevitably, history would repeat itself again.

But now, in the process of evolving her own thought, Montessori made use of many of Froebel's insights, combining elements of his system with ideas and methods she found in other disciplines—the practice of medicine, the teaching of the deaf and the retarded, and the use of techniques from anthropology.

As a student in the natural sciences and medicine at the University of Rome in the 1890s it was inevitable that Montessori should be a student of anthropology—a field of science in which Italians were preeminent at the time. Among her teachers, some of them early antagonists of a woman medical student, all of them finally her supporters, were the leading authorities in the fields of medical, criminal, and pedagogical anthropology—de Giovanni, Lombroso, and Sergi.

67

MARIA MONTESSORI: A BIOGRAPHY

The anthropology that Montessori studied, taught, and wrote about was not the anthropology that we are most likely to think of today, when cultural and social anthropology are the dominant fields, but physical anthropology, a basically biological discipline which had begun in the seventeenth century with the idea of classifying the varieties of mankind as the zoologists and botanists were classifying fauna and flora. It was rooted in a new view of man as a biological organism and a proper object of scientific study in which the classification of the races would be undertaken by means of the development of quantitative techniques for measuring anatomical and morphological variation such as facial angles and skulls.

In the nineteenth century physical anthropologists spent most of their time collecting observations and measurements which they recorded on minutely detailed scales and charts. One striking thing about the study of anthropometry—the measurement of human physical characteristics, with its apparatus of meter sticks, calipers and tapes, its painstaking record keeping—was that it trained an observer like Montessori to look at things. It further reinforced the habit, begun with the study of medicine and clinical training, of observing, comparing, recording, which she would eventually transfer from the study of physical forms and structures to the study of behavior.

Achille de Giovanni was a physician and medical educator whose influence Montessori had felt as a young medical student. Unlike many professors of his day, he had a strong clinical orientation and was responsible for directing medical studies toward the naturalistic point of view, emphasizing the study of the individual, stressing the observation of pathology in the particular patient. It was de Giovanni who introduced into the medical clinics the techniques of anthropometry for the classification of human characteristics.

Another of the most influential of the Italian anthropologists of Montessori's day was Cesare Lombroso, who also began his professional career as a physician and surgeon. He became professor of psychiatry at the University of Turin in 1896 and professor of criminal anthropology in 1906. Lombroso believed in a biological basis of criminality, in the existence of a born criminal type who was a throwback to an earlier stage of evolution and could be identified and described by various anatomical and physical signs by means of such anthropometric data as skull measurements and facial asymmetries.

Lombroso and his followers studied the skulls, brains, and nervous systems of criminals, weighing them and measuring their height, length, and various proportions in order to discover the morphological irregularities. In these abnormalities—anomalies in the shape and size of the skull particularly—they considered that they had found evidence of arrested development, of a regression to the level of primitive man and the animals.

Physicians applying the medical model, they were studying the pathology of crime, which they regarded as an illness of society to be cured not through punishment but through prevention. They believed the morbid process could be modified in the very young before it became chronic.

Lombroso repeatedly insisted that prisons and reformatories did not cure criminality, pointing out the high degree of recidivism. He believed that the habitual adult criminal could not be cured, only removed from society; a decrease in crime and its destructive social effects could come only through the proper training of the very young.

Montessori's social thinking was influenced by this point of view, the idea that psychiatrists should abandon the old methods of the jailer and, together with social and political scientists, discover the causes and remedies of antisocial behavior in order to restore to society workers otherwise lost to disease. The criminal anthropologists were positivists who said, To deal with crime, study the criminal.

What turned out to be most significant about their scientific work for Montessori was not their conclusions but their emphasis on beginning by observing the individual rather than theorizing.

Of the leading anthropologists, the one with whom Montessori had the closest contact was her teacher Giuseppe Sergi, who was professor of anthropology at the University of Rome from 1884 to 1916 and founded its Institute of Experimental Psychology, the first in Italy, in 1876. Sergi was best known for his work on the origin and distribution of races, particularly the Aryans and the "Mediterranean race," and for his *"metodo cranioscopico,"* a geometrical description of the cerebral cranium which he considered his outstanding contribution to the development of his field, the natural study of man. Montessori took from him not his substantive ideas but the habits of scientific investigation which she would apply to the learning behavior of children.

It is fascinating to read today, in the light of his pupil Montessori's development and achievements, an article by Sergi in which he describes *"il movimento femminista"* as "a rebellion against nature, which made them women, rather than against man for subjugating them."[12]

He is not, Professor Sergi says (perhaps with a nod in the direction of his young pupil who had spoken so eloquently at the Berlin Feminist Congress two years earlier), opposed to education for women and the opportunity for them to supplement their natural family role with other social and professional roles. But the present feminist movement is actually a war against men, against human nature, and against the real differences between the sexes and therefore "eccentric." Woman is "naturally" maternal, he says, and therefore should care for home and children while man directs himself to external social matters. True anthropometrist, Sergi contrasts the feminists with "normal" women: they are asexual, frigid; they even look masculine, with undeveloped secondary sexual characteristics, thin and bony and exhibiting masculine features and gestures—especially the emancipated and successful women of North America who take such an active part in public life and who loook so different, with their flat chests and masculine characteristics, from "our well-developed women" (one thinks of Montessori, surely a well-developed woman, although a feminist). They are, he states, a third sex.

Sergi sees the women's movement as a threat to the deepest foundation of social life—the family. The woman who chooses to devote her attention to public life must turn her family over to "mercenaries" for their care and training. But men, he predicts, will not stand for this demand for a "free life" that will destroy the family, and so terrible battles are bound to take place if the movement continues to spread. "Violence will assume a terrible aspect."

Even women, he stated, won't go along with the movement for long because "They hear too deeply the voice of their nature." The education of women should be suited to feminine nature, to being a mother, child-educator, and "inspirer of her sons." It is in this role, he concludes, that woman contributes to social progress.

One wonders what Montessori thought of all this. Actually, stripped of its bombast and stated a bit less extremely, it is not a position she would have found it hard to reconcile with her own. That woman's life should be centered on the home and that social progress is to be achieved through the education of young children were essentially ideas which she shared. Although she would have encouraged the exceptional person of either sex to realize his or her potential to the fullest, she had little sympathy for the militant extremists of the women's movement. While she spoke out against the gross injustices by which she saw so many women victimized, she never saw herself as a victim. She had no sense of being confronted by obstacles she could not overcome. And she felt her own professional achievements were a more effective statement than any rhetoric about the potential of women. She was not only articulating the case for women's capabilities, she was exemplifying it, demonstrating what a woman could do instead of talking about it.

The Early Struggles

Despite the archaic character some of his views have today, Sergi played an important role in shaping his students' thinking about the applications of the study of anthropology. His most lasting contribution to Montessori's thought in particular was the idea of turning anthropology from the classification of abnormalities to the discovery of ways of preventing abnormality, through the establishment of a scientific pedagogy based on the anthropological study of children.

It was Sergi whom Montessori credited with turning her attention to the school as the environment in which the transformation of man would be effected.

4

In the two years after her graduation as a doctor, Montessori's work in medicine and anthropology, her experience working with the children from the asylums of Rome, and her study of the works of Seguin on the treatment of such children had convinced her of the need for special schools for the education and training of the mentally retarded and the emotionally disturbed child.

She continued her research at the Clinica Psichiatrica of Rome, working with a colleague, Dr. Giuseppe Montesano, also an assistant physician at the clinic, and publishing some reports of the results of their work together in professional journals. Working in the same institution, sharing a common interest in the problems of diseased and deprived children, the two young doctors spent much of their time together and gradually found their relationship becoming more than a professional one. It was a relationship that was to have a profound effect on Montessori's life. But all that the world knew of the clever and lively young Dr. Montessori's life at that time was its public side—which was becoming better known with each new accomplishment in an already impressive career.

In 1897 she was asked to speak at a national medical congress in Turin, where she called attention to the need for research into the causes of delinquency, maintaining that among them was the lack of adequate care for the retarded and disturbed children she identified as potential delinquents. This was still a controversial position in a time when many of her colleagues in the field of medicine believed delinquency to be caused by congenital abnormalities, and her speech was one of the main topics of discussion among the delegates and in the press.

In the summer of 1897, Professor Clodomiro Bonfigli, who was a member of the Chamber of Deputies as well as director of the Manicomio di Roma, the asylum where Montessori worked, had introduced in the legislature a bill to provide for the establishment of special Istituti Medico-Pedagogici. His proposal was warmly applauded by his fellow deputies but not supported by enough of their votes to become law. However, it did call attention to the question.

Now Montessori began to express her ideas on the subject in various publications. In the summer of 1898 *Roma*, a political review, published a long article by her titled "Social Miseries and New Scientific Discoveries." The issue entirely sold out and the article was widely quoted in the general press and reprinted in its entirety in an educational journal with the appropriate title of *Educational Awakening.*[1] In addition, she was devoting her energies to enlisting the interest and support of influential people—academics, philanthropists, politicians, educators—in the cause.

In September 1898 Montessori was chosen to bring the message to the nation's teachers at a national Pedagogical Congress held in Turin. The congress was concerned with public school policy and participants included some three thousand educators in various fields who had come to discuss not just theoretical matters but practical reforms for a school system that was generally acknowledged to be badly in need of them.

That summer there had been a wave of disparaging references to the Italians in the European press following the murder of the Austrian empress Elizabeth, the third successive assassination of a European monarch by an Italian. The Italian press responded by turning on its educators. In Turin, where teachers were assembling for the Pedagogical Congress, editorial writers asked, "What are we teaching in our schools? Are we educating killers?" The delegates to the congress, put on the defensive, discussed the weak points of the system, the large number of intractable children, the lack of effective moral education. When Montessori appeared on the scene, they responded to her enthusiastically both because she seemed a symbol of national potential, a figure in whom they could take pride, and because she gave them a starting point for change when she told them that any attempt to reform the schools would prove useless unless the "degenerate" children were first separated from the normal pupils.

Once again, as in Berlin two years before, her appearance was a public triumph. The speech she gave, essentially the article she had written for *Roma,* was to have a decisive effect in bringing into being the kind of institution she was urging and set the direction for her own career in the next few years.[2]

In it, she brought to bear everything she had learned—from medicine, from anthropology, from education, from Seguin in particular, and from her own recent practical experience in the field—on the problem of the vast class of children Italian society didn't want to recognize. Variously referred to at the time as "frenasthenic," "intellectual idiots," "moral imbeciles," or simply "deficient," they were a mixed bag we would probably identify today as the retarded (both the organically impaired and the victims of severe poverty and cultural deprivation), the emotionally disturbed, the delinquent.

Recent scientific studies, she maintained, had shown that these children were educable in varying degrees, and society owed it not only to them but to itself to create the kinds of educating institutions necessary for their intellectual and moral rehabilitation.

She described the existing conditions in which young children unable to function on the lowest level—to communicate, to distinguish objects or understand their meaning, to feed or clean themselves, or in some cases even to walk—were confined to asylums where they were thrown together with the insane and received no care beyond what was required to keep a vegetable alive. Others, able to take minimal care of themselves but unable to learn in a normal school situation, vere expelled from school to roam the streets, ventually becoming thieves, drug addicts, prostitutes, even murderers. These were Lombroso's "congenital delinquents," often born of alcoholics or epileptics, destined to fill the jails and end their days in mental asylums, no better off than in the days when the insane were condemned to spend their lives in chains.

In the preceding century, she pointed out, Italian moralists and legal scholars had been among the first to maintain that society's attitude toward the congenital moral imbecile should be one of understanding rather than punishment, "and yet today our country practices a barbarism in this regard that should make us blush."

The study of penology, she pointed out, had shown that punishment does not provide a deterrent to criminality. "The criminal, like the insane, behaves destructively because of the nature of his feelings and his reasoning. His perceptions will not be altered by punishment. Therefore we need to find another solution, another formula for social justice." The answer, she maintained, was in identifying the potentially criminal personality from childhood, before it had been further influenced by the wrong environment. Science could outwit nature. If anthropological studies had failed to solve the problem up to now, it was because they had been misapplied. They had concentrated on adults, already contaminated by the life of the streets and jails and no longer capable of being changed. The solution would be found by shifting the focus to the child, on whom the environment had not yet had an unchangeable influence.

She reminded her audience that as early as 1831 Seguin had shown that "the idiot is not incapable of learning but only incapable of following the common methods of education," and that he had developed new methods for the education of deficient children that were being used in special institutions throughout Western Europe, England, and the United States. She referred to the impressive results of these institutions, "returning to society thousands upon thousands of useful human beings able to live honestly on their own work, while Italy still possesses not a single such institution."

She quoted statistics—how many gardeners, farm workers, carpenters, masons, tailors, shoemakers, maids, nurses' aides had been trained by these institutions and how much they were able to earn by their labors, while in Italy their counterparts stayed at home to grow up helpless, "worthless," passive consumers of society's goods, or preyed on the community as criminals.

"The intellectual idiot and the moral imbecile," she told her audience, "are capable of being educated and have instincts that can be used to lead them to the good." She distinguished between different levels of severity among the retarded. There were those who could be given some elementary instruction in arithmetic, history, geography, and even some vocational training. Many could learn a craft. Almost all could be trained to do simple manual work such as candle making, rope making, caning chairs, making brooms, working as domestics or in dairies and on farms. "In certain kinds of work requiring mechanical repetition," she told them, "it is even an advantage to have imbeciles trained to do the work; since they do not tire of such tasks as quickly as intelligent people, they can keep at the work longer and thus increase production."

This has an insensitive ring to our twentieth-century ears, but she was promulgating a social program to a public which up to then had been content to ignore the fate of the disadvantaged, and she was probably correct in her assessment that they would be more impressed if charitable appeals to their hearts were supplemented by pragmatic references to their pocketbooks. Throughout her speech she stressed the advantages to the nation of transforming a class of public charges and criminals into productive members of society. And while praising the good works of the philanthropic women whose committees were responsible for such few local programs as did exist to help poor, sick, and orphaned children, she suggested that their charity would be more effective if enlightened by modern scientific knowledge about the real needs of such children.

"Our efforts will have to go into gaining an understanding of those children who have the most difficulty adapting to society and helping them before they get into trouble."

For those with less severe difficulties she urged the creation of special "joint classes" such as those in existence in England, France, Germany,

Switzerland, and Austria, where those children who were disruptive or unable to keep up with the others were gathered together in separate classes. This, she argued, would be better for all children, since the teachers of regular classes would be able to teach more effectively without having to cope with serious discipline problems—a matter of special interest to the classroom teachers and school administrators in her audience—and the children in the special classes would receive more attention and be happier together where they could proceed at their own pace.

She urged special courses for teachers in pedagogic methods designed for the retarded along Froebelian lines. Such methods, she explained, were developed by observing what resources these children had and then deciding how best to make use of them. For instance, their marked tendency to imitate others made it advantageous to educate them in groups.

Once the problem children were identified and brought together, the efforts of the teacher would have to be supplemented by those of the pediatrician and the psychiatrist, specialists who would make differential diagnoses to determine the individual needs of each child and who would prescribe the hygienic measures necessary to maintain in these constitutionally weaker children the level of physical health necessary to make learning possible. First the care of the body, then the training of the mind.

Here, in the context of the special medical-pedagogic institution where the deficient children would be gathered together under the supervision of doctor-teacher teams, Montessori was developing the principle that was to inform her later work in the education of normal children: *First the education of the senses, then the education of the intellect.*

She spelled out the program in detail.

> The children should be occupied from morning to evening without being over-tired and without being isolated. First we have to teach the simplest things—walking in a straight line toward a goal, use of the toilet, use of the spoon—and then we try to fix their attention on their sense perceptions, taking them for walks in a garden, for example, to stimulate their senses of sight and smell by means of flowers of different sizes, colors and perfumes. Gymnastics for the training of their muscles. For the training of their tactile senses, a variety of objects of various textures, capable of attracting their attention and holding their interest.
>
> Once the education of the senses is underway, along with the arousal of interest, we can begin real instruction. We can introduce the alphabet, not in a book, but on a little table on which are raised letters, painted different colors, that can be touched and traced with the fingers. We

gradually follow with manual instruction and eventually moral education, the final goal of the scientist as well as the philanthropist.

To work effectively with these children, she added, in a note that was characteristic of her thinking and would become more so, "the physician must love not only science but the individual. Here religious feeling becomes an indispensable auxiliary of science."

In her articles and her address at the Turin congress Montessori saw herself bringing together the points of view of the positive scientists and the socialist thinkers in the belief that social ills could be solved by reason and science properly understood and applied.

Her watchword was progress, and she was insisting that it was the function of the state to ensure it through publicly supported educational measures. She urged the formation of special institutions for "degenerates" not as a purely medical matter, not as a charitable duty, but as a matter of political economy, necessary for the progress of civilization. To her and to her late-nineteenth-century audience, the possibilities of human perfectibility and infinite social progress were assumed—the question was only how to go about attaining them.

The constitutionally weak and the disadvantaged, her argument ran, produced nothing—at their least harmful only consuming what others produced, at their most harmful, damaging it as a criminal class. Every productive citizen had the right to be protected against parasites and criminals. Special institutions for deficient children would gather all the destructive elements of society early enough, remove them from further weakening influences, and give them a new kind of education designed to make them productive and honest. Then they could be returned to society to make a contribution rather than remaining a charge and a burden. Modern science, joined to modern political thinking, would benefit not just the individuals who would be served by the establishment of these special classes and special schools, but society as a whole.

Her speech had an invigorating effect on the congress. The delegates responded not only to her argument but to hearing it from this young, attractive, and impassioned spokeswoman. Her concluding words—"No one who fails to support this program has the right to be called a civilized person in this day and age; this is not sentiment or rhetoric but sanity and science"—were followed by a resounding ovation and by passage of a resolution to be presented to the minister of education in which the nation's teachers unanimously approved her proposal for the establishment of separate classes and medical-pedagogical institutions for the various kinds of deficient children as well as special courses designed to prepare teachers to work with them. This resolution was the main accomplishment of the congress, and it received nationwide publicity.

As at Berlin, there was applause and praise, the congratulations of colleagues, interviews with the press about the resolution urging the government to act on her suggested reforms.

It was a coincidence that must have been an added source of private satisfaction to even the high-minded young Montessori that the minister of education to whom the congress of educators submitted her proposal for action was Dr. Guido Baccelli, the professor of medicine who, eight years before, had interviewed her in his office at the University of Rome and told her politely that, as a woman, she should forget about studying medicine there.

When the congress ended in mid-September, Baccelli responded to the resolution voted at Turin by officially requesting Montessori to give a series of lectures in Rome beginning in January 1899 to the teachers and student teachers at the Scuole normali di magistero, the teacher-training school of the Collegio Romano, on special methods of education for retarded children.

By the end of the year 1898 a committee had been formed to generate public support and raise funds for a national medical-pedagogical institution. Headed by Professor Bonfigli, La Lega nazionale per la educazione dei fanciulli deficienti (the National League for the Education of Retarded Children) included other members of the Chamber of Deputies as well as senators, prominent editors and publishers, scientists, doctors, lawyers, and wealthy society figures including a sprinkling of the nobility. Montessori was one of the more active members.

Reports of the league's founding and articles about its aims—a number of them written by Montessori—appeared in newspapers and magazines throughout Italy.

Then, in mid-February 1899, Montessori set off on a two-week lecture tour that took her to Milan, Padua, Venice, and Genoa. She gave two talks in each city.[3] The proceeds from the first, titled "The New Woman," were to go toward a local cause—in Milan La cucina dei malati poveri, a public kitchen to feed the sick poor, and L'Albergo popolare, a shelter for the indigent. The other, on "Modern Charity," would raise funds for the league as well as calling the attention of the public to its work.

Everywhere, she spoke to capacity audiences, the halls always crowded with the city's leading citizens, including most of the prominent women of the community. Newspapers gave advance news of her appearances and reported in detail on her talks, sometimes reprinting them in full. Everywhere the comments were the same—the audience had been completely won over by her youth, her beauty, her charm, her sincerity. It was sometimes hard to believe they were not describing a diva of opera or the stage. But there was always praise for the message as well as the messenger. Reports of her effectiveness as a propagandist on behalf of the causes for which she spoke also went into detail about the causes themselves.

She had become a well-known personality and the public turned out to see and hear the winning feminist cum physician, the "beautiful scholar" they had read about.

By now she had become completely identified with the cause of special education for deficient children. Appearing in public, she represented the league, which in turn was set up to forward the program she had articulated. Everything she had done in her work up to now—in medicine, pediatrics, psychiatry, anthropology, education—had directed her attention to special educational methods in an environment designed to meet the needs of abnormal children.

She was always gracious in crediting Bonfigli as the originator of the program, the first to call attention to the problem nationally, and in praising Baccelli for his support.

And everywhere she spoke, she left behind converts to the cause of feminism and new members for the league, which was already training a group of teachers and making plans to open a school in Rome.

In Milan, where she gave her first talks, the meeting room of the city's leading hotel was crowded with local notables—especially women—who had paid three lire for a ticket admitting them to both lectures, which were also to be reprinted in pamphlet form by the feminist press, the proceeds to go to the league and the kitchen for the poor.

She came to the podium elegantly dressed, wearing a large fashionable hat and gloves, smiled at her audience, with a gracious gesture quieted the applause and the buzz of admiration ("how young she is, how graceful, how unlike the usual feminist . . .") and began to speak, glancing occasionally at some notes, in as clear and unhesitating a flow of sentences as if she were reading them.

Her subject was "The New Woman," and she began by reviewing past and current theories about the inferiority of women with a quiet sarcasm that delighted her audience.

It is not science that is against women, she told them, but the male scientists. The most eminent thinkers in every branch of philosophy and psychology, when they turn to the question of women, fall into the most ridiculous errors. No matter how well they reason on other topics, when they begin to talk about women they become obsessed, delirious with their prejudice. "It is certainly true that men lose their minds over women." Attempting to prove the absurdity of the feminist position, they had ended up making themselves ridiculous.

There was the historian Michelet, who maintained that woman's constitutional weakness doomed her to eternal tutelage and made any effort to emancipate her pointless, and Proudhon, according to whom women could either remain at home as housewives or, if they left the home, become prostitutes. There were the paternalistic ideas of Comte and Fourier, with whom she dealt gently, saving her sarcasm for her contemporary fellow countrymen Lombroso, Venturi and Sergi. Lombroso's ingenious view was that woman was an incomplete organism, a case of infantilism—in effect, a man in a state of arrested development. Venturi went all the way back to the invertebrates, the groundworm and the snail, to establish the physiological inferiority of women. Sergi was convinced that the movement to grant social equality to women would destroy the institution of the family and threaten the very basis of society.

Only recently, at a scientific congress held in Vienna, an attempt had been made to explain the natural inferiority of women in terms of the smaller amount of phosphorus to be found in their brains. It was even suggested that a woman who used her available energies to study would have none left over for procreation, a statement which Montessori delighted in reporting had been challenged by a woman scientist in the audience who rose and said, "Friends and colleagues, please disprove my nine children."

How were women to defend themselves against such arguments? Not, she suggested, by an appeal to sentiment, but by the use of reason. Women themselves must enter the field of positive science, must argue with their brains, not their hearts. Women would have to confront men, to debate with them, to work alongside them, to join them in discovering the truth. Women would have to study women themselves.

> I wish [she told her listeners] that I could make all women fall in love with scientific reasoning. It doesn't suffocate the voice of the heart but augments it and supports it.
>
> For instance, you ladies go on declaiming against war, which tears away your beloved children and leads them to an undeserved death. What effect do you expect your voices to have if society is not touched by the youths themselves, sent to be slaughtered, if it has no pity for the tears of their fathers, no less burning than those of their mothers?
>
> Try arguing with your brains, not just your hearts. You'll have more chance of succeeding when you demonstrate that every war is followed by a period of decadence, that in wartime women are subjected to such severe strains that the next generation is born wretched and sickly. . . .

By the same token, it's not enough to deplore the fact that women are overworked. We must demonstrate scientifically the terrible consequences of that fact—the statistics that show that women exhausted by fatiguing labor give birth to degenerate children, that while vice and crime claim even more victims among the young than war, the effects of overwork claim twice as many as war and vice together.

In short, we must show that war and inhuman working conditions will produce a sick, degenerate society in which there are more miserable children, more idiots, more delinquents, more of the insane, all of whom will have to be provided for in jails or hospitals or asylums at great cost to society. . . .

Feminism would triumph, she insisted, not as a result of progaganda, not because of lectures or newspaper articles, but because it was a social inevitability. As mechanical progress diminished the work of the housewife, as the new inventions left more of her time and energy free, she would begin to participate in the new movement spreading through every class, first in the towns and industrial centers, eventually in the farmhouses and fields. She talked about the women's study groups that were being formed in Rome, in Milan, and predicted that

the movement itself will disappear when it has succeeded in persuading men that women can and should do more with their lives than what they are allowed to do today.

Eventually, the woman of the future will have equal rights as well as equal duties. She will have a new self-awareness and will find her true strength in an emancipated maternity. Family life as we know it may change, but it is absurd to think that feminism will destroy maternal feelings. The new woman will marry and have children out of choice, not because matrimony and maternity are imposed on her, and she will exercise control over the health and well-being of the next generation and inaugurate a reign of peace, because when she can speak knowledgeably in the name of her children and in behalf of her own rights man will have to listen to her.

The theme of children and peace was one she would still be talking on to their grandchildren, two world wars later.

To critics who ridiculed a version of the future in which women, equal to men in every way, would be expected to wear soldiers' uniforms and judges' robes, Montessori pointed out that the new woman would evolve in a new social environment. There would be no need for women to bear arms when war was abolished, no need for courts of law when science had been applied to perfecting mankind. "We will have no need for judges or jurors when there are no criminals, no delinquents."

She saw the women's movement as gradually preparing the way "by

81

struggling against all the barriers to liberty of thought and action. In the meantime, what we see is not yet the new woman, but a woman in transition. The woman who emerges from the home today enters society with no preparation. She has to have exceptional strength. She is an anomaly—not yet the new woman but the pioneer who blazes the trail. She has forfeited the rights given her on the basis of her weakness but not yet gained her new place."

The description of the woman of the future, liberated by technology from domestic work and able to dedicate herself to the scientific study of the needs of children, is of course a description of Montessori herself.

Montessori spoke for over an hour, repeatedly interrupted by furious applause. When she finished, many of the women in the audience rushed forward to surround her. One of them, Ada Negri, a famous young socialist poet and passionate feminist, was moved to tears and jumped to her feet, weeping and crying, "Brava! Brava!"

All but the most rabid antifeminists were won over by her. The journalists described her as "the apostle of a new movement on behalf of unfortunate children," "vibrant," "erudite," "as convincing as she is admired," and added that "she herself is the most persuasive argument for the feminist movement."

She was already considered important enough to be attacked in some detail by writers who accused her of being naïve in her belief that science could identify potential criminals in early childhood, that the establishment of special schools would do away with the necessity for jails, that children who tortured animals or women who became prostitutes were casualties of their environment. She had too much study of science, grumbled one critic, and too little experience of life.

Through it all, she kept her equanimity. When a reporter referred to her as *medichessa* she let it be known with gentle courtesy that she preferred to be designated by the same word used for male doctors—*medico.*

Publicity and word of mouth brought out an even larger audience to hear her second lecture, "Modern Charity." In it she told her listeners that the old idea of the aim of charity as the relief of existing social miseries must be changed in the light of modern scientific knowledge to include the aim of preventing them.

Hospitals, institutions with their roots in the middle ages, had been established to cure illness; the need now was for research and for institutions designed to apply the understanding gained on the causes of disease in such a way as to prevent it. If more money were spent providing adequate nutrition for the poor instead of only providing medicine for them when they were already sick, many hospital beds would remain empty.

As examples of the kinds of preventive institutions she had in mind, Montessori cited the Cucina dei malati poveri and the proposed Albergo popolare, set up to offer the poor a wholesome diet and sanitary shelter with the idea of preventing tuberculosis—in the long run a more economical expenditure of public funds than waiting to treat it in hospitals—as well as the proposed *istituti medico-pedagogici*. She pointed out that in Italy at that moment there were sixty-five thousand deficients, eighteen thousand of them classified as idiots. In a single city, Turin, there was a prison population of five thousand, two thousand of them minors, and a large number of these mentally deficient. They formed an army of extrasocial and antisocial beings who in turn continued to add to society an increasing contingent of the insane, the tubercular, the epileptic, the delinquent, and no provisions existed for them beyond thrusting them out of the school system and eventually receiving them in jails or asylums. All civilized nations of the world had established institutions for the education and training of these unfortunates. Only Turkey, Spain, and Italy lagged behind.

This preventive charity could not remain the work of a few sentimental souls; it would have to become a duty of the community. "We have already learned much about the causes of our social ills; it is time to use what we have learned in order to prevent them."

The lecture ended with the distribution of membership forms for the league, and with the same ovation, the same rush afterward by admiring women in the audience to surround her and congratulate her, the same favorable press reports as her first talk.

She repeated both lectures in Padua, where the local sponsoring organizations which would share the proceeds with the league were the Dante Alighiere Society and a school for professional women, and where she was the first in a series of speakers which later in the season would include professors Lombroso and Venturi, whose edifying ideas on the women's movement she had dealt with in her first lecture.

A few days later, in Venice, she repeated her lectures. She was introduced by the president of the university to an enthusiastic audience that included all of the civic leaders, the local notables of government, the educational establishment, and society. Again, she appealed to the audience and the press to publicize the cause; again, they did so, and publicized her as well. She was hailed as an effective propagandist for the cause of applying scientific knowledge to the establishment of institutions for the prevention of retardation, disease, and crime, and as a living example of what the women's movement was all about.

In Genoa, where she wound up her lecture tour, she was introduced by the distinguished head of the Scientific Society, Professor Enrico

Morselli, in the old-fashioned florid oratorical style that was as typical of academics of the time (and beside which her speech was strikingly simple and direct) as was the condescending nature of the compliments he paid her. "Although up to now a woman entering the professions has been seen as a challenger, a competitor of men in areas up to now reserved exclusively for them, we must admit that in medicine women are often more effective than men because they bring, in addition to the contribution of their minds, that of their hearts."

In all of the cities in which she spoke, Montessori used her time to visit the local hospitals, clinics, and sanitoria for nervous diseases and the university departments connected with their study, making note of anything that might be helpful in planning the league's institution in Rome.

She left Genoa in a train compartment filled with flowers brought by admirers who came to see her off. She was visibly moved by their tribute and, never one to let an opportunity slip by, made a last plea for support for the league's work. Among her listeners was a young woman medical student, one of those for whom Montessori had paved the way.

Her lectures had a discernible impact in every city where she appeared. They stimulated numerous articles in the Italian press on the problems of retarded and delinquent children as well as on her own significance as an example of the role women were capable of assuming in society. Her ideas—as well as her youth and charm—were topics of discussion before classes and meetings, after dinners and parties, in medical and academic circles throughout the country.

By the end of June 1899 she had been elected, along with an assortment of princes, professors, senators, lawyers, and physicians—one of whom was her co-worker at the psychiatric clinic, Dr. Montesano—to the board of the league. Bonfigli was to serve as president with Baccelli as honorary president. The league was moving ahead with plans for the opening of its institution in Rome as well as for the establishment in existing elementary schools of classrooms especially adapted for the needs of older, less severely abnormal children.

That same month, Montessori was in London as a delegate to an international congress of women, feted at the Rothschild estate, received at the Royal Institute, and invited to Windsor on a special train, to be received at court with the other delegates with full pomp and ceremony by Queen Victoria, with whom she managed to have a few words of private conversation.

It was an exciting experience for a young professional not yet turned thirty. While in London, she addressed the membership of the English Association for Promoting the Welfare of the Feeble-minded, telling them about the efforts begun in Italy during the past year to help the sixty-five thousand deficient children who up to then had been neglected by the state and private charity alike.

In her address to the congress she gave a moving description of the conditions of child labor in the mines of Sicily. Her plea to end the exploitation of children by industry was warmly supported by her fellow delegates.

During the weeks she spent in London that summer she tried to find a copy of Seguin's second book, which had been published in English thirteen years earlier but which she had been unable to find in any library in Italy. She called on every physician she knew was interested in deficient children, as well as the superintendents of special schools, but was unable to find anyone who had a copy of the book or had even read it. "The fact that this book was unknown in England," she said, "although it had been published in the English language, made me think that the Seguin system had never been understood."[4]

It was her hunch, having been unable to locate a copy of Seguin's second book anywhere in Italy, France, or England, that although he was quoted in all the writings about institutions for deficient children, and his didactic apparatus was used at the Bicêtre, his methods were not really being used. The techniques of his followers were "purely mechanical, each teacher following the rules according to the letter" but missing the spirit.[5]

On her return to Italy at the end of the summer Montessori found herself to be a well-known public figure. Her ideas were being discussed in the press all over the country. Critical articles appeared attacking her proposals as too costly; they were followed by rebuttals pointing out the social gains that would result from the expenditure of public funds she advocated. Other articles reported on the activities stimulated by her visits to the cities where she had spoken—the schools started, the branches of the league formed.

In the fall of 1899, in addition to her hospital work and practice and her activities on behalf of the league, she took on a new position. By now a specialist and acknowledged authority on the nervous diseases of children, she was appointed lecturer in hygiene and anthropology at the Regio Istituto Superiore di Magistero Femminile, one of the two teacher-training colleges for women in Italy, the other being at Florence. The course of studies at the Istituto was on an equal level with that of the university and its diploma was required for teaching in the secondary schools. There were about two hundred and twenty students enrolled at the time Montessori joined the faculty.

In addition to her teaching responsibilities, she also read students' theses as part of the committee of examiners which granted diplomas in pedagogy and morals. Another member of the committee was the playwright Luigi Pirandello.

Although she was teaching as a physician, she was teaching in a school of education, and her contact with faculty and students and her involvement with their curriculum as well as her responsibilities as an examiner meant a growing familiarity with the history and methods of education.

In December came a new honor. She was presented with an award for outstanding service in the hospitals where she had worked as a medical assistant since 1895, the year before her graduation.

By the spring of 1900 the league had opened a school in Rome, a medical-pedagogical institute, to train teachers in the care and education of deficient children, with a practice-demonstration school in which twenty-two young pupils were enrolled. Montessori was appointed director of the school.

It was a natural choice. Her speeches and articles had called attention to the need for such an institution. She had become the spokeswoman for a new kind of education for problem children. Now she would be given an opportunity to experiment with the kinds of sensory teaching materials developed by Itard and Seguin: three-dimensional shapes and letters to be felt, matched, set into holes of corresponding shapes; beads, cloths, and laces to be threaded, buttoned, and tied; a whole series of objects of differing sizes, shapes, colors, textures to be distinguished and handled so as to develop skills in both perceiving and performing. She would be able to modify these materials in her own way as she observed the reactions of the children, constantly adapting the objects to the pupils' needs as these became apparent to her.

Montessori's colleague and research associate at the psychiatric clinic and fellow member of the league, Dr. Montesano, now chief physician of the Rome mental asylum, the Manicomio di Roma, was appointed co-director of the school. In their capacities as joint directors of the new institution, Montessori and Montesano would be working together closely in daily contact as they developed a program and plans for implementing it. Whatever their titles suggested, of the two it was Dr. Montessori who was the better known and who exerted the greater influence.

The institution was known as the Scuola Magistrale Ortofrenica, the Orthophrenic School, taking its name from the term "frenasthenic" (*i frenastenici*) coined by the alienist Andrea Verga in 1874 to denote the entire class of abnormalities including idiots and imbeciles as well as those less severely retarded but still unable to function up to average levels.

The Early Struggles

There were sixty-four teachers being trained in the first term, men and women already teaching in the regular Rome schools as well as school administrators, teachers from special institutions for deaf-mutes, and some forty newly licensed teachers with no previous classroom experience. The children were drawn from the regular schools, where they had been unable to function. There were three classes. The first began their preparation for learning by sensory stimulation. Its aim was to awaken their capacities to perceive and make distinctions among the objects in their environment. The second and third classes corresponded to the first two elementary grades with a similar program but special teaching materials and methods. Manual work and gymnastics played an important part in the children's curriculum. The teacher trainees were given courses in general psychology, in the physiology and anatomy of the nervous system, in the psychology of retarded children. They were trained to make anthropological examinations of the children, recording their measurements, and to make close observations of their individual behavioral characteristics. Lectures on the causes and characteristics of mental deficiency and special methods of instruction were given by Montessori and Montesano. The core of the curriculum was based on the lectures Montessori had given to the teachers at the Scuole normali.

The school had been set up along the lines of a teaching hospital. Following the clinical model, the pupils were instructed by apprentice teachers under the supervision of Montessori and her colleagues, just as patients are treated by medical students, interns, and residents under the supervision of experienced senior faculty in a hospital setting. Its twofold purpose was to provide care—special education for abnormal children—and train practitioners in the methods that proved successful in this special setting. It was, in its time and place, a unique institution. And it worked. From the beginning, results were impressive.

Government officials including Baccelli, the minister of public education, came to visit the school. All of them left with nothing but praise for the program and Montessori's guiding role in it.

At the end of the first term, in July 1900, officials of the ministry of education, the league, the city council, the University of Rome, and the Chamber of Deputies attended a demonstration of the school's accomplishments to date. Montessori spoke briefly about the children and the methods used to instruct them. Members of the teaching staff answered questions on the physiology and psychology of retarded children and then the young pupils themselves were asked to show what they had learned. The visitors were amazed at the results that had been achieved with these children in the short space of three months, and the enthusiasm of all the officials present was recognized as a sure sign that their future support could be counted on.

When, later in the month, examinations were given the student teachers for the purpose of granting them certification to teach deficient children, the board of examiners consisted of some of the most distinguished figures in the fields of education, psychiatry, and anthropology at the University of Rome, including the noted Professor Sergi, as well as government officials from the ministries of education and health. The examiners granted licenses to all of the teachers, many with honors, and expressed official satisfaction not only with the results of the examinations but with the general direction of the institution which had been able to accomplish so much so quickly.

On her thirtieth birthday, in the first summer of the new century, Montessori's father presented her with an enormous, beautifully handtooled leather volume in which he had pasted clippings of articles about her from newspapers published in Italy, Germany, France, and England over the past eight years, from the time she had been chosen as a young medical student to present flowers to the queen through her triumphs as director of the Orthophrenic School in Rome. They were all beautifully numbered in his elegant handwriting and in the front of the book he wrote in flowery letters:

Cara figlia,
A pile of newspapers has accumulated in our house over these last years thanks to some of your many friends and admirers.

These newspapers contain souvenirs which are as dear to me as to you, because they demonstrate your genius and record your activities, but kept in as disorderly way as they were, they might not have been preserved.

I decided to collect these souvenirs in a volume and present it to you on the occasion of your thirtieth birthday, with the hope that you will look through it with pleasure.

Rome 31 August 1900

Tuo padre

He had written out a table of contents listing each of the more than two hundred items and giving the name of the newspaper or journal from which it came, the city, the date of publication, title of the article and author, all in the old-fashioned calligraphy in which he had entered so many figures in ledgers over the years. It was a labor of love, a proof of pride, and perhaps an apology.

5

Montessori spent two years in the medical-pedagogical institute known as the Orthophrenic School evolving and training teachers in a special method of observation and education of feebleminded children, those from the elementary schools who could not function there as well as those who had been sent to the asylums as idiots. She went to London and Paris, visiting all of the existing institutions for deficient children and paying particular attention to what was being done at the Bicêtre, where she found that the methods described in Seguin's first book were no longer followed and that his second book was unknown there.

On her return, she tells us, "I gave myself over completely to the actual teaching of the children, directing at the same time the work of the other teachers in our institute."[1] She was there from eight in the morning to seven at night, teaching, observing, experimenting with different materials and methods, trying everything she had found in her long line of predecessors in medicine, education, and anthropology down to Seguin and Froebel and Sergi.

At night she made notes on what she had observed during the day, read everything she could get her hands on in the professional literature dealing with special education, wrote out her own ideas, made sketches and models for teaching materials until she felt she had hit on what worked best. "Those two years of practice," she later said, "are my first and indeed my true degree in pedagogy."[2]

What worked best worked so well that the children who had been classified as unteachable in the elementary schools and those who had been assigned to the asylums as idiots were able to master skills that had been thought totally beyond their capabilities. A number of them actually learned to read and write. When they were able to pass the same examinations given to normal children in the primary grades—at that time still the highest level of formal education reached by the majority of their countrymen—Montessori had proved her point. She had also acquired a new professional identity. No longer primarily a physician, she had now become an educator.

Based on the apparatus developed earlier by Itard and Seguin to teach deficient children, modified by her own observations of her pupils' reactions, she developed a set of teaching materials which she had manufac-

89

tured and which she found "became in the hands of those who knew how to apply them, a most remarkable and efficient means, but unless rightly presented, they failed to attract the attention of the deficients."[3] It was this apparatus and this presentation which later, adapted for use with normal children, became the Montessori materials and the Montessori method.

It was characteristic of her way of designing materials and evolving methods for their use—really two aspects of the same process rather than separable ones—that she developed her method for teaching writing and reading on the basis of her observations of the behavior of the children to be taught.

An eleven-year-old retarded girl was unable to learn to sew or even to darn, no matter how many times she was shown. Montessori then tried her with Froebelian mat weaving, threading strips of paper horizontally in and out of vertical slots in a mat. When the girl had mastered the weaving, Montessori gave her the needle and thread again, and found she was now able to darn, a more refined version of the same activity. From then on, sewing lessons were always preceded by mat weaving, but Montessori did not stop there. She generalized the principle involved to other kinds of activities: "We should really find the way to teach the child how, before making him execute a task."[4] The way to teach a skill was not by having the child repeatedly try it, but by having him repeat an exercise that prepares him for it. "Pupils could then come to the real work, able to perform it without ever having directly set their hands to it before."[5]

Her next thought was to apply this principle to writing. She had a three-dimensional wooden script alphabet made, with the vowels enameled red and the consonants blue. Since they had to be made by hand, she could afford only one set. The children practiced touching the model letters over and over, following their contours, until eventually they had learned to make the movements necessary to reproduce the form of the letters and were able to write them with chalk on the blackboard.

She experimented with various ways of guiding the children more efficiently, adding some painted alphabet cards and other refinements of technique, and when she felt she had found the best method, taught it to the teachers at the Orthophrenic School. The lectures were printed and distributed to about two hundred elementary teachers. They constituted a method for teaching reading as well as writing: "Looking becomes reading; touching becomes writing . . . some learn to read first, others to write."[6]

Experimenting on her own, she had gone beyond either Itard or Se-

90

guin in developing a method by means of which retarded children could be taught to read and write. And when she presented some of her eight-year-old "defectives" for the state examinations in reading and writing they passed, doing as well or better than "normal" children.

Her own reaction to this accomplishment, hailed as miraculous by everyone around her, was to wonder what it implied about the education of the normal children whose achievements her idiots had been able to equal. What if these same methods were used with *them*? What if normal children were stimulated in their development instead of being "suffocated, held back"?

To Montessori it was clear that "the boys from the asylums had been able to compete with the normal children only because they had been taught in a different way . . . I found myself thinking that if, some day, the special education which had developed these idiot children in such a marvelous fashion could be applied to the development of normal children, the 'miracle' of which my friends talked would no longer be'possible. The abyss between the inferior mentality of the idiot and that of the normal brain can never be bridged if the normal child has reached his full development.

"While everyone was admiring the progress of my idiots, I was searching for the reasons which could keep the happy healthy children of the common schools on so low a plane that they could be equalled in tests of intelligence by my unfortunate pupils!"[7]

The peculiar tension in Montessori between scientist and mystic, between reason and intuition, was already present when she wrote about her success with the children so many others had given up on: "We must know how to call to the *man* which lies dormant within the soul of the child. I felt this, intuitively, and believed that not the didactic material, but my voice which called to them, *awakened* the children, and encouraged them to use the didactic material, and through it, to educate themselves. I was guided in my work by the deep respect which I felt for their misfortune, and by the love which these unhappy children know how to awaken in those who are near them."[8] She spoke of her "belief that we must act upon the spirit" as a "secret key" that had opened the way to the results she had been able to achieve, and added that "while my efforts showed themselves in the intellectual progress of my pupils, a peculiar form of exhaustion prostrated me. It was as if I gave to them some vital force from within me."[9]

Now, in 1901, Montessori left the institute and school, at what would seem to have been her moment of triumph, for reasons which have never been made clear. The explanation she herself gave later and which has been repeated ever since is that she decided to leave the field of medicine and special education in order to begin to educate herself all over again in the education of normal children.

While that is indeed what she did afterward, it was not the reason for her decision. Montessori left the school for a personal reason—to remove herself from a relationship and a situation which had become intolerable. At some point she had formed a close friendship with her colleague Dr. Montesano, which grew into a love affair, and she had borne his child.

Everything we know about her makes it unbelievable that it could have been a casual liaison; she must have been drawn to him as a man she respected, perhaps found herself involved in an intellectual adventure which grew into a deep emotional involvement before either of them had given enough thought to whatever they later decided made a permanent union impossible.

Why they did not marry is not clear. According to her son, Dr. Montesano's family and his mother in particular opposed their marriage, but Montessori herself, strong-willed and used to overcoming obstacles and forging ahead to achieve her own goals, already accomplished at persuading others to her purposes, must have had her own reasons for not marrying the father of her child. In any case, after his birth, which her son dates as March 31, 1898, the child was sent to stay with a wet nurse in the country. He believes it was a plan that was urged by Montessori's mother as well as Montesano's, and that Montesano made it a condition of legally granting the child his name that the birth be kept a secret from all but the families and closest friends of the pair. He was also told that they made a promise to each other never to marry and that it was Montesano's betrayal of that promise by marrying someone else that was the crisis to which Maria Montessori responded by leaving the school where they had worked together in daily contact.

Reviewing the known facts of her public life in those years it is hard to see how she could have been pregnant from the summer of 1897, been confined, and given birth in the spring of 1898, a period in which she seems to have been quite visible in her capacities as a physician in practice, working in hospitals and the psychiatric clinic of the University of Rome. It is easier to suppose that it was the pregnancy and birth itself that, in 1901, caused her to leave her position at the Orthophrenic School and drop from public view for a time. That is the first explanation that occurs when one is faced with the fact of her decision to leave. However, if her child was indeed born early in 1898, the only explanation left for her departure and what can only be described as her retreat is that given by her son: the traumatic event was not the birth of her child but the betrayal by his father.

At any rate, Montessori seems for the only time in her life to have given in to the pressures of others—her family and friends—and agreed to have her child in secrecy and send him away to be discreetly brought up by a family in the countryside near Rome. According to her son, those who were closest to her next to her parents and who knew of his existence included Montessori's good friend Donna Maria Maraini and later her close associates Anna Maccheroni and Anna Fedeli. Seventy-five years ago the knowledge that she had had a child out of wedlock would have shattered any woman's career; it would have ended all Montessori's hopes for the future, all possibility for her to make the contribution she had come to see as the real purpose of her life.

The child whose name in the world would be his mother's—Mario Montessori—has shadowy memories of visits from time to time from a "beautiful lady" who was never identified. The family romance that is a universal fantasy of children was for this child a reality. The ordinary people with whom he lived were not his real parents; his own mother was someone far more special. His later impressions of those years include having had the conviction that it was so, as well as a recurring dream in which he found her. One of the remembered events of that far-off childhood, even more mysterious than the passage of time makes everyone's, was a visit from the beautiful lady one day while he was playing with his pet bird. Annoyed at being interrupted at his play to be given the present she had brought him, he remembers breaking the elaborate toy. Whether a memory or a fantasy, it reverberates with ironies. One sees reflected in the story Montessori's later concern with the inappropriateness of conventional toys, her stress on the child's need to exercise his attention on whatever has engaged it for as long as he remains absorbed in his activity, her sense of herself as an observer of children.

At seven, Mario was sent to a boarding school near Florence. Occasional visits from the unidentified lady continued, but no explanations of her presence or her interest were given the boy during his childhood, and he was left to his dreams and fantasies of who she might be. And during the years of his infancy and childhood Montessori must have had, in the midst of all her work and her success, dreams of her own, and who knows what regrets. They can only be guessed at from the pattern of her interests, the shape her life took from then on. Deprived of the experience of caring for her own child, she was to turn her attention increasingly to ways of meeting the needs of other children. And this focus of her intellectual energies was accomplished by a gradual change in the character of her views as well. Having begun her adult life as a free-thinker she gradually became more religious. During the years following Mario's birth she made a spiritual retreat for two weeks every summer at a convent near Bologna, withdrawing to meditate among the nuns.

No one can know what the experience of her tragic affair or its after-math cost her. We only know that she decided to leave the institution where she worked beside the father of her child, now another woman's husband, and refocus her interests and energies. It was, as it turned out, a momentous decision, for her and for the world.

All the world could see at the time, however, was that it was an unusual, a surprising decision. From her position as a public figure, director of a highly respected institution, she withdrew to the academic life and the status of a pupil.

She was now thirty years old, a well-known authority in her field, an extraordinary success for a woman of her time and place. At this point she gave up not only the directorship of the school but also the practice of medicine, in order to study anthropology, experimental psychology, educational philosophy, everything she thought could help her in her search for the reasons why schools were failing the children they were supposed to be helping. Whatever complex personal reasons existed for her decision, it was of momentous significance in the context of her life's work. It was her first real educational project—the education of herself. No institution of learning, no curriculum existed to teach her what she needed to know, so she made her own.

She enrolled at the University of Rome again, this time as a student in the faculty of philosophy. The major psychological theories of the time had their roots in the German idealism of Herbart and Wundt and were taught not as branches of natural science but of philosophy.

She felt that Seguin's "physiological method" of education, with its stress on the training of the senses and the importance of approaching abstractions through concrete forms a child could see and touch, must be based on the psychological principles developed by Wundt as a "phys-iological psychology," and she set herself the goal of discovering the con-nection and its application to the education of normal children.

"A great faith animated me," she wrote of this time, "and although I did not know that I should ever be able to test the truth of my idea, I gave up every other occupation to deepen and broaden its conception. It was almost as if I prepared myself for an unknown mission."[10]

She took courses in pedagogy, in hygiene, and in experimental psy-chology, then a new field in the Italian universities, continued her studies in anthropology and did anthropological research in the elementary schools as a way of learning more about normal children and how they were educated.

She visited elementary schools, sitting in the classrooms noting how teachers taught and how children learned in the traditional setting. What she saw were large groups of children ranged stonily in row after row, repeating in unison the words of the teacher or an assistant, a system which had spread throughout the schools of the Western World from its beginnings in industrial England, where the monitorial techniques of the Lancasterian system had been introduced as an economical way to instruct large numbers of pupils at the same time. It became clearer and clearer to her that it was a system that repressed everything she wanted to elicit from the children, who, "like butterflies mounted on pins, are fastened each to his place, the desk, spreading the useless wings of barren and meaningless knowledge which they have acquired."[11]

The physical immobility, the enforced silence, the use of rewards and punishments all seemed to her as degrading, as destructive of the child's natural abilities, as the sexual slavery of women she had spoken out against at the beginning of her career.

She was appalled not only by the methods employed in teaching and discipline, but with the poor hygienic conditions she observed, and she continued to write articles pressing for better sanitary conditions and improved health care.

A second national pedagogical congress was held in Naples in 1902 and there Montessori summarized the results of her work in medicine and teaching in a report titled *Norme per una classificazione dei deficienti in rapporto ai metodi speciali di educazione* ("Rules for a Classification of Deficients with Reference to a Special Method of Education") in which she discussed Seguin's methods as a point of departure from which she went on to outline systematically her own program for stimulating the latent capacities of "unteachable" children.

Her experience with Seguin's methods had justified her earlier belief in their validity, and now, feeling, as she put it, a need for meditation and for more thorough study, she sat down and translated the books of Itard and Seguin into Italian in her own careful handwriting, "in order that I might have time to weigh the sense of each word, and to read, in truth, the *spirit* of the author." She was, as she said, "making for myself books as the old Benedictines used to do before the diffusion of printing."[12]

She had just finished her handwritten translation of the six hundred pages of Seguin's French book when a friend in New York sent her a copy of the 1866 English volume which had turned up among the books discarded from the private library of a New York physician. The book was falling apart, so dusty and soiled that Alessandro Montessori insisted on having it disinfected before he would let his daughter handle it. With the help of an English friend she translated it, and found that after his thirty years of work with deficient children Seguin had reached the same conclusion she herself had recently come to: his physiological method for educating abnormal children, based on the understanding of the individual pupil, would, if applied to normal children, lead to "a complete human regeneration." Here was confirmation—from the source she respected most—of the idea that she had arrived at herself.

Her background in physical medicine and her social reformer's outlook had led her to the problem of mentally deficient children. In solving that problem with the tools of physical anthropology and psychological pedagogy, she had been led to the problem that now absorbed her—how to educate normal children in order to create a better society.

"From the very beginning of my work with deficient children," she wrote later, "I felt that the methods which I used had in them nothing peculiarly limited to the instruction of idiots. I believed that they contained educational principles *more rational* than those in use, so much more so, indeed, that through their means an inferior mentality would be able to grow and develop. This feeling, so deep as to be in the nature of an intuition, became my controlling idea after I had left the school for deficients, and little by little, I became convinced that similar methods applied to normal children would develop or set free their personality in a marvelous and surprising way."[13]

In December 1904, at the recommendation of Sergi, Montessori was appointed to give a university course for students in the faculty of natural sciences and medicine in the Pedagogic School of the University of Rome, a position she held until 1908.

Her lectures dealt with the history of anthropology and its application to education, aspects of general biology, and those characteristics of the individual to be studied by the anthropologist as educator: stature and weight; the head, brain, and face; the thorax, pelvis, limbs and skin; types of malformations; techniques of anthropometric measurement and statistical methodology and—the culmination of all this data—the biographical chart of the pupil.

She gave three lectures a week, the first dealing with the observations, the second with the techniques used in gathering the data, and the third with clinical demonstration of normal and abnormal children drawn from the elementary schools in order to present as wide a variety of children and educational methods as possible. The aim of the course was "to lay practical foundations of a far-reaching reform in our schools."

The lectures were reprinted later in a volume titled *L'Antropologia Pedagogica*[14] (which appeared in English as *Pedagogical Anthropology*). It is hard to find a book more dated in its style, more obsolete in its factual content, and yet the general principles on which it is based—that the nature of education should follow from an understanding of the nature of the child to be educated—was a significant innovation at the time. From references to her later work it is clear that Montessori added to the text of her original lectures at the time they were published, but the book probably still gives a good idea of what the lectures were like, in content as well as style.

One thing that distinguished them was her use of what is called today in the jargon of professional educators "visual aids," ranging from charts and graphs to photographs and diagrams. A typical "teaching aid" was a drawing of an infant body and an adult body side by side, both exactly the same size, to illustrate the difference in proportions by way of introducing a discussion of the difference in functioning. To illustrate, to make the material interesting to the student, so that he learned because he wanted to rather than because he was forced to, was a method she recommended to teachers of children and used herself in teaching teachers.

As a member of the university's faculty, Montessori stood out just as she had as a student at the same institution. Many of her colleagues took their teaching responsibilities lightly, repeating the same set of lectures year after year and showing little interest in their students. For many, the position was little more than a comfortable lifetime sinecure. Her lectures were always fresh, profusely illustrated with example and anecdote, and delivered in her compelling style. The enthusiasm of the students was reflected in their attendance. Students told other students about her lectures and her courses were always full. One of the people who came to hear her was a young woman named Anna Maria Maccheroni, who became a lifelong friend and collaborator. She described the occasion in a memoir she wrote some forty years later:

> The hall was large, and over the lecturers' chair was a canopy. Having taken a place on one of the two benches at the right side of the platform I could see the hall crowded with young people of both sexes. The lecturer herself stood, looking eagerly at them, with her searching look. . . . She could take in each one, individually. . . .
> Of course I noticed at once that she was a very good-looking woman, but what impressed me even more was that she was not following the

general custom of the learned women of her time. They were few, and chose to dress in a rather masculine style. Not she! In her attire, however simple it was, she retained a feminine and elegant touch. And she was smiling.

She spoke—not about anthropology, but about schools. She told us what a school should be like. . . .

She was a most attractive lecturer; her language was so simple, so clear, her delivery so animated, that even the poorer students could understand her. All that she said had the warmth of life. I remember some students saying, 'Her lectures make us want to be good.' . . .

When she had to show any special piece of apparatus, for example a prepared brain, she wore the white overall commonly used by doctors.[15]

As a teacher of teachers, Montessori had a clear sense of herself as a reformer dedicated to innovation rather than a transmitter of a body of knowledge and teaching techniques inherited from the past.

She was concerned less with tradition than with change. The industrialization and urbanization that were taking place in Italy meant that as more people moved from the country to the city and more women as well as men went to work outside the home in factories, a new system of education was called for that would look to the socialization of young children, teaching skills, imparting discipline that had once been the exclusive province of the family and the church in a more stable, traditional society with less change and less mobility.

The new science of education, Montessori told her students, would turn anthropology from the study of the origins of man to the future of man; the observations of biologically and socially caused abnormalities should yield data to be used for "the regeneration of mankind," to be accomplished through education, in the environment of the school. The content of the science of pedagogy would be derived by the experimental method from the anthropological observation of children in the laboratory of the school.

"In order to educate, it is essential to know those who are to be educated,"[16] says Montessori, and she quotes her "master," Sergi, who says, "Taking measurements of the head, the stature, is, to be sure, not in itself the practice of pedagogy. But it does mean that we are following the path that leads to pedagogy, because we cannot educate anyone until we know him thoroughly."[17]

She told her young teachers, "The subject of our study is humanity; our purpose is to become teachers. Now, what really makes a teacher is love for the human child; for it is love that transforms the social duty of the educator into the higher consciousness of a *mission*." And she suggested what was to them a new way of looking at their chosen work—as social engineering:

> Scientific pedagogy must concern itself before all and above all, with *normal* individuals, in order to protect them in their development under the guidance of biological laws, and to aid each pupil to adapt himself to this social environment, i.e., to direct him to that form of employment which is best suited to his individual temperament and tendencies."[18]
>
> The teacher ought to make the anthropological study of the pupil precede his education; he should prepare him for whatever he is best adapted for, and should indicate to him the paths that are best for him to follow, in the struggle for existence.
>
> To aid the physical development of the child under the guidance of natural laws is to favor his health and his growth; to aid his natural psychic tendencies is to render him more intelligent. This principle has been intuitively recognized by all pedagogists, but the practical application of it was not possible, excepting under the guidance of scientific pedagogy, founded upon a direct knowledge of the human individual. Today it is possible for us to establish a regime of liberty in our schools, and consequently it is our duty to do so.[19]

The lectures are full of anthropometric measurements in centimeters of the maximum transverse diameter of the cranium, of the degree of prognathism (how far the facial features protrude beyond a perpendicular line from forehead to chin), of patterns of hairline, teeth, and fingers, of measurements of the auriculofrontal radius and the width of the ocular rima, and such niceties as the formula for the facial index:

$$Fi = \frac{\text{bizygomatic diameter x } 100}{\text{ophryo-mental diameter}}$$

Tabulations of "the psycho-physical characteristics of juvenile delinquents" provide statistics on the frequency in boys of such items as "fond of wine and gluttonous," "desire to play the spy," "obscene writings in copy-books," and "frequently absent from school, to play games of chance"; and girls, of "immoderate vanity," "theft, limited to pens," "lascivious love letters," and "hatred of beautiful things."[20]

Whimsical as these items sound, they were put to a sensible use. The observations on these children were compared with notes on their homes and parents in order to show a connection between the child's behavior and his environment. That the child who is "bad" is really sick—the product of an unhealthy environment—was not a commonplace in turn-of-the-century Italy. What Montessori was telling her students was that the school, and through it society, could be reformed "by means of the scientific trend which pedagogy is today acquiring through the study of the pupil. The teacher must assume the new task of repairing what is

99

wrong with the child, through the aid of the physician, and of protecting the normal child from the dangers of enfeeblement and deformation that constantly overhang him, thus laying the foundations for a splendid human race, free to attain its foreordained development."[21]

The tool by means of which this task would be accomplished was, she told them, the biographic chart, a record of observations about the child, his background, physical growth, and behavior in school. In place of the report card, part of a system of rewards and punishments, it would serve as an aid to the teacher in guiding the child's development.

She described the biographic chart as a technique for social change grounded in the study of the individual. "The reform which has begun with the introduction of an anthropological movement into the school and the establishment of biographic charts, is nothing less than a reform of science as a whole. Medicine, jurisprudence, and sociology as well as pedagogy, are laying new foundations upon it."[22]

Do the exhaustively detailed tabulations of weight and stature, the measurements of maximum horizontal circumference of the head in centimeters tell anything really significant about the individual? No, but having collected them and made her general points, Montessori seems to have ignored them or at least made mercifully little real use of them.

The real point she was making was that the abnormal should not be handled like criminals but *treated* like the sick. Through scientific pedagogy "the education of the mentality in children who are thus predisposed, constitutes a great work on behalf of the defense of society."[23]

She used the technique as a jumping-off point in her crusade to free the schoolchild. When she has recorded and compared measurements of chests, with charts and diagrams, she inveighs against the unhealthy effects of the stationary school bench. "Deficiency of the thorax is one of the stigmata left by the school, which in this way tends to make the younger generation feeble and physiologically unbalanced. . . . We condemn children to death, under the delusion that we are working for their moral good; a perverted human soul may be led back to righteousness; but a consumptive chest can never again become robust."[24]

For all her talk of science and the use of its techniques, she is constantly invoking religious or mystical bases for her recommendations.

In urging a system of free lunches for schoolchildren she gives not only a rational reason, in terms of a social problem to be solved, but a spiritual one, in phrases like "the necessity of eating is itself a proof that the matter of which our body is composed does not endure but passes like the fleeing moment. And if the substance of our bodies passes in this manner, if life itself is only a continual passing away of matter, what greater symbol of its immateriality and its spirituality is there than the dinnertable? '. . . the bread is my flesh and the wine is my blood; do this in remembrance of what life really is.'[25]

"We must today regard the serving of food in the schools as a necessity of the first order; but it is well, in introducing it into the schools, to surround it with that halo of gladness and of high moral significance that ought to accompany all manifestations of life. The *hymn to bread*, which is a human creation and a means of preserving the substance of the human body, ought to accompany the meals of our new generations of children."[26]

She gives rules for school meals: children should never be given stimulants like alcohol, tea, or coffee; they should be given sugar and simple broths "since heat is as essential as sugar for organisms in the course of evolution," but not meat. Her facts seem as quaint today as do the endless charts and statistics. But one of the things that made her lectures so interesting was her tendency to digress on the topics that interested her most, drawing her own conclusions from the data as she observed it. Describing a photograph of a family of Neapolitan peasants used to illustrate her lecture on craniology, she says:

> The man, or rather the beardless youth who is just beginning to feel himself a man, and therefore hopes for independence, holds his head proudly level; but the very pretty woman seated beside him holds her head gracefully inclined forward. For that matter, this is woman's characteristically *graceful* attitude. She never naturally assumes, nor does the artist ever attribute to her the proud and lofty attitude of the level head. But this graceful pose is in reality nothing else than the pose of slavery. The woman who is beginning to struggle, the woman who begins to perceive the mysterious and potent voice of human conflict, and enters upon the infinite world of modern progress, raises up her head—and beauty is enhanced, rather than taken away, by this attitude which today has begun to be assumed by all humanity: by the laborer, since the socialistic propaganda, and by woman in her feministic aspirations for liberty.
>
> Similarly in the school, if we wish to induce little children to hold their heads in the position of orientation, all that is necessary is to instill into them a sense of liberty, of gladness and of hope. Whoever, upon entering a children's classroom, should see their heads assume the level pose as if from some internal stimulus of renewed life, could ask for no greater homage. This, and nothing else, is certainly what will form the great desire of the teacher of the future, who will rightly despise the trite and antiquated show of formal respect, but will seek to touch the souls of his pupils.[27]

And her lecture on "The Application of Biometry to Anthropology for the Purpose of Determining the Medial Man" included an aside in which she announced that the moral revival of the future "revolves around the struggle against the sexual sins" of a society in which women are slaves and men are "lords, in a barbaric sense, of sexual life."[28]

"The wife is a slave, for she has married in ignorance and has neither the knowledge nor the power to avoid being made the instrument for the birth of weakly, diseased or degenerate children; and still more deeply enslaved is the mother who cannot restrain her own son from degradations that she knows are the probable source of ruin of body and soul."[29] Social progress depends on "the emancipation of woman, the protection of maternity and of the child."[30]

She constantly seesaws between the approach of the quantitative scientist and the mystical rhetoric of the romantic.

> Beneath the pathological facts and the social injustices, there exists something more profound which, for the sake of simplicity we may call the *soul of humanity*. Something which responds from soul to soul. . . . Unknown profundities of the spirit, that seem to merge into the eternity of the universe itself and unexpectedly produce new forms as in a chemical reaction. And this is what we really mean by 'moral education.'
>
> In order to accomplish such a lofty work, we do not need to find a *method*. Method is always more or less mechanical. Here, on the contrary, is the supreme expression of human life—an evocation of the superman. What we need to find is not a method, but a *Master*.[31]

And she quotes Seguin on the characteristics required of the teacher of abnormal children:

> He must have been born with special gifts, as well as to have perfected himself for this high task. He ought to be handsome in person, and strong as well, so that he may attract and yet command; his glance should be serene, like that of one who has gained victories through faith and has attained enduring peace; his manner should be imperturbable as that of one not easily persuaded to change his mind. In short, he ought to feel beneath him the solid rock, the foundation of granite on which his feet are planted and his steps assured. From this solid base, he should rise commandingly, like a magician. His voice should be gentle, melodious, and flexible, with bursts of silvery and resounding eloquence, but always without harshness. . . . The perfect teacher must possess something more than physical beauty and acquired art; he must have the loftiness of a soul ardent for its mission. . . . When such a man speaks, the words seem, as if by magic, to touch the profoundest

recesses of the heart. Hypnotists and magicians! Conquerors of souls!
Valiant souls themselves; souls with a great mission![32]

Today it takes an effort to overlook the style. Her students loved it. To
her, and to the young educators she inspired, the teacher was a "redeem-
er of mankind."[33] She sent them off to schools all over Italy with a sense
of mission—they had a calling, they were not mere technicians.

In addition to her lectureship at the university, Montessori continued
to teach at the Istituto Superiore di Magistero Femminile until 1906, and
in that year was appointed to the board of examiners for the degree of
natural science in anthropology, a considerable academic distinction.

During these years she continued to practice in the hospitals and clinics in Rome, although she had less and less time for private practice.

By now, in addition to the printed versions of speeches she had given
at various congresses, she had published a number of professional papers. Their titles indicate the shift of her interest from physical to social
problems: "Bacteriological Research on the Cephalo-Rachitic Liquid in
Paralytic Insanity," "A Case of a Solitary Tubercle in the Middle Brain,"
"Anthropometric Characteristics in Relation to the Intellectual Standing
of Children in School," "The Influence of Family Conditions on the Intellectual Development of Schoolchildren," "Physical Characteristics of
the Young Women of Latium," "The Importance of Regional Ethnology
in Pedagogical Anthropology."[34]

PART II
The Children's House

6

In 1906 Montessori was, at thirty-six years, an established professional, a scientist and academic of distinction, well known and highly regarded by colleagues in her several fields of interest and by a wide circle of Roman civic figures and social leaders. Toward the end of the year she returned to Rome from Milan, where she had been invited to serve on an awards committee at an international meeting on pedagogy and psychology, and it was then that the opportunity came her way for which everything she had done till now seems like preparation.

Rome, like the entire country, was experiencing a new sense of possibility.

The late 1890s had been a period of widespread social disorders, brought on by economic distress. Crop failures had led to a rise in the price of bread. There was rioting in Milan and workers struck in Rome, protesting against the high cost of the government's colonial policy in Africa and the vast fortunes made by speculators while peasants died of hunger and children labored in factories. The ministry of education at Bologna was mobbed by students and at the University of Rome soldiers were posted in the lecture rooms. In the spring of 1898 the university was closed down and the city itself was in a state of siege for several days. Widespread repressive measures were taken by the government against protesting groups of Catholics and peasants, opposition newspapers were suspended, and martial law was established to combat the threat of socialism. But the socialist point of view continued to spread, nowhere more so than at the University of Rome, where Labriola introduced Marxist thought to the academic world and such influential professors as the anthropologist Lombroso were strong sympathizers of the socialist cause. In this atmosphere of grinding poverty, disease, and high taxation, not only in the historically impoverished south but among the sharecroppers and migratory agricultural workers of the Roman campagna, socialism seemed increasingly to be the only remedy to both the rural and the urban poor. A Bolognese count was widely quoted as saying, "The real and most dangerous agents of rural socialism are the primary teachers."[1]

The climate of political agitation was intense and bitter and culminat-

107

ed in the assassination of the king, Umberto I, in 1900. He was succeeded by his son, Victor Emmanuel.

In 1903 prime minister Giovanni Giolitti took power with the aim of democratizing and thus saving Italy's liberal institutions by means of a series of social, economic, and financial reforms; his educational reforms included subsidies for building schools, raising teachers' salaries, and introducing changes in methods and curriculum in order to improve the quality of elementary education.

By 1906 the Giolittian era of reform was at its height, especially in the areas of education and low-income housing. The reforms enacted in Italy during the next three years were the most impressive in the whole period from unification to World War I. After the depressed 1890s, it was a period of relative prosperity. The gradual industrialization of the Italian economy had improved the lot of the Italian masses. There was a decline in infant mortality and in deaths from infectious and parasitic diseases and the conditions of elementary education were improving. Children were healthier and the old battle against illiteracy was on the way to being won.

Throughout the 1880s and '90s Rome had faced all the social problems caused by its rapid growth into a crowded modern city whose population had doubled in the years since Alessandro Montessori had brought his family there to live. Waves of immigrants arrived from the impoverished countryside looking for a better life and finding only a different kind of misery.

One effect of the rapid growth of the city was a dramatic race by entrepreneurs to take advantage of the increased need for housing in order to turn a fast profit. New apartment buildings and new bridges went up all over the city in the eighties.

Looking back from the vantage point of the next decade, a Roman commandatore recalled:

> We were too hasty and too extravagant in our building plans. We tried to turn ancient Rome into a great modern city overnight. Many immense works were projected and undertaken all at once in a fever of enterprise. Speculation was encouraged and fanned to fever heat. Every promoter was eager to build. Princely parks and villas were subdivided and sold. Speculative banks grew and so did debts. So many buildings went up they threatened to exceed the number of tenants.[2]

In the atmosphere of uneasiness that developed, credit was withdrawn, individual projects began to collapse, and there was a wave of failed enterprises that ended in a full-scale crash. Banks and loan societies received unfinished apartment houses, which stood empty, their large square white or yellow façades staring blankly over the city, until inevitably they were invaded by squatters.

One of these projects stood between the old Roman wall and the modern cemetery, in the San Lorenzo district, near the gate where the tram line to Tivoli had its starting point. It was one of the last areas to be developed as land in Rome became scarcer and scarcer, probably because of its proximity to the cemetery and the superstitious fear of ghosts as well as the more rational fear of unhygienic conditions. But it was a beautiful and historic spot, and at the height of the building craze one of the building societies decided to risk its capital on a project there, consisting of several buildings, each five or six stories high with several apartments on each floor. It was a huge undertaking for the time, and before it could be completed the bubble burst and the building society went into bankruptcy, leaving just the skeletons of the buildings, the walls full of open holes where doors and windows had been planned, and no plumbing and no source of heat or light.

The abandoned structure did not remain empty for long. Beggars and criminals found it a convenient shelter and hiding place. Thousands of the homeless poor crowded in, and the police were reluctant to penetrate what were described as "these grim walls of crime and horror." With no sanitation and no policing, it became a hellhole of infection and prostitution, an abode of the dead as well as the living. The bodies of those who had been murdered for a bit of loose change lay around next to those of men, women, and children who had succumbed to disease. The press referred to the Quartiere di San Lorenzo as "the shame of Italy."

Eventually, another group of wealthy bankers known as the Istituto romano di beni stabili (the Roman "Good Building" Institute, perhaps better translated as the Roman Real Estate Association) decided to undertake an urban renewal scheme that might prove both a civic feather in their cap and profitable as well. They undertook to renovate some of the buildings to the extent that would be necessary to accommodate about a thousand people. No one but the poor could be expected to live in San Lorenzo, and this meant that improvements could be minimal: a coat of whitewash, the installation of doors and windows, water pipes and drains.

Jerry-built structures which had accumulated in the original central courtyard were torn down, providing the apartments with air and light, and the large suites of six or seven rooms, in which whole families and sometimes groups of strangers had occupied a single room, were divided into small apartments of one, two, or three rooms and a kitchen for each family. There were communal bathrooms with hot and cold water and fountains in the courtyard for washing clothes. The builders provided trees and plants for the courtyard, and the tenants themselves were responsible for the building's maintenance.

As tenants, the directors chose employed married couples, who would seem to be the most stable elements of the local population. Among the families who moved into the renovated apartments were about fifty children, who created something of a problem for the owners. During the days while their parents went out to work, those children old enough to get around but too young for school ran wild throughout the building, defacing the newly whitewashed walls and using their ingenuity on whatever other petty acts of vandalism they could invent. Something had to be done with them to protect the investment of the builders, and the directors decided the most effective solution would probably be to gather them together in one place and keep them occupied there all day. A woman could be hired to supervise them in an empty ground-floor room set aside for the purpose: the expense would be minimal and the savings significant. In fact, the building's owners calculated that the cost to them of providing working parents with a day nursery would be met by what they saved on leaving the tenants responsible for the care and maintenance of the buildings, for which incentives included a yearly prize for the best-kept building in each block.

It is not really surprising that the directors of the Beni Stabili should have thought of Maria Montessori. The American writer Dorothy Canfield Fisher, who spent her winters in Rome, saw that "Rome is, at least from the standpoint of a New Yorker or a Chicagoan, a small city, where 'everyone who is anyone knows everyone else.' Although the sphere of Signor [Edouardo] Talamo's activity was as far as possible from that of the pioneer woman doctor specializing in children's brain-centers, he knew of her existence and naturally enough asked her to undertake the organization and the management of the different groups of children in his tenement houses, collected, as far as he was concerned, for the purpose of keeping them from scratching the walls and fouling the stairways."[3]

Montessori had an interest in trying out some of her educational ideas on normal children. The directors of the concern needed someone to oversee the children's center, and they offered her what seemed clearly a mutually advantageous arrangement. She would have full charge of the children's care in return for keeping them out of the hair—and away from the walls—of the building directors.

She was a logical choice to approach for advice on the matter, a lecturer in education and hygiene and an official of the Italian Red Cross, having been since 1903 a medical assistant first-class of that organization. And while the real estate men may have been surprised at her decision to undertake such an insignificant task herself, they were decidedly pleased, and gave her a free hand.

As it happens, they gave her little else. They were not prepared to spend a penny on toys or equipment of any kind, and there was no money for meals. There was a room, provision for one supervising adult, and fifty wild children ranging in age from two to six.* It would probably have seemed preposterous to anyone—with the possible exception of Montessori herself—that what went on in that room would become known all over Italy within a year and all over the world within five more.

Friends could not understand how she could involve herself in such insignificant work as that of a schoolteacher of ordinary children—not even interesting by virtue of any dramatic defects—in a slum school. For a university professor, it was unthinkable. Her medical colleagues were equally disapproving. She told an interviewer some dozen years later that "one of her own chiefs in the medical schools told her, in so many words, that she was lowering the prestige of the medical profession by making of herself *una maestra di asilo infantile*."4 This was not science; this was child care.

She insisted on some provisions for food and sanitation and set about enlisting the support of society women she knew to be interested in social projects, asking them to help collect funds for toys and materials. And she found an untrained woman of about forty named Candida Nuccitelli, the daughter of the building porter, and put her in charge of looking after the children under Montessori's "guidance and direction."

It was decided that the woman in charge of the children's room should always be someone who lived in the tenement house, and it was planned that eventually every house owned by the Beni Stabili group would have such a room, under the supervision of a building tenant. At this time the group owned some four hundred tenements in Rome, fifty-eight of them, comprising some sixteen hundred apartments, in the San Lorenzo district, and plans were already being discussed for the opening of sixteen "schools within the house" in that district alone. Little wonder that to Montessori "the work seemed to offer tremendous possibilities of development."5

A woman who was a mutual friend of Montessori and Edouardo Tala-

*Accounts—even by Montessori herself—differ on the number of children (sometimes given as fifty, sometimes as sixty) and their ages (sometimes two to seven, sometimes three to six) in the original group.

mo, the director general of the Beni Stabili, suggested a name for this new kind of schoolroom—Casa dei Bambini, Children's House. Both Montessori and Talamo liked the name, and decided to use it.

On January 6, 1907, the first Casa dei Bambini was officially opened in the tenement at 58 Via dei Marsi with a formal inauguration ceremony. It was the day of the Feast of the Epiphany, commemorating the arrival of the three kings with their gifts for the infant Christ, and in Italy traditionally an important festival for children.

Montessori described the entrance of the children: "They were dressed all alike in some thick, heavy blue drill. They were frightened and being hindered by the stiff material, could move neither arms nor legs freely. Apart from their own community they had never seen any people. To get them to move together, they were made to hold hands. The first unwilling child was pulled, thus dragging along the whole line of the rest. All of them were crying miserably. The sympathy of the society ladies was aroused and they expressed the hope that in a few months they would improve."[6]

Montessori had been asked to make a speech.

She read the lesson for the day from her mass book: "Arise, be enlightened, O Jerusalem; for thy light is come, and the glory of the Lord is risen upon thee. . . . Lift up thine eyes and see; all these are gathered together, they are come to thee: thy sons shall come from afar, and thy daughters shall rise up at thy side. Then shalt thou see, and abound and thy heart shall wonder and be enlarged. . . ." Inspired by what she had read and carried along by her characteristic enthusiasm, she made a prediction she described on the anniversary of that day thirty-five years later:

> I don't know what came over me but I had a vision and, inspired by it, I was inflamed and said that this work we were undertaking would prove to be very important and that someday people would come from all over to see it. The press said that Dr. Montessori had made a beautiful speech, but what an exaggeration in what she had said!
> It was from then that the real work began.[7]

She herself was still occupied with her many other responsibilities—teaching, research, practice. The children were left to the care of the woman in charge, with Montessori stopping in when she could—sometimes only once a week—to hear a report of what had been going on and make her own observations. She brought in some of the teaching materials based on those Itard and Seguin had designed for the feebleminded, which she had modified in her work with the children at the

Orthophrenic School, and asked her assistant to make them available to the children. "I placed no restrictions upon the teacher and imposed no special duties."[8] "I merely wanted to study the children's reactions. I asked her not to interfere with them in any way as otherwise I would not be able to observe them."[9] There were also some toys which friends had donated and some paper and colored pencils. The only furniture at first were some large rough tables, of the kind used in offices, at which three children could be seated, a desk for the teacher, and a massive storage cabinet in which the toys and materials could be locked at night.

Gradually over the next weeks Montessori noticed certain changes taking place. The sullen, the disinterested and withdrawn, and the rebellious children showed a remarkable interest in the didactic materials, which they chose over the toys or drawing materials. Unlike her retarded children, who had to be coaxed into paying attention, these normal children immediately began to place wooden cylinders in the corresponding holes in a board, arrange cubes in descending order of size to build a tower, put circles, squares, and rectangles into spaces of the same shape in a wooden tray. Not only did they prefer these materials to dolls or balls or little wagons, but once involved with them they would persist at a task until they had succeeded in fitting everything into its proper place and then go on repeating the process over and over again. Along with developing unsuspected powers of concentration, they began to change socially as well. Although at first there had been no change in their diet or the amount of time spent outdoors or in exercise, they all looked healthier. "From timid and wild as they were before, the children became sociable and communicative. They showed different relationships with each other. Their personalities grew and they showed extraordinary understanding, activity, vivacity and confidence. They were happy and joyous."[10]

One day while she was visiting the Casa Montessori noticed a little girl of about three intently fitting the graded cylinders into their proper places in the containers, taking them out, mixing them up, and then starting all over. She kept repeating the exercise over and over again, seeming to be totally involved in what she was doing and oblivious to everything that was going on around her. Montessori began to count the number of times she repeated the process of taking out, putting in.

> I then decided to see how concentrated she was in her strange employment. I told the teacher to [have] the other children sing and [march around]. But this did not disturb the child at all in her labors. I then gently picked up the [little] chair in which she was sitting and set it on top of a small table. As I lifted the chair she clutched the objects with

which she was working and placed them on her knees, but then continued with the same task. From the time I began to count, she repeated the exercise forty-two times. Then she stopped as if coming out of a dream and smiled happily. Her eyes shone brightly and she looked about. She had not even noticed what we had done to disturb her. And now, for no apparent reason, her task was finished. But what was finished and why?[11]

While she was observing the children's responses to this new environment in which they had been placed and wondering what they meant, Montessori was also making some changes. She would talk with the teacher about how the children used the material, watch them herself when she was there—sometimes now for hours at a time—and she was continually making slight modifications in the materials in order to adapt them to normal children's use.

She was no longer the blooming girl who had astonished her elders just after her graduation by being attractive as well as articulate. In her late thirties, she was a somewhat portly figure, still handsome but putting on weight, still self-assured but a shade more dignified. She would come into the classroom wearing a simple but stylish dark-colored dress or shirtwaist, her dark hair piled neatly on top of her head, and smile at the children. And they would respond in a way that surprised her. "When I entered the room, all the children sprang to greet me and cried their welcome. Nobody had taught them any manner of good behavior."[12]

Their behavior probably had less to do with a conscious desire to be mannerly than with their admiration of this striking woman and the effect she always had on peers and pupils, strangers who became her devoted followers, listeners who came to hear her and with striking frequency spoke of being "converted," "enlightened," of having their way of seeing things—sometimes their entire lives—changed by her presence. It was not just her message, just as with children it was not just her method. She had the kind of personality that invites identification.

Some of the anecdotes she told about those early experimental days in the first Casa are revealing not only about the behavior of the children but about her own—the style with which she approached and dealt with them. One day she came into the classroom holding in her arms a tightly swaddled four-month-old baby girl she had taken from her mother in the courtyard to show the children.

> She was so still that her silence impressed me greatly and I wanted the children to share my feelings. "She is not making a sound," I told them. And jokingly I added, "None of you could do so well." To my great surprise I saw that the children were looking at me with an extraordinary

114

intensity. They seemed to be hanging on my lips and to be feeling keenly what I was saying. "Notice," I continued, "how soft her breath is. None of you could breathe as silently as she." Surprised and motionless, the children began to hold their breath. At that moment there was an impressive silence. The tick-tock of the clock, which was not usually heard, began to become audible. . . . No one made the least perceptible movement. They were intent upon experiencing the silence and reproducing it. . . . The children all sat perfectly still breathing as quietly as possible, having on their faces a serene and intent expression like those who are meditating. Little by little in the midst of this impressive silence we could all hear the lightest sounds like that of a drop of water falling in the distance and the far-off chirp of a bird.

That was the origin of our exercise of silence.[13]

The "game of silence" became part of the school day, an exercise in concentration not unlike meditation. Montessori saw it as "a most efficacious preparation for the task of setting in order the whole personality, the motor forces and the psychical."

On another day, "I decided to give the children a slightly humorous lesson on how to blow their noses. After I had shown them different ways to use a handkerchief, I ended by indicating how it could be done as unobtrusively as possible. I took out my handkerchief in such a way that they could hardly see it and blew my nose as softly as I could. The children watched me in rapt attention, but failed to laugh. I wondered why, but I had hardly finished my demonstration when they broke out into applause that resembled a long repressed ovation in a theater."[14] Montessori thought she had touched on a particularly sensitive point with these children, who were always being scolded and ridiculed for having running noses but whom no one had ever bothered to teach how to use a handkerchief.

When I tried to do so, they felt compensated for past humiliations, and their applause indicated that I had not only treated them with justice but had enabled them to get a new standing in society. . . .

When I was on the point of leaving the school, the children began to shout, "Thank you, thank you for the lesson!" When I left the building they followed me in a silent procession until I finally told them, "When you go back, run on tiptoe and take care that you don't bump into the corner of the wall." They turned around and disappeared behind the gate as if they were flying. I had touched these poor little children to the quick.[15]

What she had done was treat them with respect. It was a new experience for these children and, at the time, for most children.

115

As the months went on, Montessori not only observed the way the children worked with the "sensory materials" she had provided, modifying them until she felt she had hit on the right thing, but began to add to the classroom a number of things of her own design.

In order to take the measurements that were recorded on the biographic charts she was still using, she designed a special anthropometer. She had scales installed in the bathroom so the children could be weighed before being given a weekly bath. No practical detail was too small for her attention. She even designed and had constructed special tubs with separate compartments so several children could be bathed at once. She arranged for a physician to examine the children at regular intervals, and had special charts printed up for keeping track of their developmental histories. She got rid of the old tables and chairs and replaced them with some she designed and had specially made: child-sized lightweight tables and chairs that even the smallest child could move about and a few comfortable little armchairs, some made of wood and others of wicker. The small-scale furniture eventually included little washstands where a three-year-old could clean up by himself, using his own soap, brush, and towel, kept in a little cupboard. And she replaced the large locked cupboard with long, low ones so the children could select and replace the materials they chose to work with by themselves.

Since there was no money available from the building group for furnishings and equipment, Montessori called on her friends for contributions and used her own resources to supplement what her committee of ladies provided. She brought potted plants and small animals the children could tend themselves, and hung blackboards around the room at the children's height. And she hung a reproduction of Raphael's "Madonna della Seggiola," in which she saw the figure of Saint John as representing humanity paying homage to maternity, "the sublime fact in the definite triumph of humanity."[16] This idealization of motherhood, so characteristic of her, may have originated in a sense of having sacrificed her own; that which has to be relinquished is always somehow more precious. Then too, she had not experienced motherhood as a mundane business of day-to-day care, never had to take care of her child's bodily needs, cook his meals, quiet his tantrums, balance disappointments against delights. Her idea of motherhood was both greater and less than life because it was idealized, unreal.

Montessori was constantly watching the children, learning from them. She noticed that they were more interested in the challenge presented to them by the self-correcting material than in toys, that they wanted to do things for themselves, that they were not interested in rewards given for

116

working but in the activity itself. This seemed to her like an inherent characteristic of the child, and she decided that the children's education should proceed in such a way as to provide an environment in which the spontaneous activity of the child would be left free to manifest itself.

She worked out a way of teaching and had her assistants (she soon acquired a second pair of hands belonging to a seamstress, who had had some education but no previous experience that would spoil her for doing things Montessori's way) follow it. "This is red," the teacher would say, holding up a colored square. "This is blue." "Give me the red." "Give me the blue." If the child faltered or made a mistake, he was never criticized; the material was put away until another time, when he was "ready"—when the material at hand caught his interest. The teacher would show the child how to use the materials, arranging them by size or color, distinguishing hot from cold, perceiving different sounds, matching and sorting, and leave him to himself. Starting with the simplest things, the children gradually went on to more and more complicated perceptions and manipulations. And always, they experienced the sense of mastery that came from feeling they had done it themselves. They worked not out of fear of punishment or anticipation of rewards, but for the sheer pleasure of the activity itself.

Gardening, gymnastics, tending plants and pets, preparing and serving a communal lunch were all gradually added to the day's activities. And the classroom acquired an atmosphere of order and quiet—every child going about his business, intent on his task of the moment—that was singularly impressive to the visitors who began to appear, having heard about the unusual educational experiment under way in the San Lorenzo tenement.

The children were free to move about, to choose their material and work at it as long as their interest held out. To those who questioned the lack of discipline they saw in this absence of a continually imposed external authority, Montessori replied, "A room in which all the children move about usefully, intelligently, and voluntarily, without committing any rough or rude act, would seem to me a classroom very well disciplined indeed."[17]

However, freedom was not to be confused with anarchy. There *was* authority, although it did not have to be continually expressed since the children had no need to be in revolt against it. What Montessori meant by freedom was a very different thing from what such radical libertarians as Rousseau before her or Summerhill's A. S. Neil after her meant. It was a freedom to take action of certain kinds within certain well-defined limits. And she had no compunctions about defining those limits: "We do not speak of useless or dangerous acts, for these must be suppressed, destroyed."[18]

Her school is child-centered in the sense that the nature and needs of the child are the starting point for what is taught, but it is *she,* and not the child, who decides. No one who understood anything about her background or character could have supposed her to mean, as some critics did, that the school should be child-centered in the sense that the child could do *anything,* in any way he wanted to. She rebelled against her Catholic, traditionally conservative background in the sense that she extended it; she never was a rebel in the most radical sense. And she was, after all, a physician and approached education with the attitude of a doctor treating patients. She knew best what was good for them. Like many rhetoricians of freedom she was herself something of an autocrat.

> When the teachers were weary of my observations, they began to allow the children to do whatever they pleased. I saw children with their feet on the tables, or with their fingers in their noses, and no intervention was made to correct them. I saw others push their companions, and I saw dawn in the faces of these an expression of violence; and not the slightest attention on the part of the teacher. Then I had to intervene to show with what absolute rigor it is necessary to hinder, and little by little suppress, all those things which we must not do, so that the child may come to discern clearly between good and evil.[19]

If the use of the terms good and evil has a familiar ring in the classroom it should not lead one to think that she was really not changing much. The *way* in which she used them was different. "The task of the educator lies in seeing that the child does not confound good with immobility and evil with activity as often happens in the case of the old-time discipline. Our aim is to discipline for activity, for work, for good; not for immobility, not for passivity, not for obedience."[20]

While the children were not forced to sit still and do what they were told to do at a given moment, there were definite expectations of how they would behave. They were free to do the "right thing," a peculiarly Catholic concept and one that could work only assuming certain attitudes toward grown-up authority on the part of these children. Montessori could count on the attitudes they brought with them from home, and she made it clear to the parents what was expected of them.

A set of rules was drawn up and posted in the Casa dei Bambini. It spelled out clearly the responsibilities of the parents:

> The parents who wish to avail themselves of the advantages of the Casa dei Bambini pay nothing. They must, however, assume these binding obligations:

(a) To send their children to the Casa dei Bambini at the appointed time, clean in body and clothing, and provided with a suitable apron.

(b) To show the greatest respect and deference toward the Directress and toward all persons connected with the Casa dei Bambini and to cooperate with the Directress herself in the education of the children. Once a week, at least, the mothers may talk with the Directress, giving her information concerning the home life of the child, and receiving helpful advice from her.

There shall be expelled from the Casa dei Bambini:

(a) Those children who present themselves unwashed, or in soiled clothing.

(b) Those who show themselves to be incorrigible.

(c) Those whose parents fail in respect to the persons connected with the Casa dei Bambini or who destroy through bad conduct the educational work of the institution.[21]

Montessori showed what was for an "authority"—a teacher or doctor or in fact any professional at the time—a unique respect for the parents of the children she worked with as well as the children themselves. She never talked down to them, criticized them, or told them they were wrong. From her earliest days in the pediatric clinics through her years in the schools she founded, it was the example of the care she gave, the concern she showed them, and the respect with which she treated them that impressed them and often changed them, altering the way they treated each other until the change in relationships changed the quality of their home life. Bringing the parents of the slum children in the first Casa dei Bambini into the schools at all and involving them in the school life of their children—even though they had to hew to the rules as she set them down—was an innovation. For working-class parents to be expected to confer with their children's teachers about their children's education was revolutionary in 1907.

Her aim was to make the children independent, to teach them to do things for themselves. "No one can be free unless he is independent."[22]

Every educator has in mind an ideal type of person who should emerge at the end of the educational process. Usually it is a person who bears a rather striking resemblance to the educator himself. Montessori's ideal is like no one so much as Montessori herself—a self-controlled, competent, independently functioning individual. A woman of the Victorian age in a strongly traditional and socially backward country, she had freed herself by learning, at every stage of her life, how to do what she wanted to do—for herself.

She once told a friend she thought everyone ought to start the day by making his own bed. "We often believe ourselves to be independent simply because no one commands us, and because we command others; but the nobleman who needs to call a servant to his aid is really a dependent through his own inferiority. The paralytic who cannot take off his boots because of a pathological fact, and the prince who dare not take them off because of a social fact, are in reality reduced to the same condition."[23]

She knew it was harder to teach a child to feed, wash, and dress himself than to do those things for him, "but the former is the work of an educator, the latter is the easy and inferior work of a servant."[24] It hindered the child's development rather than fostered it.

When Montessori found the teacher had made medals to give the children as rewards for good work she watched to see what would happen. The children accepted them politely but with little interest; they were more interested in being allowed to get on with the work itself and one little boy even carelessly offered his medal to a classmate who was being punished by having to sit still with nothing to do. "The dangling cross could satisfy the child who was being punished, but not the active child, content and happy with his work."[25]

The only punishment for misbehavior was inactivity—being given nothing to do. The obstreperous child was treated like a sick child and isolated. He soon recovered.

Housekeeping chores, which became known as "exercises of practical life," became part of the school day. The children learned to button and lace their clothes, practicing first on pieces of cloth set in wooden frames, and took care of dusting, serving lunch, and cleaning up.

Montessori was always observing the children and learning from their own behavior what they needed. When she noticed that when they got tired of games or marching they liked to move themselves along sideways on a fence rather than sitting down to rest, she designed a special fence of parallel bars and upright poles to meet the particular physical need she thought was involved—one of many kinds of gymnastic equipment she invented and had made for "furnishing the child with a proper outlet for his individual activities."[26]

What later became "the" method for doing things in every Montessori classroom around the world began as ways of doing things suggested by Montessori's observation of the behavior of the San Lorenzo children. At this stage of her career she was still the experimenter, her ideas still evolving in response to her experience.

At first, the directress distributed the various materials to the children and when they were through with them, collected them and put them away. Montessori noticed that the children always followed her to the cupboard, guessed that they wanted to put the things away themselves, and from then on let them do so. It became clear that they loved putting things in their proper places, ordering the environment. They made a game of straightening up. When the embarrassed directress dropped a box containing about eighty little cards of various shades of different colors, the children quickly sorted them out and returned them to her in proper order.

When the directress rushed in a bit late one morning to find that the children had gone to the cupboard in her absence and were already removing the materials themselves and going off with them, she accused them of stealing and referred to them as little thieves. Montessori saw it differently and responded to their demonstration by allowing them to choose their own materials from then on. Now they could freely select what they preferred to work on and keep at it, repeating the same thing over and over, for as long as they wished, and she could see what they found interesting and what gathered dust and could modify her materials accordingly.

The materials that came to be known as the "didactic apparatus" were designed to be self-correcting. Through trial and error the child rectified his own mistakes until he got the cylinder in the right hole, the rods in the right order of length. He was refining his perceptions at the same time that he was gaining a sense of autonomy, of mastery over the objects in his environment. The teacher's job was to observe the child, to show him how to use the material, and then leave him to try it himself without interfering in his efforts. She was to remain in the background, letting the child in fact teach himself. In Montessori's view of education, "a man is not what he is because of the teachers he has had, but because of what he has done,"[27] a doctrine which came to be stated as "things are the best teachers." In the light of current psychological understanding, this seems to leave a great deal out—the whole process of identification by which children form attachments and learn by modeling themselves on those for whom they have developed positive feelings. It seems to leave out a whole dimension of being human—the emotional. Like most reforms, it was a position adopted in reaction to abuses at the other extreme—in this case the dependence on rewards and punishments in which a child learned only for the sake of approval, to gain love, rather than learning to love accomplishment for its own sake. But while Montessori's theory stressed the relationship between the child and the material, other developmental processes were undoubtedly at work at the same time, even though they were not what interested her.

"With my methods," she said, "the teacher teaches little and observes much; it is her function to direct the psychic activity of the children and their physiological development. For this reason I have changed the name of teacher into that of directress."[28]

Nowhere is the nineteenth-century attitude toward social work among the poor made clearer than in Montessori's description of the role of the woman who supervises the children:

> The directress is always at the disposition of the mothers, and her life, as a cultured and educated person, is a constant example to the inhabitants of the house, for she is obliged to live in the tenement and to be therefore a co-habitant with the families of all her little pupils. This is a fact of immense importance. Among these almost savage people, into these houses where at night no one dared go about unarmed, there has come not only to teach, *but to live the very life they live,* a gentlewoman of culture, an educator by profession, who dedicates her time and her life to helping those about her! A true missionary, a moral queen among the people, she may, if she be possessed of sufficient tact and heart, reap an unheard-of harvest of good from her social work.[29]

7

On April 7, 1907, three months after the opening of the first Casa dei Bambini, a second one was opened in another of the San Lorenzo tenements. For the occasion, Montessori delivered an inaugural address[1] in which she described the Casa as a new kind of educating institution, part of a broad social program "directed toward the redemption of the entire community. . . . The Casa dei Bambini is earned by the parents" who have a responsibility for "the physical and moral care of their own children."

> This is not simply a place where the children are kept, not just an asylum, but a true school for their education. . . . We see here for the first time the possibility of realizing the long-talked-of pedagogical idea. We have put the *school within the* [home]; and this is not all. We have placed it within the [home] as the *property of the* [community], leaving under the eyes of the parents the whole life of the teacher in the accomplishment of her mission.
> This idea of the [community] ownership of the school is new and very beautiful and profoundly educational.
> The parents know that the Casa dei Bambini is their property, and is maintained by a portion of the rent they pay. The mothers may go at any hour of the day to watch. . . .

By transforming the school in this way, she believed it possible to reach into the home, and thus "modify directly the environment of the new generation."

She spoke of this "socialization of the [home]" as a way of freeing women, who could go off to their work with easy minds, knowing they had left their children "like the great lady" in the care of the directress and the house physician. She compared the benefits of this "communizing of persons" to the collectivization of utilities or of mass transportation. It would equalize the social classes, enabling women to work outside the home without abandoning their children to inferior care. It was not just the poor who needed this; since the reports of the first Casa had appeared, she had been deluged with letters from middle-class women, women who taught, who "worked with their brains" out of choice, wanting to know how they could set up such facilities where they lived.

"We are then, communizing a 'maternal function,' a feminine duty, within the [home]. We may see here in this practical act the [solution] of many of woman's problems. . . . "

Her sensitivity to the problem of others taking over the "maternal function," to the quality of care given to the children of absent mothers, was certainly a reflection of the concern—and perhaps also the sense of loss—she must have felt during these years at her own inability to mother her young child. If the school could provide the nurturing traditionally assigned to parents—and do it even better—the parentless child was not really deprived.

Eventually, not only the school but also the infirmary for the care of the sick, the kitchen for the preparation of wholesome food, washing and bathing facilities for improved sanitary conditions, libraries and social clubs, all would be established and maintained collectively.

> Thus the tendency will be to change the tenement houses, which have been places of vice and peril, into centers of education, of refinement, of comfort. . . .
> The new woman, like the butterfly come forth from the chrysalis, shall be liberated from all those attributes which once made her desirable to man only as the source of the material blessings of existence. She shall be, like man, an individual, a free human being, a social being, a social worker; and, like man, she shall seek blessing and repose within the [home], the [home] which has been reformed and communized.

In the coming years Montessori would extend the application of her method to older children as well as to children of the middle and affluent classes. But what she was doing and saying here about her work with the deprived children of the rock-bottom poor anticipated in a very specific way the social concerns of a later time—our own. Half a century later concern would focus on what she was talking about here—the role of early stimulation as the basis for later learning, the use of prekindergarten training to make up for deficits in the previous experience of children from impoverished backgrounds, and the school as an integral part of the community, the matrix of learning experiences provided by a variety of institutions—including the family, the church, the press—of which the school is only one.

Teaching the slum children of San Lorenzo to distinguish the shapes and sizes and colors of objects and to use the symbols of language and number skills, developing their self-respect and sense of competence through their ability to affect and to some extent control their environment, she was demonstrating how the school could be the intervention point at which society could provide the children of poverty with what their parents were not equipped to give them. She was more than a teacher; it was her reformer's vision that the educational process could in this way improve the world by improving men and women.

Again at this second Casa, Montessori chose an untrained—therefore, from her point of view, unspoiled—young woman as directress, and again the children who came on the first day disorganized, bewildered, and often sullen immediately showed a spontaneous interest in handling the materials, gradually worked their way from the simpler to the more complicated ones on their own, and soon became cheerful and responsible as well as strikingly competent at their tasks.

More and more visitors—educators, journalists, religious leaders—hearing about the interesting experiment under way in San Lorenzo, came to see what was going on.

By spring what they saw in each Casa was a model class of children, almost unbelievably interested in their work/play, almost unbelievably well behaved and cooperative in the care of their surroundings and equipment. No one left unimpressed.

The children loved having visitors and a number of accounts of those early visits indicate that they rose to the occasion in ways that understandably surprised and amused the guests. They greeted everyone who came—unless they were busy working, in which case it would wait. Queen Margherita was ignored by one little girl who was busy repeating her arrangement of squares and circles. The other children had all gone back to their work after greeting her and the queen was sitting quietly looking around when the girl, having finished her task, ran up and kissed her.

The children offered the visitors chairs, thanked them for coming, and were polite about accepting their occasional gifts of toys or candy but were clearly not as interested in them as in their rods and cylinders. They would put the candy aside, or use it as a pointer in figuring out the division of the number rods, and the dolls and dollhouses and china tea sets, Montessori tells us, stood unused. They preferred solving the puzzles, playing the games that were the sensory materials, and they had real dishes to carry and serve from when it was time for their midday soup. When a dignitary of the Church came to visit, bringing a bag of cookies that had been shaped with geometric cutters, no one thought to eat them. "Look, that's a triangle!" "I've got a circle!" "Cosmo has a rectangle!" Hard to believe, but attested to over and over again by visitors to Via dei Marsi.

When the prime minister's daughter arrived one morning with the Argentinian ambassador in tow and found the school closed for a local holiday, some of the children in the courtyard came up to them and offered to get the key from the porter. They rounded up all the others they could find, showed the guests into the schoolroom and made them comfortable, chose their materials and set to work so the visitors who had come such a distance could see how things worked there. Montessori's explanation of their consistently cheerful, cooperative attitude was simple. "The children found no obstacles in the way of their development. They had nothing to hide, nothing to fear, nothing to shun. It was as simple as that."[2] Well, perhaps not quite that simple. They also, it must be added, had a sense of being important. They felt well treated, they knew they were being watched with interest, and their response seems due to something more than the absence of frustration. Whether it was spelled out or not, they had a sense of positive expectations and certainly a rough idea of what kind of behavior was valued. It doesn't seem to diminish the result, but rather to add a dimension to it, to say that their behavior was more than a matter of removing the impediments to their innate natures. They had made a positive identification with nurturing adults, and education was taking place. Along with sensory training and cognitive skills, it involved emotional growth, another aspect of what is today called ego development.

Up until now, Montessori had presented the children only with the graded, self-correcting sense-education materials and the practical-life activities. She had made no effort to introduce reading and writing, sharing the common belief that these skills should not be taught before the age of six—that younger children were not yet ready to master them.

But the children, who had already made such surprising strides—who, at three and four, could bathe and dress themselves, sweep, dust, and straighten up the classroom, put away their materials in the proper places and manage the keys in the locks, care for their plants and pets, and, as Montessori put it, "knew how to observe things, and how to see objects with their hands"[3]—wanted to go further.

According to her later account, some of the children began to ask to be taught to read and write, and tried to persuade her by showing that they could make an O on the blackboard. And the mothers begged her too. They were impressed with their children, whose extraordinary development was a matter of so much public interest, and in many cases had begun to change themselves in response to their own small children, who had become critical of sloppy housekeeping, rudeness, and rough ways. Flowerpots had begun to replace washing in the windows of the apartments of families with children attending the Casa; the mothers began to dress with greater care and the fathers to walk with their heads up. In addition to the influence of the children and the habits and attitudes they brought home from school, the parents were in at least weekly contact with the directress. Now some of the mothers, illiterate themselves, asked Dr. Montessori to teach the children to read and write because they seemed to learn things so easily at the Casa; if they waited until they started elementary school they would be exhausted by the effort involved in learning in that setting.

She was interested in the suggestion that the children might be able to learn reading and writing effortlessly through methods similar to those she was using to involve them in gaining perceptual skills, making increasingly subtle discriminations of size, shape, pattern, and color by themselves. She thought about the results of her work with deficient children, whom she had managed to teach to read and write using the three-dimensional models of letters. And she decided that after the August vacation, when classes began again in September, she would give it a try.

As September approached, she decided instead to take up after vacation where the children had left off before the interruption, and to start the reading and writing program in October, at the same time that the public elementary schools would begin their instruction of first-graders. It would provide a basis of comparison and give her attempt the character of a controlled experiment.

When school resumed she began to look around for someone to manufacture the letter models she had in mind, but no one would undertake the job at a price she could afford. Then she decided she could make do with the enameled letters used to spell words on shop windows, but these were available only in block letters and she wanted script. October came and went, and still she hadn't managed to find the right thing. Meanwhile, the elementary-school children had already filled whole copybook pages with vertical strokes, loops, and curves.

Finally she decided just to cut out large paper letters in script form, which she had one of her assistants color blue. She cut another set out of sandpaper and glued these onto smooth cards. She soon realized that her makeshift materials were superior to the elaborate kind she had originally wanted and would have been using by now if she had been able to afford them. The paper alphabet could be reproduced easily in quantity so that many children could be working with the letters at once, and the sandpaper ones were a tactile exercise that would train the sense of touch in addition to that of sight in recognizing and reproducing the shape of the letters.

In the late afternoons, when the children had gone home, she and her assistants, in their long skirts and with rolled-up sleeves, sat on the small chairs and cut out letters, painted and glued them. One of her pupils at the teacher-training institute, Anna Fedeli, who was one of a group of young women students who surrounded her and who remained a long-time companion, suggested a couple of improvements. A paper strip pasted across the back of the letter would make it clear which way the letter went, so the child wouldn't be holding it on its side or backwards. And a compartmentalized case she made out of an old cardboard box she found in the courtyard made it possible to keep all the letters in order so the child could select the ones he needed. Signora Fedeli apologized, laughing, for the primitive character of the case she had made, but Montessori was impressed, and adopted both ideas. She kept that original cardboard case for years; it was the prototype for the wooden case of letters that shortly became standard equipment in Montessori classrooms all over the world.

Montessori liked to show the old cardboard case and tell how all this had come about and how her pupil had been responsible for modifying what eventually became such a widely used bit of apparatus. It is one of the few instances in which she seems to have had a collaborator—rather than followers, implementers—in even the simplest aspects of her work. And it was only on this level—practical, mechanical detail—that anyone could change or modify the materials or the methods once she had established them to her own satisfaction. Eventually she came to feel that she had found what worked best on the basis of observation, trial and error, and proven results—scientific pedagogy. No more changes were needed. Further modifications would only be distortions, deviations from the ideal.

But in November 1907 she was still experimenting. Already an authority, she was not yet the unquestioned one she would become. And she began, with the improvised materials and the San Lorenzo children in her specially designed classroom, the phase of her experiment that would make her world famous.

The children traced the letters with their fingers and later with pencil or chalk, learning their sounds, first vowels and then consonants. Italian is a perfectly phonetic language, and there was no ambiguity about the sound of an "A" or an "E." After repeated practice, they were able to identify, and then produce themselves, the letter for every sound.

They took enormous pleasure in the game by means of which they were teaching themselves what children two and three years older were learning so laboriously in the regular schools.

One day Montessori was sitting with a little boy of two and a half whose mother had left him with her for a while. She was sorting the paper letters, arranging them in their compartments, while the little boy watched. Finally, he picked up one of the letters, an "F," and held it up to look at it. Some of the children playing nearby began to call out "F! F! F!" He paid no attention, but replaced the letter and took out another one. The older children called out "R! R! R!" Again he took out a letter and the children, who had stopped running around and gathered around him, called out the sound. He began to get the idea that each shape he chose elicited a corresponding sound from the children, and the game went on, to their mutual delight, for three quarters of an hour. Finally, he chose a letter he had held up several times already, and identified it himself, saying "F! F! F!" Not yet three years old, he had been able to take the first step toward learning to read, something no one would have considered possible at the time, but which came about as Montessori observed the children's free behavior given the right materials under favorable circumstances—what she came to call spontaneous activity in the prepared environment.

As the weeks went on, the children learned the sounds of all of the letters of the alphabet and gradually began to combine them into syllables and then words. Without really knowing it, repeatedly following the shapes of the paper letters until they could reproduce them themselves, they had, as Montessori saw, "mastered all the acts necessary to writing." And suddenly, it all came together.

> One beautiful December day when the sun shone and the air was like spring, I went up on the roof [terrace] with the children. They were playing freely about, and a number of them were gathered about me. I was sitting near a chimney, and said to a little five-year-old boy who sat beside me, "Draw me a picture of this chimney," giving him as I spoke a piece of chalk. He got down obediently and made a rough sketch of the chimney on the tiles which formed the floor of this roof terrace. As is my custom with little children, I encouraged him, praising his work. The child looked at me, smiled, remained for a moment as if on the point of bursting into some joyous act, and then cried out, "I can write! I can write!" and kneeling down again he wrote on the pavement the word *mano* (hand). Then, full of enthusiasm, he wrote also *camino* (chimney), *tetto* (roof). As he wrote, he continued to cry out, "I can write! I can write!" His cries of joy brought the other children, who formed a circle about him, looking down at his work in stupefied amazement. Two or three of them said to me, trembling with excitement, "Give me the chalk. I can write too." And indeed they began to write various words: *mamma, mano, Gino, camino, Ada.*
>
> . . . It was the *first time* that they had ever written, and they traced an entire word, as a child, when speaking for the first time, speaks the entire word.[4]

To the children it seemed as though they had acquired some marvelous new power in the same way that they grew taller or sprouted new teeth. "Not being [aware of] the connection between the preparation and the act, they [had] the illusion that, having now grown to the proper size, they knew how to write."[5]

> The child who wrote a word for the first time was full of excited joy. He might be compared to the hen who has just laid an egg. Indeed, no one could escape from the noisy manifestations of the little one. He would call everyone to see, and if there were some who did not go, he ran to take hold of their clothes, forcing them to come and see. We all had to go and stand about the written word to admire the marvel, and to unite our exclamations of surprise with the joyous cries of the fortunate author. Usually, this first word was written on the floor, and, then, the child knelt down before it in order to be nearer to his work and to contemplate it more closely.
>
> After the first word, the children, with a kind of frenzied joy, continued to write everywhere. I saw children crowding about one another at the blackboard, and behind the little ones who were standing on the floor another line would form consisting of children mounted upon chairs, so that they might write above the heads of the little ones. In a fury at being thwarted, other children, in order to find a little place where they might write, overturned the chairs upon which their companions were mounted. Others ran toward the window shutters or the door, covering them with writing. In these first days we walked upon a carpet of written signs. Daily reports showed us that the same thing was going on at home, and some of the mothers, in order to save their floors, and even the crust of their loaves upon which they found words written, gave their children presents of paper and pencil. One of these children brought to me one day a little notebook entirely filled with writing, and the mother told me that the child had written all day long and all evening, and had gone to sleep in his bed with the paper and pencil in his hand.[6]

The experiment which had had its beginnings in a landlord's desire to keep the children from scribbling on the walls had had a somewhat unexpected result: they had learned to write on them.

Order was soon restored as the "explosion into writing," as it came to be called, became an accepted fact of life in the Casa. By Christmas, less than six weeks later, while the first-graders in the public elementary school were still laboring over their pages of slanted lines, curves, and hooks, two of Montessori's four-year-olds wrote letters on behalf of their classmates to Signor Edouardo Talamo, thanking him and sending holiday greetings. "These," Montessori tells us proudly, "were written upon note paper without blot or erasure and the writing was adjudged equal to that which is obtained in the third elementary grade."[7]

The next accomplishment was reading, which, Montessori found, contrary to the accepted idea of the time, was best learned *after* writing.

She set to work again after school hours cutting paper into little cards on each of which she wrote in large, clear script the name of some toy in the classroom—a doll, ball, sheep, soldier—placing the card in front of the object. The children already knew how to read the sounds of the individual letters; now they put the sounds together and connected them with the thing named. The child began by translating the word slowly into individual sounds, not understanding at first, but repeating the series of sounds over and over, faster each time, until "finally the word bursts upon his consciousness. Then he looks upon it as if he recognized a friend, and assumes that air of satisfaction which so often radiates our little ones. This completes the exercise for reading. It is a lesson which goes very rapidly, since it is only presented to a child who is already prepared through writing. Truly, we have buried the tedious and stupid ABC primer side by side with the useless copybooks!"[8]

Just as the children had "exploded" into writing, they now began to read everything in sight. They amazed their parents by stopping in the street to read the signs in shop windows. Those whose parents were literate read their parents' mail and their shopping lists.

One of Montessori's early attempts to find a painless way of teaching the children to read whole words involved a game using some of the toys that had been contributed by wealthy friends and well-wishers when the Casa was first opened. A child drew a card from a basket and if he could read clearly the name of the toy printed on it, he was entitled to take the toy and play with it for as long as he wished. A surprise to her at the time as well as to us today, the children were not interested in playing with the toys. "They explained that they did not wish to waste time in playing, and, with a kind of insatiable desire, preferred to draw out and read the cards one after another."[9]

It may have been the novelty of this newly acquired skill; it may even have been, in some way she did not recognize, a response to her, a reading of her implicit values and a bid for her approval and love, but she interpreted their behavior as a proof of an inherent desire to learn: "I watched them, seeking to understand the secret of these souls, of whose greatness I had been so ignorant! As I stood in meditation among the eager children, the discovery that it was knowledge they loved, and not the

131

silly *game*, filled me with wonder and made me think of the greatness of the human soul!"[10]

If these events and even the techniques used sound familiar today, it is because they have long since been adopted and adapted by school systems all over the world. In 1907 they were revolutionary, and the four- and five-year-olds who learned to write in less than two months and to read in a matter of days after that astonished the world.

8

A group of devoted followers began to gather around Montessori, young women who found in her a combination of mother and teacher. In her work they found a cause that gave meaning to their lives. Some of them stayed, some came and went, but for the rest of her life she was surrounded by followers of various ages and social conditions. Her constant companions were always less her intellectual peers than they were her zealous helpers.

Anna Maccheroni described her meeting with Montessori, the beginning of a lifelong relationship between the two women that was characteristic of many of the relationships Montessori had with younger women throughout her life.

It was in November 1907 and Maccheroni, who had attended Montessori's lectures on pedagogical anthropology at the University of Rome the year before and been deeply impressed ("It was as if I had been thirsty and had found pure water"[1]), had returned to Rome after a seaside family holiday. She was at loose ends about her own life plans and decided to ask Montessori for advice about pursuing a teaching career.

She made an appointment to see Montessori at her home. Waiting in the drawing room she wondered why she had come and when Montessori entered the room and politely asked what she wanted, she said she really didn't know.

"She then looked at me with the greatest interest, and made me sit down beside her on the sofa. It was an extraordinary moment indeed. All that I had kept in my heart, as under a heavy stone, came pouring out."[2] The younger woman told about her unhappy family life, her desire to teach, and her misgivings about what she would be doing in the traditional schools.

"An hour afterwards, when taking leave, I apologized for the time she had lost with me. 'It is not lost time,' she said earnestly, and not as if she was paying a compliment."[3]

Montessori asked if she had ever thought of teaching mentally defective children, and suggested that she read Seguin. And she told her about the Casa dei Bambini experiment which had now been under way for several months and invited her to visit San Lorenzo.

Maccheroni came to the Casa and watched Montessori working with a three-year-old who was learning to identify circles, squares, and triangles. She saw her calm, patient introduction of the shapes and their corresponding words and was struck by the child's reaction. "He looked satisfied and happy, just as if he had been given chocolates instead of two new words."[4]

Her response to Montessori as a teacher was one that was repeatedly described in similar words throughout the years by many of those who saw her work with children or heard her talk. "This experience gave reality to what I had seen in my mind in listening to Dr. Montessori's lectures, which answered so exactly to my inner need. I had a calm sense of security, a serene and sure feeling that I was on the very spot I had been looking for. . . . Seeing the first Montessori school I felt as if I had entered into my own kingdom."[5]

She made her own set of the materials she saw Montessori using—the wooden geometrical insets and sandpaper letters—and set about using them to teach two microcephalic children at the school where she was teaching French. In ten days the children—who had been considered unteachable—had learned to recognize several letters and even read a few syllables. She was struck by their joy, which to her seemed "as if they felt some inner conquest, the setting free of some power they had not hitherto been able to use."[6]

It is this almost mystical enthusiasm that characterized so many of the reports of those who found a purpose for their lives in Montessori's system of educating young children.

Maccheroni continued to visit the Case, and little by little began to take on responsibilities as an assistant to Montessori and to spend more and more of her time at the Montessori home.

And there was more responsibility to be shared every day as newspaper reports spread the word of the "miracles" accomplished in the two little schools of San Lorenzo. According to Dorothy Canfield Fisher, "By April of 1908, only a little over a year after the first small beginnings, the institution of the Casa dei Bambini was discovered by the public, keen on the scent of anything that promised relief from the almost intolerable lack of harmony between modern education and modern needs. Pilgrims of all nationalities and classes found their way through the filthy streets of that wretched quarter, and the barely established institution, still incomplete in many ways, with many details untouched, with many others provided for only in a makeshift manner, was set under the microscopic scrutiny of innumerable sharp eyes."[7]

When in the fall of 1908 a Casa dei Bambini was opened in Milan, Montessori sent Maccheroni to be in charge. It was the first Casa established outside Rome and Montessori evidently felt that she could trust Maccheroni's understanding of her principles to carry out the work there as she herself would have done it. This confidence was not lost on the younger woman, who eagerly gave up her position as a secondary-school teacher to go to Milan and undertake the care of forty-six children under the age of six, at a lower salary for a ten-hour day from eight in the morning until six in the evening, living in a ground-floor apartment next to the Casa, with the help of one untrained woman. With a fervor that was typical of the young women who became Montessori's followers and assistants, she considered it a mission to which she was privileged to dedicate herself.

The Milan Casa was established by the Società Umanitaria—the Humanitarian Society—the outstanding philanthropic institution in Italy at the time. Founded by Jewish socialists, Umanitaria was a center for working-class families that provided modern housing and such social services as occupational training in model workshops, employment referral, and adult education facilities. Montessori later noted that one of the members of Umanitaria's staff was an obscure young journalist named Benito Mussolini.[8]

The directors of Umanitaria, dedicated to the "moral elevation" of the workers as well as to improving their lot in material ways, saw the school as one of the pivotal points of their efforts. Montessori was well known to them as a spokeswoman for social reforms as well as for the miracles she had already accomplished with slum children, and they invited her to Milan to lecture under the society's auspices in the spring of 1908. Hearing her account of the San Lorenzo experience decided the Umanitaria officials to ask her cooperation in establishing a Casa dei Bambini there modeled on those in Rome.

Montessori welcomed the opportunity to undertake a further experiment in her method. In September she returned to Milan to give three lectures to educators and civic leaders, as well as a talk in the tenement on the Via Solari in which the Casa would be located, at which she spoke about the potential capacities which could be stimulated in young children to a highly interested group of working people—the parents and neighbors of the children who would attend the new Casa. Members of Umanitaria undertook to manufacture the teaching materials in the society's workshop for the unemployed, the Casa di Lavoro—the House of Labor.

The Milan Casa was opened on October 18. It was the beginning of a longstanding relationship between Montessori and Umanitaria, which over the years was to establish other Montessori schools and sponsor teacher-training courses, conferences, and exhibitions of the didactic materials.[9]

Meanwhile, the British ambassador, Sir Rennell Rodd, had started a Casa dei Bambini in the embassy on Rome's Corso d'Italia, and on November 4, 1908, a fifth Casa, the fourth in Rome, was opened in a modern building in a middle-class neighborhood, the Prati di Castello. And in January 1909 the Italian part of Switzerland began transforming its orphanages and kindergartens into Case dei Bambini, using Montessori methods and materials in place of Froebelian.

In the summer of 1909 Maccheroni and a few others of Montessori's intimate circle of young women joined her as guests of Barone Leopoldo Franchetti and his American-born wife at their villa, La Montesca, near Città di Castello. The Baronessa, the former Alice Hallgarten, was a nature enthusiast as well as a passionate amateur of rural educational reform. The Barone was a leader in the movement for agrarian reform in the Mezzogiorno, the backward south, and his estate was a model of modern farming methods as well as living conditions for the peasants who worked on his land. The Barone welcomed his energetic wife's interest in establishing a primary school for the children of the peasants on his estate and when the Franchettis met Montessori in 1908 they saw in her a kindred spirit. They found her ideas helpful in their school and undertook to offer her encouragement and support in her work.

Montessori's circle included Elisabetta Ballerini, whom Maccheroni had met at the school for defective children where she had worked and who had come with Maccheroni to hear Montessori and stayed to become one of her assistants, a directress in the Casa in the Franciscan Convent on the Via Giusti. Another was Anna Fedeli, who also became a constant companion and assistant to Montessori. She directed the second Casa in Milan, opened in 1909, and remained a close associate through the years until her death in the early 1920s.

Here at Città di Castello Montessori gave her first training course for about a hundred students, most of them teachers, including some of her pupils from the Magistero. The Barone had stimulated the interest of the local education authorities, some of whom attended the lectures, and arranged to have a few local children present so that Montessori could demonstrate the use of the materials. Both of the Franchettis attended every lecture.

Describing the response of the students at this first course, Maccheroni said, "The teachers seemed to accept the Montessori idea with great interest and hope. . . . The child was considered from a point of view so different from what was at that time to be found in books for teachers, that the students felt as if they were breathing bracing air."[10] She mentioned a Signorina Costagnocchi, "who got rid of her heavy indecision about her future, found fresh confidence in herself,"[11] and after taking a degree at the university opened a Montessori school in Rome for children of well-to-do families.

It was a pleasant summer for Montessori, surrounded by her enthusiastic young companions and admirers discussing her lectures on the terrace overlooking the beautiful hills, and with the solicitous Franchettis as gracious hosts. The Baronessa was always urging her to rest, sometimes removing the books from her room, closing the shutters and drawing the draperies, but Montessori was never able to do nothing for long. For her, inactivity was not restful; what was refreshing was "spontaneous activity" under the right conditions.

And here she found the right conditions for a piece of work that would carry her name around the world.

The Franchettis, full of enthusiasm for Montessori's work, had urged her to put her ideas and methods into a book, and offered to help arrange for its publication. Montessori, who had been speaking and writing about her work for years now, and who organized and expressed her thoughts with ease, sat down and, within a month, wrote *Il Metodo della Pedagogia Scientifica applicato all'educazione infantile nelle Case dei Bambini* (*The Method of Scientific Pedagogy Applied to the Education of Young Children in the Case dei Bambini*, which later appeared in English translation as *The Montessori Method*).

In it she defined the new science of pedagogy, traced its lineage from Itard and Seguin, gave the history of her own work and its culmination in the Casa dei Bambini, and told the story of what had happened there. She explained her methods in detail, describing the teaching materials and how they were to be used, first in the education of the senses, later for the teaching of reading and writing and eventually arithmetic, and spelled out the other aspects of school life as well: the furnishings of the schoolroom, the exercises of practical life, gymnastics, the care of plants and animals to teach nature and foster responsibility, the use of handwork such as pottery and building.

But the heart of the book was its statement of her educational philosophy.

> The transformation of the school must be contemporaneous with the preparation of the teacher. For if we make of the teacher an observer, familiar with the experimental methods, then we must make it possible for her to observe and to experiment in the school. The fundamental

137

principle of scientific pedagogy must be, indeed, the *liberty of the pupil*—
such liberty as shall permit a development of individual, spontaneous
manifestations of the child's nature. If a new and scientific pedagogy is
to arise from the *study of the individual,* such study must occupy itself
with the observation of *free* children.[12] . . .

We must not start from any dogmatic ideas which we may happen to
have held upon the subject of child psychology. Instead, we must proceed by a method which shall tend to make possible to the child complete liberty. This we must do if we are to draw from the observation of
his spontaneous manifestations conclusions which shall lead to the establishment of a truly scientific child psychology. It may be that such a
method holds for us great surprises, unexpected possibilities.[13]

An essential aspect of her idea of education, and one which sharply
distinguished it from the regular schools of the time, was the idea that
the school must not impose arbitrary tasks on the pupil but provide the
means for him to develop his own natural tendencies. The aim is "spontaneous self-development," and it follows from the observable psychological nature of the child, who

despises everything already attained, and yearns for that which is still
to be sought for. For instance, he prefers the action of dressing himself
to the state of being dressed, even finely dressed. He prefers the act of
washing himself to the satisfaction of being clean: he prefers to make a
little house for himself, rather than merely to own it. His own self-
development is his true and almost his only pleasure. The self-development of the little baby up to the end of his first year consists to a large
degree in taking in nutrition; but afterwards it consists in aiding the orderly establishment of the psycho-physiological functions of his
organism.[14]

The child has to be allowed to repeat, as often as he needs to, the selected activities which are right for him—which interest him at a particular moment in his growth. "It is necessary to offer those exercises which
correspond to the need of development felt by an organism, and if the
child's age has carried him past a certain need, it is never possible to obtain, in its fullness, a development which missed its proper moment."[15]
This was a point which she would return to later and amplify as the idea
of "sensitive periods."

She did have a unique capacity—clearly intuitive and a product of her
personal genius although she liked to think of it as a product of her
scientific training—for defining the kind of activity that would stimulate
the mental growth of children at different stages of development. And
she was able to work out ways of presenting such activities that would

stimulate the child's interest, leading him to invest his energy and foster his own growth.

She often told the story of one of the children in the early days of the first Case dei Bambini who, when asked who had taught him to write, replied, puzzled, "Who taught me? Nobody taught me; I learned."[16] Self-educated herself, having set her own goals and fashioned her own curriculum, she had a conviction that the only kind of education that was of value to the individual was auto-education.

To be in control of one's self was for her the ultimate end of the process of education. It was what she had achieved in her own life and what she wanted to make possible for the children in her schools. She saw it in the four-year-old who walked carefully carrying the big soup tureen at lunchtime in the Casa, resisting the temptation to brush a fly from his face, to run or skip, until he had set the tureen down and served the soup at each of the little tables. She saw it in the child tracing the forms of the letters over and over until suddenly he realized he could write them himself. "To the casual onlooker the child seems to be learning exactitude and grace of action, to be refining his senses, to be learning how to read and write; but much more profoundly he is learning how to become his own master, how to be a man of prompt and resolute will."[17]

Like everything else, this was to be learned not by precept but by practice, and her three- and four-year-olds were practicing the exercise of their resolute wills, controlling themselves out of choice, not fear, because they were given adequate scope for activity of a satisfying kind. Their spontaneity was apparent to visitors—and it was the thing that struck them first—in their personalities as well as their work. They were open, not what Montessori referred to as "that moral monstrosity, a repressed and timid child, who is at ease nowhere except alone with his playmates, or with street urchins, because his will power was allowed to grow only in the shade." She compared such children—and she included most of the children of the time—to court dwarfs, museum monstrosities or buffoons, and she blamed their condition on "scholastic slavery," for which "the remedy is simply to enfranchise human development."[18]

Her view of history and of human nature are inextricably related, and explain her unclouded optimistic belief in the possibility of progress toward human and social perfection, which would result from the freeing of the natural (and for her, natural means "good") tendencies of man.

All forms of slavery tend little by little to weaken and disappear, even the sexual slavery of woman. The history of civilization is a history of conquest and of liberation. . . . Even as life in the social environment triumphs against every cause of poverty and death, and proceeds to new conquests, so the instinct of liberty conquers all obstacles, going from victory to victory. It is this personal and yet universal force of life, a force often latent within the soul, that sends the world forward.[19]

It is hard to say how much of this is rhetoric—decoration intended to make her message more attractive to her readers—and how much it really reflects another aspect of her mind at work—a mind that could often be tough and questioning. After all, from the beginning of her unconventional career, she had had to use persuasion to make her way past barriers guarded jealously by men, starting with her father and including officials of the educational and political establishments of the society she lived in. And who knows how she had come to terms with the feelings of bitterness and betrayal she must have felt toward the father of her child?

The Montessori Method is full of the kind of mystical thought and flowery sentiment that set hard-headed readers' teeth on edge even then, and later came to characterize her writings even more. "The scientist," she writes, "is not the clever manipulator of instruments, he is the worshipper of nature and he bears the external symbols of his passion as does the follower of some religious order.[20] . . . We must make of [teachers] worshippers and interpreters of the spirit of nature."[21] Throughout the book, her "scientific pedagogy," we find such statements as "All human victories, all human progress, stand upon the inner force.[22] . . . Humanity shows itself in all its intellectual splendor during this tender age as the sun shows itself at the dawn, and the flower in the first unfolding of the petals; and we must respect religiously, reverently, these first indications of individuality.[23] . . . Life is a superb goddess, always advancing, overthrowing the obstacles which environment places in the way of her triumph.[24] . . . These methods tend to guard that spiritual fire within man, to keep his real nature unspoiled and to set it free from the oppressive and degrading yoke of society."[25] She was fond of quoting from Wordsworth's "Intimations of Immortality" the lines "Shades of the prison-house begin to close/Upon the growing boy."

Read today, *Il Metodo* appears a combination of good practical sense and valuable insights about fostering the development of children on the one hand and on the other rhapsodic passages of flowery prose and vague philosophical underpinning that add nothing to the thought and are most charitably ignored. It is hard to realize today how radical many of its statements were at the time, because so much of it has become part of our body of received ideas. To understand its impact, one has to go back to the days of schoolchildren fixed at their desks in frozen rigidity repeating group lessons by rote in a relentlessly inflexible routine, the legacy of a system that in its own day had been a reform—an answer to the problem of teaching large groups of the illiterate poor at once with few teachers. Now, in the historical process by which every educational solution eventually becomes another time's problem, Montessori sought to free the children from physical and mental restraints, change them from passive, dependent creatures to active and independent individuals.

No details of the child's daily life in school are beneath her consideration, and the book includes instructions in the matter of diet (for children three to six, "the quantity of meat should correspond to 1 gramme for every cubic centimetre of broth. . . . The best way of feeding eggs to a child is to take them still warm from the hen and have him eat them just as they are, and then digest them in the open air. . . . After the age of four, filet of beef may be introduced into the diet, but never heavy and fat meats like that of the pig, the capon, the eel, the tuna, etc., which are to be absolutely excluded along with mollusks and crustaceans (oysters, lobsters) from the child's diet. . . . All cheeses are to be excluded from the child's diet. . . . Children must never eat raw vegetables, such as salads and greens, but only cooked ones; indeed they are not to be highly recommended either cooked or raw, with the exception of spinach which may enter with moderation into the diet of children"[26] as well as clothing ("Short and comfortable clothing for children, sandals for the feet, nudity of the lower extremities, are so many liberations from the oppressive shackles of civilization"[27]).

Her sense of the practical is that of a woman who practiced medicine among the poor and knew the facts of an impoverished life but also kept one foot in the nineteenth-century niceties of domestic arrangements and personal refinements. For her there was a connection between manners and morals, between how children learned and how they lived. Her efficiency expressed itself in the double layer of every thing she invented, every lesson she gave. In a reading game that was an early attempt to teach the children to recognize whole words, each child drew the name of a classmate from a basket and then offered that child a toy. Characteristically, Montessori saw the reading game as a way of teaching two things at once. In addition to learning to recognize words, "We taught the children to present these toys in a gracious and polite way, accompanying the act with a bow. In this way we did away with every idea of class distinction, and inspired the sentiment of kindness toward those who did not possess the same blessings as ourselves."[28] Putting away the materials in their proper place was a perceptual exercise; it also developed a sense of personal orderliness. An exercise in refining the sense of taste involved experiencing various solutions of bitter and sweet, acid or salty flavors. The children learned to fill a glass with lukewarm water and carefully rinse their mouths after each test. "In this way the exercise for the sense of taste is also an exercise in hygiene."[29]

She was never far from a concern with the application of learning to everyday life. Sense training was important not only as the basis for cognitive development but as a means by which the consumer defends himself against the tricks of big business and advertising:

> Almost all the forms of adulteration in food stuffs are rendered possible by the torpor of the senses. . . . Fraudulent industry feeds upon the lack of sense education in the masses. . . . We often see the purchaser depending on the honesty of the merchant, or putting his faith in the company, or the label on the box. This is because purchasers are lacking in the capacity of judging directly for themselves. They do not know how to distinguish with their senses the different qualities of various substances. In fact, we may say that in many cases intelligence is rendered useless by lack of practice, and this practice is almost always sense education.[30]

She insists on the literal, and has little feeling for the use of symbols or the value of fantasy.

A child who draws a red tree is making a mistake in his apprehension of reality, just as if he responded with the wrong choice when the teacher said, "Give me the red." A teacher who demonstrates blue by referring to the color of the sky and of her apron is confusing the child, deluging him "with useless, and often, false words."[31] Metaphor (the example she gives is a teacher calling the sound of a mandolin string being plucked that of a baby crying, to illustrate the nature of sound) is "ridiculous," serves only to impress the figure of the teacher on the child's mind—as someone who makes foolish mistakes—rather than the object of the lesson itself. In her system there is no place for serendipity; what is learned must always be what she intended to teach. To make sure this is so—and that therefore the child can go on to the next lesson—everything must be as direct and as simple as possible. What is valuable is what is practical, familiarizes children with reality, is "so closely related to daily life that it interests all children intensely."[32]

She does not mean to banish fantasy—the symbols of poetry, the imaginative flights of the fairy tale—from the child's life, but only from school, where, as she has defined the function of the school, it has no business.

Although the mainstream of psychology was moving in directions of which she remained either unaware or unaccepting—it is sometimes hard to believe that she worked and wrote throughout the years in which Freud was developing and demonstrating the nature of the unconscious and the existence of infantile sexuality and its role in psychic conflict— and although she seems to have neglected both the role of interpersonal relationships and the imagination in education, her basic premise, discovered and expressed in her own way, was sound and consistent with other innovations in twentieth-century thought. Stated most generally, it was the crucial importance of early experience. In the early years of the century it was not yet a commonly held belief—and if it sounds to us today self-evident, she helped to make it so—that "many defects which become permanent . . . the child acquires through being neglected during the most important period of his age, the period between three and six, at which time he forms and establishes his principal functions."[33] She knew this was the most significant finding of her educational experiments. "It represents the results of a series of trials made by me, in the education of young children, with methods already used with deficients."[34]

She thought it a mistake for boys and girls to be segregated in the early childhood years and for their early training to be different. In the Casa, boys and girls shared the responsibility of housework, preparation of meals, and care of the animal pets. She believed in teaching adolescents of about twelve or thirteen how to care for babies, and felt that such training would help "to produce that ideal type of father who can give the baby its bottle and is not ashamed of pushing the pram."[35]

She was aware that she was open to the criticism that after only two years of intensive work with abnormal children, and only ten years after she had left medical school, she had put forward an ambitious plan for reforming society through a method of educating young children. Her rejoinder to this criticism was that "my ten years of work may in a sense be considered as a summing up of the forty years of work done by Itard and Seguin. Viewed in this light, fifty years of active work preceded and prepared for this apparently brief trial of only two years."[36]

There was no area of life that would not be reached and improved by the transformation of the school, the system of educating the senses through training and practice, taking advantage of the child's spontaneous interest in mastering his environment through self-directed activity. Women would be freed from age-old slavery, children would grow up healthy, independent yet cooperative, able to make intelligent choices as workers, consumers, parents, and citizens, and ultimately the secrets of nature would be discovered and channeled for society's benefit.

If this sounds like a great deal to expect of schooling, we must remember that to Montessori the school was a laboratory in which a great social experiment would be carried out. It would perform many of the functions that had traditionally belonged to other educating institutions of society—home and family, church, child-care and child-saving centers, and asylums—not in order to replace them but to build on them. In the school the child would acquire the capacities of judgment necessary to order the experiences the rest of his life provided. Society would be given its direction by the school as the center of the life of the child, forming character as it trained the body and taught cognitive skills.

It seems clear today that such a large order would be harder to fill than Montessori supposed, that she failed to reckon with some of the complexities of life—both of individuals and societies—apparent to our more well informed and more skeptical age.

But if the experiment did not result in changing the world, it did contribute to changing the quality of life in school for young children—no insignificant matter—and demonstrated the possibility of a more effective kind of learning, a set of principles for the education of freer and more productive men and women.

9

When the course at Città di Castello ended there was a diploma-awarding ceremony at the villa with the Baronessa dressed in white, wildflowers in her hair. Two years later she died, and Montessori dedicated the English edition of *The Montessori Method,* published in America in 1912, to her memory.

The summer of 1909 ended with Montessori and her companions traveling to Perugia and visiting the other little hill towns around Assisi.

In the fall she returned to Rome and began making plans for two courses she would give in the spring, one a training course for teachers, the other for nonprofessionals—parents and others who were interested in the method that was gaining such renown through published reports and word of mouth.

Maccheroni and Fedeli returned to Milan, where a second Casa was opened in October 1909 with Fedeli as directress. Then, at Easter 1910, both returned to Rome to assist Montessori in the courses. They were joined by Ballerini, who died not long afterward, and Lina Olivero, another member of the circle of young women followers that had formed around Montessori, working and living with her. They were like daughters to her. Everyone else called her "Dottoressa." To them she was "Mammolina."

Maccheroni took charge of a Montessori class in the Franciscan convent, the Convento delle Suore Francescane Missionarie di Maria, on the Via Giusti, a beautiful old building with plenty of space and lovely gardens. Here the nuns had taken in more than a hundred little girls among those left orphaned by the 1908 earthquake that had devastated Messina in Sicily and parts of Calabria. They provided a large, sunlit room for the Montessori class formed for the youngest of the orphans, aged three to seven, and Queen Margherita provided the little chairs and tables and the didactic materials. Some of the poor children from the surrounding neighborhood also joined the class.

By 1910 Montessori was no longer directly involved in the school at San Lorenzo, according to Dorothy Canfield Fisher, who had spent time in Rome visiting the schools and talking with Montessori, "as a result of an unfortunate disagreement between Signor Talamo and herself."[1] Years later, it was revealed that the "disagreement" resulted from Talamo's resentment of the publicity which centered on Montessori's educational experiment rather than, as he had hoped, on his housing experiment in which it took place. According to Montessori, she was actually locked out. When she was almost eighty years old, Montessori told an interviewer, "I stayed with them for two years, until the porter was instructed by the contractors not to let me into the building," because her work was "causing such a newspaper sensation that the businessmen who paid for the construction claimed she was using the project as a personal advertising campaign." Looking back, she was able to say, "These closed doors are providential. They always make for progress."[2]

Was she perhaps also thinking, all those years later, of the doors that had closed behind her even earlier when she left the Orthophrenic School? That too had been a "providential" departure, one from which she had gone off in a new direction to begin her work on the education of normal children, the work in which she would make her real contribution and for which she would become world-famous.

The new Casa at Via Giusti, where she was aided by the Franciscan sisters, later became the demonstration school for Montessori's 1913 and 1914 international courses. Her students came to observe there, as well as other visitors interested in seeing for themselves what went on in the increasingly famous Case. On some days there were as many as a hundred visitors, who were able to look on in the large old halls of the cloister, with its graceful archways, fountains, and gardens, without disturbing the children's concentration on their activities.

After the long school days, the young women would join Montessori at the apartment where she lived with her parents and talk over the events of the school day. Renilde Montessori still took a lively interest in her daughter's work and was always part of the discussions.

Remembering these early years Maccheroni told how

> one day, looking at her hands, Dr. Montessori said, "How many things they have already done, these hands!" I asked her, "What is it you would like to do with them now?" She considered a moment and said, "To prepare sterilized milk for children." [One wonders: Was she thinking of her own child, disguising a wish that she could feed him, care for him?] She then described to me the life of solitude, the delicate care and scrupulous cleanliness required in milking the cows and bottling the milk, raw milk but free of germs. Now at the time she said this, she had already started with her method and movement which obliged her to be continually in contact with the public. I remember how she enjoyed getting free for a quarter of an hour to indulge in the retirement and the humble work she felt she needed. "Quick, quick! Give me my wooden shoes and the water," and she set to work to wash, with the

146

greatest care, the pavement of her terrace looking out on the Pincio. She was never awkward, never splashed herself or bumped the broom against the pail.

On another occasion, "a number of us returned with Dr. Montessori from a reception held in her honor. She invited us all to come home with her. But it was the cook's day out. Without changing her dress, Dr. Montessori put on a white apron and cooked us spaghetti al sugo, cutlets, fried potatoes, and I forget what else besides. I noticed with what ease, grace and exactness of movement she did everything. The dinner was excellent."[3]

At night Montessori would plan her lectures for the two courses she gave in that spring of 1910.

According to Anna Maccheroni, who attended both courses, they were parallel, but not identical. Montessori never repeated the same lecture, always varying the material for the two different audiences.

An American writer, Josephine Tozier, described Montessori's method of teaching her method to teachers: "She does all she can in training her teachers to understand [her] theory: she reiterates, she repeats, she emphasizes, she reproves; she goes personally into the classes to show her teachers how to handle the children."[4]

Among those who attended the lectures and came to observe at the Via Giusti were the Baronessa Franchetti and Donna Maria Maraini, Marchesa Guerrieri-Gonzaga, the Roman socialite and philanthropist who was one of Montessori's oldest friends and at whose villa at Palidano Montessori was a frequent guest. Queen Margherita and members of her court were also frequent visitors, and the queen invited Montessori to the palace on several occasions to discuss her work.

The visitors were particularly interested in coming at lunchtime, when they could watch the little children serving each other. A few of the children would eat first, so they could serve the others, most of whom remained outdoors except for a few whose turn it was to set the tables. When all the children were seated, the little waiters would carry in the soup tureens and put them on the tables, where each child helped himself. Accounts by those early visitors mention over and over again how impressed they were with the pride and seriousness—as well as the efficiency—with which four-year-olds carried out this responsibility.

Montessori's book was being widely read, reviewed, and talked about, and translations began to appear in other countries. After the first English version came French, Spanish, German, Russian, Polish, Rumanian, Danish, Dutch, Japanese, and Chinese editions, and eventually over the next few years *Il Metodo* would be translated into over twenty languages.

Visitors began to appear at the Case dei Bambini in Rome from all over the world, just as a century earlier they had come to see Pestalozzi's school at Yverdon, study his method, and return to found Pestalozzi schools in their own countries.

The journey to Rome was made by journalists, professors of education, diplomats and crowned heads of Europe, classroom teachers, government officials, religious leaders, social workers, physicians, philanthropists. Intrigued by what they had read, they came out of curiosity, stayed to marvel, and returned to start Montessori schools and societies throughout Western Europe, in the United States and England, in China, Japan, Canada, India, Mexico, Syria, Australia, New Zealand, and South America.

Visitors sometimes waited in Rome for days for a chance to see and talk with Montessori. Those who could not come, wrote. Letters asking for information about the method, how to start a school, where to find a Montessori-trained teacher, arrived every day from all parts of the world. They came from Catholics, Theosophists, Bolsheviks, Social Democrats—all of whom found in Montessori's system an answer to the ills of society. She was inundated with such a volume of correspondence—from as far away as China but by far the largest part from England and America—that she soon became unable to handle it all herself.

A Montessori society was founded in Rome, among its influential patrons Queen Margherita. Soon branches were founded in Naples as well as Milan, along with Montessori schools.

Ernesto Nathan, Rome's mayor, was enthusiastic about the Montessori experiment and called it to the attention of other government officials. Influential Romans began to take an interest in Montessori schools— which seemed to promise and to accomplish so much—for their own children. The wives of government ministers and Roman aristocrats organized Montessori classes in their homes. The class the British ambassador had started for children of his embassy staff had grown into a school for children of a number of members of the diplomatic corps stationed in Rome and was now housed in a villa on the Pincian Hill and held under Montessori's supervision. The children from the various embassies all spoke different languages and came from homes with differing customs. According to a journalist's report at the time, "Confusion reigned at first; but before a month had passed this Tower of Babel" had been converted "into a community of happy, busy children."[5]

The Children's House

Montessori had two classes in her own apartment near the Piazza del Popolo, one for poor children and another to which some of her wealthy and titled friends and sponsors sent their own children to learn with the advanced materials she was beginning to work out for the later elementary grades. She was now experimenting with methods for children six to nine.

She had designed a new set of materials, the advanced apparatus, for teaching arithmetic. There were plane insets, bead bars, chains, squares, and cubes for teaching multiplication, fractions, geometry, but once again Montessori had difficulty finding workmen willing to take the time and trouble to produce the equipment she had designed. In order to persuade an ironmonger to make the plane insets she gave him an explanation of their use that amounted to a geometry lesson. He enjoyed the experience of being a Montessori pupil so much he agreed to take on the job.

Just as she had adapted what she had learned from abnormal children to normal ones, Montessori now applied what she had learned working with deprived children of the poor to the advantaged children of the well-to-do. The general principles always remained the same, and they continued to work with the same success.

In October 1911 a Casa dei Bambini for forty-five children, most of them six-year-olds, from the dark, narrow streets of the dirty, disease-ridden quarter of Pescheria, the medieval Rome ghetto, was established by the Roman board of education at the urging of the principal of a girls' public school. The municipal officials were finally persuaded to allow her to use a room in the St. Angelo school but provided nothing more—no furnishings or equipment, not even the didactic materials at first. Montessori was particularly interested in this experiment with children so impoverished that two of them did not even have homes, but slept at night with their mother in the hallway of a tenement building on a mattress of straw which, along with a pan for burning coals and a cooking pot, made up their entire inventory of household goods. Even before the teaching materials were provided, the story of San Lorenzo had repeated itself at St. Angelo. The children proudly learned order and cleanliness, had some training in movement and speech, and "by the time the materials arrived, a happy discipline was completely established in the school." They "exploded," on schedule, into reading and writing, and at the end of the year an American observer, Anne E. George, spoke of "the life, the joy, the individual independence which I saw in the children themselves and in everything they did. . . . During the year spent there these little waifs of the Ghetto had found that personal liberty and self-

149

control that alone make it possible for any human being to do his best work and to adapt himself to the conditions of the life about him."[6]

Another visiting American, Professor Florence Elizabeth Ward, wrote: "The schools established in the slums several years ago reach now to the other extreme of the social stratum. In the Casa dei Bambini on Pincian Hill one sees the carefully reared scions of the exclusive aristocracy using the didactic materials and receiving the social training provided for the children of the Ghetto at the Municipal School of St. Angelo in Pescheria, a most poverty-stricken quarter. Between these extremes there are such schools as the one in Via Giusti."[7]

Accounts in the Italian press and reports by early visitors led to a number of articles in other countries, especially England and the United States.

The first discussion of Montessori's work in an American publication appeared in a professional educational journal. Montessori was introduced to American teachers in a series of articles by Jenny B. Merrill in *The Kindergarten-Primary Magazine* beginning in December 1909.[8] The magazine was a monthly "devoted to the child and to the unity of educational theory and practice from the kindergarten through the university." Dr. Merrill, a member of the magazine's editorial committee, was supervisor of kindergartens in Manhattan, the Bronx, and Richmond; other members of the committee were on the faculties of Teachers College and the New York Froebel Normal School. Some of Dr. Merrill's earlier contributions to the publication had been articles on "Suggestions for the Hudson-Fulton Celebrations in Kindergartens" and "Fall Walks," and typical articles by other contributors around this time included "Ethical Lessons from Froebel's Mother Plays," "The Doh-Doo Fairies," and "New Music Plays for the Kindergarten," as well as suggestions for songs such as "The Good Cobbler and the Children," "My Ball, I Like to Bounce You," and "Come, Little Leaves."

Into this sentimental atmosphere came Dr. Merrill's news of "A New Method in Infant Education" and it was indeed a striking contrast to the character and tone of what kindergarteners were used to. Merrill got her information from an article which had appeared in *The London Journal of Education* and from Baronessa Franchetti.

The Merrill article started off with the news that in Italy "an able woman physician, Dr. Med. Maria Montessori, Docente all'Università di Roma, has modified the kindergarten methods to such an extent as to warrant the title of this article" and went on to explain Montessori's success in the use of Seguin's methods in the training of defective children and her subsequent modifications of those methods for use with normal children. She quoted the *London Journal* article's statement that the fundamental principle of Montessori's method was "liberty, the free development of the spontaneous individual manifestations of the child" and noted that while this was an idea all Froebelians held in theory, Dr. Montessori was justified in pointing out that, in spite of theory, education in fact was still infused by the spirit of slavery, typified by the school desk and the immobility it forces on the child.

Merrill pointed out that in the new Italian system the teacher played a more passive role—that of observer. "Her office is rather to direct than to instruct. Her active intervention is to be reduced to a minimum and her art lies in knowing just when her help is necessary to spur on the developing intelligence of a child and when he may be safely left to himself"—surely a new, and perhaps somewhat disquieting, concept of her role to the American kindergarten teacher reading the article.

The article described the Montessori classroom with its child-sized furniture—the small tables and little chairs, the low washstands, and the garden and pets. It explained the "exercises of practical life" and how the children were led first of all to make themselves independent and masters of their surroundings by learning to dress and wash themselves, tidy their cupboards, and dust the furniture. (A not uncommon reaction to this activity by teachers hearing about it for the first time was that it sounded like a training school for hotel waiters or housemaids.) It described some of the materials, the buttoning and lacing frames, the sandpaper letters and cylinders, and concluded, "The Baroness Franchetti says the Montessori occupations need to be seen to be fully appreciated."

A second article in the following issue dealt with the development of reading and writing in the Montessori class. "Our kindergartens," it said, "have succeeded in *excluding* reading and writing and have emphasized the principle so well enounced [sic] by Froebel, 'The ABC of things should precede the ABC of words.' It did seem that we had succeeded in cutting out the three R's, but Dr. Montessori has put them back in the infant school in Rome and we must convince our Italian friend of the error or let them [sic] convince us. Altogether it behooves us to be liberal, not dogmatic, and to listen to the tale with interest."

The article described, with many exclamation marks, the route by which four-year-olds moved from feeling letters to writing words in six weeks. "It is said that they leave toys for letters. Is this desirable in four-year-olds?" It is a question that would be asked again and again in this country over the next few years in discussions of the Montessori method.

Miss Merrill reprinted the daily schedule of exercises in a Montessori school ("translated for me from the original" by a teacher at P.S. 125 in Manhattan) and ended her second article with the somewhat school-marmish exhortation, "We ask kindergarteners to study it for it contains admirable suggestions. Comparison of methods is valuable."

A third installment of this introduction of Montessori to American teachers appeared in the February 1910 issue. In it the author turned from the somewhat disquieting subject of early reading and writing to a more "reassuring" topic, the role of nature in education—"work in gardens such as Froebel urged and all kindergarteners believe in."

She urged the construction of model tenement houses in New York City, opening into gardens. "It is delightful to realize these happy interchanges between the kindergartens of different speaking people," she wrote, "and to know that nature that 'makes all the world akin' is the best connecting link."

"In the first garden thus planned for the children in the heart of Rome," she told her readers, "the surrounding neighbors, as they have here in New York, despoiled it with refuse thrown from the windows. Soon, however, little by little, the children themselves so interested their parents in their garden that this annoyance ceased." She concluded, with typical Froebelian stickiness, that "There are heart gardens as well as flower gardens."

After describing how children in a Montessori class kept track of the seeds they planted, recording their observations and drawings in a note-book, Miss Merrill told her readers how the Baroness Franchetti, who was on a visit home to America and touring some of the New York City schools, "spoke most feelingly to a class of little boys in P.S. 68, Manhattan, about this work of the children in Italy who live upon her estate."

Here the article was touching on something that tied in with the American urban ideal of public education at the time—the school as a force for socialization of different backgrounds, Americanizing all, bringing everyone into the mainstream. According to this way of thinking, there was one cultural ideal and the well-to-do and well-educated classes were patrons of this public system of schools for the less privileged. While their children did not attend them, their taxes paid for them and their civic associations supported them. This system for coping with the challenge of the waves of new immigrants arriving from Europe in the years around the turn of the century was faced with a similar challenge in a later generation—educating the children of the severely economically deprived and socially disadvantaged populations of the urban black ghettos after World War II. When that problem reached crisis proportions almost half a century after Merrill wrote these articles, Montessori would be rediscovered and have a second introduction in U.S. education.

Meanwhile, Merrill continued to describe Montessori education to American teachers through the spring and into the summer of 1910, expressing some of the reservations that many of her readers of the time would also feel about Montessori and the American child. Clay modeling, for instance, should emphasize expression, not the product. The making of vases in the Montessori class was more like "useful work" than the "play spirit of the kindergarten." Merrill, the American supervisor of kindergartens, says, "We fear she is getting too near child labor."

In her last article Merrill referred to the Montessori system as "an Italian modification of Froebelian methods," and to the didactic apparatus as "educational playthings." Speaking of the New York teacher who translated Montessori for her, she unselfconsciously expressed the well-meaning attitude of patronage the American public school teacher shared with the American-born Italian baroness toward the children in her classroom. "Miss Schell has mastered the Italian language for the sake of doing efficient work in her locality. She dearly loves the Italian children." She probably did—as she probably also enjoyed exercising her benign authority over them. It would be hard for her and others like her to give up their position at the center of the classroom stage and accept what could only seem to them a far less exalted role—that of observer and guide in a process by which children made use of materials designed to enable them to educate themselves. Merrill reported "much of interest in the method to Miss Schell as well as to myself but her general criticism is that the devices seem to be too scientific and she misses the play spirit." Their feeling was that the use of the didactic materials resulted in an emphasis on "training" at the expense of "free self-expression." They "deplored the absence of the use of the building instinct appropriately exercised with blocks," those blocks so dear to the hearts of kindergarten teachers. It was hard for them to replace one set of ritual objects with another.

The Merrill series ended with "the hope that our traveling kindergarteners will endeavor to visit these new institutions in Italy." How many of them would do so, and how impressed they would be, she could hardly have suspected.

Throughout the next four years, and especially in the years 1911, 1912, and 1913, when Montessori finally came to America, reports of visits to Montessori schools and discussions of the method, the philosophy behind it, and its application to the American kindergarten scene by educators and journalists appeared in scores of articles and reviews of her book and of books about her in newspapers, popular magazines, and cultural reviews, as well as in professional journals and bulletins published by the U.S. Bureau of Education. The method was discussed at professional meetings of state teachers' associations as well as the prestigious National Education Association.

American teachers and teachers of teachers began to arrive in Rome in droves. Early visitors to the Case dei Bambini included child psychologists Arnold and Beatrice Gesell, publisher S. S. McClure, and such prominent professors of education as Howard Warren of Princeton, Arthur Norton of Harvard, Lightner Witmer of the University of Pennsylvania, William Heard Kilpatrick of Columbia University's Teachers College, and delegates from the Massachusetts Institute for Abnormal Children, Pratt Institute, Iowa State Teachers College, Miami University, and the universities of California, Arkansas, and Michigan. In February 1911, Professor Henry W. Holmes of Harvard's Department of Education wrote to Montessori expressing interest in her book and in the publication of an English translation under Harvard's auspices. Among the other luminaries of American education who were expressing interest in introducing the Montessori system in public and private schools and settlements were G. Stanley Hall, the Clark University professor who had pioneered the child development movement and had brought Sigmund Freud to the United States to lecture; Ella Flagg Young, the controversial superintendent of the Chicago public schools; and Jane Addams, the social work pioneer of Hull House.

The Montessori system offered a program of reform to a reform-minded age. Through a new kind of educational institution—which seemed to have proved itself beyond anyone's wildest expectations in an unbelievably short period of time—it would be possible to mold a new generation of children—independent, productive members of society—and at the same time solve many of the problems of the day, social inequities of class and sex among them.

Educators of all kinds—teachers, legislators, doctors, parents, writers—were fascinated by the promise of the Case dei Bambini. They came to see them with their own eyes and when they left they spread word of the experiment throughout the civilized world.

The system was introduced in schools as far away as those of Australia and Argentina, and in St. Petersburg a Montessori class was started in the imperial gardens for the children of the czar's family and the court. Tolstoy's daughter came to Rome to visit the Case and interest in Russia ran so high that five different translations of Montessori's book were published.

Montessori classes had already been imported to England. Bertram Hawker, a wealthy Englishman on his way to Australia to look after his property there, stopped in Rome and was shown the Casa by British ambassador Rodd. Hawker was so intrigued by what he saw that he postponed his sailing in order to meet Montessori. After talking with her he put off his departure again, missed ship after ship, and finally canceled his trip altogether in order to return to England to found the first Montessori class there in his home at East Runton. In 1912, with other enthusiasts, he founded the Montessori Society of the United Kingdom, which came to include members of the British educational establishment—policy-making government officials and staff members of the influential *Times Educational Supplement.* Soon everyone who taught infant or elementary school in London either taught or talked Montessori.

By the end of 1911 the Montessori system had been officially adopted in the public schools of Italy and of Switzerland; two model schools had been established in Paris, one under the direction of the daughter of the French minister to Italy, who had taken Montessori's course in Rome; official preparations were under way to introduce the method in England; and plans were being made for opening Montessori schools in India, China, Mexico, Korea, Argentina, and Hawaii.

In the United States the first American Montessori school had already been opened in Tarrytown, New York, and a second one started in Boston. The boards of education of Des Moines, Iowa, and Omaha, Nebraska, were considering the adoption of the method in their schools; plans were under way for opening Montessori schools for the socialites of Newport, Rhode Island; and more than four hundred city and county superintendents of public schools in various states had requested information about the method. Since the publication of the Merrill articles and others that followed, Montessori had received requests to study with her from teachers in almost every state in the union. The demand from English and American teachers for training in the method had been so great that Montessori was planning a course in Rome for English-speaking teachers.

Now, at the age of forty, Montessori took another of those steps which would shape the rest of her life. She made the decision to give up all other work in order to devote her full time and energies to the schools and societies of what was becoming the Montessori movement, to oversee the

training of teachers in her methods and the dissemination of her ideas—
"the task of keeping in touch with these various movements, of guiding
this vast wave of international enthusiasm, and of keeping it true to her
principles." Her official biographer, Standing, wrote of this decision, in a
passage she herself approved: "Her mission in life had crystallized.
. . . She felt the duty of going forth as an apostle on behalf of all the
children in the world, born and as yet unborn, to preach for their rights
and their liberation."[9] It is one of the striking ironies of Montessori's
life—like her vehement early decision to pursue some career other than
teaching—that, unable to raise her own child, she saw her life as devoted
to the welfare of children everywhere.

She resigned from her University of Rome lectureship and removed
her name from the list of practicing physicians. Some of her friends
were apprehensive and thought she was being imprudent, but her mother approved and supported this decision as she had earlier ones.

As Montessori put it, she began to spend time on propaganda that she
would gladly be giving to research. But it was necessary, she felt, in the
cause of the child, who would be saved by the proper implementation of
her discoveries about the nature of learning, but only if they were not
distorted or diluted.

The decision to give up both an academic career and the practice of
the profession she had fought so hard to enter in order to devote herself
to the spread of her ideas—to training teachers herself and overseeing
the various Montessori societies and keeping them on the track, true to
the faith—had certain consequences. From now on she would support
herself and her dependents on the proceeds of her training courses and
the royalties from her books and didactic materials, a situation which
lent her activities a certain commercial aspect they would not have had if
she had remained a salaried academic propounding her ideas in an academic framework. The movement became a business, a kind of franchise operation in which Montessori had a vital stake in such matters as
copyright of the materials and official certification of teachers. Her name
became a brand name which could not be used without her permission,
surely an anomalous situation in the world of ideas and one which contributed to maintaining her work as a separate movement outside the
mainstream of educational thought in the years following World War I.

A certain pattern to her life was already taking shape. She was beginning to receive invitations to give lectures or training courses all over the
world from government officials of education, educational societies, and
interested groups of all kinds. Over the years she would give courses not
only in Italy but in England, France, Holland, Germany, Spain, Austria,

India, and Ceylon. She would lecture in the United States and South America. Everywhere she went there were official receptions to welcome and honor her and she was the guest of wealthy patrons, a public figure less and less in touch with intellectual developments outside the world of her own movement.

Like her earlier two-year experiment with the deficient children of Rome's institutions, she considered her two years of direct daily involvement in the San Lorenzo Case dei Bambini the practicum on which all her later work was based. After 1908 and her break with Talamo she was not directly involved on a day-to-day basis with the operation of any of the Case dei Bambini but with the training of teachers for Montessori schools and increasingly with overseeing the various Montessori societies all over the world.

Despite the increasing amount of her time which was devoted to lecturing, to her training courses, and to writing, she did not entirely abandon her academic career during the years between the establishment of the first Casa and the time of her return from America and subsequent move to Spain in 1916.

She had continued in her position as external examiner in anthropology at the university and in 1907 was appointed a member of the examination commission on history and natural science for teachers in training. In the fall of that year she was also made a member of the committee which appointed teachers of gymnastics for the schools. In 1911 she was named *professore straordinario,* or outside lecturer, in anthropology and hygiene at the Istituto Superiore di Magistero Femminile. Following a leave of absence she resumed that position in 1913 and held it until her move to Barcelona in 1916, after which she was full-time leader of the international movement that bore her name.

10

Closely connected with the changing view of the school's role in society—the greater responsibility assigned to it and the new ideas about how it should go about meeting those responsibilities—was the rise of the printed mass media of communications in Europe and the United States in the years following Maria Montessori's birth.

Before unification there were only three newspapers in Italy, all organs of the Vatican. When Montessori started school there were about seven hundred and fifty periodicals being published in Italy. Twenty years later, when she graduated from medical school, almost two thousand newspapers, magazines, and quarterlies were appearing regularly. Many of them were concerned with social causes and all of them were looking for good copy—subjects that would interest their growing readership.

Turn-of-the-century Italy was, in fact, a nation of newspaper readers. There were some fourteen hundred papers, many with distinctly individual characters, and every Italian had his favorite, to be waited for all afternoon, read in the cafés, and quoted later at dinner. The most serious and influential journals were published in Rome, the political capital, and Milan, the industrial capital. Among Roman papers the *Tribuna* was the voice of government policy—whatever government happened to be in office—with good coverage of foreign affairs. The *Giornale d'Italia*, a more liberal paper, was known for its literary and scientific articles. *Avanti* was the Socialist organ. *Messaggero* was the leader in the sensational field. The most respected journal was Milan's *Corriere della Sera*. Its writers included statesmen, scientists, and literary figures as well as some of Europe's most distinguished correspondents. Milan's *Secolo* was the organ of the Radical party.

All of these had published accounts of Montessori's work from the early days of her speeches on the rights of women and the needs of deficient children to her successes at the Orthophrenic School and now the "miracle in San Lorenzo" and the Via Giusti. From Rome, news of this latest miracle spread to the rest of Italy and was picked up by the press of Europe, Great Britain, and especially the United States.

The phenomenon itself was not new. Not only had Montessori's early speeches, writings, and teaching successes been widely publicized, but as far back as the 1850s articles on Froebel and his kindergartens by authors ranging from anonymous scribblers to such well-known writers as Charles Dickens had appeared in the popular magazines of the time and had spread the word about experiments in schooling to a growing world of interested readers, including many who might never had read a book on education. What was new was the scale of the phenomenon and its impact.

In America particularly, the proliferation of popular newspapers, general magazines, special journals, and books of all kinds, the development of newspaper chains and wire services carrying news and ideas about the news around the world, had a revolutionary effect on education. In their hunger for interesting material to fill their pages and increase their circulations, publications were quick to note and report on anything new. Developments that might have passed unnoticed by any but a few only a half century before by the beginning of the twentieth century became the breakfast-table conversation of millions almost as soon as they had taken place.

The press was not responsible for all the changes that marked the vast social upheavals and evolutions in institutions but it was accelerating the pace at which they occurred. A new kind of educating institution in themselves, newspapers and magazines spread the call for and the news of educational reforms. Whether attacking or generating enthusiasm, the press was reporting on what was happening—and sometimes causing it to happen. It had itself become an important agency of public education as well as a catalyst for change in the schools, from the nursery to the university and professional levels.

Whether you were a reader of such special periodicals as *American Education*, the *Journal of Educational Psychology*, the *Kindergarten Review*, *Pedagogical Seminary*, the *American Primary Teacher*, or such popular ones as *Ladies' Home Journal*, *Woman's Home Companion*, *Good Housekeeping*, *Dial*, *Scientific American*, the *Delineator*, *Contemporary Review*, you could not have avoided reading about Montessori schools and Montessori methods by 1912.

But the single most influential publication for the Montessori method in America was a series of articles that appeared in the spring of 1911 and the winter of 1911–12 in *McClure's Magazine* and were reprinted in England in the *Fortnightly Review* and *The World's Work*. It was the *McClure's* articles that really launched the Montessori movement in America. Already known to professionals and experts in the field of education, the Montessori phenomenon now burst upon the American public consciousness.

159

MARIA MONTESSORI: A BIOGRAPHY

S. S. McClure was one of the most influential journalists of his time. He introduced syndicated material to metropolitan newspapers, invented the Sunday supplement, and brought out the first of the low-priced mass-circulation magazines which served as a powerful instrument for social and political reform by exposing corruption in industry and government.

McClure's genius was an intuitive feeling for what would capture the public imagination. He was able to identify and articulate public concerns. Like all successful innovators, he was in touch with the temper of the times. And although he had been warned by his journalistic colleagues that an article about an educational experiment in Italy could not possibly interest the mass reading public, he thought otherwise.

In London in the winter of 1910, Mary L. Bisland, McClure's representative there, whose job was to keep an eye open for new material, told him about the work Montessori was doing in Rome with young children. She had heard about it from a friend, Josephine Tozier, who had spent some months in Rome talking to Montessori and visiting her schools.

It was through another American, the Marchesa Ranieri di Sorbello, that Tozier had first heard of what she described as "this precious boon to little children, and saw, in the nursery of her *palazzo*, two sturdy little sons who by its help had made a leap on the road of education several years in advance of their peers. Without realizing that they had as yet done anything more than play, these two boys, the youngest of whom is only three and a half, can read and write both in English and in Italian."[1]

McClure commissioned Tozier to write an article on the method and from the violently conflicting reactions of the educational authorities he asked to read the manuscript, he knew he was onto a controversial and therefore provocative subject.

In his autobiography, published in 1914, McClure described the events leading up to his magazine's introduction of Montessori to her largest American audience.

> Everyone in the office said a pedagogical article could not possibly be interesting . . . I commissioned Miss Tozier to write an article on the Montessori method of teaching young children. . . . When Miss Tozier's article was completed, it was carefully compared with Mme. Montessori's book—then untranslated—by the English critic, Mr. William Archer, who assured me that it adequately represented Mme. Montessori's theories. Before the article was published it was submitted to several authorities of kindergartening and pedagogy in the U.S. These experts, I found, greatly differed in their estimates of Montessori's methods. Some of them were very antagonistic in their attitude, and declared that, because Mme. Montessori recognized and valued the

work of great educators of the past, there was nothing new about her method.

Miss Tozier's article appeared in the May number of *McClure's*, 1911, and immediately letters of inquiry began to come into the office in such numbers that it was impossible to answer them all. Mme. Montessori, in Rome, found herself engulfed in such a correspondence as threatened to take all her time. It seemed as if people everywhere had been waiting for her message. . . .[2]

The Tozier article in the May 1911 issue of *McClure's* described, in nineteen pages and almost as many photographs of the children and the materials, how young children learned in the Casa dei Bambini. It gave a brief account of Montessori's background and how she had adapted the sense-training system of Seguin to achieve the remarkable results illustrated in the pictures of three- and four-year-olds reading and writing.

Extra editions of the issue had to be printed and the overwhelming response in the form of letters from parents, physicians, psychologists, and teachers and school officials led McClure to assign Tozier to write two more long articles on the Montessori phenomenon to be published the following winter. In the meantime, the magazine published in the fall of 1911 some general information in response to the many questions about when a translation of Montessori's book would be available and how the didactic materials could be obtained. It reported on the translation then in progress under the direction of Harvard's Professor Holmes and that negotiations were being conducted in correspondence between Montessori and American manufacturers for the distribution of the didactic apparatus in this country.[3]

McClure's also published some samples of the hundreds of letters from readers anxious to put the new ideas into practice. Some wanted to find out about study and training with Montessori, others wanted to enroll their children in Montessori schools, still others wanted to use it in kindergartens, in day nurseries, in schools for backward children, or in their own homes. A typical letter read, "You have made in me, not merely an interested inquirer, but an ardent convert."[4]

The second Tozier article, in the December 1911 issue of *McClure's*,[5] went into greater detail about the principles of Montessori's philosophy of education, particularly her ideas of liberty for the child and its social implications. And it told the story of the St. Angelo school, where the San Lorenzo experiment had been replicated among even more deprived children and under far less favorable conditions. It was a story that went from abject misery to happy ending, and could not fail to touch American readers.

It was followed in January 1912 by an article in which Tozier described the Montessori materials in detail.[6]

McClure's followed up the Tozier articles with one by Montessori in the May 1912 issue,[7] the first article by her to appear in an American publication. Entitled "Disciplining Children," it was included as the last chapter in the American edition of her book, published at almost the same time. The editors introduced it as the "latest word upon education . . . by this great educational genius."

The December 1911 issue of *McClure's*[8] had reported the opening of the first Montessori school in America that fall.

Anne E. George, an elementary teacher at Chicago's prestigious private Latin School, had been interested in the use of play in early childhood education and in the spring of 1909 an American friend in Italy wrote her about the Case dei Bambini in Rome and Milan. Intrigued, she went to Rome that summer and visited the Casa at San Lorenzo, which was still under Montessori's direction, and met and talked with Montessori.

Anne George, who spoke no Italian, had been told that she and Montessori would be able to carry on their conversation in French. "This proved true of the Dottoressa, but I found that phrase-book French furnished small material for a discussion of the problems related to child education. I managed to say that I was a teacher, then we sat and mutely looked at each other for what seemed to me an endless age. I have since learned that the Dottoressa is always unresponsive if she suspects a visitor of being interested only in the fact that her children read and write an early age. To take a superficial attitude toward her methods is to place a wall between your mind and hers."[9]

Determined to break through that wall, the younger woman plunged desperately into an account of her own ideals as a teacher, and some of the things that were being done in American schools.

"I shall never forget the smile with which she welcomed me then, nor the sincerity with which she talked to me of her work and her hopes. Busy as she was,"[10] "Dr. Montessori took me to her schools, showing me in detail how she gave her lessons. The impression made by those mornings has stayed with me and has been my guide in all my work since. Dr. Montessori's simplicity was a revelation. Whenever we entered a classroom, I distinctly felt that a new and sweeter spirit pervaded the place, and that the children were, in an indescribable way, set free. Yet there was order in everything. With a straightforwardness often stripped entirely of words, Maria Montessori taught, or, to use her own word, 'directed,' her children. She treated the children, not as automatons, but as individual human beings. She never forced her personality or her will upon them, and made none of the efforts to attract and interest which I had often made use of."[11]

"I returned to America," the young teacher said, "to prepare myself to become her pupil,"[12] much as Montessori herself had undertaken almost ten years earlier to prepare herself for a new kind of work by turning to the writings of Itard and Seguin. Miss George, however, had found a living master.

She brought back to America with her a copy of *Il Metodo* and a complete set of the Materiale Didattico from the Casa di Lavoro in Milan, "determined to study the work as thoroughly as possible, and as the language was a serious barrier between me and the Dottoressa, from whom alone this new experiment could be learned,"[13] set about learning Italian in order to master the text.

She returned to Italy the following summer to perfect her Italian and in the winter of 1910 enrolled in Montessori's eight-month training course in Rome as her first American pupil.

It had been a busy year for Montessori, and when Anne George reappeared the Dottoressa had some difficulty recalling her. "I reminded her of our visits to the schools. Suddenly her face cleared and she said, 'Oh, is it the *simpatica Americana* who spoke such funny French, come back?' "[14]

George was welcomed, was taken home to meet Montessori's parents, and soon became a member of the circle of young women who studied and worked with Montessori by day and spent their evenings at the Montessori apartment with the family.

When the course ended, George returned to America, the first Montessori-trained American teacher, and in October 1911 she started the first Montessori school in the United States with twelve children in the home of Edward W. Harden in Tarrytown, New York. Like the impoverished children of San Lorenzo, the Tarrytown pupils, all "from cultured families whose greatest ambition it was to give their children everything possible in the way of education and rational enjoyment,"[15] settled into a self-established order and discipline, worked their way with intense absorption through the sensory materials, and "exploded" into reading and writing.

It was a newsworthy experiment, and accounts of her success in transplanting the Italian educator's methods to a new culture, among upper-middle-class children in a beautiful house overlooking the Hudson, appeared in profusely illustrated detail in *The New York Times* in the winter of 1911[16] and in an article by Anne George entitled "The First Montessori School in America" in *McClure's* in June 1912, as well as in a piece published the following month in *Good Housekeeping.*

In November *McClure's* published "The Montessori Method and the American Kindergarten" by Ellen Yale Stevens,[17] an elementary-school principal who was a student of Dewey and Thorndike at Columbia University's prestigious Teachers College, who had visited the Rome Case dei Bambini and urged the introduction of the method in kindergartens and of the theories in the teaching of psychology and was writing a book, *A Guide to the Montessori Method,* to be published in 1913.

All this was enough to make Montessori's name familiar on the American scene even if nothing else had appeared in the press, and there is no doubt that Montessori was both deeply grateful and warmly disposed to publisher McClure at this point in their relationship, the later vicissitudes of which would influence the eventual fate of the Montessori movement in this country.

Among the prominent Americans who were intrigued by the news appearing about the Montessori method was the wife of Alexander Graham Bell.[18] Bell, the inventor of the telephone and one of the most idolized Americans of his time, had begun his career as a teacher of the deaf. The son of a world-famous speech teacher who invented a phonetic alphabet system known as Visible Speech, whereby the sounds of any language could be written by means of a few symbols, the young Bell made use of Visible Speech to teach deaf pupils before beginning the scientific experiments which would result in the transmission of vocal sounds over electric wires. Throughout his long life he retained an interest in the education of the deaf. His wife, Mabel Hubbard Bell, was deaf, and Bell took a great interest in the young Helen Keller and her teacher Annie Sullivan.

Bell's father-in-law, Gardiner Hubbard, had been a founder of the National Geographic Society and in the late 1890s Bell, who became president of the society on Hubbard's death, was instrumental in transforming the society's magazine *National Geographic* from a dry, sober, technical journal into an attractive, lively periodical, profusely illustrated with photographs, for the general public. His plans for the magazine were carried out under the editorship of a bright young man named Gilbert Grosvenor, who became the Bells' son-in-law.

One of Bell's many friends and associates in the world of communications was Samuel S. McClure. It was a series of articles on Napoleon written by Ida Tarbell in 1894 and illustrated with a group of Napoleonic prints that had been collected by Gardiner Hubbard that had given the fledgling *McClure's Magazine* its first great journalistic success.

Both Bells took an active interest in the education of their several grandchildren. Bell's experience as a teacher of deaf children informed his philosophy of education, which was antiregimentation and favored the encouragement of the child's natural curiosity. Bell was highly critical of "the system of giving out a certain amount of work which must be carried through in a given space of time, and putting the children into orderly rows of desks and compelling them to absorb just so much intellectual nourishment, whether they are ready for it or not," which he compared to the forced feeding of geese to produce *foie gras.*

Nothing could have been more natural than that all these strands should come together in an enthusiastic response on the part of the Bells to the Montessori system as described in Tozier's 1911 *McClure's* articles.

In the spring of 1912 a Montessori class was set up for two of the Bell grandchildren, joined by a half dozen of the neighbors' children in the Bells' Washington, D.C. home. That summer the class was moved to the Bells' summer home on Cape Breton in Nova Scotia, where five local children joined seven Bell grandchildren in the first Montessori class in Canada. Bell took a great interest in the children's progress, conferring regularly with their teacher, Roberta Fletcher. The results of the experiment in what the scientifically minded Bells liked to call the "Children's Laboratory" rather than a Children's House impressed them and led Mrs. Bell to ask Roberta Fletcher and Anne E. George to start a Montessori school in the Bells' Washington home that fall. By spring, it was clear that there was enough interest on the part of Washington parents to warrant opening a larger school in permanent quarters and Mrs. Bell subscribed $1,000 toward the establishment of a private Montessori school.

The Bells knew everyone of importance in Washington, and a project in which they were enthusiastically involved was sure to receive press coverage that would stimulate wide public interest as well. It was a pattern that was to repeat itself over and over in the history of Montessori's early successes: the interest of influential people—outside the educational establishment itself—who started classes in their homes for their own children and then took an active interest in spreading the word of the method's unique advantages by organizing various Montessori groups and associations.

In his autobiography McClure said, "Alexander Graham Bell told me that he considered the introduction of the Montessori system in the United States as the most important work that *McClure's Magazine* had ever done."[19] It was an impressive statement considering that Bell was talking about the magazine that had published articles that led to legislation reforming municipal government, the railroads, the steel industry, and the United States Navy, that had exposed the shame of the cities and had helped to break the stranglehold of the giant trusts.

Plans had gone ahead for the preparation of an American edition of Montessori's book under the auspices of Harvard's Division of Education and in April 1912 it was published by the Frederick A. Stokes Company in a translation by Anne E. George, at that time the only teacher in America who had been trained by Montessori herself and whom Montessori considered the only one qualified to teach a Montessori class of children. She did not consider that anyone else, even trained by her, could train other teachers. That only she could do. This meant that in all the United States, with the great groundswell of interest in her method, there was a single Montessori-trained teacher of children—although plans were already under way for a course which would train more Americans—and no one qualified to teach other teachers.

The book appeared with the somewhat unfortunate title *The Montessori Method*, which reinforced other tendencies suggesting the aspect of a closed, rigidly defined, personally owned system.

By the end of 1911 arrangements had been completed for the manufacture and sale of the Montessori "didactic apparatus" by the House of Childhood in New York, under the management of Carl Byoir.

The brochure issued by the manufacturer stated it as Dr. Montessori's wish that "the apparatus be kept together as a complete method or system" and said, in what critics described as "language suggesting the vending of a patent medicine,"[20] that "infringers and imitators will be vigorously prosecuted." It is clear that Montessori feared the dilution of her method through the indiscriminate use of what she saw as "didactic apparatus" by others who might consider them simply as toys or games. She had evolved them for use in a particular way, and used only in that way would they achieve the results for which they were intended. It is also clear that if the objects themselves as a patentable system were to become the focal point of the method, instead of the principles on which their development and use had been based, the result would be something closer to a business than an idea, a commercial venture rather than a chapter in the history of education which, like all intellectual developments, would have to be rewritten and succeeded by later chapters in an ongoing work.

The pamphlet, which was issued for trade purposes, explained that "the Montessori Didactic Apparatus is not a set of separable toys. It is a system for sense training, and while the sequence is not dogmatic it should be presented to the child in a regular order. . . . These materials should not be purchased by any one who does not intend a careful, intelligent use according to the principles of the Montessori method."

Many educators shared the view expressed by William Boyd, a professor of education at the University of Glasgow and the author of a widely read book, *From Locke to Montessori*, published in London in 1914, of the marketing of the Montessori materials as an example of "the rather sordid commercialism involved in patenting an educational method and the slight on the intelligence of teachers who are expected to use apparatus which they are not allowed to modify or improve in any way."[21]

The Montessori Method was the first translation of *Il Metodo della Pedagogia Scientifica applicato all'educazione infantile nelle Case dei Bambini* to appear, although it was soon followed by others in numerous languages. The first edition of five thousand copies was sold out in four days and interest was reinforced by Montessori's article in *McClure's*, which appeared immediately afterward, in addition to those by Tozier, George, and Stevens. Reviews appeared everywhere—in newspapers, magazines, and professional journals. It was a saturation effect for the media of the time, and it was effective. By summer, less than six months after publication, a sixth edition of the book was in circulation, and it had become a best seller, edging out titles by such notables as Arnold Bennett, Jane Addams, and Henry Bergson to reach second place on the list of nonfiction best sellers of 1912[22] with a total sale for the year of 17,410 copies,[23] not much by today's standards but a smashing success for the time.

It is an interesting detail that tells something about the time that the number-one nonfiction best seller of that year was Mary Antin's *The Promised Land*, an account of the immigrant experience that was also largely a book about education. The autobiography of a Jewish girl who had come to America in the 1890s, written when she was not yet thirty years old, it is full of descriptions of her educational experience as a child in the Russian Pale ("we had never been to a Froebel kindergarten") and contrasts the narrow learning opportunities available to her in the religiously oriented ghetto of the Old Country with the world that opened before her in Boston, where the public school system "made an American" of her. She even sounds a little like Montessori when she talks of "the joy of doing common tasks well" and of her belief in the promise of education in the New World where, when she graduated from grammar school, she tells us, a school official described her as "an illustration of what the American system of free education and the European immigrant can make of each other."

Americans saw their schools as giving everybody what one of the characters in *The Promised Land* refers to as the chance to "be somebody. . . . In America, everybody can get to be something, if only he wants to." The same reading public that flocked to buy Mary Antin's testimonial to the value of public education rushed out to buy *The Montessori Method,* which it saw as offering a blueprint for just how the American school could go about helping to "secure for a promising child the fulfilment of the promise. That is what America was for. The land of opportunity it was, but opportunities must be used, must be grasped, held, squeezed dry."[24] The Montessori method would show them how to use, grasp, hold, squeeze dry the opportunities the American school offered the new American child.

Montessori dedicated the American edition of her book to Alice Hallgarten,

> who by her marriage to Baron Leopold Franchetti became by choice our compatriot. Ever a firm believer in the principles underlying the Case dei Bambini, she, with her husband, forwarded the publication of this book in Italy, and, throughout the last years of her short life, greatly desired the English translation which should introduce to the land of her birth the work so near her heart. To her memory I dedicate this book whose pages, like an ever-living flower, perpetuate the recollection of her beneficence.

In her preface, Montessori wrote:

> The book itself I consider nothing more than the preface to a more comprehensive work . . . the educational method for children of from three to six years set forth here is but the earnest of a work that, developing the same principle and method, shall cover in a like manner the successive stages of education. Moreover, the method which obtains in the Case dei Bambini offers, it seems to me, an experimental field for the study of man, and promises, perhaps, the development of a science that shall disclose other secrets of nature.
>
> I know that my method has been widely spoken of in America, thanks to Mr. S. S. McClure, who has presented it through the pages of his well-known magazine. Indeed, many Americans have already come to Rome for the purpose of observing personally the practical application of the method in my little schools. . . .
>
> To the Harvard professors who have made my work known in America and to *McClure's Magazine,* a mere acknowledgement of what I owe

them is a barren response; but it is my hope that the method itself, in its effect upon the children of America, may prove an adequate expression of my gratitude.[25]

Harvard's Professor Henry W. Holmes provided the introduction. In it he wrote:

An audience already thoroughly interested awaits this translation of a remarkable book. For years no educational document has been so eagerly expected by so large a public, and not many have better merited general anticipation. . . . The astonishing welcome accorded to the first popular expositions of the Montessori system may mean much or little for its future in England and America; it is rather the earlier approval of a few trained teachers and professional students that commends it to the educational workers who must ultimately decide upon its value, interpret its technicalities to the country at large, and adapt it to English and American conditions. . . .[26]

He described Montessori's work as

remarkable, if for no other reason, because it represents the constructive effort of a woman. We have no other example of an educational system—original at least in its systematic wholeness and in its practical application—worked out and inaugurated by the feminine mind and hand . . . it springs from a combination of womanly sympathy and intuition, broad social outlook, scientific training, intensive and long-continued study of educational problems, and, to crown all, varied and unusual experience as a teacher and educational leader. No other woman who has dealt with Dr. Montessori's problem—the education of young children—has brought to it personal resources so richly diverse as hers. These resources, furthermore, she has devoted to her work with an enthusiasm, an absolute abandon, like that of Pestalozzi and Froebel, and she presents her convictions with an apostolic ardour which commands attention. A system which embodies such a capital of human effort could not be unimportant. Then too, certain aspects of the system are in themselves striking and significant: it adapts to the education of normal children methods and apparatus originally used for deficients; it is based on a radical conception of liberty for the pupil; it entails a highly formal training of separate sensory, motor, and mental capacities; and it leads to rapid, easy, and substantial mastery of the elements of reading, writing, and arithmetic. . . .

None of these things, to be sure, is absolutely new in the educational world. All have been proposed in theory; some have been put more or less completely into practice.

Holmes pointed out that much of the Montessori material had been in use at the Massachusetts Institution for the Feeble-Minded at Waverley

169

by Dr. Walter S. Fernald, Seguin's successor there, and that Fernald had long suggested that it could be used effectively in the education of normal children. He conceded that many other educators had been advocating formal sense-training. But he pointed out that Montessori was the first to combine these elements and put it into practice in schools. This system, he wrote, "is indeed the final result, as Dr. Montessori proudly asserts, of years of experimental effort both on her own part and on the part of her great predecessors; but the crystallisation of these experiments in a programme of education for normal children is due to Dr. Montessori alone." She had taken over various features from other educators and unified them; "as a system it is the novel product of a single woman's creative genius."

Holmes urged students of elementary education to study the system, to try it out in the kindergarten. "It is highly probable," he said, "that the system ultimately adopted in our schools will combine elements of the Montessori programme with elements of the kindergarten programme." He believed that education must always be eclectic. "An all-or-nothing policy for a single system inevitably courts defeat."

After comparing the Montessori school with the kindergarten in America, he concluded that "since the difference between the two programmes is one of arrangement, emphasis, and degree," with the former characterized by greater liberty for the pupil, formal sense-training, and direct preparation for academic skills, and the latter involving more group-teaching, creative activity, and scope for the imagination, "there is no fundamental reason why a combination especially adapted to English and American schools cannot be worked out," with the inevitable modifications of the Montessori scheme "which differing social conditions may render necessary."

He predicted that in such adaptations the Montessori principle of freedom would have to be worked out in ways that would vary from school to school depending on the characteristics of the children and teacher and what had to be taught in the time available, while the use of the Montessori apparatus for sense-training would be valuable for all children from three to five regardless of differing school conditions. And he suggested combining the two systems by making use of the Montessori apparatus and approach in the first year and gradually making the transition to the use of the "far richer variety" of the Froebel gifts in the second, when the Montessori exercises which lead the way to writing would also be introduced. Stories, artwork, and games would have a place throughout the curriculum. In this plan, the Montessori method and materials, which would predominate in the first year of the kindergarten, would become a preparation for the predominance of the Froebel material in the second, with neither system being used exclusively at any one time. To Holmes, "the material is by no means the most important feature of the Montessori programme. . . . If parents shall learn from Dr. Montessori something of the value of child life, of its need for activity, of its characteristic modes of expression, and of its possibilities, and apply this knowledge wisely, the work of the great Italian educator will be successful enough."

Holmes had made several points which were prophetic and which came to read with a certain irony in the light of the later history of Montessori in America. (The introduction was dropped from reprints of the book published in the second wave of interest in Montessori in America which followed the long period of obscurity between the two world wars.)

First, he saw that the real future of the movement would depend not on popular interest but on the professional teaching community. Second, he realized that it would have to be adapted to differing local cultural conditions and would inevitably have to be combined with other systems rather than remain forever fixed in its present form. Third, he was aware of the apostolic character of the movement. And finally, he recognized that it was the principles—how children learn and what they need for their fullest development—not the specific materials themselves, which would prove Montessori's real and lasting contribution, and that these could be transmitted and applied without the direct hand of Montessori herself or someone personally trained by her.

Interest in the Montessori phenomenon ran so high at U.S. schools of education by 1912 that lectures were being given, often by "authorities" who had never visited the schools themselves but relied on secondhand press reports and magazine articles for their information. Florence Elizabeth Ward, professor of kindergarten education at Iowa State Teachers College, was one of the interested educators who decided to find out about the method for herself and, in the spring of 1912, after visiting Anne George's school in Tarrytown and talking with Holmes in Cambridge, Massachusetts, she sailed for Italy. Aboard ship she read one of the first copies of the English translation of Montessori's book. By the time the ship reached Naples, the book was worn and dog-eared, having been borrowed and read by many interested passengers. In Rome, she waited days to see Montessori. She found herself "surrounded by Americans whose purpose was the same" and "soon realized that one's presence there did not insure illumination on the subject of the

Montessori method. No training courses were being offered for teachers; the Dottoressa was difficult of access. . . ."

However, "once admitted, one was treated with the greatest cordiality. 'I am willing to see those who are here in search of truth,' said Dr. Montessori, 'but many come out of curiosity or with a passion for the new and the unusual. I cannot meet these purloiners of time. If I saw all callers and answered all letters, I should have no time for experiment and study, and my system is not yet completed."[27]

After conferring with Montessori and visiting the Case, Ward returned to the United States and delivered an enthusiastic report to the 1912 meeting of the National Education Association which she expanded in a book, *The Montessori Method and the American School,* published the following year, strongly recommending that the Montessori principles be brought into American education.

Meanwhile, in the early spring of 1912, a Montessori American Committee was formed and its existence announced in the June issue of *McClure's.* The members included Anne E. George, S. S. McClure, publisher William Morrow, and one Edith Sharon, whom the committee recommended to Montessori as director of the first training school in New York. McClure left for Europe, intending to confer with Montessori in Rome.[28]

Montessori was furious at what she considered a breach of an agreement between her and McClure that no public announcement of the committee's formation be made until she had agreed with them on a constitution. On June 5 she fired off an angry telegram to McClure:

> INDIGNANT ANNOUNCEMENT/CONTRARY CABLED ORDERS AND WHAT AGREED PERSONALLY MCCLURE/ANNOUNCE JULY NUMBER COMMITTEE ANNOUNCEMENT PREMATURE/THAT SEPTEMBER ARTICLE WILL GIVE MY IDEAS FULLY.[29]

McClure managed to mollify Montessori and in July she wrote to him saying "it will be a short time until the Institute will come into being," a reference to a plan she had discussed with McClure for establishing in America a training institute for research and teaching in her methods, and referring to a "pecuniary guarantee for three years" given her by the recently formed English society.

The American committee set to work and organized the first international training course in Rome, to begin in January 1913. Eventually eighty-seven pupils were enrolled—sixty-seven of them from the United States.

Other books about Montessori's work began to appear and were widely reviewed. One of the first was Dorothy Canfield Fisher's *A Montessori Mother* in the fall of 1912. It was a charming, easy-to-read little book, refreshing in its freedom from the kind of rhapsodizing in which so many of Montessori's followers and explicators indulged. It described the Casa dei Bambini from her own observations of the amazing goings-on at the Via Giusti, explained Montessori's principles and their application in the use of the didactic materials and the exercises of practical life, and made some suggestions for American mothers who wished to adapt the Montessori principles and practices to the raising of their children.

What she extracted from all the details and all the philosophy was the idea that children should be helped to become independent, and she explained what she meant in unpretentious language and close-to-home examples.

> Very little children have no greater natural interest than in learning how to do something with their bodies. We all know how much more fascinating a place our kitchens seem to be for our little children than our drawing-rooms. . . . One morning spent in the Casa dei Bambini showed me the true reason. . . . The drawing-room is a museum full of objects . . . enclosed in the padlocked glass-case of the command, 'Now, don't touch!' while the kitchen is a veritable treasure-house of Montessori apparatus.[30]

While Dr. Montessori has "systematized and ordered, graded and arranged the exercises which every child instinctively craves,"[31] in any household "the various exercises for the sense of touch can be elaborated as one's own, or what is more likely, the children's inventiveness may make possible,"[32] using the bag of salt and the box of oatmeal, a pillow or some old clothing with buttons and laces, or just—and most important of all—having the patience to let little children accomplish for themselves such tasks as dressing themselves, putting the child's developmental needs before the regularity of household routine and resisting the urge to constantly do things for him. "We must take care that we mothers do not treat our children as we reproach men for having treated women, with patronizing, enfeebling protection."[33]

It was a nice little book, and did much to make Montessori's ideas understandable and palatable to American parents by distilling the philosophy to its basic principles and suggesting that the principles might be used freely in the home with a little goodwill and ingenuity, "in ways which [Montessori] has not happened to hit upon."[34]

The suggestion did not sit well with Montessori or her disciples. And when Mrs. Fisher followed her first book with a second entitled *The Mon-*

tessori Manual for Teachers and Mothers, explaining the didactic apparatus and its uses, it was disowned by Montessori and her followers.

This rejection of popularizers and interpreters certainly had a basis in the sincere conviction that the ideas so carefully worked out by Montessori were being distorted in this way—at the very least, oversimplified; at the worst, destroyed by misinterpretation. But there was also the charge of exploitation and the increasing need to retain for Montessori herself the benefits—whether royalties, fees, or even the prestige on which they ultimately depended—accruing from the dissemination and use of her ideas as well as her materials. It began inevitably when she gave up all other work, academic appointments as well as practice, to devote herself to the spread of her ideas as a "movement." But although it began with an understandable impulse for protection, its end effect was destructive. There are no monopolies in the commerce of ideas.

Montessori took pains to repudiate personally the second Fisher book, as she did all "unauthorized" expositions of her ideas. When *Dr. Montessori's Own Handbook* appeared in 1914, she wrote a letter to the *Times Educational Supplement* in London which that respected periodical printed in full in which she said in part:

> I have taken the pains to prepare myself a handbook to fulfill exactly the task which Mrs. D. Canfield Fisher's book has the pretension of fulfilling. I should be very glad if you would give me the opportunity of saying that I have not deputed—and do not propose to depute—to others the work of a practical popular explanation of my method, as I have taken great pains to do this myself. I hope my system will not be held responsible for any want of success that may arise out of the use of other books than my own in connection with the Montessori apparatus.[35]

Ironically, one of the best descriptions of Montessori's situation in those early years was given by Dorothy Canfield Fisher in 1912, when she wrote:

> Now, only five years after [the first Casa dei Bambini was opened], there arrive in Rome, from every quarter of the globe, bewildered but imperious demands for enlightenment on the new idea. . . .
> Her laboratory doors are stormed by inquirers from Australia, from Norway, from Mexico, and, most of all, from the United States. Teachers of district schools in the Carolinas write their cousins touring in Europe to be sure to go to Rome to see the Montessori schools. Mothers from Oregon and Maine write, addressing their letters, "Montessori, Rome," and make demands for enlightenment, urgent, pressing, peremptory, and shamelessly peremptory, since they conceive of a possibility that their children, their own children, the most important human

beings in the world, may be missing something valuable. From innumerable towns and cities, teachers, ambitious to be in the front of their profession, are taking their hoarded savings from the bank and starting to Rome with the naive conviction that their own thirst for information is sufficient guarantee that someone will instantly be forthcoming to provide it for them.

When they reach Rome, most of them quite unable to express themselves in Italian or even in French, what do they find, all these tourists and letters of inquiry, and adventuring school-mistresses? They find a dead wall. They have an unformulated idea that they are probably going to a highly organized institution of some sort, like our huge "model schools" attached to our normal colleges, through the classrooms of which an unending file of observers is allowed to pass. And they have no idea whatever of the inevitability *with which Italians speak Italian.*

They find—if they are relentlessly persistent enough to pierce through the protection her friends try to throw about her—only Dr. Montessori herself, a private individual, phenomenally busy with very important work, who does not speak or understand a word of English, who has neither money, time, or strength enough single-handed to cope with the flood of inquiries and inquirers about her ideas. In order to devote herself entirely to the great undertaking of transmuting her divinations of the truth into a definite, logical, and scientific system, she has withdrawn herself more and more from public life. She has resigned from her chair of anthropology in the University of Rome, and last year sent a substitute to do her work in another academic position not connected with her present research—and this although she is far from being a woman of independent means. She has sacrified everything in her private life in order to have, for the development of her educational ideas, that time and freedom so constantly infringed upon by the well-meaning urgency of our demands for instruction from her.

She lives now in the most intense retirement, never taking a vacation from her passionate absorption in her work, not even giving herself time for the exercise necessary for health, surrounded and aided by a little group of devoted disciples, young Italian women who live with her, who call her "mother," and who exist in and for her and her ideas, as ardently and whole-heartedly as nuns about an adored Mother Superior.[36]

Her "disciples" could not protect Montessori from the interest in her work which, by 1912, as a result of a worldwide publicity, was at flood tide.

In America, one educator commented, "In the recent political campaign one was continually surprised to discover this friend an ardent Roosevelt man and that one as ardently opposing him. In educational circles one meets the same kinds of seemingly incongruous opinions regarding Mme. Montessori and her so-called system."[37]

The British government had sent a representative, Edmond G. A.

Holmes, to Rome to investigate the new schools and on his return issued, in the fall of 1912, a special report on Montessori classes for the Board of Education in England entitled *The Montessori System of Education.* In it, Holmes stated that while the system had up to now been chiefly applied to children of kindergarten age, "the principle is applicable to children of all ages and will bear its best fruits in the higher classes."

Schools were being established not only in England, the United States, and numerous countries of Western Europe but in India, China, Mexico, Korea, Japan, Syria, Australia, New Zealand, Argentina, and Hawaii and were continuing to spread. In addition to private schools, the governments of Switzerland and Australia and of the cities of London, Rome, Stockholm, and Johannesburg had officially adopted the Montessori method in their school systems. Montessori societies were being formed all over the world, and the need for teachers trained in the method was acutely felt, and by no one more than Maria Montessori.

11

On December 20, 1912, Renilde Montessori died at the age of seventy-two. During her last days she lay in bed unable to move, and Maria sat for hours at her right side, to which her mother's eyes were turned. "For three days after her mother died," according to Maccheroni, "she could take no food. She was not crying, was not depressed. We insisted, 'Just take a little food.' 'I can't,' she said simply, with no emotion. . . . When the coffin was set in the vault at the cemetery, she just put her head into the hollow and stood so for a minute or two. No tears, no showing of emotion. . . .Then she took her father and us to a seaside place for a few days."[1]

Montessori's remedy for grief, as for so much else in life, was work. On their return to Rome, she and her faithful little band of followers plunged into the task of giving the first international training course for teachers in the Montessori method, which had been organized by the Montessori American Committee, whose members included the Bells, McClure, Professor Holmes, William Morrow, Anne E. George, and Ellen Yale Stevens.

The Montessori family had moved from an apartment on the Corso Vittorio to more spacious quarters on the Via Principessa Clotilde overlooking the Piazza del Popolo and the Pincio, and it was here that the classes were held, beginning in mid-January 1913. "That year," Maccheroni remembered, "we had snow in Rome."[2]

The students came from all over the world—from Germany, Switzerland and Ireland, from Australia, Africa, and India, as well as England and the United States, which sent the largest number. There were sixty-seven from the United States, from New York and California, Illinois, Ohio, Virginia, Massachusetts, and the District of Columbia, and others from the Philippines, Panama, and Canada. The contingent of American women traveled together on a ship appropriately called the S.S. *Ancona,* the name of the province that was Montessori's birthplace. From Naples they proceeded by train to Rome, where they were received by Montessori, wearing deep mourning even to a black pocket handkerchief.[3] Montessori had had little memorial mass cards printed up with her mother's picture on them, bordered in black, and she gave one to each of the students.

MARIA MONTESSORI: A BIOGRAPHY

The large room in which the lectures were given could barely accommodate the eighty-seven students and the distinguished visitors who included members of Roman officialdom and the nobility. On one occasion Queen Margherita came, and was greeted by Montessori with a graceful curtsey.

Montessori adopted a method of lecturing which she would follow through countless courses for the rest of her long career. An imposing figure, now grown more stout and with a dignified, authoritative air, dressed in the black which she continued to wear after her mother's death until the years in India near the end of her life, she stood beside a translator on a raised platform in an alcove in one of the corners of the large room. She spoke slowly and carefully, with gesture and expression, in her musical Italian, pausing after each sentence for her interpreter to repeat what she had said in English. Her English-speaking students would make notes of what she had said after the translation, while she was giving her next thought in Italian. Over the years many of them learned Italian listening to the immediate translations, and there is no doubt that she learned English, although she always claimed not to know the language and refused to speak it, at least in public, until near the end of her life. She was fluent in French and Spanish while still a young woman, but seems to have acquired her English in the same process by which her students learned their Italian. Some of them remembered her, in courses she gave in the ensuing years, listening intently to the translation and, if she did not think a word was right, frowning, interrupting her interpreter, and correcting the word or phrase.

Montessori's American pupils found themselves presented with an entirely new concept of the teacher's role. The directress was not to "teach," she was to present and to observe and allow the chldren to teach themselves as they worked with the materials that made up the properly prepared environment for their spontaneous activity.

Montessori told her students: "When you are in a Casa dei Bambini to observe the children, you are working and laboring to learn something which I do not give, which an assistant does not give, which no one else gives—the capacity, the sensitivity which permits your learning the intimate facts revealed by the children themselves. You alone can prepare yourselves to observe, just as the children must develop themselves by their own experience. This is what the teacher must know—*how to observe.*"[4]

She had accomplished her own education, defining it as she went along. She had evolved a system in which all children would educate themselves. And now she told those who would teach it that they too must educate themselves in the skills they would need to draw on in order to help each child to be free to learn for himself. They would need to be able to observe the individual differences of each child in order to help him when—and only when—that help was needed. Otherwise, they would only interfere with his learning. To teachers who had been trained to follow a set curriculum, a set of rules to apply to all children of a certain age, this was a breathtakingly new way of looking at their work.

English editor Sheila Radice described those days in the Montessoris' home: "Her house was at the service of multitudes—a *va e vieni* all day long. A lady from America once waited seven hours to see her, forgotten by the maidservant and waiting on patiently, uncomplainingly, while the hours went on and the room grew dark."[5] She described the course itself as "a pilgrimage from all parts of the earth, with all the accompaniments of a pilgrimage—faith, fervor. Strangers gathered about Dr. Montessori, hoping for some lesson from her, scarcely as yet knowing what."[6]

Many of them found in the course not just an educational method but a philosophy of life, even a religion. Despite Montessori's early positivism, the legacy of her postunification anticlerical background and her scientific training, she gradually returned to religion, to the Catholic Church and to the more personal form of the deepening mysticism of her later years when she was associated with the Theosophists. The return to the faith in which she had at least been nominally trained as a child, as were most Italians of her time no matter how liberal their families, was part of her response to the great personal crises of her young adulthood—the birth of her child and later her mother's death. At one time she contemplated founding a religious order dedicated to the service of the child, and the little band of women living and working with her at the time—Maccheroni, Fedeli, Ballerini, Oliveri—whom Dorothy Canfield Fisher had compared to "nuns about an adored Mother Superior," actually took vows of dedication to this cause, but the idea was never carried out formally through the Church.

Some of the students who took the first international course became close associates of Montessori's, including Helen Parkhurst, who was to work with Montessori in America for a time before going on to develop her own system of education, which came to be known as the Dalton Plan. Another young woman was Adelia McAlpin Pyle, the daughter of an American millionaire related to the Rockefeller family, who joined Montessori's intimate circle and served as her translator for years during lectures and courses. Among the English students was Claude Claremont, who remained a lifelong associate, a leader of the Montessori movement in England, and head of the Montessori teacher-training colleges that were later established in London.

She was creating her own following, outside the framework of any existing institution. Her students were just that—*her* students, not those of any university or department of education. Her funding, since it did not come from any academic institution, would have to come from students' fees and royalties on books and materials. The business of "propaganda," of spreading information about the "movement," would be undertaken by the various Montessori societies organized locally but "authorized" by her and responsible to her alone.

And always, support would come from private patrons, interested individuals who lent their often distinguished names and their prestige to the cause, enthusiasts who would eventually come to outnumber professionals of the academic world of education.

In Rome the American Ambassador attended a special showing of what *The New York Times* correspondent described as "magnificent cinematograph films taken to illustrate all the different phases of the method," also reporting that "the Marchesa di Viti di Marco, formerly Miss Etta Dunham of New York, who is well known here for her interest in every new development, intellectual or eduational, was also present, and explained from personal experience the wonderful results obtained by the simple but scientific mode of training the minds of children through their senses."[7]

In America, meanwhile, the Alexander Graham Bells' enthusiasm did not stop with the establishment of their school. By the spring of 1913 the Montessori Educational Association, an outgrowth of the Montessori American Committee, had been formed by a group of Washington parents with Mrs. Bell as president. The board of trustees included, in addition to the Bells, Dorothy Canfield Fisher, and McClure, such personages as Philander P. Claxton, the United States Commissioner of Education, Margaret Woodrow Wilson, the President's daughter, and various educators, bankers, attorneys, and foundation executives. Montessori agreed to recognize the association as an organization for the spread of her ideas in the United States. Mabel Bell was instrumental in obtaining a building for a larger Montessori school in Washington in the fall of 1913, spoke at parent groups, and started a Montessori Educational Association news bulletin to publicize the method.

Others were interested in starting societies too. The New England Montessori Association was formed in the spring of 1913 and in New York City the head of the Scudder School for Girls gave a course of lectures for teachers, one of whom returned to Maine to direct a public Montessori class there. Myron T. Scudder wrote to McClure inviting him to "a Montessori evening, with stereopticon views, and a discussion as to the value of the method in America," to which he had also invited members of the Teachers College, Columbia, and New York University faculties as well as a representative of the New York City Board of Education. He added optimistically, "I feel now that misunderstanding will vanish, that harmonious relations will be established among those who are interested in the Montessori movement," and that he looked forward to "a wise propaganda of publicity and education regarding the method."[8]

From Montessori's point of view, what mattered was not that Scudder was gaining exposure for her work among the educational establishment, but that he was not authorized by her to do so. No one but she could give a Montessori training course, and she fired off a letter to *The New York Times* to say so. After giving some idea of the spread of the method throughout the world, the schools established, the societies formed, the translations of her book being published, the requests for information constantly being received, she concluded:

> In view of this widespread interest I feel that the public should be able to obtain accurate information about those teachers who have been specially trained by me. Owing to the short period of the training course it has been possible to give, and also to the fact that the method has not yet attained to its full development, I feel it would be premature to establish training schools which were not under my direct supervision, so that for the present no training course for the preparation of teachers except those held here in Rome, will be authorized by me.[9]

To many, it seemed hardly appropriate that an educational method should be made into a closed system with the head of a hierarchy having the sole power to determine who could disseminate it. To American educators it was unseemly and more suggestive of a church than of what the schools should be.

By 1913 there were nearly one hundred Montessori schools in America and the Montessori system was well enough known to have become a subject of controversy, a target of attack as well as a focus for reformers' hopes. A typical letter to *The New York Times* from an alienist in North Dakota accused the Montessori method of being "based on the fallacy that will-power and self-control are developed by self-indulgence. . . . Instead of being trained to be a member of the family the boy of today is taught to be President of the United States. The children are being petted and allowed to have their own way until they get an exalted idea

181

of their importance."[10] The result, he predicted, would be a generation of conceited, hysterical egomaniacs.

The issue was joined by a Montessori supporter who replied, in a letter published the following week, that the Montessori method "teaches self-reliance and not self-indulgence, and gives full sway to the child's bent, always with a life-size picture of old George B. Consequences in the background," and that it was "destined to become one of the most democratic institutions in the world."[11]

Such arguments could only increase public interest in the method and its inventor.

By now there was a growing feeling among Montessori's supporters in the United States that Montessori's presence would be an invaluable aid to acceptance of her ideas in this country. She was a fascinating personality, an impressive speaker, and if she herself were to come here and speak about her work it would do more than anything else to stimulate interest in the method. At first, Montessori said no. She had no desire to come to the United States. She was busy with her training courses and preferred carrying on her work to talking about it.

She had made some films, then a very innovative undertaking, of children at the Case which showed the method in action. Hearing about this, McClure thought he saw a way to do something for the cause and at the same time do something about his own problems.

McClure was an erratic man, a more talented editor than businessman, and by 1912, under a crushing burden of debt, he had lost control of his magazine and taken to the lecture platform to earn his living, speaking at colleges and on the Chautauqua Circuit and to business and professional clubs under the managership of Lee Keedick. In 1913 the new fad on the lecture circuit was the motion picture, and McClure, looking for a way to expand both his repertory and his income, hit on the idea of bringing Montessori to America to lecture and show her films under his auspices.

He went to Rome in the fall of 1913 to put his proposition to Montessori. Unaware of the real state of his affairs, she still thought of him as the influential journalist who had introduced her work to the American public. Now he was suggesting that she accompany him to America where, in his manic way, McClure sketched plans for a joint lecture tour of major American cities, the establishment of Montessori schools and a teacher-training institute, arrangements for a company to manufacture and distribute the didactic materials, and a future in which primary education in America would be made over in the image of the Montessori method.

Maria Montessori at 16, a student at technical school.

In 1913, Maria Montessori examines the first copies of a new edition of her book, *The Montessori Method*, first printed in 1912.

With her son, Mario
Montessori, in1930

In 1919, the year she began her first training
course in England.

At the International
Montessori Congress in
1949

Circa 1950

With Roman children on one of her last visits
to their school, circa 1951.

Perhaps naïvely, Montessori was attracted to McClure's vision, and agreed to his plan. Her trust in his judgment was at least in part based on a picture of him as a wealthy and powerful figure who would be undertaking this project out of devotion to the cause rather than for any personal gain.

McClure wrote to his wife from Rome on November 15, 1913:

> At 5:15 yesterday I finally concluded matters after a heart-breaking week. Thursday night I thought it was all off.
>
> It seems that people in Rome have not been slow to spread the news of my downfall. The Dottoressa was pulled hither and thither. It seems that even Morrow had spoken against me. The Donna Maria and her husband were loyal believing the Dottoressa always remembered how good my advice was & especially in regard to her school last year, when others opposed and she retained her faith in me in spite of powerful adverse influences. If I had failed in this contract it would have been a serious disaster. My trip cost $500 to Lee Keedick. I had urged it. Now that I have won it is a tremendous thing. Sole rights in her films in America! Think of that. Then she comes and lectures in cooperation with me & the films for three weeks & in the future we control her lectures & the films for her school for all time & perhaps for the whole world. This is how I imagine it. Carnegie Hall. I speak forty minutes telling of our visit to Rome May 1911 & in connection with our visit give the essence of her principles. Then I show the moving pictures, with brief explanations. The children in the moving pictures look sweet and dear. Then I introduce the Dottoressa and she speaks half an hour. Then I or Miss George (or I hope in New York City Mr. Howells) give the gist of her talk. . . .
>
> She is to be announced as under the auspices of the American Montessori Assn. [sic] & I give the introductory address as a Vice-president of the Assn. and representing the Assn. and the pictures are produced by the authority of the Assn. & have been made by the Dottoressa & under her supervision. So you see there will be no loss of dignity & nothing to make any college professor annoyed.[12]

Of the film, he wrote, "I think it will be a money-maker."[13]

McClure succeeded in getting the exclusive rights for the showing of the films in North America as well as Montessori's agreement to come and lecture in the United States in December 1913 for $1,000 plus expenses for herself and a teacher. The lectures would be arranged under the management of Lee Keedick and McClure would share in the profits. He was "pretty sure Keedick and I will make a great deal of money on her talks."[14] McClure was to pay Montessori a percentage of the profits from any lectures he gave as well as from any showing of the films. Their contract called for her to receive an $800 advance against 60 percent of the net profits from her lectures. McClure would get 20 percent and Keedick the other 20.[15]

The New York Times carried the news that Montessori had finally been induced to come to America, where she would give a series of lectures in principal cities beginning in Washington, D.C., where a reception was being arranged in her honor at the White House by Margaret Wilson. It was reported that Queen Margherita was among those who congratulated Montessori on her decision to bring her message personally to the New World.[16]

Montessori set sail with McClure from Naples on November 21 on the steamship *Cincinnati*. Word that the famous Dottoressa was aboard reached the passengers, and a delegation was formed to request McClure to speak to them about her work during the voyage. So jealously was his status as her exclusive agent-spokesman being guarded that they found it necessary to draw up a petition to present to McClure formally making their request.

On a piece of stationery bearing the flag of the Hamburg-America Line they wrote:

> We the undersigned passengers on the steamship Cincinnati being deeply sensible of the great gift which is being brought to America through the instrumentality of Mr. S. S. McClure of not only the works of Dr. Maria Montessori but the presence of the gentle teacher herself—Do hereby respectfully request Mr. McClure to make us a talk upon the System and to tell us something of the stupendous plan which he is about to inaugurate at such time and place during the voyage as may suit his convenience.[17]

The document was signed by over fifty of Montessori's and McClure's fellow passengers. It was an indication of the kind of interest with which Americans awaited her arrival on their shores and the wild enthusiasm with which they would greet her.

Some time in the year following her mother's death, Montessori brought her son Mario to live with her. This seems to suggest that it was her mother who was most strongly opposed to the child's being brought out into the light of Montessori's public life, and it is a possibility that seems consistent with what we know of Renilde Montessori's ambitions for her daughter, the sense she must have had of sacrifices made and hopes placed on the achievements of her special child. These must not be jeopardized by rumors, shattered by a scandal.

But while the death of Montessori's mother may have made it possible for her to bring her son home, it was the boy's own confrontation of his mother—in a recognition scene reminiscent of classical drama—that finally decided the matter.

Mario Montessori's memory is of a spring day in 1913 when he was about fifteen, seeing on a school outing the lady whose visits had punctuated his childhood and been explained in his fantasies. A car stopped where he was resting; she got out, and he went up to her and said simply, "I know you are my mother" and told her he wanted to go with her. She made no objection, he got into the car with her, and the scene ended as all such tales should—they went off together to live happily ever after. From then on, Mario remained beside her, part of her life, increasingly as she grew older assuming the functions of a devoted son but never—as most sons do—leaving her. He had begun as less than a real son; from now on he would be more than sons usually are—if not the only man, certainly the most important one, the closest other in her life.

Mario's father, Dr. Montesano, had agreed to give the child his name on condition that he be sent away—hidden, in fact—and that the facts of his birth be kept secret. From the time that he joined his mother Mario used her name—Montessori—as though symbolically denying that he belonged to anyone but her. It was not only a way of keeping the promise of secrecy she had made, of continuing to protect the father of the child who now became visible, of not embarrassing the man who now had a family of his own. It was also a denial that there had ever been a sexual relationship with a man in her life, a father of her child.

When Montessori left for America Mario remained with her father in Rome. He was also looked after by old friends like Donna Maria Maraini and Anna Maccheroni. But his existence was not known to the public at large, to which Montessori was becoming better known each day, more famous with every new edition of the morning papers in cities all over the world.

12

While Montessori was en route to America, the Montessori Educational Association was making plans for her arrival. Official greetings from the government were sent to her while she was still aboard ship, and major newspapers in New York, Washington, and Boston carried the news that she would be arriving to give lectures in cities from the east coast to Chicago over the next three weeks and that a gigantic reception had been arranged for her at the Alexander Graham Bells' home in Washington on the evening of December 6. The press referred to her as "the most interesting woman in Europe,"[1] "a woman who revolutionized the educational system of the world . . . who taught the idiot and the insane to read and write—whose success has been so wonderful that the Montessori method has spread into nation after nation as far east as China and Korea, as far west as Honolulu and south to the Argentine Republic."[2] Editorial writers predicted that her theories of "auto-education" would appeal to the individualism of this nation and added "there can be little doubt that she will have a favorable reception."[3] The purpose of her trip was described in detail. She was coming to study American school systems, to see the work done by her own students now teaching Montessori classes in various parts of the country, and to create interest among American parents and educators in a projected laboratory school in Rome, "a model school for every branch of psychological research in child development,"[4] an international pedagogical clinic with branches in every country for children of different nationalities, social backgrounds, ages, and degrees of normality.

"Three years ago," said Margaret Naumburg, who had been one of Montessori's pupils in the first international training course and founded the progressive Walden School in New York, "no one over here even knew of her existence. Today the newspapers use her name as a leader. This wildfire spread of Montessori's ideas could have happened only in the twentieth century. Wireless and cable and quick translation have put the world in touch with Maria Montessori."[5]

The *Cincinnati* docked on Wednesday morning, December 3, at her pier at the foot of Thirty-third Street in South Brooklyn and Montessori came down the gangplank, accompanied by McClure. Beside her, McClure appeared slight, wispy, almost insignificant, all but overshadowed by the impressive figure of the Dottoressa. Since she spoke no English, McClure spoke for her, introducing her as "the woman who studies children as a naturalist studies bees"[6] and giving, for the benefit of the reporters, a brief explanation of her system and of her plans for establishing an international educational research institution.

She was an impressive figure. Her abundant wavy dark hair, now streaked with gray, set off the expressive eyes in her full face with its calm smile. Her matronly body in its black dress was wrapped in dark furs against the New York winter chill. To waiting reporters she appeared as "motherly looking," "a very pleasing picture," "a regal figure," "a galleon under full sail."

When she stepped onto the dock she was immediately surrounded by a group of young women who had been her pupils in Rome the previous winter and were now using her methods to teach in this country. Among them were Adelia Pyle, who as one of her close circle served her as interpreter as well as companion, and Clara Craig, superintendent of the Rhode Island teacher-training schools, which had already officially adopted the Montessori system. She kissed them affectionately and then turned and greeted the scores of reporters and local dignitaries who had come to the pier to meet her. A welcoming committee from the Montessori Educational Association included William Morrow, Ellen Yale Stevens, and Anne George, who, along with McClure, was to accompany her on her tour, and there was a delegation of leaders of the Italian-American community including the Italian vice-consul and a member of the New York Board of Education.

Without speaking a word of English, Montessori made it evident to the furiously scribbling members of the press who reported on her arrival that she had had a good trip, that she was intensely interested in her first glimpse of New York, and that she was pleased by her reception.

After some initial confusion, the usual red tape was waived by the Customs officials, who allowed Montessori to carry off with her the two thousand feet of films of her pupils' work, which would normally have been held for clearance at Customs for several days but which she planned to show at her lecture in Washington three days after her arrival.

Then, the large box of films in tow, and accompanied by McClure and Anne George, Montessori was swept off to the Holland House, one of the city's more elegant hotels.

There, later in the afternoon, she encountered her first taste of American publicity. About a dozen reporters and photographers crowded her suite, along with the little band of her American students who had met her at the ship but had come on to the hotel separately, only to find that they could not get up to see her. So many people had crowded into the hotel that the staff began turning away everyone without proof of an appointment. In order to get past them, some of the young women, including Adelia Pyle, went out for some dress and hat boxes and, carrying the boxes and pretending they were milliners and dressmakers making deliveries, managed to get past the hotel clerks and the curious bystanders and join Montessori in her suite. She greeted them wordlessly, as intimates who can part and then, after months of interruption, take up exactly where they had left off. There was no excited expression of greeting, no look of surprised recognition, just her serene smile and a kiss on the cheek before she turned to resume her answers, sometimes in Italian, sometimes in French, to the reporters' questions.

Montessori patiently posed for picture after picture, seeming a little amused, while her entourage bustled about the cluttered hotel rooms. The photographers skittered about, suggesting one pose after another, and although the Dottoressa presumably understood no English, she responded calmly but promptly to every request.

What was most striking about the heavily built woman with her smooth, unwrinkled face and bright, clear eyes was her poise and serenity amid the confused babble of voices and the distracted bustle of people. She seemed curiously detached. It was not that she seemed aloof—she was obviously interested in all the odd things going on in this noisy place—but she gave the impression of being somehow apart, beyond and untouched by it.

"Her eyes," said the reporter for *The New York Times*,[7] who had been granted a half hour's interview with Montessori, "are the expressive part of her face. They seem always to be working out formulae about you. She smiles slowly—her face changes expresson almost imperceptibly. There is no rapid alteration of mood." Her calmness reminded him of the "*silencio*," the period of meditation practiced by the three- and four-year-olds in the Montessori method, and when he mentioned this, Montessori smiled her quiet smile and told him that the children's silence was not a passive, enforced, paralyzed silence. "It is a voluntary, active thing. Meditation means something growing. It opens up an unsuspected inner world."

A perceptive observer, aware that critics of the Montessori method insisted that its main defect was its dependence upon personality, a criticism which Montessori firmly denied, the *Times* writer concluded that "half an hour spent with the world-famous educator establishes the fact that the method is Montessori and Montessori is the method, and one may well have grave doubts about how it will go with 'auto-education' when Maria Montessori's personality is removed.''

Between photographs she answered numerous questions about her method and her plans, with Anne George translating first the questions and then her answers. She spoke slowly but unhesitatingly, always watching the questioner's face closely, occasionally emphasizing a point with a shrug or an expressive gesture of her hands. She explained the reasons she had come to speak here, drawing a black shawl closer about her shoulders with just a glance at the windows, as if to add that she had certainly not come all the way to America in order to freeze to death.

"America more than any other country outside of my own has been interested in the method as I have worked it out in the Casa dei Bambini. I have come to understand the spirit of this great interest with which I have been in touch, though somewhat remotely, in the teachers I have trained for their work in America. . . . A flashlight? How is that?"

A photographer had lunged forward and a bulb had flashed in her face. George was explaining in Italian. "Si, si," Montessori said, nodding, and turning without annoyance to the camera again, went on with the conversation as though nothing unusual had occurred. "I come first to America because the work is progressing here more rapidly and I want to be sure that it develops in the right way."

She explained her idea for a laboratory school where the Montessori method would be extended to older children and children of different cultural backgrounds, a center for "experimental science in pedagogy where I hope to bring out more clearly the close relationship between physiological and mental growth." It was the foundation of this institution that was her most cherished dream, and the carrot at the end of the stick that had brought her to America. It was McClure's assurances that she would find support for her project in this country, more than anything else, that had decided her to come.

The meaning of the results obtained at the Case dei Bambini? "We merely allowed the child to discover itself. We saw them despising playthings which gave them no chance to exercise their powers of reason. That is why children break their toys: because they are moved by an intellectual curiosity to know what is inside them."

"Reporters?" The Dottoressa asked the word in English, looking over at the little knot of young women at the doorway trying to quiet the racket in the corridor. More of the press was clamoring to get in.

"Si, si," she said. The door was opened and the reporters descended on her. She seemed to enjoy it. For every question she had a calm, unhesitating answer.

Five reporters at once asked if she were a suffragist.

"Ah, naturally," she replied, this time in French. "As one of the great social and political developments of the age, one must be in sympathy with the woman's movement. Anything which broadens the race and the individual must be supported. But, you understand, I am not a militant."

When would the Montessori-trained children be ready for college?

"That is a difficult question for me to answer. The college as it stands now is not at all compatible with such a system as we are teaching. It is totally different. With education carried on as I believe it should be, when a system is established for the complete education of the individual, there would be no colleges as they exist now. We would have no need for them."

Should mothers work? The role of women in society was as much an issue of that moment as it is of this, with the difference that it was more controversial. The reporters waited for her answer with lifted pencils and bated breath.

"In the continual social progress of the world women are more and more taking up different lines of work. Anything that tends to broaden the mother is of advantage to the child." The woman of broad interests and intelligence, she explained, is a better mother.

Not all mothers, she felt, understood how to care for their children. The experience of the Case dei Bambini showed that children could develop outside their homes, and in fact that when the children returned home their mothers and families were educated through their children. The important thing was that mothers and teachers should cooperate in helping the child to become independent.

Why were some children bad?

They were not, she explained. "Even babies are perfectly good if they are treated properly." She described the obstetrical ward in Rome where the newborns never cried. "Sixty babies and not a sound. If they desire anything they ask for it. They are separated from their mothers, who are poor and ignorant women and would not understand that they must be left in peace. There is no reason but ignorance of child hygiene why babies should cry, and a study of rational feeding has done away with the need for it. They are fed every two hours and when that time comes they make a slight noise with their lips, but they do not cry." And she told how she had observed infants less than a week old responding to a ray of light and fixing their attention on it. "The baby, lying peacefully in his crib, exercises his senses by about his seventh day of life. Their psychological life has already begun. From this earliest age they can be kept busy adjusting themselves to the external world." The reporters busily taking notes on these unusual-sounding ideas had no way of knowing that she was anticipating studies of infant development by some half century, observing what psychologists like Jerome Bruner and others would conclude about the sucking and looking behavior of neonates from experiments conducted in the laboratories of cognitive-studies departments like Harvard's in the 1960s.

Ellen Stevens had added a word of explanation about the way the Montessori system of auto-education worked, and the reporters turned their attention to her. Left alone for a moment, Montessori leaned back in her chair and closed her eyes.

"Tired?" someone asked her.

"No," she said, smiling, although it was late afternoon and since she had walked down the gangplank that morning she had been in the midst of a continual commotion. And then she added softly, "They do not ask what I think of America, of education here. That is sensible. But I should like to say that while I have been too absorbed to keep in close touch with the educational influences at work here in the United States, I have been watching the larger, general trends with great interest, and I heartily endorse the methods of education which have been developing here."

A photographer wanted to take another picture in the next room and she got up with no sign of irritation and followed him calmly, making her way through the little knots of people without falling over the five separate pieces of furniture which tripped up the cameraman as he led the way. Behind her, visitors had a last glimpse of Montessori standing at a window, looking out with a smile. All they could see outside the window was a blank gray wall, but she seemed to one of them "to be seeing something invisible to the rest of us."

Not all of the reporters were equally careful listeners, and in any case what they had come for was good copy—something to catch the reader's attention. In *The New York Herald* the next day Montessori was quoted— or misquoted—as having said, "We believe in taking the baby away from his mother just as soon as he is born. The mother does not know how to care for her offspring. Parents require much training before they are to be trusted with their infants," and, "After my method has been taught there will be no college education necessary."[8]

Such arrogant-sounding pronouncements were hardly likely to endear her to the general public, and there was a further misunderstanding centering on her attitude toward women's rights. The Women's Political Union had announced that Dr. Montessori would address them at the St. Regis on the following Monday, an announcement which was fol-

191

lowed by a statement issued by a spokesman for the Dottoressa to the effect that she would do no such thing. "Dr. Montessori has accepted no invitations except one from Thomas A. Edison."[9] The suffragist organization, piqued and somewhat embarrassed, let it be known that it had announced the lecture with the consent of Montessori's manager. Already, she must have begun to experience a first twinge of feeling exploited by McClure and Keedick, who were, after all, out to promote her as a celebrity in order to fill the lecture halls.

In one newspaper account she was referred to as an Italian countess.[10] She was described as "a woman easily entitled to her place among the half dozen most prominent in the world . . . a woman of wonderfully attractive personality . . . on the highest pinnacle of feminine attainment both in this country and abroad, [whose] methods of juvenile upbuilding already have taken a place in history next to those of Rousseau, Pestalozzi and Froebel" and "give promise of assuming a worldwide predominance."[11] Perhaps under the influence of a physical anthropology only half understood, one account of her appearance added to the usual remarks on the attractions of her face and manner the comment, "Her nose is prominent and pointed, indicating extreme sensitiveness to impressions, which is borne out by the long, intelligent fingers."[12] But most of the accounts described her in such terms as having done "more constructive scientific work than any other living woman, the creator of a system of education that will within a few years modify all existing educational systems and theories and as it is developed, take their place, thereby evolving a new and higher type of thinking and acting man."[13]

The publicity—compounded of fact and error, intriguing description and enthusiastic prophecy—did its job. An eager public discussed what was reported about her ideas and methods—and lined up to buy tickets for her lectures.

The day after her arrival, accompanied by McClure and Anne George, Montessori went on to Washington. She visited the Montessori school Mrs. Bell had helped establish on Kalorama Road, where she watched the children at work closely and was visibly impressed. It was the first time she had actually seen her own methods in use in a country outside of Europe and their success confirmed her often-stated belief that they were not limited to any one class or condition of children but applied universally to all children.

A case of flu prevented the President from keeping an appointment to meet her. Wilson, who had been an academic before he became a politician, was something of a frustrated educational innovator himself and had taken an interest in what he had heard about the wonder-working

Italian educator. His daughter Margaret shared his interest. Margaret Wilson, who had been enthusiastically involved in the Washington Montessori activities, took Montessori sightseeing in a White House car and arranged for her to meet a number of influential government figures, including Philander P. Claxton, the U.S. Commissioner of Education, who later issued a statement saying he was in favor of the introduction of the Montessori system in the public schools and suggested beginning with the school system of New York.

Margaret Wilson was one of a number of well-connected individuals, close to the seats of power and wealth, who at various times and in various places throughout Montessori's life took up her system as a cause and used their influence to interest others. Sometimes their interest persisted and they became members of the Montessori world, which became an increasingly special one, but often—sometimes after personality clashes, sometimes as a result of conflicting ideas, sometimes in the course of developing new interests—they moved on to other things. Like many of the Americans who took up Montessori in the years before World War I, Margaret Wilson was to lose contact with the movement later. Her interest in Montessori was one of many passing enthusiasms, like her chairmanship, that same winter, of a group known as SPUG (the Society to Prevent Useless Giving), a women's civic organization dedicated to de-emphasizing the commercial aspect of Christmas.

On Saturday evening, December 6, Montessori gave her first lecture in America, at the Masonic Temple in Washington, D.C. It seemed as though all of Washington society and officialdom came to hear her describe her method in words translated by Anne George and illustrated by the films of children in the Case dei Bambini, and that the cream of those came on to the reception held in her honor afterward at the Alexander Graham Bells' mansion on Connecticut Avenue.

Four hundred guests nodded, spoke to, or shook hands with Montessori as she stood in the receiving line in a black chiffon gown unrelieved by any touch of color, next to the Bells, Mrs. Bell resplendent in lavender satin and lace. Also in the receiving line were McClure, Dr. Claxton, Margaret Wilson, and Mrs. Franklin Lane, wife of the Secretary of the Interior. Crowded around the sumptuous buffet tables were society leaders, cabinet members, and foreign diplomats, including the secretaries of the Navy, Commerce, and Agriculture, the Surgeon General of the Public Health Service, the Bishop of Washington, the ambassadors of France and Germany, and high officials of the British, Russian, Italian, Spanish, Swedish, Greek, Norwegian, Peruvian, and Uruguayan embassies.

But Washington was only a prelude to the main event, and after the weekend in the capital Montessori returned to New York on Monday for a triumphal appearance such as few heroes—and fewer heroines—had enjoyed there. McClure and Keedick had done their work well; the press had fanned the already existing interest in the Italian woman whose classroom methods with young children promised to change the world, and a crowd estimated at about a thousand had to be turned away from Carnegie Hall, where one of the largest audiences in its history filled every seat and rows of people four and five deep stood in the galleries. The boxes were crammed with teachers, college students, and parents who, according to *The New York Sun,* "were eager to hear Dr. Montessori explain how she was able to make children advance rapidly in learning, make them polite, self-reliant and charming by giving them complete liberty and without rewards or punishments."[14] Who could resist such a promise?

The stage was hung with American and Italian flags, and over it a huge banner read, "America Welcomes Dottoressa Montessori." Professor John Dewey of Columbia, philosopher, dean of American educators, and president of the National Kindergarten Association, presided, and on the platform were such dignitaries as Henry Fairfield Osborn, president of the American Museum of Natural History; Frederick A. Stokes, Montessori's American publisher and president of the American Publishers Association; as well as the dean of the School of Pedagogy of New York University; professors from such prestigious schools of education as those of Princeton and Harvard; the heads of the leading kindergarten training schools, public and private; and representatives of the Montessori Educational Association and various civic organizations.

After a few words of welcome from Dewey, McClure introduced Montessori as "the greatest woman educator in history" and finally the overflow crowd got its first glimpse of Montessori herself as she came forward, soberly regal in a black lace and chiffon evening dress, a black chiffon scarf over her shoulders, its jet tassels swaying as she held out her arms to receive several large bunches of flowers.

When the initial burst of wild applause had died down, she began to speak in her measured, expressive Italian, pausing for Anne George, who stood beside her, to translate sentence by sentence. She said little about the materials used in the Case, preferring to dwell on the significance of her method as a step toward a new science which would explore normal development just as abnormal development was already being studied. It would be based upon observation and experimentation and "through the lessons learned from it a finer, stronger race will be devel-

194

oped, more courageous, more capable of carrying on the work of the world."[15]

She told how she had discovered by observing little children "an independent intellectual and spiritual life" unconnected with any of the efforts of their teachers, "a growth from within." (This emphasis on the child's development proceeding primarily from the liberation of innate capacities rather than from external influences—interaction with nurturing adults—may have been particularly appealing to Montessori because it minimized a sense of what her own child might have missed since she could not raise him herself, shape his development in day-to-day contact.) She repeated her reply to visitors to the Case who wondered why the children were not kept busy every minute: "Let them meditate." And she told a fascinated audience how the children's interest in work surpassed their appetite, how these children of poor families, who seldom got treats, identified and arranged the circle- and rectangle-shaped cookies they were given instead of grabbing and eating them.

She concluded by saying, "The development at which I aim includes the whole child. My larger aim is the eventual perfection of the human race."[16]

Her talk lasted more than two hours, interrupted by frequent bursts of applause, followed by the films showing the children exactly as she had described them—absorbed, enthusiastic, intent on their work, orderly without supervision. To those who left Carnegie Hall in the winter chill late that December night it seemed they had heard a really original voice, seen a glimpse of a possible future.

With the interest in hearing Montessori surpassing anything McClure and Keedick had dared to count on, arrangements were immediately made for a second New York lecture the following week. Meanwhile, still admitting no fatigue and eager to see more of America and Americans, Montessori left for Philadelphia, where she repeated her triumph on the lecture platform and met with another of the world's most famous women of the moment, Helen Keller.[17]

It was a strange meeting. The two women had long known about and admired each other, the one whose interest in education had begun with the possibilities of educating the handicapped and whose mentor, Seguin, had been primarily a teacher of the deaf, and the other who could neither hear nor see but had become civilized, literate, even cultured.

Now, in Montessori's Philadelphia hotel suite, they communicated through a double process of interpretation, Montessori's words translated into English by Anne George for Anne Sullivan Macy, Keller's teacher, who then spelled them in the manual alphabet into Keller's hand. It

195

was hardly a process that could encourage much subtlety of expression, and it was not surprising that what was said amounted primarily to an exchange of compliments and a vague agreement that socialism would be the tool for building a better world. What was extraordinary was not what was said but that it could be "said" at all.

After an embrace and a confused greeting, Keller referred to herself as "a product of the Montessori method." Montessori told her that she was dedicating her new book, *Dr. Montessori's Own Handbook,* to her and Keller said they were both fighters for freedom, Montessori for the freedom of children, she for the freedom of their parents by means of a new industrial revolution.

"I began," Montessori said, "as a sympathizer with political revolutionists of all kinds. Then I came to feel that it is the liberation of this"—putting her hands to her bosom—"what we have in our hearts—that is the beginning and end of revolution."

Keller: "But surely, we can never have the Montessori system or any other good system of education so long as the conditions of the home, of the parents, of the workers are so intolerable."

Montessori: "Certainly, certainly, that is true. But we must educate children so that they will know how to free themselves and others from bondage."

It was a chicken-or-egg argument, and could end only in a smiling impasse. The two women parted with Montessori's apologies for Keller having had to come to the hotel to see her ("When I first came to America I felt that I must rush to you to render homage") and Keller's hope that the next time they met they would be able to dispense with one step in the translation of their words—that they would converse in Italian, in Rome, where she hoped to "see," through her teacher's description, the Montessori children at work in the Case.

From Philadelphia Montessori returned to New York, where she again received visitors and the press in her rooms at Holland House and was entertained by members of old New York society at select little gatherings in their east side mansions with such guests as Nicholas Murray Butler, the distinguished president of Columbia University. She had been in America a week, during which time it was impossible to pick up a newspaper without seeing her name, if not in the news columns, on the society page, or to move among men and women in the academic world or talk with ordinary schoolteachers or parents without hearing her name.

Some indication of the influence Montessori was felt to be having at the time was given by a letter from a kindergarten teacher to *The New York Times* during the first week of Montessori's American tour, objecting that, "It does not seem common sense to apply one fixed sequence to all children" and culminating in "my earnest plea that the open-minded kindergartener may be permitted to procure such features of the Montessori material as she feels capable of using for the ultimate good of the minds in her charge."[18] The letter writer sounds like someone who feels she may be standing in the path of a tidal wave.

Montessori had returned to New York to appear at the Brooklyn Academy of Music under the auspices of the Institute of Arts and Sciences. Again, the large hall was filled to overflowing and a rapt audience listened as McClure, who had a touch of Barnum in him, described Montessori as "the greatest woman in the world" and predicted that her work would "revolutionize education in our time."

It was to happen more slowly, less directly, and less systematically than he hoped, but a Montessori revolution in education did not seem an unreasonable prediction to the audience who listened to him say, "As an editor for thirty years I have found that the only true test of real greatness and permanent worth is the approval of the masses of people"[19] and attribute Montessori's ability to arouse popular interest to the recognition on the part of the masses of parents and teachers of the great truths that she had discovered. When Montessori came on stage at the conclusion of McClure's remarks the audience rose spontaneously and applauded for several minutes. As usual, she was dressed wholly in black, even to black gloves, and appeared self-contained and calm, smiling slightly at the enthusiastic ovation but not appearing surprised or embarrassed. By now, she was used to this kind of reception.

Anne George, like all of Montessori's protégée-interpreters, knew Montessori's thoughts so well that she repeated her statements in unfaltering English without any hesitation as Montessori talked about her concept of liberty—the freedom of the child to develop according to his own nature—and explained that it did not mean letting a child indulge every impulse of the moment, that it was necessary to check destructive tendencies and encourage "useful and admirable" ones.

"Instead of imposing on children the results of someone else's experience from without, children should be stimulated and allowed to explore for themselves, so that their experience makes their knowledge real and a part of themselves, rather than a matter of memorized formulae."[20]

After her talk and the showing of the films and the by-now-usual ovation, Montessori remained on stage to receive special dignitaries and members of the American committee, who were soon joined by a good part of the audience, pressing forward to shake her hand or express their enthusiasm for her ideas.

After her Brooklyn appearance, Montessori went on to Boston, where she gave two more lectures and met with members of the Harvard faculty. She went to Providence, where she was welcomed by the governor of the state and met with the members of the Rhode Island Board of Education who had already adopted her system, and to West Orange, New Jersey, where Thomas A. Edison showed her around his workshops and laboratories. Everywhere, the time between public appearances was taken up with conferences and meetings with local educational leaders. When she was not talking to audiences or in small informal groups, she was making notes of her impressions or of ideas for future work. At one point she mentioned wistfully that she would like to hear an opera in New York and see a typical American play, but there never seemed to be time.

The end of her second week in America found Montessori back in New York, where the papers carried advertisements announcing the repeat performance of her Carnegie Hall triumph.

Last Appearance
at
Carnegie Hall
Monday eve., Dec. 15, at 8.15
Great Public Demand Has Caused
Dr.
MONTESSORI
To Consent to a Second Lecture
Carnegie Hall Box Office Open To-day (Sunday)
Seats 50¢, $1, and a few at $1.50
Mail Orders Promptly Filled
Order Now and be sure of your seat.
Hundreds were turned away from the first
lecture. Auspices of Montessori Educa-
tional Association.[21]

The second Carnegie Hall lecture was a repeat of the first only as far as the crowd and its enthusiasm for Montessori's words was concerned. The words themselves were different. As always, she spoke extemporaneously, without notes, never repeating her thoughts in exactly the same way.

"The primal impulse of the child," she told her attentive listeners, "is to become a man, and he must have liberty to find those conditions and that help which will enable him to become in the fullest possibilities, the man he was destined to be."[22] She did not think it necessary to spell out that by "man" she meant to refer to "woman" as well; what she had to say was revolutionary enough. She took issue with statements of contemporary psychologists to the effect that between the ages of three and six a child's attention was hard to hold, making schooling impractical. On the contrary, if the child were given appropriate materials to handle and work with, he would fix his attention on them for unexpectedly long periods of time. And she told about the little girl in the Casa dei Bambini who was so engrossed in her activity with the cylinders that she could not be interrupted and remained impervious to the other children's singing and marching and even to being bodily moved in her chair from one spot to another while she repeated the exercise more than forty times. "Surely this shows with what intensity a child rivets its attention on something in which it is interested. This constancy is the essence of children's spontaneous development and they should be allowed to repeat the work which interests them."[23]

She criticized the misplaced discipline of parents who would not allow children to touch objects on a table or desk—"It is not naughtiness but his way of learning; the child at this age learns through his sense perceptions by touching things, whereas adults have outgrown this stage of development"—and took issue with the view of young children as naturally destructive.

The instinct to pull an object to pieces is the natural result of giving the child something it cannot understand. Most toys given to children are too complicated. Instead of expecting children to amuse themselves with toys they do not understand, mothers should assume more responsibility for their children's entertainment. The mother who drives her child away from her side when she is working makes a pitiful mistake. It is impossible to estimate the effect upon the child's mind if he were never turned away, if he could always be sure of sympathy and understanding from the person he loves most of all.

Confidences would come more easily in the years when they are longed for if they were invited in the years when living was exciting and every act a great adventure. The child should be allowed to work with the mother. Imitation is the first instinct of the awakening mind.

The child wants to do something sensible. Useless play without a meaning does not appeal to him: neither do so many of the tasks set for children in the ordinary schools. That is why children are rebellious and naughty.

People often say to me, "What about the naughty child? Your method may do very well for the young angel, for the child who is naturally gentle, who is capable of happy mental development. What about the rebellious child, the suspicious, headstrong child who cannot be managed by gentleness?" I answer always, "There are no bad children. What seems like caprice is really only rebellion against the denial by their parents of their desire for a natural environment." I have come to this conclusion only after several years of the most careful observation.

At first when people asked me that question I made no answer. It seemed hardly possible that I was right. I would not make the statement until I was sure. But now I know. If children are allowed free development and given occupation to correspond with their unfolding minds their natural goodness will shine forth. This I have called the conquest of goodness. It is fact, not theory.[24]

The newspapers let out all the stops reporting on her lecture the next day. A typical article was headed, "Smash Your Toys if You Want To. Dr. Montessori Gives Children Leeway to Wreck Christmas Presents. Mothers Alone to Blame, She Says. They Don't Pick Gifts that Appeal to Infantile Mind, Woman Teacher Asserts."[25]

Despite the inevitable exaggerations and distortions, Montessori went on receiving reporters and trying to explain her ideas as well as answering their questions about her impressions of America. It is hardly possible to know exactly what she said in these interviews and how much was lost in the process of translation from Italian to English to newspaperese, but she was reported to have described Americans as "the most intelligent people in the world," responding more quickly to "fineness of thought" (an understandable view in the light of the enthusiasm with which they were responding to her own thought at the time) than the people of any other country in the world and without having to travel the long road necessary for those under less enlightened governments.[26]

The interest Americans took in their children was, she felt, the token of a great race and bespoke a great future for them. The intelligence of any country was in direct proportion to its interest in the welfare of its children. Historians, she was quoted as having said, had traced the downfall of the civilization of Egypt directly to its neglect of the child.

There began to creep into her public pronouncements the kind of modesty which is assumed only by those who have become used to hearing themselves repeatedly described as great men or women. "All the homage which the American people have lavished on me," she said, "I accept not as tribute to me personally, but as homage to the child."

She was asked questions about American customs as well as American institutions, and she gave her views on everything, the trivial as well as the serious.

Asked what she thought of the slit skirt then fashionable in America, she looked puzzled and shook her head. Anne George, interpreting for her, illustrated in pantomime just what a slit skirt was and Montessori, after a moment's thought, pronounced demurely, "Anything is good which adds to comfort. If the skirt as you describe it gives freedom, and permits the wearer to receive more pleasure from walking, it is to be commended. I often think that it is the men who have all the comfortable things to wear, while women have to sacrifice every comfort to beauty." Then, apparently deciding that if she were to be asked such questions she might as well enjoy herself answering them, she added playfully, "Look how easy it is for a man with his short hair to take off his hat. Is this not unfair, that the man should have all the comfort of short hair himself and the pleasure of looking at the beautiful long hair of women?"

She was delighted by the American custom of shaking hands. "We never do that in Europe. It is never possible to meet people so intimately, to be able to tell how sympathetic they are from the contact of their hands and the expression of their eyes. That is how I feel I understand the American people, though I cannot speak their language."

Of American schools, she remarked on "the magnificence of the palaces you have erected to your children. I marvel at their grandeur." As for her general impressions of America, "It has been mostly a feast of Tantalus. So many beautiful cities. So many people with whom I should have liked to talk, but always I must hurry away. Your skyscrapers impress me tremendously, especially at night, when they are lighted. We have nothing like them in Rome."

Those who were under the impression that the aesthetic aspects of life were neglected in her idea of education she reassured that "It should be a part of every child's education to understand the principles of beauty in every form. Dancing and art appreciation should be a part of every school program. However, beauty is not the most essential thing. We must not return to the pagan conception of things," and she illustrated her point with an old Italian folk saying: "The woman, it goes, may have beauty. That in itself is zero. She may have charm, zero. She may have talent, wit, intelligence—all these are zero if they stand alone. If she has a great soul, however, that counts as one. And then you can add all the zeros, and you have a great sum."

All of the speaking—the public moments on stage and the no less public ones off, constantly surrounded by admirers, meeting officials, explaining her work, answering reporters' questions—the whole pace of the tour was beginning to be felt. After New York, Pittsburgh; and after Pittsburgh, Chicago. Another train trip. Another reception, another lecture, more interviews.

In Chicago visitors including local dignitaries and figures prominent in the educational world came and went all day in her suite at the Blackstone Hotel. She gave two lectures to standing-room-only audiences at the Illinois Theater, which was filled to capacity over an hour before they began. At the first lecture she was introduced by Ella Flagg Young, the ardent feminist who became superintendent of the city's schools, and at the second by Jane Addams of Hull House fame.

After her Chicago appearance on the twentieth, Montessori retreated to Battle Creek, Michigan, where she enjoyed a weekend of seclusion at the Battle Creek Sanitarium as the guest of breakfast-cereal millionaire J. H. Kellogg. Rested, she returned to New York for a last look around the city and a glittering evening farewell reception in her honor at the new Women's Cosmopolitan Club before sailing, in the early hours of the morning of Christmas Eve, on the *Lusitania.*

At the pier to see her off were McClure and a committee from the Montessori Educational Association. Admirers had filled her cabin with baskets of flowers and fruit and brightly wrapped Christmas gifts. The farewell and the flowers were reminiscent of the days of her first Italian lecture tour in 1899. The reporters were there too, and before the whistles blew and the gangplanks were drawn up, Montessori made one last statement:

"Your wonderful country is one of the hopes of the civilized world. The feel of youth is in the air and soil. You will rear here the greatest race the world has ever known. It is in your blood. The mixing of the peoples of the earth will produce a great posterity. No country has the heritage to leave to its children like the heritage of the American people.

"America is glorious! Glorious because of its achievements, of course, but more than that, glorious because of the thought it has taken for its children. And I must bow with humility to the American mother. She is one of the greatest wonders of your growing men." [27]

Then it was over. Montessori had spent three weeks in America, hardly a long time, but long enough for her to have fanned the already existing interest in and enthusiasm for her work among public and professionals alike to such a degree that it seemed reasonable to suppose that the influence of Montessori in America could only increase.

The Washington correspondent of the London *Times* wrote in January of 1914:

> There are abundant signs that the United States will be the first country to experimentalize with the Montessori system on a large scale. It is clear that she has compelled the interested attention of specialists the country over.
>
> Already there are over sixty Montessori teachers at work in private

schools, and with special classes. . . . Los Angeles, Boston and New York have experimental schools in full swing. . . . A National Montessori Association [sic] has been established in Washington with powerful backing; and it is significant that since Mme. Montessori's visit the education boards of practically all the States have applied for information. Various universities have taken the system up in an experimental way. At the University of Chicago, a young Hindoo student who has been trained by Mme. Montessori and who hopes eventually to introduce the system into India, is holding two classes, one of deficient, the other of normal children. . . . It is hoped that eventually a [teacher-training] school will be established here.

This enthusiasm is natural. The United States is a great educational laboratory. The fact that each state manages its own school system, the liberality of state and private support of education, and the passion of Americans for improvements of all kinds guarantee a fair field for new ideas. . . . The field has also been prepared by the wave of radical social reform which in the last few years has swept over the land. Questioned by an interviewer as to the difference between her system and the kindergarten system of Froebel, inasmuch as Froebel also designed that children should "work in freedom," Mme. Montessori replied:

> Ah, but whose freedom? Froebel's, not the child's. He came to the child with his philosophy about the child. I go to the child to get mine. He imposes his imagination upon the child. The result is to confuse the child. . . . It is false psychiatry. Not in that way was a Dante made. The imagination must be the child's. He must first of all see clearly. Then out of the whole world of metaphors and comparisons he may choose what he likes.

It may easily be imagined how an idea of that kind appeals to a people who are feverishly, though often subconsciously, trying to reconcile with the individualistic traditions of the "free-born" citizen the paternalism implied by statutory eugenics, sex hygiene, and all the stock-in-trade of the modern Radical who would reform society. One sees that in the way the Press treated Mme. Montessori. . . .

And if the teachings of Mme. Montessori are in sympathy with the spirit of the times, they are also consonant with some of the favourite conceptions of American education. . . . The general tendency of American schools for young children is towards freedom and liberty. . . .

But enough has been said to show that it is safe to prophesy that the Italian example is bound to find many followers here.[28]

In fact, the American interest in Montessori was at its height, and would never again in her lifetime be as great.

When Montessori left America at the end of 1913 she still had, she told McClure, "unlimited confidence" in him, and felt that they were joined "dans un idéal d'humanité, qui élève les coeurs."[29] On January 5,

1914, she sent him a telegram reading "Arrived happily everybody here loves and admires you. Montessori."[30]

After her departure McClure went on lecturing and showing her films. He seems to have had a sincere interest in her work and in presenting it to the American public, but he was also after a slice of the pie. Many people saw the profitable possibilities in exploiting the method, the materials, and Montessori herself, and she was well aware of this. Approaches to her were many, and it wasn't difficult for her to see that for each one who was interested in education there was another interested primarily in cashing in on a good thing.

McClure's lectures, in which he showed Montessori's films, were now for his own profit. McClure's biographer, Peter Lyon, says, "Never had he been dishonest; but he had been naïve, which, in the circumstances, was worse. His gravest offense was his failure to make his position clear; she had imagined him to be her Maecenas, while in fact he was only a promoter diligently delving for an honest dollar."[31]

During the spring of 1914 McClure continued to send Montessori newspaper cuttings of articles reporting on the lectures he gave in high school auditoriums, Baptist temples, and Rotary meeting halls across the Midwest. In small towns like Logansport, Indiana, regular school sessions were adjourned so teachers could hear about the wonders produced by the Montessori system of education.[32]

McClure made one last effort to retain his position as Montessori's associate. If he could succeed in persuading her to make the United States the center of her growing movement, he could, he felt, play a decisive role in its future.

Montessori had returned to Rome to take up her work there, and the second international training course was held, at nearby Castel Sant'Angelo, from February through June. Students from fifteen countries were enrolled, forty-five of them Americans. During this second international course the International Council of Women held a congress in Rome and Montessori gave a reception for the American delegates. It was an opportunity to return some of the hospitality she had enjoyed on her American tour and to make new American friends for the method. Since she spoke no English, Montessori received the Americans flanked by her friends Donna Maria Maraini and the Marchesa Etta de Viti de Marco, a wealthy former New Yorker married to an Italian nobleman.

American friends and supporters were urging Montessori to return and give a training course in the United States, since no one but she could give such a course and it was clear that the movement could not hope to spread without trained teachers to carry on the classroom work.

204

McClure decided to try to interest her in establishing the research center she dreamed of—an idea they had first discussed in the spring of 1912—in America rather than in Rome. Judging by her recent reception there and the extent of Montessori activity already under way in American schools, it seemed highly likely that support could be found for such a project.

In April 1914 McClure sent his brother Robert to Rome to approach Montessori about returning to the United States. Anna Maccheroni described Robert McClure's arrival:

> I well remember the day he came. Dr. Montessori was seated in an armchair shelling peas. How she liked manual work, neatly done, with exact movements. She was putting the peas in one china bowl, the pods into another. The maid came in. "Well," said Dr. Montessori, looking at the peas, "I must finish this."
>
> So she did. Then she sent the bowls to the kitchen and got ready to receive this visitor who had made the journey to Europe in order to see her.[33]

McClure's offer was an impressive one. He proposed the establishment in New York of an institute which she would head and where she could experiment further with the development of her ideas for the education of children and train teachers. At first, she seems to have been enthusiastic about the idea, and even made some preliminary plans for the kind of school, for both normal children and for the retarded, blind, and deaf, which would be part of the institution. But after some days of negotiation she decided to decline the offer.

Maccheroni described the occasion as the only time when she saw Montessori actually depressed. (There must have been another time as well—the occasion when Montessori, stricken by Montesano's marriage and betrayal of their pledge, left the Orthophrenic School and began what was essentially a new career, the study of normal children's needs and the development of an educational method for meeting those needs. But if Maccheroni remembered that earlier time she could not refer to it publicly, even when both she and Montessori were already old women.) The only clues she offers to the reasons behind Montessori's decision—and they are probably more related to Maccheroni's own romantic fantasies about events than to the actual workings of Montessori's mind—are that she preferred to remain "free," to go on "talking, preaching" to the varied groups of students of her training courses, and to remain in Europe rather than to relocate in America.

It is highly probable that the fact that she had a child living in Italy at the time may have played a role in her decision. To leave him behind would be unthinkable; to bring him with her could only call attention to a relationship and perhaps even create a scandal about it which would be certain to interfere with the effectiveness of her work—what she saw by now as her mission in life.

Maccheroni says that Montessori's depression lasted only an evening, and then "she was her own bright self" again. "Somebody mentioned the enormous amount of money she had refused. With a very small movement of her shoulders she pushed aside such a matter and went on with her courses."

Robert McClure had a somewhat different and more concrete explanation when, informed of Montessori's decision, he wrote to his brother from Rome:

> Something has happened to completely change Montessori's attitude towards you. . . .
> The non-return of the negative on demand, and Keedick's method of charging her expenses seemed to them matters of grave dereliction. (They made me feel as if they thought there was almost an attempt at fraud.) . . .
> I cannot help thinking someone in America has been poisoning her mind and that that influence together with this distrustful attitude of her entourage in Rome has made her thoroughly dissatisfied with her arrangement with you. . . .[34]

Montessori complained that she had received no share of the proceeds of McClure's lectures using her films, and that McClure had exceeded his authority in negotiating on her behalf with the House of Childhood, the company that was to manufacture and distribute the didactic materials in America. She insisted that the Montessori American Committee be dissolved, that all existing contracts for lectures and film showings be cancelled, and that McClure should try to secure better terms for her with the House of Childhood.

> If all these conditions were met she would talk about a training school, but it must be understood that it was *she* who was organizing the class, that it was *her* enterprise, that if we had anything to do with it it was to be as her agent, everything must be submitted to and approved by her. . . .
> She had said that other people had offered to pay her to come to America to teach, that schools had been offered to her and that in short she did not need anyone to help her in getting up a class. . . .[35]

Two things stand out in this situation. It *was* Montessori's work, her ideas, which were being exploited for profit, whatever interest McClure may have had in the work for its own sake. And this odd state of affairs followed from the Montessori work being treated—by everyone involved, including Montessori and her associates—like a commercial franchise, a patentable business, rather than an educational theory and practice to be tested and developed in a scholarly context of university departments of education and demonstration schools by teachers and teachers of teachers whose interest in educational techniques would have no immediate material aspect. The insistence that only she could train teachers in the proper use of her method and materials, and on controlling the manufacture, distribution, and use of the materials, made of the Montessori method a business, with her as the head of the enterprise. Eventually, the business would also take on the characteristics of a church, with Montessori as priestess, pope, and messiah to her followers. Even in the short run, it was one of the factors that contributed to the decline of the movement in this country, keeping it out of the intellectual mainstream of education, which in the long run proceeded from teachers colleges and university departments of education rather than from public forums and the mass media, which could serve to stimulate interest but not to institutionalize it.

The immediate result was that McClure dropped out of the picture, returning the films and relinquishing Montessori's power of attorney. He seems to have had no choice under the circumstances. He *was* a businessman, not a disciple, and he had made a bad investment. He left the fold with a total profit from his months of effort of about five hundred dollars and a residue of bitterness about Montessori.

In his autobiography, written in 1914, the very year of the event, McClure says nothing of the disappointment he must have felt at the outcome. Perhaps he showed such gentlemanly restraint because he still hoped for a reconciliation and further collaboration. Perhaps he was embarrassed to reveal the rather petty details of his falling out with the authority he himself had called "the greatest woman in the world." In any case, he mentions Montessori only in the context of how he got ideas for articles in the magazine, explaining how he came to commission the Tozier articles which did so much to stimulate interest in Montessori in this country.[36]

Some of Montessori's other American supporters were also becoming disenchanted. Late in that same year, 1914, Mabel Bell's son-in-law, Gilbert Grosvenor, editor of the *National Geographic* and one of the original members of the Montessori Educational Association, wrote to Mrs Bell:

> It is going to be very difficult to have any business dealings with a woman of her peculiar disposition. . . .
>
> She seems to me to lack the faculty of knowing who her friends are. We all know Mr. McClure's weaknesses, but I think his promotion of Madame Montessori and her ideas was entirely altruistic. She owes her entire success to him, and yet, because she thought he ought to have sent her $100 more than he actually did send, she writes him a most insulting letter and discontinues all dealings with him. This action on her part, in my judgment, is inexcusable. . . .
>
> My own hope is that if Montessori comes to America you will retire as the President of the Association. You gave the Association the benefit of your name and experience and financial help at a time when it sorely needed it. But the situation will be very different when Montessori reaches America. She will then be the whole movement in America, and I am afraid there may be unpleasantness. Anyway you would be worried to death over her idiosyncrasies and her utter lack of responsibility.[37]

Grosvenor's references to "unpleasantness," to Montessori's "peculiar disposition," "idiosyncrasies" and "utter lack of responsibility" are the angry reaction of the benefactor spurned. Montessori's insistence on controlling all aspects of the work carried on in her name, whether in teaching her method or publicizing it, and her charge that she was being exploited whenever she was not consulted, struck many of those who felt they were being generous in supporting her work as unjustifiable ingratitude. The wealthy Americans who used their influence to promote her ideas expected thanks, not criticism. Instead of appreciating all they had done for her, they told each other, she turned on them.

Montessori's behavior may have contributed to this attitude, but the situation has to be seen from her point of view too. She was totally dedicated to the success of her work, surrounded by enthusiasts who, in their messianic fervor, believed that her method promised a reform of the schools and, through the education of a new kind of child, of society itself. And she and her followers sincerely believed that her ideas could be put effectively to use only in the exact way she had evolved them. To Montessori, her method was more than a theory about education drawing on the child's spontaneous desire to learn when given freedom to use self-correcting materials in an unrestricting environment, a theory to be further modified by experience in various cultural contexts and integrated into the mainstream of early childhood education. It was a system for effecting such education which she had perfected and which had to be protected both from distortion and exploitation.

Shortly after her return from America in 1914, Montessori had published her second book about the method, *Dr. Montessori's Own Handbook*. The first of her books to appear originally in English, the *Handbook* is a guide to the didactic materials, their nature and use.

To Montessori, her technique was inseparable from her method. It was neither arbitrary nor provisional, since it followed "the natural physiological and psychical development of the child."[38] What does not seem to have occurred to her is that our knowledge of both the physiology and psychology of the child, like any kind of knowledge, is never complete and that as knowledge evolves, so must theories and techniques.

But while it is hard to take seriously today some purists' insistence on the necessity of using the identical materials in exactly the same way that Montessori used them in 1907, what is impressive is how these materials have stood the test of time. By and large, the skills they develop, and their progression from the simple to the complex, meet the needs of children today just as they did in the first Casa dei Bambini.

The first group of materials are those designed to develop motor education, the child's ability to manage his environment. These involve the activities of everyday life, such as dressing and washing, housekeeping, gardening, and the serving of meals. There is manual work such as clay modeling; gymnastic exercises involving apparatus like the fence from which the children hang, taking the weight off their legs when they are tired; and rhythmic movements like marching to music. There are framed pieces of cloth with buttons, laces, and hooks which the children learn to fasten and tie and from which they go on to being able to manage their own clothing, and there are the ordinary household objects— washbasins, dishes, gardening tools. There is no limit to this kind of equipment in a Casa dei Bambini because the children use real implements to perform real tasks in what Montessori called "a living scene."

The materials for what she called "the education of the senses" are designed to develop the ability to perceive distinctions and to manipulate various kinds of objects skillfully. They begin with a series of solid insets—wooden cylinders of different sizes to be inserted in holes of the same size in a block of wood. Then there are ten pink wooden cubes of graduated size with which the child builds a tower, then knocks it down, scattering the pieces, and rebuilds it. There are ten brown wooden prisms and ten red rods with which the child builds a broad stair and a long stair respectively. There are geometric solids (pyramid, sphere, cone, etc.), little boards with rough and smooth surfaces and others of different weights and colors, and pieces of fabric of different textures. There are the wooden plane insets, a little cabinet of drawers each containing framed geometrical figures—blue triangles, circles, squares of different sizes—to be taken out and replaced correctly in their frames. There are cards with paper geometrical shapes pasted on them, a series of cylindrical boxes filled with different materials that make different sounds when shaken; sixty-three little tablets in nine different shades from light to dark of seven different colors; and a series of musical bells used together with a wooden board that has the musical staff lines on it and a set of wooden disks to represent the notes.

The materials for language development, which prepare the way for writing, reading, and arithmetic, include the sandpaper letters, boxes of colored cardboard letters and numbers, and counting rods—square-sided sticks of different unit lengths in different colors representing different numbers—as well as strings of different lengths of various numbers of beads of different colors.

All of the materials are available to the child in low cupboards from which he can take them himself to the child-sized tables and chairs where he will work with them until he is ready to replace them and start on something else.

These are the elements of the responsive environment of the "Children's House" with which the child interacts and, in the process, educates himself. They are all intrinsically interesting to the child at various stages of his physical and mental growth. Once he is shown how to use them, they are designed to allow him to master their use himself by observing, correcting, accomplishing. The result is pleasure in that accomplishment, and then the desire to go on to something else.

Of course there is much overlapping between the motor, sensory, and language materials. The kinds of perceptions and manipulative skills developed in the "sensory apparatus," for example, also develop the skills that lead to writing and reading.

In the *Handbook,* Montessori not only describes the materials but explains how they are to be used by the directress, the "non-teacher" who demonstrates their use to the child and leaves him to master them on his own and at his own speed while she remains essentially an observer of his progress, ready to help him at the right times but careful "never to be the obstacle between the child and his experience."[39]

The Children's House

The objects that make up the Montessori materials described in the *Handbook* had their beginnings in Itard's improvisations with the wild boy of Aveyron almost two hundred years ago; they can be seen today in countless adaptations in the puzzles and games sold in every toy store in the world.

13

When Montessori returned to America the year following her first triumphal tour, it was not under the sponsorship of either McClure or Mrs. Bell's association. She came under the auspices of the National Educational Association to demonstrate her work to educators and the public at the Panama-Pacific International Exposition in California.

The Exposition opened outside San Francisco early in 1915. Nominally its purpose was to celebrate the building of the Panama Canal, but like all such ventures, it was sponsored by local government and commerce to boost the city where it was held and attract visitors from all over the world. In the midst of war in Europe and economic depression, more than 18 million people visited the Exposition in the nine months between its opening and closing. There were impressive scientific exhibits and meetings of academic and professional groups, but the Exposition attracted the public primarily by being an entertainment, a fair if not actually a carnival. It was marked by such occasions as Prune Week and Hawaiian Pineapple Day. Events ranged from the appearance of world-renowned pianist Ignace Paderewski, who gave a concert to call attention to the ruin of his native Poland, to the proclamation of "Dixie Day," on which occasion the mayor of Atlanta spoke in defense of the mob which that summer had abducted a prisoner named Leo Frank from the Georgia State Prison Farm, where he was serving a life sentence of murder, and lynched him. The United States was moving closer to involvement in the war raging in Europe, but the mood in San Francisco that summer was antiwar and the aim was to have fun while stimulating trade and progress. In Europe, the Italians had begun their offensive against Austria. In San Francisco, the event shared newspaper space with the announcement of blackberry-pie and marshmallow-cream eating contests at the Exposition's Food Products Palace.

Among the more serious groups participating in the Exposition was the National Education Association, which held its fifty-third annual convention in Oakland in August. Fifteen thousand teachers attended, and there were delegates and speakers representing almost thirty countries. A number of other educational organizations held their meetings in and around San Francisco to coincide with the NEA congress, including the International Kindergarten Union. Montessori was invited to ad-

212

dress both groups and to set up a model Montessori class to be run under her supervision from August through November in the Palace of Education on the Exposition grounds.

In addition to the model school, Montessori arranged to give a course for teachers, her third international training course, in San Francisco from August through November. She planned to give four lectures a week and personally supervise the students, who would observe the work of the children in the demonstration class.

Arrangements for the course had been made by Katherine Moore, a pupil of Montessori's who had returned from the international course in Rome to teach the first Montessori class in an American public school, on Seventh Street in Los Angeles. Enrollment in both the training course and the children's class was handled by M. Beulah Townsend and her husband James R. Townsend, equally enthusiastic advocates of the Montessori system and the Socialist party. Mr. Townsend had been a candidate for the state senate on the Socialist ticket in 1912. The Townsends had established a Montessori school in 1911 so their own small children could be educated by means of the method, and the first name Mrs. Townsend entered for the course was her own.

Montessori arrived in New York late in April, inspected the Montessori classes being held in the John Jay Dwellings and visited P.S. 45 in the Bronx, where she talked with principal Angelo Patri, a popular education writer of the day, about the Gary system then being introduced in the public schools, praising the newly installed workshops and gardens that were part of the Gary plan ("You are preparing children to meet the realities of life"). Afterward she told a newspaper reporter, "The mere habit of obedience is not preparation for life in a democracy. In Italy there is universal suffrage for men. Even idiots may vote. They vote as they are told. But the safety of democracy depends upon the intelligence and independence of the voters. Intelligence can be developed only by allowing young people to deal with actual life problems."[1]

Montessori reached San Francisco on April 26, stopping only a day before leaving for Los Angeles, where she was to begin a course on May 1. She was whisked away by automobile to be shown around the grounds of the Exposition, admired its pastel-colored halls and palaces, the lush gardens dotted with statuary, and was guest of honor at a luncheon at which she was introduced by Ernesto Nathan, whom she had known as mayor of Rome. He was now Italian Commissioner to the Exposition, in which capacity he expressed his great pleasure at greeting his old friend and distinguished countrywoman here in California—"a land so like our Italy in color, climate, and tone." The luncheon was followed by a reception in her honor at which she was besieged by admirers eager to meet her—as one reporter of the event put it, "to get from her a word that they might treasure," adding that "unless they spoke Italian they had to be content with a bow and a smile in addition to the customary handclasp."[2]

Then she left for Southern California, visiting Pasadena and San Diego before settling down in a house on Virgil Street in Los Angeles for the next two months. The house had a little garden, and when neighborhood children began wandering in and stayed to play, the educator could not resist organizing an informal little class in which she found American children just as responsive to the elements of the prepared environment as their counterparts in Italy and the rest of Europe. The youngsters who had come out of curiosity found their curiosity channeled in surprising ways. They had become Montessori pupils.

Montessori spent the month of July in San Diego, where some students were allowed to begin the training course in order to finish by the end of October. When the San Diego course ended, she went back to San Francisco. With her was young Mario, who was at first introduced as her nephew, and later as her adopted son. It was the first time he had traveled with her publicly. For some reason, Montessori no longer felt it necessary to hide his existence. Perhaps she thought his presence would be less noticed in a "liberal" America than in her tradition-bound Catholic homeland. Perhaps it was simply that Mario, having discovered the identity of his real mother and joined her, refused to be denied a place in her life any longer. In any case, now a young man, he was given that place. Also staying with them that summer were Anna Fedeli and two of the Americans who had taken Montessori's first international training course in Rome the year before—Adelia Pyle and Helen Parkhurst.

Like so many others, Parkhurst, who was then teaching at the State Teachers College in Wisconsin and had come to Rome to study with Sergi, went to see the Montessori method in operation for herself and stayed to become an enthusiastic disciple.

"I found you can't learn very much about the Montessori method," she later said, "by just going to an occasional lecture. You have to follow. And so I joined the course."[3]

Parkhurst, an ebullient young woman with a quick smile who always seemed to be talking, became a member of the little group around Montessori, in which she soon stood out as the most aggressive intellectually. She herself explained that when it came to interpreting Montessori's lectures, the others, like Adelia Pyle, made literal translations of Montessori's words, while she, Parkhurst, put the statements into educational language.

Parkhurst, whom she called "Margherita," was Montessori's natural choice to direct the demonstation class at the Exposition, the closest thing to an alter ego she could find among those she had trained to do her work. It was a difficult situation for Montessori, who would have liked to conduct the class herself, having to depend on someone else to demonstrate her methods before the eyes of the world—educators, public, press, all seeing the much-talked-about system in actual operation for the first time. It—and she herself—would be judged by the success or failure of this demonstration of her method.

Unfortunately, Parkhurst's leave of absence from her Wisconsin position was due to expire three weeks after the class began, so as soon as they arrived in San Diego, Montessori began looking for someone who could take over when the three weeks were up.

With Parkhurst in tow, she visited the classes of all the likely prospects, the California teachers who had taken Montessori's training course in Rome. At one school, according to Parkhurst, "There was a child using the long stair [a series of ten rods of different lengths which the child arranges in order, with the shortest at the top, to form a set of steps]. A week later we went back and the same little boy was working with the same long stair in the same way. There was repetition, but no progress in the repetition. Montessori said it was like pulling a child's tooth to keep it in the milk stage, and then she got down on her knees and knocked the stair down and scattered the material all over the room."[4]

Montessori's dramatic outburst was not repeated, but none of what they saw inspired much confidence in either of the two women.

When the time came for the class at the Exposition to open, Montessori, who had still found no suitable replacement, said to Parkhurst, "Margherita, you do it for three weeks. Then, if you have to go back to Wisconsin, the school will just have to close." As things turned out, Parkhurst stayed for the entire four months in which the school operated.

Some funds had been allocated for a building to house the Montessori school, but it was not enough. Montessori had no money to add, so, according to Parkhurst, "Delia [Pyle] and I got money to build the school from our families." She added, "Neither of us received any pay for our work with Dr. Montessori—just her grateful thanks and a great deal of inspiration, which we felt fully repaid us."

There was still not enough to construct a separate building, so it was decided to erect a glass-walled structure on a raised platform in a corner of the Palace of Education, making it possible for visitors to observe the children in action. Someone was found to donate the small-scale furniture they needed in addition to the didactic materials.

The class met daily from nine to twelve. Outside the glass walls were tiers of seats from which hundreds of visitors could look into the classroom. One observer referred to them as the "bleachers," and added that the class "is producing as warm a coterie of fans as any home club with a winning streak ever drew inside a baseball grounds."[5] Visitors were fascinated by the sight of the very young children immersed in their work, apparently oblivious to the constant crowd of observers beyond the glass walls.

While a pudgy three-year-old girl built a tower of pink cubes, knocked it down, and carefully began all over again, an owlish four-year-old beside her, oblivious to her alternating efforts at construction and destruction, picked letters out of an alphabet box to form the sounds of his name. Other children were equally absorbed in buttoning frames, counting rods, and matching colors.

The class soon became one of the most popular attractions of the Exposition, particularly toward noon, when the children could be seen serving their own lunch, washing their dishes and putting everything away in proper order. Visitors began lining up early to be sure of a seat. Those who came late were glad to find standing room from which they could see into the classroom. Many of the visitors stayed whole mornings.

The class consisted of twenty-one pupils between the ages of three and six, none of whom had ever been to any kind of school before—a condition on which Montessori had insisted. They had been chosen from among more than two thousand applications from parents eager to enroll their children in a class to be held under the supervision of the world-famous educator whose method promised to turn their offspring into what one enthusiastic journalist described as "the perfect mental and physical child"[6]—and all in four months.

The children spoke several languages and began by communicating in sign language. Among them were some from less well-to-do homes as well as the sons and daughters of prominent San Francisco families, diplomats, officials of the Exposition, and little Margaret Pershing, daughter of then Brigadier General John J. Pershing, commanding a brigade on the Mexican border and later to head the U.S. Army forces in World War I. Late in August three-year-old Margaret was killed, along with her mother and two sisters, in a fire in their home at the Presidio, and the class was reduced to twenty.

Teachers who had come to San Francisco to attend the NEA and International Kindergarten Union meetings were spellbound by the intensity of the children's enthusiasm for what they were doing and the ordered calm in which they all worked away under Parkhurst's practiced eye. They flocked to a joint session of the two educational groups to hear Montessori herself, although she spoke in Italian without a translator this time. Her talk had been printed in English and distributed to the members of both organizations earlier, and few of them understood Italian, but they came anyway, to see the famous Dottoressa in person. The usual articles in the local press, in addition to the word-of-mouth reports of those who had studied with her or heard her before, created an enormous interest not just in her work but in her as a personality. For every sober article explaining the Montessori system there was another like the one in the *San Francisco Chronicle* headed, "She Insists Upon 'Madama' Title/Dr. Maria Montessori is Yet Single, But Adopts the Matrimonial Prefix."[7] According to Parkhurst, it was commonly understood, although not publicly spoken of, that the adolescent Mario who accompanied Montessori was her own son.*

In the evenings Montessori wrote affectionate letters home to her father in Rome, full of news of the Exposition, her course, and what young Mario was up to. In one of them she mentions with fond parental amusement that Mario has decided to keep a diary of the summer's events "from which to write a book (no less!)."[9]

Montessori told the teachers taking her course, "When you have solved the problem of controlling the attention of the child, you have solved the entire problem of education. The ability to recall a wandering and scattered attention, always ready to vanish, is the real root of judgement, character and will. To be able to choose objects that will interest and hold the attention of the child is to know the means of aiding it in its mental development."[10] What they had seen in the schoolroom that morning, she told them, was a pedagogical laboratory in which the first

---

*Fifty years later, Martin Mayer wrote in the introduction to a new American edition of *The Montessori Method*, [8] "thinking back recently to what had happened to Montessori's reputation in the United States, Miss Parkhurst blamed its collapse less on any arguments against her procedures than on the educational community's discovery that Dr. Montessori's companion on her American trip was her natural son." Parkhurst was never reluctant to offer an opinion—often a somewhat idiosyncratic one—on any matter at hand, and it seems doubtful that Mario's presence was as widely noted or as decisive a factor in the outcome for Montessori in America as Parkhurst later made it out to be.

step was being taken toward developing a science of man which would systematically influence human development.

The Montessori materials, she explained, were instruments geared to the child's level of development in such a way as to lead to the spontaneous acquisition of knowledge—"discovery which evokes in the child enthusiasm and joy."[11] It was precisely these qualities of enthusiasm and joy which were so conspicuously absent from the classrooms most of them had left to come to San Francisco, and which were so strikingly evident in the classroom they had observed that morning. And what educator in the America of the early years of this century, with its cheerful belief in the promise of progress through efficiency, could resist a system which, by freeing children to learn for themselves, would lead them to accomplish more—"to lessen effort while at the same time increasing output"?[12] If this phrase, which appeared in the *Proceedings* later published by the NEA,[13] was indeed a faithful translation of Montessori's words, it indicates a shrewd sense of what would appeal to her American audiences at the time.

Montessori appeared on the opening day of the school, her ample figure formally attired in her usual long-sleeved black silk relieved only by a bit of lace and a jeweled broach at her throat and wearing a commanding hat with sweeping feathers that seemed to defy gravity as she bent to demonstrate to a besmocked little boy how to use the cylinders. But after that introductory appearance, her role in the schoolroom remained a supervisory one. Her own teaching was reserved for the teachers enrolled in the training course.

According to Parkhurst,

> It was a terrible time for her. She had sent for me because I had studied with her in Rome and she knew I was experienced and she felt she could depend on me. But when you are going to depend on somebody for thousands of people daily, you eye that person with a great deal of suspended judgement.
>
> I had to get up very early to go to the Exposition. Every morning Dr. Montessori padded out and got breakfast for me—toast and coffee with egg and a little syrup in it—and we would sit together without much conversation. I would keep my thoughts to myself, because after all I had to go down and face the Exposition.
>
> Dr. Montessori would eye me. She was not usually a demonstrative person. She moved into a situation like a battleship. She was very keen, always alert, always very honest, but this was a special situation. I felt just as I had when I went to Rome and wrote my family, "I wonder what Dr. Montessori will think of me."
>
> Fortunately, the school was a success. But even though I felt perfectly confident in what I was doing, it was very difficult to look out and see

those hundreds of eyes day after day—all those heads, like bunches of grapes. It was like a nightmare. I was giving my all to help get Montessori's message across, and I was so tired. After almost three weeks, I was just about ready to give up when Dr. Montessori said to me one morning at breakfast, "Margherita, I am coming to the Exposition today. And I want to have lunch with you afterward." That didn't disturb me at the time. I thought the children would give a good demonstration. But later, when I looked out and saw her there, I found myself wondering, "Oh, dear, what will she think?"

When the session ended at twelve o'clock, Montessori came over to Parkhurst and said, "We will go to lunch now, Margherita." They went to a restaurant and when they were seated, Montessori looked at her and said, "I've never seen you before, Margherita." She paused, eyeing Parkhurst coolly, and then said, "You know, when I watched you today I thought, With that child, if Margherita would just . . . And you would turn and do exactly what I would have done. It's never happened before. It was marvelous. Margherita, *will* you stay on?" It was an irresistible request, and of course Parkhurst agreed. And then, in an extravagant gesture of gratitude Parkhurst remembered as quite unique for Montessori, the older woman bought her an expensive present—a watch of gold and diamonds with a sapphire stem.

Parkhurst often saw Montessori upset in the early part of that summer, pressured from many directions. She had given up her practice and her university position, and was supporting herself, her father, and her son on the proceeds from her books, her training courses, and the materials. She dreamed of an institution in which to carry on her research with children and her training of teachers, but everyone who offered to help seemed to want a share of the control as well as the profits. And she was not always the best judge of character.

"People would write to her," said Parkhurst, "and she'd be taken in. Or somebody she met at a hotel would tell her what they were going to do for her and how much she'd make. Money was a crying need and there was really no one to advise her. And we all felt McClure had treated her very badly."

During the first anxious weeks in Southern California, when Montessori lost control of herself, usually when some promise of support had fallen through, or when she felt her supporters, like the Bells or Anne George in Washington, were taking action without consulting her, or when the debts began to grow and there seemed no way of paying them, it was, said Parkhurst, "as if a great storm had come and everything was cracking up about her." Then Mario, who was seventeen at the time, would put his arms around his mother and hold her tightly and in a few minutes she would regain her calm again. Then she would smile and say, "Well, let's put on perfume and go to Catalina." The phrase became a kind of family slogan for the little group.

With the chronic shortage of money, the bills began to pile up and there was nothing to pay them with. Fedeli would bring them to the two young Americans and Adelia Pyle would hide them under the rug to keep Montessori from seeing them. Then she and Parkhurst would write to their families for money and when the bills had been paid they would tell Montessori, "We were wrong about those bills, they didn't amount to so much after all," and she would smile, relieved, don one of her imposing black hats, and say, "Let's put on perfume and go to Catalina." To Parkhurst, "She looked so beautiful, even though I thought she was as old as God [Montessori was forty-six and Parkhurst was twenty-eight at the time]. Then we'd all go out to Catalina in the glass-bottomed boats and have a big dinner and Delia and I would pay."

In a picture taken at a public lecture Montessori gave that summer, we see her standing beside Adelia Pyle, who was translating for her. The two women are on a stage, framed by the elaborate decorative detail surrounding a huge pipe organ in one of the Exposition's outdoor plazas. It was an uncomfortably hot and windy day but a large crowd stayed following an organ recital to listen to the famous Italian educator through her American interpreter.

They are a striking pair, both round-faced and plump, the elder all in black and the younger in white or some pale shade that looks like white in the photograph, their sleeves full, their skirts voluminous, and the dark-and-light theme carried out even to the ornate plumed hats they each wear. In the photograph they look enough alike for the young woman to be the daughter she had assumed the role of in relation to Montessori, to whom at this point she had all but dedicated her life. It was a kind of dedication Montessori inspired in many of her younger followers—at least for a time.

There is no doubt that among all her protégées, Helen Parkhurst played a very special part in Montessori's life that year—the daughter she never had, the disciple who would carry on her work in America. But the very qualities that distinguished Parkhurst from the other young women who gathered around Montessori—her strength of mind, her independence, the sense of purpose and the will to carry out her ambitions that made her so like Montessori herself at that age—also made it unlikely that she would be satisfied to remain anyone's second-in-command for long.

While they worked together, Parkhurst managed to maintain a certain distance from Montessori—and Montessori seems to have respected her for it. "She could erupt like a volcano," said Parkhurst later, "but never at me. We never had words, never at all. I was always cool. The others worshiped. And then I was away all day, teaching the class."

But Parkhurst, who was direct and outspoken herself, sometimes to the point of seeming abrasive to others, found herself in a difficult position as the favorite among "Mammolina's" children. "There was great emotion around her; there were many satellites. Some of the others who hadn't my teaching experience resented me for being first, for being able to do what I did. There were so many who wanted to take my place—and there were times I wished somebody *could* take my place. But I did my job as best I could, and it came off well."

It came off so well that when the Exposition ended, the Montessori class received both of the only two gold medals awarded in the field of education.

There were many offers to remain in the United States and give training courses, including one from Margaret Wilson, who offered the prestige of the White House along with her sponsorship, but Montessori doesn't seem to have considered any of them seriously. And then, at the end of November, word came of the death of Montessori's father in Rome. She left San Francisco immediately on the first leg of the long trip across the country to New York and passage back to Italy. Although she returned on unpublicized personal visits, the last one in 1918, during the thirty-six remaining years of her life she never returned to teach or work in the United States and gradually her American followers lost touch with her and went off in other directions. America was developing its own educational leaders with their own ideas, and Montessori seemed, for most of the time between the two world wars, to have fallen out of the mainstream of American educational thought and practice, to belong to the faraway world of a Europe Americans were increasingly eager not to be "entangled" with as they went their own way. Ironically, a quarter century later Americans were again involved in a war in Europe and a few years afterward, when she was already dead, Montessori's ideas crossed the Atlantic again and were received with the same enthusiasm she herself had enjoyed in an earlier generation.

When Montessori left America at the end of 1915, she left Parkhurst in charge of the movement here. To Helen fell the tasks of overseeing the various schools and societies, starting new ones, raising money—in short, carrying on the work and spreading the message.

The last time they saw each other before Montessori's departure,

Parkhurst told her about a dream she had had in which she felt very cold and "a big ball of fire came down and went along beside me," warming her. Montessori said, "Margherita, I was the ball of fire." Then she put her hands on Parkhurst's shoulders and said, "Margherita, I will never leave you but you will leave me," and going over to a picture of Saint Anthony holding the infant Jesus, she said, "Saint Anthony, why did you do this to me?" It was a rare display of self-pity—indeed, a rare display of personal emotion—but understandable in a woman to whom children were the most important thing in life but who had not raised her own child and who saw so many of those who were for a time like children to her drift away. And she does seem to have pinned special hopes on Parkhurst—to have hoped, in fact, that "Margherita," of all her family of surrogate children, would inherit her mantle and wear it for more than a brief season.

But without Montessori's presence on the scene the various Montessori societies became competing factions and soon floundered altogether. Parkhurst left to develop her own system, which became known as the Dalton Laboratory Plan. The intervention of the Great War further increased the lack of communication between Montessori and her followers here.

For a time Parkhurst was in charge of Montessori activities in New York. In Washington, Alexander Graham Bell had accepted the presidency of the Montessori Educational Association early in 1915, and there were groups in other cities as well. It was Montessori's idea that various regional organizations would oversee the work in different parts of the country. But jealousy and competition soon arose. There were quarrels over politics—who was in charge of what—and money—how much of what was raised should be paid to whom, and what share should be sent on to Montessori. When Parkhurst looked back at the personal tensions and financial difficulties that beset the movement in those years she said of Montessori, "She was part of the crack-up."

The story of the collapse of the Montessori Educational Association is interesting because of the light it sheds on a pattern that was to be repeated over and over again in different times and different places. Schisms came to be a characteristic feature of the history of the Montessori movement—just because it *was* a movement, defined early in its history as more than a body of ideas, as an institution with a leader, with ritual objects, with the need to be certified by a recognized authority if one was to use the name of its inventor—all phenomena which seem somehow inappropriate to a body of ideas in the history of thought.

Of course, Montessori, who began as a clinician, had developed not only a theory of education, but a technique for putting that theory into practice. She believed in the "scientific" truth as well as the importance of her ideas and she believed that she had established the best way to implement them. But just there is the catch. It is hard to understand how anyone of her intellectual background and sophistication could have failed to see that in all the history of human thought, no idea and no system has not been modified over time as more has been learned and as it has been applied by people with changing needs.

In 1915, while Montessori was in the United States, the Montessori Educational Association (MEA) sent a representative, Bailey Willis, to California to talk with her and try to straighten out the misunderstandings between those who felt they were trying to help carry out her work and Montessori herself. Willis reported afterward that they had discussed Montessori's ideas for organizing a center and local societies and her own relationship to such organizations. They talked about the role of such groups as the MEA in educating teachers as well as the public about the Montessori system, the question of training teachers, whether the Montessori method should be combined with the kindergarten, "the exploitation of Dr. Montessori's name by unauthorized persons for personal advantage," and the questions of the "loyalty . . . and possible dissolution" of the Washington organization.

Willis came away with the impression that "Dr. Montessori's attitude was one of well-feigned ignorance of the Association's purposes, and of desire to be informed. She was sincerely anxious about the misuse of her name, the purity of her method."[14]

Today, one wonders whether this concern with the "exploitation" of her name, the "purity" with which her ideas and methods were applied, could even have presented itself as a problem if Montessori had chosen to carry out her work as an academic in a leading university department of education anywhere in Europe or America. There she could have published books and articles, taught her theories, and let those theories stand or fall in the normal competition of ideas. If those ideas had been referred to by some generic name rather than bound together with materials and technique in a closed system referred to by her own name would the movement have fractured? John Dewey's ideas as practiced came to be known as progressive education, not Deweyism; over the long haul, what worked with children and suited the needs of society became incorporated into the general system. What was faddish, just plain wrong, or tied to a particular cultural moment melted away.

But Montessori did not see it that way, and her followers, most of whom were worshipful enthusiasts who saw her system as an answer to the social ills of the world, did not disagree with her. If they did, they ceased to be her followers. Those who broke away, taking with them what they found valuable in her method, were always seen as betrayers by the keepers of the flame, the "true Montessorians."

It was Montessori's conviction that her ideas would be distorted unless they were practiced exactly as she had translated them into classroom method. And while there was some justification for her fears of distortion and exploitation, of a cheapening of the ideas in the hands of those who did not really understand them and used their name for their own purposes, the price paid for the purity gained through private institutionalization was a certain rigidity, sometimes even atrophy.

After listening politely to what Willis, the MEA representative, had to say on behalf of the Washington group, Montessori handed over a copy of a memorandum she had drawn up headed "General Regulations for the Formation of an Authorized Montessori Society." The memorandum stated that the only teachers authorized to call themselves Montessori directresses would be those who had taken the training course from the year 1913 on. This would eliminate Anne George, who had not only opened the first Montessori school in America but had done much to publicize the method. She had been one of Montessori's earliest and most enthusiastic supporters here, but she had taken the course with Montessori in 1911, and the regulation would mean she was no longer authorized to call herself a Montessori teacher. Montessori seemed to feel that even George was using her, to doubt whether the members of the Washington group were really acting with the best interests of the movement, as she saw them, in mind.

Her statement went on to spell out a "program for propaganda," in which local societies would try to recruit as members lawyers who would concern themselves with "the legal defense of the Method [and] of the name Montessori" so that no school or society could use her name without her authorization; journalists and editors "who will be ready to lend their assistance in a just and righteous propaganda"; businessmen to study "the best means, from an economic and social standpoint, of diffusing the practice of the method"; and prominent authorities in science, letters, art, and especially the educational and political world, all of whom would contribute to the "just and righteous propaganda," which she defined as "public lectures, benefits, popular meetings, regular visiting days in the schools so that the method may be seen in operation, and articles for the papers."[15]

The Bells felt Montessori's lack of confidence in their organization but were reluctant to dissolve the association they had done so much to build up over the last three years and which they felt had done so much to stimulate interest in the method in this country. There were now more than seven hundred members of the Washington group and it was publishing a news bulletin. It seemed to the Bells that "any indication of friction between the MEA and Dr. Montessori herself would be liable to injure the Montessori movement in America."[16]

What they could not understand was that some of the efforts they had undertaken on their own on behalf of the Montessori movement were greeted with suspicion rather than enthusiasm on her part. She did not welcome the publication of anything that dealt with her work—even a news bulletin—unless she had an opportunity to check it and approve its contents.

Before any clear understanding could be arrived at between the MEA members and Montessori, the news of her father's death reached her and she returned to Italy.

Mario stayed on in the United States, and in 1917 started a Montessori class in California to which such Hollywood film stars as Douglas Fairbanks and Mary Pickford sent their young children. He later remembered hearing a local Catholic priest denounce Montessori from the pulpit on the grounds that her educational philosophy ignored the concept of original sin. Mario pursued the matter until a retraction was made. It is an incident that illustrates both the ambivalence of the relationship between Montessori and the Church and the tenaciousness with which Mario was to protect and defend his mother for the rest of his life.

When Montessori left the United States she authorized the formation of an organization to be known as the National Montessori Promotion Fund, with herself as president, and delegated Helen Parkhurst to be in charge, headquartered in New York. Three months later, Mrs. Bell, who had succeeded her husband as president of the MEA, complained that she had still received no official notice of the formation or aims of this organization from Parkhurst, whose official designation was corresponding secretary of the Fund, or any word from Montessori as to the relationship between the two organizations. As the gap widened, the Bells decided to send Anne George abroad to see Montessori and try to clarify matters on behalf of the MEA.

George reported that she was received well by Montessori and that Montessori wanted both organizations to go on functioning in the United States. However, it was becoming increasingly clear to the Bells and the others in the MEA that the activities of the two groups overlapped and that the Fund had more money, had a connection with the House of Childhood, which distributed the Montessori materials, and that Montessori was keeping in closer touch with the Fund. It was finally decided to dissolve the MEA and in the fall of 1916 Mrs. Bell agreed to become a member of the Fund's board of trustees at the invitation of its treasurer, Adelia Pyle's mother.

But the fragmented American movement was falling apart. By early 1917 Parkhurst was considering splitting off from the Western U.S. groups because of policy disagreements and lack of financial support. There was constant bickering about who was in charge of what aspects of the "propaganda"—who spoke for the movement and how funds should be distributed among the various groups.

Parkhurst, strong-willed and ambitious, was becoming more and more restive in the position of a representative of Montessori and an agent for her movement here and more and more interested in pursuing her own independent interests in education. Late in February the president of the Fund's board of trustees wrote to Mrs. Bell that their job had been done and the trustees were dissociating themselves from the organization; shortly afterward Parkhurst made the decision to leave the Fund and strike out on her own. Montessori, to whom this was a defection if not a betrayal, considered that Parkhurst had "torn up her contract" with her, Montessori.[17] Parkhurst said of the break, "We came to a crossroads. She was going on with the materials. I wanted to do something else with the prepared environment." And she added, "Her ideas were not extended, just revisited."[18]

The Bells' son-in-law's judgment that Montessori lacked "the faculty of knowing who her friends are" seems to have had some truth to it. She had set up the Fund because she felt she did not have enough direct personal control of the Association, which had done so much to further her work in America, and the result, after a year of bickering and misunderstandings, was that no one at all was left with authorization to represent her in America. And yet no one could teach, publicize the movement, or organize local groups without such authorization.

Montessori was, from this time forward, to concentrate her efforts elsewhere. Although she traveled all over the world during the remaining years of her life, she never returned to the United States again after World War I. It was, in more than one sense, the end of Montessori in America, at least during her lifetime. The movement which had seemed to promise to take hold so effectively began to wither away in the face of a lack of local leadership and an intellectual and social climate increasingly disinterested in both the Dottoressa and her educational system.

14

Early in 1914 a typical magazine article on "Montessori's Educational Crusade" spoke of the universality of the appeal of "the Italian apostle of a new libertarian education" to Americans and noted that her recent visit had "unloosed a thousand tongues and a thousand pens."[1]

There seem to be a number of reasons for this failure of the Montessori movement to sustain the interest generated in the years before World War I. Some of these reasons have to do with Montessori herself, some with larger issues in education and in American society as a whole.

There was the fact that Montessori was a woman, a foreigner, and a Catholic. She was at the least an outsider, at the most an anomaly. There was her insistence that her system be bought as a whole package or not at all. And there was her autocratic way of dealing with those who were most interested in the spread of her ideas here. Montessori, with the compelling personality that attracted so many followers wherever she spoke and taught, remained absent from the American educational scene after 1915 and no strong individual or group was left to carry on. Her remaining supporters in the world of American education were women teachers without great influence; her critics were some of the leading scholars and educators in the country. There were no facilities here for training teachers in the use of her methods and materials, and the certificate obtained by taking her training course abroad was not recognized here as accreditation for teaching in the public school systems.

Even at the height of the prewar interest in her work, critical voices began to be heard in certain quarters. The most influential of these was that of William Heard Kilpatrick, a disciple of John Dewey and the best-known teacher of education of his generation. Kilpatrick held sway at Columbia University's Teachers College, the leading teacher-training institution in the country. His influence on an entire generation of educators was enormous. Students came from all over the world to study with him, and his lectures had to be limited to the number who could be accommodated in the auditorium; no classroom was large enough to hold them. The tuition fees paid to the university by his students were so great he was called "the million-dollar professor." This stellar figure took a dim view of the Montessori phenomenon. He visited the Casa in Rome and returned to write a little book, *The Montessori System Examined,*

227

published in 1914, in which he dismissed Montessori's thought as fifty years behind the time and her methods as unduly mechanical, formal, and restricting.

While paying lip service to Montessori's emphasis on providing more freedom for the child, Kilpatrick criticized her system for not providing more situations for social cooperation and imitative play. He characterized the Montessori materials as a "meager diet" affording "singularly little variety. . . . So narrow and limited a range of activity cannot go far in satisfying the normal child. . . . The imagination, whether of constructive play or of the more aesthetic sort, is but little utilized."[2]

Disagreeing with her view that sense training was the basis for other, more general forms of learning (a view with which psychologists today would agree, although they would state it in more sophisticated form than she did), Kilpatrick stated categorically for the teachers of America "that Madam Montessori's* doctrine of sense-training is based on an outworn and cast-off psychological theory; that the didactic apparatus devised to carry this theory into effect is in so far worthless; that what little value remains to the apparatus could be better got from the sense-experience incidental to properly directed play with wisely chosen, but less expensive and more childlike, playthings."[3]

The reasons he found for the groundswell of enthusiasm for her methods served at the same time to justify his own hero:

> A simple procedure embodied in definite, tangible apparatus is a powerful incentive to popular interest. Professor Dewey could not secure the education which he sought in so simple a fashion. Madam Montessori was able to do so only because she had a much narrower conception of education, and because she could hold to an untenable theory as to the value of formal and systematic sense-training. Madam Montessori centered much of her effort upon devising more satisfactory methods of teaching reading and writing, utilizing thereto in masterly fashion the phonetic character of the Italian language. Professor Dewey, while recognizing the duty of the school to teach these arts, feels that early emphasis should rather be placed upon activities more vital to child-life which should at the same time lead toward the mastery of our complex social environment.[4]

Kilpatrick's conclusion was that Montessori "belongs essentially to the mid-nineteenth century, some fifty years behind the present development of educational theory. . . . Stimulating she is; a contributor to our theory, hardly, if at all."[5]

*Kilpatrick refers to her throughout his book not as "Dr." but always as "Madam" Montessori.

Kilpatrick's book was widely read by the teachers of teachers, those who held policy-making positions in the educational establishment. In the perspective of the time, Kilpatrick was the authority. He gave the word, it was No, and while it is hard to say exactly the degree to which his verdict was responsible for the loss of interest in Montessori in this country, it certainly had some influence.

Other critics followed suit.

When the National Kindergarten Association sent a representative to Rome to observe the Montessori schools, she reacted much as Kilpatrick had. Her report, published in a Bulletin of the U.S. Bureau of Education in 1914,[6] while praising the "tendency toward freedom from rigidity," criticized the emphasis on individual rather than group work and the lack of creative expression. These were the criticisms that began to be heard more and more often in professional comments on Montessori: the didactic materials were too rigid and limiting; the demand that the materials be used exactly as prescribed by Montessori was insulting to the intelligence and creative talents of teachers and prevented their being adapted to different children in a different cultural milieu; there was insufficient scope for the free play of imagination, for the dramatic and poetic instincts of the child—in short, while the kindergarten as it existed in the United States could profit from some of the insights and techniques of Montessori, American educators would not buy them on an all-or-nothing basis.

Americans, then as now, tended to focus much of their thinking about social problems on the question of the schools—what they should be doing and how well or badly they were doing it. The kindergarten movement was in a state of flux, under attack for its outdated Froebelian sentimentality by educators who saw the "gifts" and such activities as paper weaving as irrelevant to the needs of twentieth-century urban education. But Montessori seemed to go too far in the opposite direction. To the question of what should be the goals of primary education in a democracy, it was John Dewey who seemed to American educators to have the most persuasive answer. The school's function was to socialize, to prepare the child to participate in the institutions of life in a modern democracy. The reform of society would be achieved through the public schools, which were seen as the logical agency for assimilating large groups of immigrant children into the larger society.

Montessori was not politically oriented in the same way that the progressive educators were. When Dewey criticized education that was "merely symbolic and formal" it seemed to many that Montessori's kind of education fit that description. Her social aims were very real but they

229

were vaguely stated and provided no exact blueprint for the outreach of the school into the community or adjustment to any particular political ideal. She began, after all, with the orientation of a biological scientist concerned with the health of the patient, not as a social theorist concerned with the health of the body politic.

Individual development was the focus of her interests, and she was convinced that it would lead to a better world, but the nature of that future world was too vaguely formulated for the spirit of the times. When she was rediscovered in this country it was at a time which had come back to where she had stood all along, emphasizing the development of individual skills and disciplines rather than social adjustment to the group. But that was not until the 1950s, when the Russians had launched Sputnik, Johnny couldn't read as well as Ivan, and the progressive education movement was blamed for stressing social and psychological adjustment at the expense of the systematic development of cognitive skills—the three Rs.

When Montessori had burst upon the American scene the kindergarten movement already had its own leadership in the schools of education that trained teachers and administrators for the public school system. Throughout the late nineteenth and early twentieth centuries education had been becoming increasingly professionalized in this country; schools of education were standardizing curricula for teachers, and professional educational societies were establishing criteria for accreditation and creating an educational elite.

A professional orientation means being centered less on a client's or consumer's opinion of one's work and more on that of other professionals. The judgment that counts is made by one's peers according to the standards they are establishing for their field. Certification is granted by the professional institutes they establish, and advertising or "propaganda," like profit making, are considered more consonant with a business than with a profession. Montessori's insistence on personally certifying all teachers and controlling the sale of the didactic materials seemed more commercial than professional, and the interest shown in her work by the popular press occasioned more scorn than respect on the part of self-conscious professionals. All of these factors helped to put her outside the pale of the dominant educational world in the United States, although in such countries as England, Holland, Spain, and Italy—wherever Montessori methods were adopted by the official school establishment—it was a different story. Here, though, where she was not programmed into the establishment but cut off from those who were carrying the field on into the future, she ceased to be a recognized force, although many of her ideas—no longer thought of as originating with her, since fewer and fewer people here remembered her—either remained around or were rediscovered by others.

Despite the widespread interest in professionalizing education, Montessori seemed to many teachers to go too far in the direction of scientific efficiency. Many of them felt threatened by what they saw as their loss of control of the classroom situation and the educational process in a school where the teacher was defined as essentially an observer and behind-the-scenes guide and in which each individual child proceeded at his own pace.

There was also some concern about taking the child out of the home at the tender age of three. It looked like social control, an un-American attack on the institution of the family.

In 1912 and 1913 the annual meetings of the National Education Association devoted to the kindergarten years had focused on Montessori's work and its implications. As the keynote speaker at the 1913 meeting of the International Kindergarten Union, Kilpatrick had stated the position he would go on to elaborate in his book the following year: except for the Case dei Bambini, Montessori's ideas were all outmoded derivations from Rousseau, Pestalozzi, and Froebel, based on a narrow view of the function of the school, and dependent on a set of too-limited mechanical devices. She had "the spirit but not the content of modern science." The lack of free play and of stories was "a lamentable defect." As for the Montessori materials, they were "based on so erroneous a psychology that we must accordingly reject the apparatus itself. In so doing," he added, "we discard probably the most popular feature of the Montessori system, a feature popular both because it can be mechanically applied and because it costs $50.00—two characteristics which suffice to commend any system of any sort to the unthinking American public."[7] It was a devastating attack, the opening shot in a campaign Kilpatrick was to wage against Montessori for several years and in which he won the battle although not, ultimately, the war.

By 1916 these meetings had turned to other topics and Montessori was no longer part of the agenda. About two hundred books and articles on the Montessori phenomenon had appeared in America and England in the years from 1909 to 1914, more than seventy in the year 1913 alone. About sixty appeared in the years between 1915 and 1918, when only five appeared. By the twenties, the flood had subsided and the name Montessori was seldom seen in print in the United States.[8]

By 1919 the definitive history *Public Education in the United States* by

E. P. Cubberley, which remained the standard work in its field for decades, repeated the gospel according to Kilpatrick: that Montessori had been "rejected" by "most American educators" because of her erroneous psychology and her system's premature emphasis on formal learning.

Looking back, it is clear that the whole American intellectual climate of the moment was inconsistent with Montessori's theoretical principles. Judging her theories to be unsound, professional educators condemned her teaching practices as well.

Eventually, the aims of American education would undergo that periodic reexamination that leads to redefinition and a change in emphases, and early learning would come into its own, along with self-motivation, programmed instructional materials, and many other features that had their origins in Montessori's work. But at the time these educational techniques were too much at variance with the prevailing American social philosophy, the late-nineteenth-century progressive movement that saw the schools primarily as an instrument of social reform and that was articulated by Dewey and his followers in the early years of this century.

In this context Montessori's ideas did seem to be foreign to the main thrust of American education, and Kilpatrick's book, widely read by educators at the time, dealt them a telling blow.

PART III
The Method and the Movement

15

The history of the Montessori movement in England—and of Montessori's role in it—contains both striking parallels to as well as differences from the American experience. It is a story that begins with the same initial enthusiasm of response to the news of the "miracles" at the first Casa dei Bambini. Here too, early accounts in professional educational journals were followed by articles in newspapers and popular magazines and, as had their American counterparts, reform-minded English educators began to make the pilgrimage to Rome, were impressed and inspired by what they saw there, and returned to start schools and societies and bring the message of a new kind of education for a new kind of child to their countrymen.

By the spring of 1912 the name Montessori was becoming familiar to readers of English periodicals and particularly of the influential London *Times Educational Supplement*, which was followed with close attention by practically all professional educators from the kindergarten or infant school to the university level.

The publication of the English edition of *The Montessori Method* and the innumerable reviews it engendered aroused both public and professional interest, which was further stimulated by the publication and discussion in the press of the official report "The Montessori System of Education," prepared by Edmond G. A. Holmes, a chief inspector of schools, for the Board of Education.[1] It seemed as though everyone concerned with schooling had read either Montessori's book or Holmes's report, an enthusiastic presentation of the advantages of auto-education, which recommended that the authorities set up classes in the public school system to experiment with English schoolchildren of nursery-kindergarten-primary age by allowing them to learn spontaneously in a prepared environment. The first printing of Holmes's pamphlet was sold out in a few days and a second was rushed to press for an eagerly waiting public.

Soon the system was being discussed, explained, and attacked at practically every professional meeting of teachers and school officials.

In March 1912 Holmes read a paper on the Montessori method to a large audience of English teachers. Holmes had been an early visitor to the Casa, along with Bertram Hawker, the man who had stopped off on his way to Australia, became engrossed in the method, and returned to England to open the first Montessori school in the drawing room of his house at East Runton, near Cromer. About a dozen village children were chosen, with the cooperation of the Norfolk educational authorities, from the East Runton elementary school, and the directress was a Miss Lydbetter, who had taken Montessori's training course and was at that moment the only bona fide Montessori-trained teacher in the country. Visitors to East Runton were impressed, and the press reported favorably on the results of this initial experiment: the children were found to be "clean, not tired, considerate, and happy"[2]—in that order.

Holmes and Hawker were instrumental, in the spring of 1912, in forming a British committee, the Montessori Society of the United Kingdom, with headquarters in Eaton Square. The society soon had two hundred members and included on its executive committee a number of wealthy, influential, and in some cases titled personages.

Journalists reported that "public interest in the movement is getting beyond the stage of curiosity"[3] and large audiences turned out for lectures on the method that Hawker gave in London, Liverpool, Sheffield, Lee, and Cambridge.

The intention of the society was to keep in touch with Maria Montessori, arrange for the training of Montessori teachers for the English schools, and educate both the teaching profession and the public about the method.

In the summer of 1912, in a letter thanking the members of the society for their interest and assistance, Montessori wrote, "I approve in substance your conditions regarding the training of teachers but I should like to have more exact information before replying to them. I should like also to know in which way the Society could prohibit the use of the name 'Montessori.' "[4]

Again, as in America, there begins the concern with the use of her name in connection with her ideas, the emphasis on protecting a system of patentable devices in addition to spreading general intellectual principles, and again one wonders if the history of the movement would have been different if Montessori had not insisted on keeping such a tight rein on all aspects of the use of her method and especially on training all teachers herself.

As a young woman she had insisted on controlling her own life and she had achieved remarkable things. Now she insisted on controlling what she had achieved. It was impossible for her to relinquish the use of her name in connection with her ideas once she became dependent on the use of those ideas for her own livelihood, her entire income, turning away from a life in which she might have done further research, written, and taught her ideas to others in some academic institution to devote herself instead to the spread of a movement she felt had to be carried on in only one "right" way.

During 1912 and 1913 the books on the method that were appearing in America were also being brought out across the Atlantic and an introduction to the Montessori system by Theodate L. Smith of Clark University,[5] another of the educators who had journeyed to Rome and then put the theory into practice in an open-air kindergarten for American children, was typical of those which, when they appeared in England, were widely reviewed and read, adding to what the press called "a growing chorus of converts."[6] Another was *Montessori Schools as Seen in the Early Summer of 1913* by Jessie White,[7] an account of how Montessori schools varied with the personality of the individual teacher directing the class.

At the same time, the publication of *The Montessori Principles and Practices* by Edward P. Culverwell,[8] a professor at Dublin University, stimulated a good deal of interest in Montessori's ideas in Ireland. A fairly balanced appraisal of the method, Culverwell's book maintained that in the end Montessori's ideas would prove right because they were consistent with the biological principles of child development and because their emphasis on liberty was consistent with the political direction in which society was moving through history.

Discussing the Culverwell book late in 1913, an English reviewer speculated that "Owing to the indiscriminate worship of blind admirers, the Montessori method may in a few years come to be looked on as a fad which has had its day," and suggested that Montessori herself was to some extent responsible for the danger: "Like a great many of her disciples, she is too apt to think or to give the impression that she thinks, that she stands alone in her knowledge and appreciation of the principles on which her system is founded." Extravagant praise of the method "by those who can see no virtue and no likeness to it in any other system must tend to irritate good teachers, and to make them, as Professor Culverwell says, not only unsympathetic, but hostile and suspicious. Those, therefore, who agree with him as to the reality of its excellence will do well to exercise in their written and spoken comments on the work of their teacher, the self-control which it is one of her chief objects to instill into the minds of the young."[9]

At numerous conferences throughout 1912 English educators discussed the merits and drawbacks of the Montessori system. The criticisms were familiar: the Montessori method catered to the "formal" and

237

ignored "the literary and artistic side of life." The appreciations were equally familiar: Education would never be the same again. "We now know that education must not begin at twelve years but at two years."[10]

Controversy raged in the columns of the staid London *Times*. Charlotte M. Mason, a now-forgotten leader in the infant school movement of the time, publicly called the method a "calamity," insisting it discarded knowledge and replaced it with "appliances and employments." The Montessori child had pretty manners, was neat and sharp-sensed, but "at the expense of another and higher sense. No fairies play about him, no heroes stir his soul; God and good angels form no part of his thought; the child and the person he will become are a scientific product . . . but song and picture, hymn and story are for the educational scrapheap."[11]

There were plenty of advocates ready to reply to this romantic—and perhaps envious—nonsense. One teacher wrote in answer to the "cheap sneers" of Mason, whose criticisms were appearing in magazine articles as well, that most children never in fact mastered the skills of reading and writing well enough to benefit from the ideas in the books they read. "The methods which prevail in the education of the young do not produce the initiative desired—the alert mind and the ready wit."[12]

In a magazine article Mason compared her own Froebelian approach with what she considered the Montessori mischief and came closer to some rational objections—if not to the method itself, then to its possible misapplications.

"It is difficult," she wrote, "to believe that a certain particular set of cubes and bricks and lacing frames and skeins of colored silks and other apparatus are the one perfect and predestined means of proper education for which the world has been waiting all these years. We must not set them up and worship them as fetishes. The danger is that some of [Montessori's] disciples may be tempted to exalt the method (the apparatus) above the principle (the freedom of the child)."[13]

Other critics said that the method had been around as long as Seguin, that Montessori had merely reedited his physiological method for defective children in the light of modern knowledge and added her own commanding personality and a certain flair for publicity. They pointed out that sense-training methods had been in use for many years in training schools for the feebleminded by devoted teachers who never thought to label these systems with their own names.[14]

The criticisms contain both a certain meanness and a certain truth. Montessori never claimed to have originated the materials of her system, but it cannot be denied that she used them for new purposes in new ways. It is also true that she cared about making the results of her discoveries known and that she impressed the world and attracted interest not only because of what she had done but what she was like. The same aggressivity that had thrust her forward, like a self-propelled rocket, from childhood, first into technical studies, then into medical school, then into public life, was applied to her later career, and the press had served throughout to make her and her work known, using her as she had used it in a symbiotic process the result of which had been to make her famous. But while she might have done her work without becoming famous, she could never have gained the fame without having accomplished what she did.

Toward the end of 1912 it was announced that the education committee of the London County Council would send one of its infant-school teachers, Lily Hutchinson, to Rome to attend the international training course Montessori would give beginning in January 1913.

As 1912 drew to a close the *Times Educational Supplement* reported that "interest in the Montessori system increases every day. The pilgrimage to Rome, where the Montessori Society of the United Kingdom have now an accredited resident representative, is becoming almost as necessary a part of the educationist's education as in the days when our great-grandfathers used to make the Grand Tour for the development of the intellect. Englishmen are learning Italian so as to be able to speak with the Dottoressa without the cumbersome intervention of an interpreter, English ladies are being sent to Rome to learn the system on the spot."[15] Culverwell's lectures in Dublin and Hawker's in various English cities were attracting audiences of as many as a thousand teachers.

The Montessori movement seemed on the brink of transforming the British educational system.

At the 1913 annual conference of teachers held by the London County Council the Montessori method was the main subject of discussion. The chairman described the method as "a subject upon which the whole educational world is agog" and suggested that council members, by virtue of their position of authority in education, "ought to know all there is to know about the Montessori method."[16]

In discussion of new ideas for classroom activities the results at the Casa dei Bambini became the standard by which teaching practices were judged. Did they train the children in self-reliance? Did they provide "a Montessori feeling"?

A dozen English teachers took the four-month training course in Rome in the spring of 1913 and returned, diplomas in hand, to set up experimental classes in public or private schools from the Hampstead Garden Suburb to the outskirts of Birmingham.

By early 1913 a London school official commented, "The topic is being everywhere discussed—at teachers' meetings, parents' meeting, educational officials' meetings, and meetings of educational amateurs and laymen. Newspapers and magazines are full of it, and there is much crash and conflict of opinion."[17]

Montessori's supporters—and young teachers in particular—pointed out that she had reversed the old doctrine which held that it doesn't matter what you teach a child so long as he hates it. But at the annual meeting of the Association of University Women Teachers at the University of London the keynote speaker attacked the Montessori system in a paper entitled "The Theory of the Primrose Path," in which she stated that "this enervating doctrine" rested on "a too ready and thoughtless identification of games with ease and mere pleasure" and an even more "fatal assumption—that all work was distasteful." This extraordinary failure to understand the most basic premise of the Montessori method—that under the right circumstances children would find work a pleasure and would pursue it for its own sake—went on to remind teachers that "pain, disagreeable effort" were "an effectual instrument for good" and to express the fear that "left to choose for ourselves, we should accomplish pitifully little." It was a not uncommon response on the part of teachers unable to tolerate the idea of "letting children sit on the floor and do what they like, as they like, when they like it, for as long as they like, and no longer."[18]

This kind of criticism on the part of the teaching establishment makes Montessori's fears of distortion of her ideas understandable even if it does not always justify her attempts to prevent it by controlling the use of her method and the spread of her ideas.

After all, there were always other voices ready to answer those of the critics. This particular diatribe was duly reported in the education columns of the *Times*, with a comment in the paper's editorial news columns which chided its author for falling into "a pitfall of logic denouncing an educational system of growing popularity on the ground that it turned work into play, that lessons cannot be worth learning if the child enjoys them! We should rather congratulate the child," said the *Times*, "on the services of a teacher who makes learning a pleasure."[19]

Now, as in America, the inevitable commercial aspects of the movement began to appear. By spring of 1913 a model Montessori classroom had been set up in the London showrooms of the firm of Philip & Tacey, which advertised "the exclusive right of manufacturing the apparatus and didactic materials for the Montessori System. Eight guineas a set."[20]

Without any salaried position, Montessori was "relying upon the support of those who believed in her, and upon fees for courses of lectures," as a member of the society put it early in 1913, announcing that the society had promised Montessori £500 a year for three years "in order to enable her to carry on her researches, to widen the sphere of her work, and to found what might in time develop into the Montessori Institute.

"In return," he said, Dr. Montessori would receive two or three picked students from England for training, who, when they returned to this country, would be able "to train teachers to work in the schools."[21]

Whether or not Montessori had actually agreed to this quid pro quo is not clear, but it was the issue over which controversy and splits inevitably occurred. It is possible that she intended only, as she later stated, to undertake to train teachers of children. Teachers themselves, she always maintained, could be trained only by her.

In January 1914, following Montessori's American tour, the London *Times* published in its regular news columns a series of articles[22] describing Montessori's enthusiastic reception by the American press and public and appraising the effects of her visit. The articles described the history, principles, and methods of the system and discussed its significance and its future, giving the subject equal or greater space than President Wilson's thoughts on the Mexican problem or the signs of war clouds gathering over the frontiers of Europe. And they made it clear that by the beginning of 1914 Montessori's ideas had had a decided influence in the infant classes of the English school system. Montessori's early English enthusiasts included a good number of the officials who ran the educational establishment.

In America, despite the interest and encouragement of some influential figures like Bell and Edison, Montessori's loyal supporters were almost exclusively women. In England, where men were not only professors of educational philosophy but where more men held administrative positions in the local schools and taught in them, it was a different story. Many of her English followers from the beginning were men, and many of them stayed with the movement through the years, unlike the American educators who fell away after her departure from the American scene.

They were men like the Reverend Cecil Grant of St. George's School at Harpenden, who told the delegates to the 1914 Conference of Educational Associations at London University that if they were to apply the scientific method to education they must call in someone who was an expert at once on the physical, mental, and teaching areas and that "God has given us that triple expert in Dr. Montessori."[23] And there was Claude A. Claremont, who took the international training course in

1913 and served as Montessori's assistant and interpreter for the 1914 course and who claimed for Montessori "a position in the education of young children such as Darwin occupied in the biological sciences."[24]

When the Reverend Grant published his *English Education and Dr. Montessori*,[25] reviewers saw in its "excessive adulation" a danger "that her more fervent admirers may hinder instead of promoting . . . by the extravagant terms which some among them are inclined to use in speaking or writing of her personality and her work."[26]

"Mr. Cecil Grant," said the *Times Educational Supplement*, "is one of those who allow their enthusiasm to run away with their judgement in this manner. There are passages in his book which can hardly fail to set people wondering whether, after all, his idol may not have feet of clay. To say that he canonizes her is to put it mildly. He is so carried away by his zeal that he regards her as a special creation of the Providence which ordereth all things in heaven and earth. She has been raised up by God 'in these last days, after much and careful preparing of the way . . . to show us how simple and inevitable, yet how new and radically change-bringing, are the required reforms.' "[27]

By the beginning of 1914 Lily Hutchinson, the infant-school teacher sent by the educational committee of the London County Council to Montessori's 1913 international training course, had submitted her report. She had, she said, gone to Rome prejudiced against the Montessori system—probably at least in part in reaction to the kind of "excessive adulation" expressed by enthusiasts like the Reverend Grant—but had returned something of an enthusiast herself. In the Casa dei Bambini she saw much that she thought could be applied with profit to the English school system. Montessori had "new theories of life and almost a new religion."[28]

Many of the sober gentlemen of the committee were somewhat skeptical. One of them remarked, "Gentlemen, this is not a report, it is a rhapsody!" They were not all as impressed as Mrs. Hutchinson, perhaps because they had not experienced Montessori's commanding presence and persuasive delivery or seen the children at work in the Casa, but most agreed with the member who felt that "in their one thousand schools the Committee might well try a small experiment in the Montessori system," and a motion was formally made that "facilities should be afforded in one of the infant schools for a trial of the new Montessori system."[29] The first Montessori class in London was set up by Lily Hutchinson—and outfitted with the materials at her own expense—in her classroom in a school on Hornsey Road.

Several English teachers were among those enrolled in Montessori's second international course in Rome from February to June of 1914 at which Anna Maccheroni directed the demonstration classes and Claude Claremont acted as English interpreter. The London *Times* carried an announcement of the course for the benefit of those who might wish to attend; tuition was fifty-one pounds sterling to be remitted to Dr. Montessori's secretary, Signorina Anna Fedeli, Via Principessa Clotilde 5, Rome.[30]

In the summer of 1914 the Montessori Society held a conference at Runton to discuss "child emancipation." Its announced purpose was "to unite educationists in a movement for freeing the children of the country from useless and cramping restriction and devitalizing pressure."[31]

It was now two years since Bertram Hawker's little class had begun here, the first Montessori school in England, and during the conference about two hundred and fifty visitors from various parts of the United Kingdom visited the class, now held in a whitewashed barn in this remote corner of East Anglia. They were drawn there, said one journalist, by "the magic word Montessori" in "the first collective tribute of educationists of this country"[32] to her work. Montessori sent a telegram in which she associated herself cordially with the conference and "gratefully acknowledged" the participants' interest in her work.

She may have felt differently at the end of the conference, when the chairman of the Montessori Society, Lord Lytton, said of the society that "its pioneer work was done and it should now develop into a larger and wider organization, embracing Montessori and other kindred movements."[33] This was precisely what Montessori did *not* want—to have her method and the movement on its behalf blend in with other theories and systems. Her insistence on the use of her name to designate her method, and her control over the use of the name and the way the method was applied, were intended specifically to retain its unique character, distinct from other systems of educaton, to keep it from being either diluted or distorted.

It was a familiar pattern, the struggle that was to repeat itself time and time again in the history of the Montessori movement. Maria Montessori could not remain associated for long with educators or supporters in any field who saw her ideas and her system of implementing those ideas as valuable more in principle than in specific practice—or, in fact, who separated the two at all. She had no use for those who saw her theory as one among a plurality of valuable contributions to a constantly evolving truth. To those whom she described as having made up their minds to

243

consider her method "on a parallel with other methods already existing in schools," she insisted that it could not be, that "it deals with a new science, tending to fix the practical principles for a reform of man."[34]

Her belief in the scientific validity of her method explains her insistence that it not be misunderstood or misapplied. What it does not explain is her seeming failure to understand the nature of scientific knowledge itself, which is constantly changing as new discoveries supersede previous ones. In the name of science she was acting like a true believer. And the religious aspect of the "propaganda" carried out on behalf of the method did not even permit ecumenism.

By the end of the year 1914 the Montessori committee had disbanded. The members resigned, a statement was issued to the effect that "it was felt that a more practical working committee would best carry on the work of Mme. Montessori in England,"[35] and a provisional committee was appointed in December to establish "rules and regulations for future work." The president of the newly formed group was Maria Montessori.

The newly organized society immediately undertook the work of "propaganda" which was its main function. There was an official "organizer," C. A. Bang, who served as Montessori's official spokesman in correspondence published in the press, where he signed himself "Dr. Montessori's authorized representative." Bang was an employee of William Heinemann, Montessori's English publisher; he had managed the Heinemann firm for twenty-five years before retiring to devote his full time to the English Montessori movement.

A London study circle was formed by Claude Claremont and other holders of the Montessori diploma to give lectures, hold discussions, and arrange visits to Montessori classes. There was a steady growth of attendance at study circle meetings and by spring of 1915 a crowded meeting of Montessorians was told by Dr. C. W. Kimmins, chief inspector of the London County Council elementary schools, that "the Montessori movement had passed through its first experimental phase in this country and now claims consideration from serious educational thinkers."[36]

In May Dr. Kimmins was able to report on the results of experiments with the method by English teachers. The Montessori children were found to be about a year ahead of others academically, more resourceful, and better able to overcome difficulties in their work. From the city of Leeds, where the method had also been tried, came reports of similar results. Montessori children were superior in "powers of reasoning and judgement, self-reliance and control, as well as patience, perseverance, honesty and industry."[37] There were those who questioned the design of the experiment—to what extent were these impressive results due to the enthusiasm of the adults and their expectations being conveyed to the children and to what extent to the system itself? There were no control groups to answer such a question. But these criticisms were all but drowned out by the chorus of enthusiastic response to a system that could accomplish so much in so short a time.

Demands began to come from teachers and school authorities for some form of practical training in the new method. Where were the facilities for training teachers in the understanding of the methods and the use of the materials that could achieve such impressive results? Some holders of the Montessori diploma announced plans to give lectures and provide practice work in demonstration schools, but Dr. Kimmins, presumably speaking for Montessori, cautioned against rushing to introduce the method without adequate preparation, lest any resultant failures "discredit a very important movement."[38]

Plans were announced for Montessori to come to London and give a training course in the autumn of 1914, but the war intervened and she did not come until five years later.

16

In every major European country and as far afield as Australia and India in the years before World War I there were private individuals, usually women, who took up the Montessori cause and enthusiastically undertook the work of establishing schools, usually privately financed, and societies.[1]

The story was always similar to that of Anne George in the United States, these early pioneers attending one of Montessori's first training courses, bringing *Il Metodo* back to their own countries, and often arranging for its translation and publication there. In France, it was a Mme. Pujol-Ségalas who took Montessori's course in Rome in 1910 and returned to Paris to open La Source, the first Maison des Enfants in France, in the Champ de Mars section in October 1911. In Switzerland, it was a Mlle. Bontempi in Ticino, and there was a Fräulein van den Steinen in Germany, a Mme. Destrée in Belgium, a Miss de Lisa in South Australia.

An account of the Casa dei Bambini published in a Moscow educational magazine in 1912 attracted the attention of Tolstoy's daughter, Countess Tatiana Tolstoy, and in December of that year she read a paper on the Montessori system at a congress of teachers in Moscow, where it caused a sensation. The first Montessori classes in the Russian empire were begun in Vilna with materials obtained from the United States. The physicist V. V. Lermontov read about the system in the English educational literature and set up experimental classes, also with materials from America, in St. Petersburg.

Even during World War I the spread of the movement, although considerably attenuated, did not come to a halt. In the spring of 1915 an idealistic young American woman in Paris, M. R. Cromwell, whom the London *Times* described as having "in memory of two of her sisters devoted her life and fortune to this cause,"[2] set up Montessori classes for refugee children and war orphans and a workshop in the rue Marbeuf where disabled and blinded veterans manufactured the materials and furniture for schools in France, Belgium, and Serbia and even taught manual work to the refugee and orphaned children. The project's committee of sponsors included the American ambassador and the philosopher Henri Bergson, and the Queen of the Belgians ordered two sets of the materials with the expressed intention of bringing influence to bear on the government to transform her country's schools into Montessori schools.

French statesman André Tardieu was traveling in California when he came across Montessori schools there and became so intrigued he sent long cables describing them to the French minister of education. Schools soon sprang up in numerous towns outside Paris and when the French edition of *Il Metodo* appeared, in a translation by Miss Cromwell, it was with an official paean of praise from the chief inspector of primary schools in France, who wrote the preface.

When Montessori returned to Europe from her second American trip it was to take up her work in what was to her a new country—Spain—at the invitation of local government officials in Barcelona.

The first Montessori schools in Spain had been started in Barcelona in 1913 by Catalans struggling to revive their cultural traditions and institutionalize them in the face of opposition from the government in Madrid.

The struggle for independence by the Catalans, Basques, and Galicians against the Castilian state—the demand for regional integrity based on race and traditions and expressing itself most dramatically in the demand for the revival of the Catalonian language and culture—dominated Spanish politics for the first four decades of the twentieth century and was to play a crucial role in the fate of the Montessori movement there. Catalonianism was a movement not of the masses of people but of the intellectual middle class; it was ultimately doomed by the economic and social unrest that spread through postwar Europe and culminated in World War II.

Interest in the Montessori method had begun in Spain as early as 1911 with the publication in a Barcelona educational magazine, *Revista de Educación,* of a translation of the *McClure's* articles. Soon the method was being discussed and debated in other periodicals as well. Among those who were intrigued by the accounts of the "miracle of San Lorenzo" was an educator named Juan Palau Vera.[3] What he read impressed but did not convince him. Thinking there must be a good deal of journalistic exaggeration—as well as a significant dose of what he called "feminine imagination"—in the reports of how three- and four-year-olds were teaching themselves to read and write, he decided to visit the Casa dei Bambini and see for himself. He persuaded the educational authorities of Barcelona to send him to Rome to report on the experiment and, like so many others, he returned a convert. He also returned with the Dottoressa's permission to set about translating *Il Metodo*. The book's publication in Spain made the method even better known. The authorities sent two teachers and an inspector of schools to the 1914 international course in Rome and approached Montessori for help in setting up a Casa dei Bambini. She agreed.

In the spring of 1915, before leaving for America and the Exposition at San Francisco, Montessori sent Anna Maccheroni to Barcelona, where, early in March, with the cooperation of the Catalan government, she opened a small school with just five children—one three-year-old and four who were almost five years old.

By October the school had enrolled over one hundred children. There had been no attempt to publicize the school and no promotion was undertaken; there were no prospectuses and no newspaper articles. The parents of the original five children told others, who brought their children to the school and asked that they be allowed to attend. The spontaneous word-of-mouth campaign was so effective that by October the school had to be moved to larger quarters. Plans were made for Montessori to go to Barcelona from San Francisco when the Exposition ended, and to give a training course there beginning in mid-February 1916.

The Catalan government, fervently interested in educational reforms as part of a broad social program intended to further the cause of regional identification and autonomy, welcomed the Montessori experiment. Here, it seemed, she had finally found the opportunity she had been waiting for, the chance to experiment on a large scale under her own control with the application of her method to children of various ages and backgrounds, and to extend the method into the program of the elementary-school years.

When Montessori returned to Europe from California she met Maccheroni at Algeciras. Adelia Pyle, who was with Montessori, wrote to Helen Parkhurst: "There was Maccheroni, the same dear old Maccheroni, her figure a little more bent, her hair a little more untidy, but just as full as ever of overflowing enthusiasm." And Parkhurst described Maccheroni, always preceding Montessori and getting things ready for her arrival, as "like a John the Baptist smoothing the way for the Dottoressa."[4]

After a short stop in the sunny port and a couple of days in Madrid, Montessori, Maccheroni, and Pyle went on to Barcelona together to make preparations for the course to be given there.

One of the students of the 1916 Barcelona course wrote home to England:

. . . The abacus and moveable geometrical forms are of course not original, but as instruments for the study of mathematics used in accordance with the Montessori principle of freedom in auto-education they take on a novel air. Grammatical analysis may seem an ambitious subject for children of from seven to ten, but for children who have been brought up in the previous Montessori schools it becomes amazingly simple. The knowledge and correct use of parts of speech is acquired as a game, leading to ease and even elegance in composition. The mere pushing about of pieces of cardboard inscribed with nouns, verbs, prepositions, etc., seems to clarify ideas and to give ease in expression. The claim of Dr. Montessori, as a follower of Seguin, that the truest system of education of children is through the senses, seemed to me to be entirely vindicated by actual results, and moreover, that the principle could be applied much further than to infancy. I had ample opportunity of observing startling results of touch as an aid to learning both in the schools in Barcelona and at a very remarkable school in Palma, Majorca, and that the whole system has a wonderful way of turning rampageous little urchins into cheerfully diligent little students, whose pleasure it is to be quiet, industrious, and well behaved.[5]

Out of the little class begun by Maccheroni in Barcelona in 1915 evolved the Escola Montessori, with infant and primary departments for three- to ten-year-olds, and the Seminari Laboratori de Pedagogiá, an institute for teaching, research, and training in the Montessori method founded and supported by the Catalan government as part of its interest in developing its own language, its own schools, its own government.

There were 185 students enrolled in the 1916 course, which had a surprisingly international character considering the condition of Europe at the time.[6] The majority were teachers from Barcelona or elsewhere in the province of Catalonia, but others had been sent by the educational authorities in other parts of Spain. Teachers were also sent from Portugal, Britain, Canada, and the United States. The course was held under the official auspices of and was partly supported by the government of Catalonia and the municipality of Barcelona, whose officials were particularly eager to welcome the British and Americans. Official hospitality was extended at welcoming receptions, and there were concerts of national folk songs and traditional dances of the Catalan villages. The mood was infectious and one student of the course wrote, "A great enthusiasm bound us all into one sympathetic body as we listened from day to day to the eloquent unfolding of her principles by the Dottoressa."[7]

The course was held in the historic old part of the city. A Catalan-style royal blue and orange armchair was provided for Montessori, who sat in it while giving her lectures in Italian, from which they were translated sentence by sentence into Catalan rather than Castilian Spanish.

English-speaking students sat at a separate table where Adelia Pyle translated into English. About half of the lectures dealt with the new elementary materials and the method of using them in the teaching of arithmetic, geometry, and grammar. It was the year of publication of *L'autoeducazione nelle Scuole Elementari*; by the following year, 1917, the book would appear in English as *The Advanced Montessori Method* and in numerous other translations.

There were two public Montessori schools in Barcelona in addition to the one directed by Maccheroni, one a state school established by the Spanish government and one a municipal school established by the Barcelona authorities, and these provided demonstration classes for the course.

The setting with which the Catalan government had provided Montessori to carry out her experiment was all she could have wished—the perfect prepared environment. The institute was housed in an old building of traditional Spanish architecture with spacious grounds, gardens, orchards, and winding, palm-lined paths. There were little pools with fountains and goldfish, sheds and cages for pets, all under the brilliant southern sky.

In the classrooms children drew at little easels, sang and played musical instruments, danced, played in sand piles, and modeled with clay, in addition to working with the materials, including the new ones Montessori was developing for the teaching of history, geography, and science.[8]

In a memoir published at the time of Montessori's death, a Barcelona teacher described the way in which the Catalans had taken Montessori to their hearts and her reaction to their adulation.

On Christmas Eve of her first year in Barcelona, Montessori attended midnight mass at the Church of Our Lady of Pompei and took communion. During the ceremony of Catalan Christmas music that followed, Montessori, seated in the midst of a group of officials, was unable to stifle her sobs. Maccheroni apologized to those around them for the Dottoressa's "weakness," explaining that she was still affected by the recent death of her father, but the Spaniards were not critical of this display of emotion, they were touched by it. "She had cried with us," said one of her admirers, "she was ours." When the service ended she was engulfed by a crowd of well-wishers offering her sympathy, expressing their admiration for her, inviting her to visit their schools and see their children.

Embarrassed at having broken down in public and overwhelmed by the number of invitations she could not possibly accept, Montessori responded much as she had to the florid praise of her charms as a young feminist twenty years earlier—by insisting on the seriousness of her purpose, the importance of her work. Leaving the cathedral, she said to Maccheroni, in words that bear the ponderous mark of having been transmitted through the years by those who revered her but that still reveal something of her own character:

> Many who haven't understood me think that I'm a sentimental romantic who dreams only of seeing children, of kissing them, of telling them fairy tales, that I want to visit schools to watch them, to cuddle them and give them caramels. They weary me! I am a rigorous scientific investigator, not a literary idealist like Rousseau. I seek to discover the man in the child, to see in him the true human spirit, the design of the Creator: the scientific and religious truth. It is to this end that I apply my method of study, which respects human nature. I don't need to teach anything to children: it is they who, placed in a favorable environment, teach me, reveal to me spiritual secrets as long as their souls have not been deformed.[9]

Years later, Harvard psychologist Jerome Bruner described Montessori as a "strange blend of the mystic and the pragmatist."[10] Her dual nature seems to have been stimulated in different ways by the cultures of the various countries between which she moved throughout her life, responding to the world around her like a pupil in a Montessori classroom to the prepared environment. Here in Spain, insisting on her identity as a scientist, she sounds like nothing so much as a mystic. At other times, in other places, it was her practicality that asserted itself in her statements about her work. If one of these was England, another was Holland.

In 1917 Montessori was invited to lecture to the Pedagogical Society of Amsterdam. It was her first visit to Holland, a country that proved particularly hospitable to her ideas and one in which her method took root early and remained alive and which she made her home during the last fifteen years of her life—although she was absent from it for longer periods of time than she was there.

The first Casa dei Bambini in Holland had been started in Amsterdam in 1914 by Caroline W. Tromp, who had been trained by Montessori in Rome. During World War I, with international communications interrupted and training by Montessori herself impossible, a teacher-training system was established in Holland which provided a regular two-year course in the Montessori precepts and methods. Thus a constant supply of teachers was provided and the movement was kept in close touch with Montessori through the dedicated Miss Tromp and her colleague Rosa Joosten-Chotzen, another of Montessori's early pupils, who also instituted a system of regular monthly meetings of Montessori teachers to share their experiences and keep abreast of new developments in the movement. Thus in Holland, unlike the many countries where the movement sprang up only to dwindle during and after the war, the system was institutionalized in the regular educational establishment and its leaders maintained constant contact with Montessori throughout the years, as well as forming a community for exchange of ideas and mutual support instead of becoming isolated and fragmented. In this fertile soil the Dutch Montessori movement flourished.

On that first visit in 1917 Montessori was introduced to Professor Hugo de Vries, the Dutch botanist, then in his seventies, who had made important discoveries in plant evolution and in 1900 had confirmed the Mendelian laws of heredity. Hearing about Montessori's work, De Vries was struck by the parallels between her ideas about the development of children and his own theories of the development of plants, and he later suggested that she make use of his term "sensitive periods" to describe her observations about the stages of children's growth and learning.

As a result of the interest aroused by her visit, the Netherlands Montessori Society was founded in 1917.

In 1916–17 Montessori visited the United States again. She spoke at the Child Education Foundation in New York, but there was no lecture tour, and little publicity.

The main source of financial support for the New York-based institution which was to carry out the Montessori work in America when Montessori left the country was the family of Adelia Pyle. But when their daughter announced her intention to follow Montessori to Europe and dedicate her life to the Dottoressa's work, converting to Catholicism to boot, the family disinherited her, dropped the name Montessori from the institution, and renamed it the Child Education Foundation. Adelia Pyle eventually left Montessori. The Child Education Foundation continued to operate under Helen Parkhurst and Anna Eva McLin, who took over when Parkhurst left to direct her own movement. In the winter of 1916–17, when Montessori lectured there, the Foundation still offered courses in the Montessori method at its headquarters on West End Avenue.

Montessori left for Los Angeles in the spring of 1917, gave a course there, and attended the wedding of her son Mario to his first wife, an American named Helen Christie, in December 1917, before leaving the United States for the last time.

While there, she issued a proposal calling for the establishment of an organization to be called La Croce Bianca, the White Cross. Its purpose would be "to treat the children of war; to gather up the new human generation and to save it by a special method of education." The plan was to train teacher-nurses to work with the depressed and frightened children of the war-ravaged countries. A free course would include first aid, nervous diseases, pediatric dietetics, psychology, domestic science and agriculture, and a theoretical and practical course in the Montessori method especially applied to these deprived and disturbed children, to be taught by Montessori herself. Working groups would then be sent out to France, Belgium, Serbia, Rumania, Russia—wherever there were refugee children of the European war. It was a plan that was never realized but that anticipated in conception the work that was done with children evacuated during the London blitz of the next war as well as numerous other programs for working with refugee children both during and after World War II. And although the White Cross never actually came into existence her plea did result in the establishment of Montessori classes in some thirty cities of France for the benefit of children who had been victims of the war.[11]

The issue of Montessori education was not forgotten in England during the war years. Throughout the fall and winter of 1915 and well into spring of 1916 correspondents argued in the columns of the *Times Educational Supplement* over the role of the imagination in the Montessori system. Critics accused Montessori of emphasizing the motoric and the realistic at the expense of the creative imagination and dramatic play. Her utilitarian position was felt by many to be too restricting to the child's mind.

What they failed to see was that she had worked out her system in a culture in which children were not sent away to live at school at an early age. In Italy, less was expected of the school, whose function was "instruction" *(istruzione)* or what Montessori called "pedagogy" *(pedagogia),* a matter of intellectual training as distinct from *educazione,* upbringing in general, including what is transmitted outside of school by family, community, and society at large. School was expected to teach one all there was to know about how to read but not necessarily all there was to know about how to live. Italian children lived at home, usually amid a large family, indulged in many ways, including stories and play, which Montessori would have thought it unnecessary to introduce into the school curriculum. School was a place for the development of cognitive skills and a self-reliant character, not because these were the only things that mattered, but because the other things were taken care of elsewhere—in the home and to some extent in the church.

While the war was raging in Europe, news of education was eclipsed by news of battles, but *It Metodo* continued to appear in new translations—by 1917 it had appeared in English, French, German, Russian, Spanish, Catalonian, Polish, Rumanian, Danish, Dutch, Japanese, and Chinese—and when a new major work by Montessori was published it was widely reviewed and discussed.

With the publication of the two volumes of *The Advanced Montessori Method—Spontaneous Activity in Education* and *The Montessori Elementary Material*—which appeared in English translation in 1917, Montessori extended the method beyond the nursery and into the elementary school, applying it to the teaching of grammar, reading, arithmetic, geometry, drawing, music, and metrics in those years.

Reviewing the book, the *Times Educational Supplement* said in early 1918 that the Montessori method "has reached a stage when it is an integral part of the new education."[12] There were criticisms too, and they had a familiar ring—there was too great an emphasis on apparatus; the methods of language teaching were too rigid.

Throughout the war years, the Montessori Society continued to meet and to stimulate discussion of the method in educational circles through lectures and magazine and journal articles. During a debate in the House of Commons in January 1918[13] a member of Parliament chided the minister of munitions because wartime restrictions prevented the manufacture of the Montessori materials, while toy trains and other trinkets were still being produced. The minister promised to look into the matter.

When the war ended in the fall of 1918 Montessori began to make plans for her long-delayed visit to England. It was decided that she would give a two-month training course in England, to begin in September 1919.

The end of the war found interest in her ideas and their application to the local schools still high in England. Articles in the press compared Montessori to Darwin and Lamarck, to Tolstoy, to Bergson and Jung, and lauded her method as a means toward liberating the individual, freeing him to work out his own destiny, an aim that suited the postwar mood. Among signs of the return to normalcy noted in the press two months after the armistice was the fact that the manufacture of the Montessori didactic material was going ahead now that wartime restraints on the necessary supplies had been lifted.

News that Dr. Montessori would come to London to give her first training course there brought over two thousand applications. From these, two hundred and fifty students were selected.

Montessori had arranged with her manager in London, C. A. Bang, for Anna Maccheroni to precede her in July, to inspect Montessori classes in London schools to be used for demonstration of the method for the training course, and to take care of other details before Montessori arrived.

When her two assistants met Montessori's boat at Folkestone, Maccheroni remembered later, "She appeared from her cabin in the ship wearing a light-colored waterproof—and I had told Mr. Bang she was always in black!"[14]

When Montessori's boat train arrived at Charing Cross on the morning of August 30, the day before her forty-ninth birthday, she was, as usual, received like a queen. It was her first visit to England since the summer, just twenty years before, when the young woman doctor had called on all her English colleagues trying to find a copy of Seguin's English book.

Waiting to receive her as she stepped from the train were officials of the Italian legation and the Montessori Society and a crowd of teachers, some of them former students now teaching with her methods in England, some of them about to become her students and eager for a glimpse of her.

She was decidedly plump now, with a dowager's bearing, a close-fitting hat on her head in place of the extravagant wide-brimmed millinery that she had worn before the war. There were the usual embraces with former students, who were always more than just students, and who had not seen her since before the war, and there was a little ceremony of welcome with a bouquet of malmaisons tied with the Italian colors, not unlike the flowers she had presented to the queen of Italy when she herself was a young medical student. Now she stood, at one of those moments of arrival in a new place that occurred over and over again throughout her peripatetic career until the very end of her life, and heard herself once again described as one of the great innovators of the age, a woman who would change mankind by changing childhood. Then the speeches ended and she thanked her admirers, smiling graciously as she stepped into a waiting car amid the cheers, to be driven off to the Ritz Hotel.[15]

The English prepared to receive her with the same enthusiasm as the Americans six years before. The world had changed. The turn-of-the-century mood of optimism and belief in the possibility of infinite social and political progress toward human perfectibility had died in the years of unprecedented slaughter. The world seemed to have been taken apart and then put back together differently. Even the relief that the war had ended was tempered by a certain disillusionment, an exhaustion that seemed more than physical. In England, it was a cold winter, plagued by labor troubles. But one thing that had not changed was the kind of response that Montessori and her message elicited from the press and the public.

Her arrival among the English was described in the newspapers as "the beginning of a great era for the children of this country," an event of significance such as the earlier visits of Garibaldi and Mazzini, "fighters also for the true liberation of mankind and for the type of freedom that precludes anarchy."[16]

Montessori gave the first lecture of her training course on September 1 at St. Bride's Foundation Institute in Fleet Street. The audience of teachers listened raptly as she spoke in her measured Italian, interpreted sentence by sentence by Lily Hutchinson, the teacher who had been sent by the London County Council to her 1913 international course. The lectures were given three evenings a week, with mornings set aside for supervision by Montessori's assistants in the use of the materials and observation of the children at work in the Council schools. There were fifty hours of lectures on the system as applied to children from three to eleven, both the method and materials having now been extended into the elementary years as described in the two volumes of *The Advanced Montessori Method.*

In addition there were fifty hours of practice teaching under the supervision of Montessori and her assistants, Maccheroni, Adelia Pyle, and Anna Fedeli, and fifty hours of observation in recognized Montessori classes. Students prepared a scrapbook on the basis of their experience working with the materials and, at the end of the course, after passing both written and oral examinations, received a diploma, signed by Maria Montessori, entitling them to teach children as accredited Montessori directresses but explicitly stating that it did *not* qualify them to train other teachers. The holder of the diploma could now open a school and call it a Montessori school, and after two years of work as a Montessori directress would have her diploma endorsed to that effect. The fee for the course was thirty-five guineas—twenty for those who already held the diploma for the infant course given in the years before she had worked out its further application to the elementary grades. The form of the course—lectures, demonstration, practice teaching, preparation of the "Book of Materials"—remained the same throughout the years in which Montessori taught, although she never repeated her lectures verbatim, speaking extemporaneously and relying on different interpreters.

Montessori's presence on the scene always made a difference. Her visit to England stimulated a widespread interest among both educators and public in her method and in the schools that had been quietly using it here and there throughout Britain over the last eight years.

The Montessori Society enjoyed a new flurry of activity now. Membership in the London group had grown to over a thousand. There were offices and a library in Tavistock Square. And there were regular reports in the press of meetings and of the formation of societies in other English cities, of lectures, study circle meetings, classes for children's nurses. Items appeared regularly throughout the fall and winter of her stay, reporting on her lectures and interpreting her ideas.

As always, she found time to talk with journalists, and she found her Boswell in one of the editors of the *Times Educational Supplement,* an admirer named Sheila Radice who wrote a series of thoughtful and sympathetic articles which appeared throughout the fall and winter of 1919 during Montessori's stay in England and were published in book form the following year as *The New Children: Talks with Dr. Maria Montessori.*

To critics who complained that Montessori reduced the world of the child to nothing but the didactic apparatus, Radice replied that "no one can continue to nurse such an absurdity who meets this clever, sensible woman-doctor and woman of the world face to face, who has listened to her terse summings-up and trenchant criticisms, and noted her kindly, sympathetic, assured manner and the occasional deprecatingly humorous glance of her dark, far-seeing eyes. . . ."

"Nothing annoys her more," Radice told her readers—and they included just about everyone in the English educational world—"though at the same time it sometimes makes her laugh, than the unintelligent swallowing of doctrine. Mothers come to her asking in all good faith whether they are to allow their children liberty to the extent of putting their feet on the table at meals. '*Per carità!* Get up at once!' she has exclaimed to a conscientious teacher found dishevelled on the ground with a class of little Bolshevists sitting on top of her."[17]

Plans for a banquet to be given by distinguished English educators in Montessori's honor in early October had to be postponed because of the labor troubles that were making normal activities impossible. The railway strike was in full swing and many of those who wanted to honor her would not have been able to attend. The dinner was put off until early December but Montessori, undaunted, managed to make her way around London and environs, Anna Maccheroni always at her side, lecturing, showing her films, talking to groups of teachers as well as at public meetings full of interested parents.

Twenty-seven hundred people came to a public lecture she gave at Westminster illustrated by her films of the children at work. She was also giving a short course of three lectures for about fifteen hundred teachers unable to take the regular training course, and attending a round of conferences, meetings, and receptions in her honor that continued throughout her stay. At a reception in October at University College she described herself as "a little overcome by the greatness of the assembly"[18] and by the fact that members of a great university had come to meet her.

She spoke with the modesty her fame had allowed her to assume, and the same gracious manner reporters had noted thirty years ago, which they now described as matronly rather than girlish charm. The times had changed more than she herself. Her speaking style now seemed a bit old-fashioned in the high-flown generalities that punctuated the passages of keen observation and shrewd common sense. "Let us call the teachers," she would say, "not to learn a new method, but to follow a new path in the light of a new hope. . . ."[19] Always, there were people who loved it, and for those who didn't, there were others around to attest to what she was like in private, when she was not stage front. Perhaps "in private" is not quite right. Few moments of real intimacy have yet been recorded by anyone who shared them with her. But at least she seems to have shown another side when she had a public of just one, such as Sheila Radice.

Sheila Radice liked Montessori and that, together with her intelligence and the English tendency to understate rather than go overboard, made her a better spokesperson for the Dottoressa than those who worshiped uncritically. Her articles provided not only a lucid and balanced exposition of Montessori's ideas in theory and in operation, they provided also a few glimpses of Montessori as a living woman and not a plaster saint.

There is Montessori sighing and saying, "Words, words, words!" as she puts down another of the innumerable commentaries on the implications of her method. "Let us leave aside these questions of historical comparison and philosophical abstraction," she says to Radice, "and get back to the living child."[20] And we see again the clinician, oriented toward observing reality rather than abstract theorizing. She watches little children's doings for hours and listens interminably to what they say.

She tells Radice that children have been taken out of the mill of industry only to be put into the scholastic mill, which, with what Radice describes as "a trained physician's eye and a great deal of Latin common sense," Montessori sees to be injuring them, both mentally and physically, almost as much.[21]

When Radice brings her a copy of Kilpatrick's *The Montessori System Examined*, "in which her doctrines were proved by the writer, with chapter and verse, to be psychologically heretical," Montessori says her only reply "is to suggest that he should open his eyes. I can't help it if things he says are impossible continually happen."[22]

It is a statement that recurs in the history of ideas with every genius— someone with the capacity to see human experience or natural phenomena in a radically new way that eventually becomes part of the way all men understand themselves and the world. It echoes Galileo, who had also been led to formulate his theories by what he had observed, seeing what no one had ever seen before in phenomena that had been there all along, insisting that the earth *does* move, despite the theological objections of the Inquisition. And Freud remembered that when he pointed out that Charcot's ideas about hysteria were inconsistent with the prevailing theories of the time, his teacher replied, "Ça n'empêche pas d'exister," a remark which, Freud says, "left an indelible mark upon my mind."[23]

Transfer of training may be theoretically impossible; Montessori sees it happening every day, in children "meeting new combinations of circumstances and overcoming them by means of aptitudes developed elsewhere."[24]

"Each impulse of the child is translated into action by means of the material, and, working itself out in repeated spontaneous exercises, trains aptitudes which will combine with other aptitudes to form new activities later on, till finally we come to the highest and most complex human activities—literature, art, craft, science, music, dancing, drama. It is all a web of phenomena—*un intreccio di cose.*"[25]

"Fortunately, the children are there, behaving as I say they behave, and people who do not believe me can go down into the schools and see!"[26]

Critics say her ideas are "too ecstatic to be scientific"? Montessori retorts that the ecstasy is in the child: "The fine differentiation that the child learns through the use of the material changes the face of nature for the child. All objects henceforth describe themselves to the child. All objects seem to say to the child, 'I am like this—I am like that.' The child follows them in a kind of ecstasy. So it discovers the world, and the world, which is infinitely richer and more logical than this material, completes its education."[27]

Radice describes the goings-on in the Montessori demonstration class at the London County Council elementary school in Hornsey Road, where a group of seven- to eleven-year-olds are at work with the advanced material. In what looks like disorder each child is making his own order, one little boy at geometrical drawings, another at word cards, others with bead frames, another reading. In the middle of the room, the children oblivious to them, are Montessori and Maccheroni, standing and talking in rapid Italian, then bursting into laughter. Later, Montessori repeats the conversation to a visitor, adding a few refinements that have occurred to her since and that start them laughing all over again.

To Radice, the atmosphere of a classroom where Montessori is present is "a sufficient comment on the ritualistic, semi-religious interpretation of the method that one sometimes sees."[28] If Montessori was becoming something of a sacred object to many of her followers, that quality does not seem to have entered into her relations with those she taught, children or adults.

Does she think all teachers should use her materials? Only if they want to get the same results that she has! She would enforce no system for which there was no demand, but she does insist on one thing—that teachers who *do* use her method make no variations in it. In one of her lectures at St. Bride's she makes very clear how she thinks about this crucial matter:

"The material has formed itself, not arbitrarily, but according to the natural reactions of the child. How did I know what to retain? The psychology of the child taught me. *La psicologia è il padrone.*" The didactic material is "a delicate instrument"; in its absence, or if it is not presented in the right order, in the right way, "the indicative reactions will not occur." The natural moment for the "explosion into writing" will be lost, the right moment for learning about colors will pass. "If he had not this simple, accessible, arithmetical material, we should never have suspected the child of eight of being so passionate an arithmetician."[29]

She believed that she had worked out a correct way of using the right materials that inevitably led to the child's orderly development. Without it, or if it were used haphazardly, the child would still learn by fits and starts, but not as much, as soon, as well. Believing that to be so—and the argument must rest on belief, since no controlled laboratory-type experiments ever established the truth or falsity of the proposition—she was bound to be chagrined by the fact that her materials were being adapted by others to use in their own way but were still referred to with her name. Toy manufacturers had not yet begun to copy elements of her system on a large scale, but there were reports of what the *Times Educational Supplement* referred to as "home-made apparatus designed on principles similar to those underlying the Montessori didactic apparatus in both nursery schools and infant schools."[30] By 1929, when a mother wrote asking "where apparatus similar to the Montessori could be bought but for a more moderate sum," an English nursery-school publication could reply: the Auto-Educational Institute, "where cheap Montessori apparatus can be bought."[31]

But Montessori never maintained that the materials were everything, and Radice pointed out to the Anglo-Saxon public that if Montessori didn't emphasize the canons of right and wrong, did not concern herself with "discipline" in the sense of proper behavior, it was because it never occurred to her it was necessary. To a member of a Catholic Latin civilization like that of Italy, "the ordinary canons of human behavior were a matter of course."[32] and were established in the home before the child ever came to school. As for the games, singing, dancing, and drawing which critics found lacking in her system, all these existed in her schools; she did not dwell on them in her lectures because she couldn't conceive of a system of education without them.

Montessori told Radice that those who were waiting for her word on secondary education and the psychology of the adolescent would have to wait a while longer. She thought even an imperfect system of secondary education would not do lasting harm to a child who had "started fair." The Jesuits said that if they could have the child from birth until the age of seven they could mold him as they wished. Montessori's idea, she told Radice, was that "if we can keep the hands of the adult generation off the child from birth until seven it will have a good chance of growing up as nature intends."[33]

It was a nice aphorism, but it betrayed two characteristic limitations of her thinking. For one thing, she minimized the role of the adult mind in her own system, the extent to which the adult prepared the environment, determined what the child would find there and how he would use it. For another, she missed the role the adult must play in any system, the fact that there is always a relationship. The child identifies, or he reacts against, but always he learns in an emotional context of his relationship with the most important others in his life—his parents or hose who come to stand for them. To say that "things are the best teachers," as Montessori liked to do, is to ignore a fundamental aspect of human development, which she does not ignore in fact, but only in theory.

She constantly stresses the negative aspect of the adult's influence on the child: "It is not the duty of the adult to develop the child, it is his duty to safeguard the child's development.[34]. . . We await the successive births in the soul of the child. We give all possible material, that nothing may lack to the groping soul, and then we watch for the perfect faculty to come, safeguarding the child from interruption so that it may carry its efforts through."[35] To talk of standing back and allowing the child to develop in relation to his mastery of the inanimate world minimizes not

261

only the role of the adult in the child's life but the very phenomenon of the child's emotional life, as though it were a thing apart from his cognitive development.

No matter what he does, or fails to do, the adult is always teaching the child—by how he takes care of him, by how he himself behaves. Only after the groundwork for his self-esteem has been laid by a certain amount of gratifying experience is the child capable of finding pleasure in achievement for its own sake. Montessori stressed that pleasure in that achievement, but played down the emotional aspect of development at that earliest stage where all living is learning. But this is only to say that she was not always clear about why her system worked, not to deny that it did indeed work.

One wonders what it was in her own early experience that took shape in her character as the need to emphasize independence above everything else—first her own, then that of children in general. Her independence was, of course, her strength. It was also, in some way, her weakness. It may have blinded her to something important about her own life and about human relationships in general. And that blindness made for a kind of loneliness that she seems occasionally to have acknowledged beneath her independence, her self-sufficiency. Throughout her career she had followers, but no peers; sycophants, but no real colleagues. Most of those who were closest to her throughout her life stood in the same relation to her as Anna Maccheroni, who referred to herself apologetically in a discussion of Montessori's work as "I who am nobody." [36]

When she was almost fifty, Montessori said:

> I don't know what to do. There is so much of it, and nobody will ever collaborate. Either they accept what I say, and ask for more, or else they waste precious time in criticizing. What I want now is a body of colleagues, research workers, who will examine what I have already done, apply my principles as far as I have gone, not in a spirit of opposition or conviction, but as a matter of pure experiment. Then they can help me with constructive criticism, after, not before, the event. I have never yet had anyone—starting from my own previous body of knowledge—work shoulder to shoulder with me in a scientific independence. Now that doctors and psychologists are beginning to take an interest in normal children, perhaps some of them will help me. At present I am in a kind of isolation, which is the last thing I desire. *Questo lavoro è troppo per una persone sola—sono troppo sola nel mondo.*[37]

Human beings do not always know what it is they really desire. Montessori said she wanted colleagues, yet it sounds very much as though what she really wanted was not an "other," but an extension of herself; not someone with different ideas to add to hers, but someone to help her carry out "my principles . . . after, not before, the event." This sounds not so much like another mind ás just another pair of hands. There can't be collaboration without differences, there can be only assistance. And time and again, when differences arose, she seemed, despite her words, to behave in a way that could only leave her "in a kind of isolation . . . alone in the world."

Though she may have lacked colleagues in the fullest sense of the word, Montessori never lacked for admirers. Everywhere she came to speak or teach, every place she demonstrated the achievements of her system, there were those who applauded and made efforts to support the work in whatever way they could.

During her stay in England in the winter of 1919 a public appeal was drawn up by a committee of Montessori enthusiasts for the purpose of collecting funds with which to found a Montessori training institute in England. It was the American plan all over again, this time presented as "a worthy war memorial for those who have given their lives for their country."

The amount the committee hoped to collect was £25,000, a small enough sum to achieve what the appeal described as "the glorious Montessori vision," nothing less than "the Kingdom of Heaven on Earth . . . this world as God means it to be. A world of beings perfectly balanced, spiritually, mentally and physically . . . knowing nothing but the joy of work and service. Dr. Montessori is proving that it is our wrong attitude of mind towards the child that has caused all the disharmonies and criminalities of the world. It is in order that parents and students may be trained to attain the right attitude of mind to free the soul of the child that such an institute is required."[38]

While some funds were collected, it was not an amount sufficient for the establishment of the proposed institute, and, as it has had to be on so many other occasions, the Kingdom of Heaven on Earth had to be postponed.

In the meantime, the subjects of what was acknowledged to be a less than perfect kingdom paid their respects to Montessori and showed their appreciation of what she had contributed to the educational realm.

Early in December she was invited to address the members of the British Psychological Society at a meeting at the Royal Society of Medicine chaired by Dr. Kimmins, the London County Council chief inspector of elementary schools. Her lecture described her system, and in particular how observations of the phenomenon of the fixation of the child's attention had guided her in designing the didactic material. She explained how this fixation of attention was both the basis of the system and the source of the child's joy in his work.

It was the experience of lecturing to her fellow medical students at the University of Rome all over again. Once again she faced a hostile audience and won them over. Once again she succeeded in taming the lions. At the end of her lecture one distinguished psychologist paid her what he must have thought was the ultimate compliment, congratulating her on the "masculine logic" with which she had stated her case.[39]

Doctors of medicine and professors of psychology said her work would eventually make the "nerve specialists" superfluous: "When the Montessori system is established in all schools, almshouses will have to be set up for the psychoanalysts."[40] Another said he had never understood how a method evolved for the study of mentally deficient children could be applied to normal children, but that before Dr. Montessori got halfway through her remarkable lecture, he was convinced.[41]

Commenting on the way in which Montessori had conquered the skeptics—"some of her most inflexible opponents in this country"—Radice said, "This happens constantly with those who hear her speak" and pointed out "how necessary it is to hear her at first hand, in order to discount that stiltedness that pervades any faithful translation of a foreign language into English."[42] But there was more than the question of translation involved. Throughout her career Montessori's conquests began with the reactions of those who experienced her personality—who saw her and heard her—from the earliest days in medical school and at Berlin and Turin. She had a presence, a combination of charm and conviction, that attracted those who heard her speak in a way that her writings alone could never have done.

On the night following her triumph among the psychologists came the climax of her English visit, when the formal dinner that had been planned in her honor and postponed on account of the autumn labor troubles was finally held at the Savoy Hotel, with the president of the Board of Education chairing the proceedings. There were messages from the Italian royal family and officials of the governments of Spain and the United States. She was toasted as one of the great educators of history, and she replied, with frequent interruptions for loud applause and prolonged cheers, by thanking those who had gathered to join with her in the work of reforming society through the reform of the school. The honor they were doing her tonight, she told them, was due not to herself but to a score or so of tiny children in the slums of Rome ten years ago who had spoken with an eloquence that had been heard by all the nations of the world, and on behalf of these boys and girls she thanked them.

She spoke to enthusiastic crowds at the Oxford Union Club, the Lord Mayor of London gave a reception in her honor, and she spoke to the Child Study Society on children's imagination and fairy tales, hoping to clear up once and for all the question of her attitude toward fantasy, explaining that she was not antagonistic to it but found it irrelevant to education, in which the child is "engaged in an immense work—*un gran lavoro*—the work of self-organization and self-discipline" in which he needs all the help adults can give him in "forming his critical and discriminating faculties, in distinguishing between the real and the imaginary."[43]

In mid-December the training course ended and Montessori personally gave an oral examination to each of the students. The final lecture of the course was canceled when word came that Anna Fedeli, who had returned to Rome, was seriously ill. Montessori left for Rome to be with her, returning in early January for a ten-day tour of English cities that took her to Liverpool, Manchester, Birmingham, Sheffield, Leeds, and Northampton. Everywhere the pattern was the same—like one of those montages in which pages of the calendar fall in succession, intercut with shots of moving trains, arrivals at identical stations to what begin to sound like the same speeches of welcome. Everywhere, a reception by the Lord Mayor, speeches to local educational groups in packed halls, interviews with the press, crowds of teachers and parents eager to talk with the great educator. And in every place that she visited, societies and schools would be set up in the months that followed, just as branches of the League for Retarded Children had sprung up in the Italian cities where as a young doctor she had spoken on behalf of the rights of women and of deficient children over twenty years ago.

Finally, toward the end of January 1920, Montessori left England, leaving the faithful Maccheroni behind for six months to oversee the new schools being opened, the lectures being given, the "propaganda" of the new societies being formed.

In a charming farewell message Montessori described her stay among the English in terms of the fairy tales about which there had been so much controversy:

"I saw mansions in the great towns open to receive and encourage me like the enchanted palaces of good magicians." England was "a country

265

of wonders, where strength of spirit and kindness unite to create things beyond expectation: perhaps that is why the English are so fond of fairy stories—because fairies, for them, are the personifications of what their souls create every day."[44]

17

Following the 1919 international training course in London, Montessori was invited to give a series of lectures at the University of Amsterdam in late January 1920. The lectures aroused the interest not only of educators at the university but of intellectuals throughout the country.

In them Montessori described her ideas about the extension of her methods beyond primary education into adolescence and sketched a program for a new kind of secondary education, later published in "The 'Erdkinder'" and other essays.[1]

One of the national characteristics which Montessori adopted from the various countries in which she spent time in the course of her peripatetic life and work was the English habit of writing to *The Times* of London. When Montessori wanted to take a position, clarify an ambiguity, or keep her followers up to date on her activities, she sent off a letter to *The Times* and over the years her correspondence appeared on Londoners' breakfast tables with almost the same frequency as reports of the first warblers sighted by nature lovers in early spring.

From Holland, following her lectures at the University of Amsterdam, she wrote in a letter published early in 1920:

> Even after England, our reception here has been sufficiently impressive, University people here being ready to recognize the scientific value of the work. The University of Amsterdam have expressed their wish that the University itself shall be the headquarters of the work that is to be done. The rector and senate of the University gave me a ceremonial reception on the afternoon of January 23 and the rector and professors have been present in person at the lectures I have given. Some of the members of the University staff, among whom is the son of Hugo de Vries, have undertaken to develop my work on university lines, and the University have signed an agreement to this effect. As for the "school" side of the matter, there is now a political movement for new legislation which will set the Dutch schools free from the rigidity of the former regime, and on January 29 the Minister of Education received me officially and agreed to press forward legislation under which new methods can be introduced into the schools.[2]

Here again, as in Spain, was the kind of recognition for which she had hungered—not just public attention but the official support and academ-

267

ic cooperation which would make it possible to extend her work in new directions, in a country where it was not likely to be blown away by the winds of political turmoil.

The interest aroused by Montessori's lectures at the University of Amsterdam led to the formation of a committee of leading academics to consider the applications of the Montessori educational system to their own particular fields—history, geography, the sciences. Unlike their more authoritarian counterparts in the universities of other European countries, the Dutch faculty members placed a great value on having students who were able to work independently, and they were impressed with the results of the Montessori system.

At first there was hostility from the teachers' unions and the press, but as impressive reports of results in the Montessori schools were made public the attitude shifted to one of neutrality and finally, over the years, to enthusiasm on the part of the press and cooperation on the part of the authorities. Articles in the newspapers and magazines familiarized the public with Montessori's ideas on the importance of early education and the role of sense-training, the building of individual initiative, and the "sensitive periods" for educating the young.

Leaving Holland, Montessori stopped first in Paris, where she was visited by the distinguished philosopher Henri Bergson and honored at the Sorbonne, and then in Italy, where she visited Milan and Rome and received reports of plans that were being made to reorganize the elementary-school system in Naples along Montessori lines. Then she returned to Barcelona.

If Montessori's dream seemed to have come true at Barcelona, she would soon be awakened again to a world less than magnanimous in what it was prepared to give her without asking something in return.

For four years the Barcelona institute and its model demonstration school flourished despite political and social unrest. Then crisis finally overtook them.

As she walked through the sunny classrooms with their atmosphere of order and harmony under the watchful eyes of directresses all trained by her, Montessori must have felt that she had finally found the perfect conditions for her work, a permanent center for continuing to develop her materials and extend her method. Visitors were surprised to find her, after the war, looking no older, seeming no less vigorous than in the days of the first Casa dei Bambini. She was eager for news, and asked a visiting English journalist to tell her all about the new developments in child psychology, listening with a smile and a raised eyebrow.

The Method and the Movement

Catalonia and in particular Barcelona was the main battlefield of the postwar economic and social struggle in Spain in which a rickety constitutional government and a weak king were eventually toppled by the economic crisis brought on by falling prices and widespread unemployment with the entrance of the generals into politics in 1923.

Labor disturbances had begun in Barcelona, the center of radical activity, almost as soon as the war was over, and passions ran high. In the spring of 1919 the long-simmering struggle between the syndicalists and factory owners erupted in a general strike in Barcelona. The propertied classes, frightened by the threat of anarchism and Communism, rapidly lost faith in the civilian government. Martial law was declared and there were massive arrests with a number of labor leaders thrown into prison. With the collapse of the government in 1919 terrorists roamed the streets and there were sporadic assassinations in retaliation for the arrests. Officials responded in turn with more wholesale arrests and shootings of workers. Feelings in Barcelona and all over Spain reached a pitch of hysteria.

In such an atmosphere it was hardly to be expected that an educational program for social reform such as Montessori's would be left to develop independently without pressures and interference. With the struggle for independence intensifying and new officials succeeding each other in power on the basis of new promises of freeing the region from the rule of Madrid, they began to demand that she take a political stand on their side.[3] The atmosphere of Barcelona was highly emotional, a state of emergency existed in the city, and executions were taking place daily. There were constant demonstrations and Montessori was expected to join them and make a public statement on the side of the Catalans and independence. She refused. The reason she gave was not lack of sympathy for the Catalans but an insistence on not involving herself in politics under any circumstances. The only cause to which she subscribed, she told them, was the cause of the child.

The issue was drawn. Authorities came into the school while she was away and announced their intention of making some changes. Montessori was furious, continued to insist that she was politically neutral and that the authorities' demands and interference made it impossible for her to carry out her work in the peace and order she needed. Official support was withdrawn from the institute and although Barcelona remained her headquarters until the outbreak of the Civil War in 1936, it was because it had become her home, not because there was any official government support for her work in the years from 1920 until the establishment of the Second Republic more than a decade later.

After the war Mario and his growing family had joined her in Barcelona and the city was now their home; she remained to be with her family. From the time they were born her grandchildren were close to her, a source of delight which must have made up in part for the years of her own son's infancy and childhood she had not been able to share.

After their departure from Italy for the United States in 1915 Montessori was reluctant to return to live in Italy because Mario would be liable for military service and her feelings about war and militaristic nationalism would not permit that. Perhaps too she felt that once having regained him she could not bear to part with him again. So she remained based in Spain, where they could live together without being separated and where her grandchildren could grow up under her watchful and devoted eye. Four children were born to Mario and his first wife, two girls—Marilena and Renilde—and two boys—Mario Jr. and Rolando. The two oldest, Marilena and young Mario, were particularly close to their grandmother, and Mario Jr. followed in her footsteps by developing an interest in psychology. He eventually became a psychoanalyst, practicing in Holland and remaining close to Montessori to the end of her life.

So although Barcelona was home to Montessori for twenty years, the place where her young family lived, from which she took off on her unending travels and to which she returned before setting off again, it was only for the first four or five of those years that she enjoyed the official recognition and support of the government and the existence of near-perfect conditions in which to carry out her work. After 1920 the system was no more firmly established in Spain than in any of the other countries of Europe, Asia, or the Americas where it had its enthusiastic devotees but where its influence ebbed and flowed with local conditions.

During the summer of 1920 Montessori's old friend and collaborator Anna Fedeli died in Italy. In October 1921 Montessori left Barcelona, accompanied by Adelia Pyle, to give a training course in Milan. With Ballerini and Fedeli dead, and Parkhurst off on her own, only Maccheroni and Pyle remained of her close followers of the prewar days. But now there was Mario, on whom she came to depend more and more as an alter ego in her work and to some extent as a buffer between her and those who were always trying to climb on the bandwagon of her fame with some profitable scheme or other.

And there were new disciples to take the place of old ones. In 1921 Montessori met Edward M. Standing, who remained a lifelong associate, collaborating in her writings, arranging for publication of her lectures, assisting her in training courses, and who eventually became her first and official biographer with his enthusiastic but somewhat impression-istic *Maria Montessori: Her Life and Work*, published a few years after her death.

By the end of 1920 the Montessori societies of the various cities of England, Ireland, and Scotland announced that they would form one national society for Great Britain and Ireland, and that "all appoint-ments and regulations will be subject to the approval of Dr. Montessori, who will be President and an ex-officio member of its Executive."[4] It was also announced that Montessori would return to give another training course in London from April through July of 1921. The announcement emphasized the fact that "the diploma will only enable students to direct Montessori schools, and not to train teachers in the method."[5]

With all the interest that had been stimulated in England, many of Montessori's admirers agreed with Lady Betty Balfour's public state-ment that "It is a pity there are hardly any Montessori teachers to be had. One difficulty is that no one can be called a trained Montessori teacher till he or she has been personally trained by Dr. Montessori. We should like to ask Dr. Montessori when she will delegate the office of training teachers to those she has already trained."[6]

To the initiate, this was heresy. C. A. Bang, the organizer for Montes-sori's English training courses, replied, "Dr. Montessori considers that no British student who has yet attended her courses is sufficiently per-fected in her method to train others."[7] He suggested that the best way of providing more Montessori-trained teachers was to make contributions toward the establishment of an institute in England where Montessori could spend several months each year training them. Neither Lady Bal-four nor any of the other interested English supporters came up with contributions sufficient to found an institution of the scope Montessori had in mind, but by the summer of 1921 a Montessori department was set up at St. George's School, Harpenden, to experiment in the exten-sion of Montessori methods to older children, with Claude Claremont as its head. It was announced that "Dr. Montessori's judgement upon all educational questions connected with the school will be final."[8] Clare-mont headed a similar department at St. Christopher's School in Letch-worth from 1923 until 1925, when he became principal of the Montesso-ri training colleges at London and Cranleigh.

Private schools through the British Isles were teaching classes mod-eled on the lines of the Casa dei Bambini and classes in which older chil-dren learned by means of the advanced Montessori apparatus. The school systems of numerous cities in England and Ireland adopted the

271

Montessori method in infant and elementary classes. And Montessori herself was a constantly returning presence to keep interest alive, giving training courses in England regularly every two years from the end of World War I to the beginning of World War II.

But while the initial enthusiasm for Montessori's ideas in England was followed by a far greater degree of establishment of her system in the schools there than in America and was kept alive by her repeated visits, the same criticisms were raised on that side of the Atlantic and the same kinds of schisms began to develop.

By the early twenties tension had begun to brew between members of the Montessori Society in London who saw their role as the carrying out of Montessori's personal directives and those—the majority of the membership—with a more generalized view of their function as an educational group.

It was a meeting of the Montessori Society in September 1921 that brought the issue to a head. Dr. Kimmins of the County Council, who had been asked to speak on "The Future of the Montessori Movement," gave a talk that was widely reported in the press in which he said, "It is always a grave misfortune for a name to be associated with a movement, because there is no finality in education and the individual teacher must vary her method as time goes on. There must be scope for the personality of the teacher in any scheme of reform, otherwise it is doomed to failure. If, however, the divergence resulting from the original scheme becomes great, the name of the founder of the original scheme should be omitted in the description."[9]

It was this distinction between the method and the movement, between Montessori's system of education and a larger trend toward reform of education beginning with that system, which became the heart of the issue from now on, and that was to split Montessori's English supporters, as it had her American ones.

The author of a letter to the editor of the *Times Educational Supplement* who signed himself "An Ex-Official of the Montessori Society" put the issue this way:

> A movement might be set up to introduce a method, but the movement and the method are two different things. A method should be able to justify itself intellectually and to demonstrate its satisfactoriness with well-authenticated facts. A movement, on the other hand, makes a moral appeal and relies very largely on suasion in which the emotions are stirred. . . .
>
> With regard to the finality of the teaching apparatus, it is impossible that Dr. Montessori should have tried every teaching appliance that the

wit of man could conceive: she could not, therefore, have found objects still hidden in the womb of time to be lacking in the power of provoking that concentration and repetition of the exercise on the part of the children which guided her selection of her didactic material. . . . She could not have rejected what she had never thought of or tested. Dogmatism on this point is among the most dangerous of all the thorns that choke the seeds of her teaching. For it has one disastrous consequence . . . it sets the workers for the movement at loggerheads . . . and they spend their energies in unnecessary differences.[10]

Like Dr. Kimmins, the author of the letter thought "the fervor and moral enthusiasm which characterize the members of the Montessori Society might be more usefully directed toward a wider movement having for its end the achievement of similar purposes, but allowing differences of method." Such a movement, known by a wider term, would include methods used by teachers who do not use the Montessori materials, "although inspired by Dr. Montessori's ideals."[11]

For about a year, there had been increasing interest in educational circles on both sides of the Atlantic in Helen Parkhurst's Dalton plan. English as well as American newspapers and magazines published numerous articles about Parkhurst's extension and adaptation of Montessori's principles into secondary education, and it was coming to be talked about by teachers, school officials, and educational theorists in much the same way that the Montessori method had been a decade earlier.

There were those who felt that Montessori's own term "auto-education" might well be used to designate a movement which would encompass both the Montessori method and the Dalton plan, relating them to each other and to systems still to come based on the same ideals, although differing in details. While eclecticism might have no place in the Montessori method, it would have a place in such a larger movement. The "grave misfortune" of which Dr. Kimmins spoke would be for Montessori's name to continue to be applied to the movement—for her and her followers to "seek to dominate the 'Montessori movement' in the way in which she has an acknowledged right to dominte the 'Montessori method.' "[12]

Montessori's response to the news of the Kimmins lecture given under the auspices of the London Society was to dispatch a letter from Barcelona "withdrawing my name from the Society and from the movement which it supports, and presenting my resignation as President of the Montessori Society of London."[13]

The resultant split in the London Montessori group was nominally over an administrative detail—whether a member of the executive committee could also serve as the Society's paid secretary. The real issue was who was to make decisions. At a noisy and disorganized meeting in October 1921, a minority of the committee, criticizing those who had "frequently flouted Dr. Montessori's wishes," resigned en masse, which placed the "official" activities of the "Montessori movement" in the offices of Montessori's publishers and in the hands of C. A. Bang, her official organizer for the London training courses. He was authorized to act as her financial representative in England and to deal on her behalf with government departments, local authorities, the press, and educational organizations, as though she were the head of a commercial enterprise with a local agent.

There were now two groups, the larger membership from which Montessori had dissociated herself, and a small group of "purists" who had removed themselves to set up shop elsewhere as a provisional committee with the aim of effecting "the restoration of Dr. Montessori as our revered President."[14]

Once again, supporters of Montessori's work, with a long record of quiet disinterested efforts propagandizing on its behalf, were spurned because they were not faithful enough in the view of her most rigid adherents and—it appears—in her own view. The affair, said one former member of the society, was "very much out of keeping with that scientific and philosophical aspect of education on which Dr. Montessori is believed to set most value." In addition, it was making the group a laughingstock. The result of the detailed reports of the squabble in the press was that "much casual amusement has been aroused, which will not help the spiritual aspects of Dr. Montessori's work."[15]

The remaining members of the society's executive committee responded to Montessori's letter of resignation in a letter pointing out that "the Society cannot take responsibility for views expressed by lecturers which it cannot foresee" and deploring her resignation.[16] In November they passed a resolution again expressing regret at her withdrawal from the presidency and recording their "unabated loyalty and devotion to the principles enunciated by Dr. Montessori and to the movement which she has inspired" and hoping that she would reconsider her decision.[17]

At its December meeting the group decided to send Montessori a copy of the resolution with a covering letter pointing out that the primary objective of the society, according to its own rules, was "to help the diffusion of the Montessori method by all possible means," and that to do so it was necessary for the society "to come into contact with other educational or scientific movements and to secure sympathetic hearing and occasional cooperation from English educationists in various departments of work, who would necessarily be in many cases as yet only imperfectly acquainted with the Montessori method. Inevitably, on some of these occasions views would be expressed which would show this imperfect understanding." The only remedy, the members felt, was "a patient and sustained effort to diffuse a more accurate knowledge of the method." The committee, the letter pointed out, was also pledged to encourage the foundation of Montessori schools, and they felt that the only way of arousing public interest and financial support for such schools was "the continuance of propaganda, which could only be successfully carried out upon a basis of trusted freedom."[18]

There was no reply from Montessori.

Much of the "casual amusement" that so distressed Montessori's English followers was occasioned by the appearance of a poetic account of the quarrel in *Punch*:[19]

CIVIL WAR IN BLOOMSBURY

(Being a faithful doggerel paraphrase of "The Montessori
Society Split," as reported in "The Times.")

Sing, Muse, the tragic story of the Montessorian split
And the lurid possibilities arising out of it,
Revealing how "paedologists," though normally urbane,
May develop, on occasion, quite a first-class fighting strain.

Opposing factions, long estranged, closed in the battle-shock
At a memorable meeting in the Square of Tavistock,
When the Dottoressa's champions, in a series of scenes,
Assailed their own executive and gave it bounteous beans.

A preliminary fusillade of protest and complaint
Was aimed against the treatment of the patron lady saint . . .

Next the dissidents demanded that the letter should be shown
Wherein the Dottoressa had resigned her London throne . . .

The Committee are empowered, so *The Times*' report declares,
To wind up the Society and settle its affairs;
To assure the Dottoressa of the fealty of her flock,
And secure the old headquarters in the Square of Tavistock. . . .

The controversy over the method and the movement continued through the winter of 1921–22, its main forum the columns of the widely read *Times Educational Supplement*. Among the points made by former members of the Montessori Society who were now its critics were that the last word on child development had not been said and that any scientific theory must remain subject to revision and progress lest it suffer the fate of the letter being retained but the spirit lost—"the ultimate result of all

275

Jacobinism, to use Matthew Arnold's term."[20] Others said that taking steps "to prevent teachers from experimenting with auto-educational methods, and educationists in general from disseminating them, unless they have attended in person a certain number of Dr. Montessori's lectures" amounted to an attempt "to create a patent in the principles which Dr. Montessori has established, and to use her name as a kind of trademark for that purpose."[21] Another added that "there is all the differences in the world between using the name of a person of recognized genius to indicate the nature of a movement or the source of its inspiration, and using that name as a trade-mark to stamp the genuineness of an article sold in the market."[22]

The faithful band headed by C. A. Bang and Lily Hutchinson was now in exclusive possession of the Montessori name, and the other committee members announced their withdrawal in order to "leave the field quite open for those who feel they can work under Dr. Montessori's Rules of Authorization," which they made no secret of finding "unworkable, because they are autocratic in conception," adding that "the rules of any Montessori Society should permit the same freedom to its members as the method permits to the child."[23] There, of course, was the central paradox. In the name of a movement dedicated to liberty, freedom not only of action but of expression was being stifled.

By spring of 1922 "The Auto-Education Allies" were meeting to discuss the Montessori method as well as other methods of independent study. Dr. Jessie White, the author of *Montessori Schools as Seen in the Early Summer of 1913* and of numerous articles on the Montessori method as well as on the now much-discussed Dalton plan, speaking of the difficulty of teachers in understanding and applying the method without enough concrete experience, said, "Now that the system has been before the world for over a decade, it is time we are quite clear and agreed on what is meant by the Montessori method, which does not change from time to time like the philosophical views of, say, Mr. Bertrand Russell." Dr. White added, "Dr. Montessori has not helped matters, for while she demands that teachers should subscribe to her principles, and seek to adopt her method in its entirety, she has continually created the impression that those who really understand her ideas can be counted on the fingers of one hand, and that, though the inadequate understanding of the rest equips them for directing children, it does not suffice to fit them to hand on a knowledge of her method to other teachers."[24]

Once again, as in the American experience, Montessori had proved her own worst enemy. Rejecting the interest and support of those who did not consult her at every turn, insisting that the method and the movement were one and the same, and that both were to be at all times and in all matters under her personal control, she ensured the purity of the method she had systematized at the price of its place in a larger movement devoted to the principles on which she had based that method.

18

After Montessori's second international course in Rome in 1914 little was heard in Italy of her, her schools, or her method. She had spent the remaining World War I years in the United States and then Spain, gradually becoming more and more neglected if not forgotten in her own country despite the continued loyalty and interest of a small group of her original friends and supporters. These included members of the influential Bertolini family, Donna Maria Maraini and her sister Donna Sofia Bertolini, Marchesa Guerrieri-Gonzaga. Before the war they had formed a group known as the Societa gli Amici del Metodo Montessori (Society of Friends of the Montessori Method), which helped to organize the first two international courses, and set up classes for their own and other upper-class children and supported the establishment of Case dei Bambini for children in poor neighborhoods. During the last months of the war before the retreat of the Austrian armies, the sisters gave their villa at Palidano, near Mantua, as a home for Italian refugee children and used the occasion to organize the children's lives, both in school and for the rest of their day, along Montessori principles.

But during the years of the war and its aftermath the Montessori schools failed to prosper or the movement to grow beyond the small circle of Montessori's original friends and Montessori became something of a prophet without honor in her own country.

In the spring and summer of 1916 she was assigned by the Italian ministry of education to supervise the implementation of her method in several classes which had been established as an official experiment in the schools of Rome. Then, in the fall of 1918, Montessori returned to Italy on a visit during which she was received by the pope, Benedict XV, in a private audience after which he ordered her works to be included in the Vatican Library. At the same time the Italian under-secretary for home affairs declared his interest in the method and in having it adopted throughout the schools of Italy, beginning with its introduction in twenty public elementary schools in Naples. There was some talk of establishing a Montessori institute, but the plan for the institute was never realized. Ironically, it remained for the Fascists to restore her system to the schools of her native land as part of what they called *nostra rivoluzione esaltante la Patria*—"our glorious national revolution."

The Method and the Movement

Despite progress in the early years of the century, particularly in the industrial north, Italy has been said to have entered the war in 1915 as the poor man of Europe and to have come out of it poorer still. The country had suffered heavy losses and the terms of the peace left widespread discontent about her share of the victory. Political and social unrest spread throughout the peninsula. The liberals, republicans, and socialists were weak and divided and the specter of Communist-inspired violence led Italian industrialists and conservatives to turn to the one party that seemed to offer them salvation from the extremists of the left—the Fascists with their particular brand of fanatical nationalism. In October 1922 Mussolini and his Black Shirts marched on Rome and the king asked the Fascist leader to take over the government. It was the end of constitutional government in Italy for a quarter of a century. During the years of World War I and of the critical social unrest and political upheaval that followed it is not surprising that a system of educational reform like Montessori's—what she herself saw as "the great movement for the welfare of young children which is gathering force all over Europe"[1]—should have fallen by the wayside.

Montessori spent part of the winter of 1921 in Italy, returning to Barcelona in February for six weeks before leaving again for London to begin her training course there in April. During this time Benedetto Croce, the distinguished philosopher and statesman, was minister of education or, as it should more exactly be translated, of public instruction. In 1922 he was replaced by Antonino Anile, a professor of history at the University of Naples, a doctor of medicine, and a friend of Montessori's.

At Anile's invitation on behalf of the Italian government, Montessori returned to Italy in the spring of 1922 to give a course of lectures in Naples, then the site of a model Montessori school in a beautifully equipped new building in a slum area, run for the municipality by one of her early students. Three hundred three- to seven-year-old children of the poorest class were enrolled, 150 of them attending daily and the others part-time. Reports were that formerly incorrigible children had become orderly, attentive, active, and happy. (Still, conservatives looked with suspicion on the unorthodox school and in the conditions of the time the results were considered less significant than the costs. Three years later the school would be closed by the local authorities "for reasons of economy.")

In April 1922, while Montessori was in Italy, Anile appointed her to inspect the municipal nursery and elementary schools in Rome where her method was being used. In none of them, even the oldest Casa dei

Bambini, had Montessori herself had any direct participation since several years before World War I. The following month he extended her inspectorate to the whole of Italy.

As a result of her officially sponsored inspection and at her request, two schools in Rome were closed because the teachers, who had not been trained by her personally and did not seem to her to be implementing her method as they should, refused to change their ways and there were no other adequately trained teachers available at the moment.

Although ambiguous press reports of the school closings led to the impression that the government was closing down Montessori schools because it disapproved of them, the fact was that the Rome school closings were part of an effort by the authorities to implement the system with Montessori's cooperation in a way that would eventually strengthen it.

In a statement issued to clarify the official position on the matter and passed along by Montessori to the London *Times Educational Supplement,* Anile said, "I hope that our country, among civilized nations, may establish these methods as soon as possible, so that our children may grow up strong and free. Italy has many scholastic deficiencies to make good, and needs to accept this teaching. The beginnings that have been successfully made have all my encouragement, and I shall be only too happy if I can be instrumental in further development."[2]

Now, with the help of a minister of education sympathetic to her aims, arrangements were made for her to give a training course for Italian teachers to be held in Naples in the autumn of 1922. By that time the Fascists had made their march on Rome and Mussolini had taken over the government.

In December 1922 Montessori had come to Italy with the plan of conducting one of a series of annual training courses under the joint sponsorship of the municipality of Naples, the ministry of education, and the Amici del Metodo Montessori. The first course was planned for spring of 1923. The courses were to be financially supported by the ministry and were to be open to Italian nationals only.

In 1923 Anile was replaced as minister of education by one of the most distinguished men in Italian intellectual circles, the philosopher Giovanni Gentile, whose conservative views led him to the tragic misjudgment that he could work with the Fascists to restore Italy to her former greatness. It was a view that many Italian intellectuals found it possible to accept in the early years of the Fascist dictatorship and for which many of them paid dearly. Gentile's debt was collected by a partisan's bullet in 1944.

On June 12, 1923, Montessori's old friend Donna Maria gave a reception for numerous high officials at which they celebrated the honor that had just come to Montessori in Britain—the granting of an honorary doctorate by Durham University.

In July 1923, after completion of the London training course, Montessori returned to Italy before going on to Holland to give a training course there in the fall. Gentile, entrusted by the new government with the task of reforming the obsolete educational system, expressed his interest in the method and his intention of officially maintaining Montessori schools and training schools for teachers under the new regime. Montessori's old friend Queen Margherita had an audience with Gentile and once again declared her intention of sponsoring Montessori's work. Gentile wrote to the president of the Montessori society in Rome wishing the society "success in the spread of Dr. Montessori's teachings"[3] and expressing the hope that he would soon be able to visit the Rome Montessori schools himself.

It seemed as though the change of government in Italy might mean the possibility of new life for the Montessori movement there. Today it is hard to see how so many Italian intellectuals could have believed that the kinds of changes for which they hoped could possibly be brought about by a government like the one Mussolini was establishing in their country, totalitarian, supernationalistic, supermilitaristic, and led by a man who could say proudly that his party had "buried the putrid corpse of liberty." But in the beginning he was able to woo many intellectuals to his cause, including the then highly respected Gentile, who undertook to provide the philosophical justification for the regime. And Montessori had always maintained that she was apolitical, that the "cause of the child" superseded ephemeral distinctions of party and nation. Today that attitude seems hopelessly naïve, but after so many disappointments and with little real interest in politics beyond how they seemed to affect the movement to which she was entirely dedicated, she found it possible to believe what she wanted to believe—that she could work with the regime and perhaps even exert an influence for the good. What she was looking for was a laboratory. What she could accomplish in it she was convinced could improve the society by improving its children.

In the winter of 1923–24, Mario Montessori wrote from Barcelona to the new head of the Italian state to point out what he referred to as the shameful fact that a system that had originally begun in Italy and had since spread throughout the rest of the world and taken root as far away as India, Siam, and New Zealand should be so relatively neglected in its founder's own native country.

Mussolini did not answer the letter but he did something the party press later described as "more practical."[4] In February 1924 he asked his foreign minister to have Italian consulates all over the world inquire into local Montessori activities and their influence. And, hearing from Gentile, who was already considering implementation of the Montessori method in Italian schools as part of his extensive plan for educational reforms, that Montessori was then in Rome, Mussolini expressed a desire to meet her. (Mussolini must have heard of Montessori in the years before World War I when he worked in Milan at Umanitaria, where a Casa dei Bambini had been established in 1908 and where she had spoken on several occasions.)

The resulting meeting led to the first official recognition and widespread establishment of Montessori's system by the Italian government, a remarkably ironic fact considering the nature of that system and of that government.

Montessori spoke to Mussolini, as she did to everyone, with compelling sincerity. It is easier to imagine what she said than what he made of it as she described the method and its history in Italy from the opening of the first Casa dei Bambini through all its vicissitudes, the many instances of schools being opened only to be closed again for lack of public financial support for their operation or of an adequate supply of teachers to run them. As for his request for information about the extent and importance of Montessori activities in other countries, she herself, she told him, did not know the full story. He would have to wait for the results of the investigation that was under way.

Mussolini listened and then promised that his "new kind of government" would support her. The newspapers of the day, all Fascist party organs, reported the encounter in lyrical terms worthy of a dramatist. In order to succeed, according to the press accounts, Montessori told Il Duce she had need of a man of will and energy, to which he responded "Faro io!" ("I will do it!")—two words, according to the official account, "which gave unforgettable joy!" It was a joy that was to be short-lived.

Mussolini was hardly interested in developing a nation of independent thinkers, in providing a prepared environment in which spontaneous activity would liberate the individual child's potential to the fullest, but he too heard what he wanted to hear in this strange encounter: children could learn to read and write by the time they were three or four. He was nothing if not practical, and to make a modern industrial state he would have to see that everyone learned to read and write efficiently, just as he would have to see that the trains were made to run on time. He would do it. And it seemed to him that Montessori would be useful. Not only that, the worldwide prestige of her name would add luster abroad—and he hungered for recognition as one of the world's great leaders of great nations—to the Italy he dreamed of building. Montessori had had her own dreams about a new Italy for almost thirty years, and they filled her mind too completely for her to see that his would be built in blood.

Perhaps what appealed to Mussolini too was what appealed to so many queens and dowagers, mothers and teachers who also never actually understood what Montessori really meant by "order" or "discipline"—the sight of all those good, neat little children, so busily occupied and so well behaved.

News of the official inquiry into the Montessori movement abroad led to a revival of the Amici del Metodo, the early group of Montessori supporters, now transformed into the Opera Montessori—the Montessori Society—under Gentile himself.

In April 1924 the government conferred a charter of incorporation on the society, which would be authorized "to raise funds and carry on the reform of education by this method and to demonstrate the method in its purity and entirety."[5] Government grants would provide part of the society's funds for the purpose of organizing schools, "protecting" Montessori schools throughout Italy, and keeping in touch with other Montessori schools and societies throughout the world. There would be an annual training course and a factory to manufacture the didactic materials. The society's administrators would include a representative of the ministry of education and one of the municipality of Rome. Montessori would be honorary president. The society was founded by royal decree of King Victor Emmanuel, still nominal head of the government, and was under the patronage of Queen Margherita.

By summer of 1924 there were once again Montessori schools in Italy where the method was being applied completely in accordance with Montessori's ideas and plans were under way for training more teachers.

By the spring of 1925 the results of the inquiry Mussolini had ordered into the degree of acceptance and application of the method outside Italy were reported to be "of a magnitude and convincingness which has surprised even the Ministry which undertook the work." According to a correspondent for the London *Times Educational Supplement*, "Signor Mussolini, after study of its contents, is reported have formulated the characteristic reply for objectors and critics, that the Montessori principle is established, and that those who fail to understand it 'display their own ignorance.'"[6] The Montessori method was in. It had official approval, official support, and for a time—until she could no longer deny what this government was really all about—it could develop in a matrix of schools for children, teacher-training courses, production of materials, publication of books about and information relating to the method and the movement, and associations of those interested in the spread of the movement.

Toward the end of the summer the municipality of Naples announced the closing of the Naples Montessori schools as part of a program of economic measures. The center of the new national Italian Montessori movement was shifted to Milan and the Società Umanitaria, where the first Case dei Bambini outside Rome had been established in 1908.

Mussolini charged officials in Milan with the task of reviving the Montessori activity that had died out in Naples. They formed an organization known as the Comitato di Milano dell'Opera nazionale Montessori, a branch of the Opera Montessori in Rome, and set about planning a national Montessori teacher-training course, to be given in 1926, to which the minister of education would send some sixty teachers; it was to be followed by a similar course the following year.

In February 1926 Montessori began the six-month training course in Milan for Italian teachers. Gentile had been replaced by Fedele as minister of education, and the latter officially appointed Montessori to direct the course. Mussolini accepted the honorary presidency of the course, for which a ministerial order established the following program:[7]

General Section

Child Psychology—Physiological study of, and care and protection of the child from birth till nine years of age; contribution of the school to the improvement of the race.

Montessori Method—Protection and care of the child's psychological development. Technique of the Montessori method and application of the method in the Casa dei Bambini and in the lower classes of the elementary school.

Previous Psychological Conceptions—History in summary form of the principal methods of education for normal and abnormal children, and their relation to the Montessori method.

Religious Education—Religious teaching, especially in connection with the education of children in the early stages.

Social Section

Domestic Economy—Domestic science applied especially to the feeding of children and the training of children in exercises of practical life.

Civic Education—Good manners and behavior, and love of country.

Artistic Instruction—Free drawing, painting, craft work, modeling, weaving, pottery, etc.

Musical Instruction—Music and rhythmic gymnastics based on fundamental movements of the body and their harmony.

Art of Diction—Training of the singing and speaking voice.

Nature Study—Farming, gardening, and observations of plants and animals.

Miscellaneous—Meteorological observations, biological study, etc.

The Società Umanitaria was entrusted with the arrangements for the course and Montessori was given full charge of the classes. Meanwhile, Gentile, as head of the Rome branch of the Montessori Society, arranged for the commune of Rome to send three teachers to the course in preparation for reopening in the following autumn the Montessori classes which had been closed there at Montessori's instigation. Twenty-five teachers were sent by the authorities of Lombardy, seventeen from the Marche, and eighteen from the Veneto in addition to a number from Milan and from various independent groups. The total enrollment was 180, 60 of them sent by the state.

In June 1926, while the course was being given in Milan, it was announced that Mussolini, now president of the Opera Nazionale Montessori, had alloted a subsidy of 10,000 lire for the society's work from his personal funds.[8]

One of Montessori's former pupils, who had come from Vienna to give the music classes for the Milan training course, remembers that there were some "nervous moments" at the beginning. After the first class, in which she had played folk songs of many nations and tunes by various classical and romantic composers, a message was delivered from government officials to the effect that the music classes would not be allowed to continue unless each class began with the "Giovinezza," the Fascist anthem, and included primarily Italian folk songs and compositions by Italian composers. "I had the feeling," the pianist recalled years later, "that the Dottoressa did not sympathize with this interference."[9] However, too much was at stake to jeopardize it all over a few songs, and Montessori failed to read the occasion as a sign of things to come. The young teacher got busy and found more suitable music, which she played from then on, and the music classes continued without further difficulties.

Vienna, where so much in the intellectual life of the twentieth century had its beginnings, was the setting for one of the most interesting chapters in the history of the Montessori movement.[10] One of the pupils of Montessori's 1921 London training course was a young woman named Lili Roubiczek who had left her upper-class home in Prague to study psychology with Karl Buhler in Vienna. An exceptionally bright student with the idealism and energy of youth, she saw in the Montessori principles of education a way of doing something to help relieve the postwar misery of Vienna's poor, and particularly the families of factory workers, by establishing a Montessori school for their children.

Defeat had left Austria demoralized and impoverished, and nowhere were conditions worse than among Vienna's working class. Roubiczek discussed her plan with Montessori, who was enthusiastic and promised her cooperation, and together with two other pupils of the course, one of them a young Australian architect named Lawrence Benjamin, she set about collecting funds for the establishment of a Montessori school in Vienna "as a measure of relief work, spiritual as well as material."[11]

With financial backing from England, they returned to Vienna to open the Vienna Montessori School—to be called the Haus der Kinder—on the outskirts of Vienna in Favoriten, the Tenth District, a factory workers' section then one of the most depressed slum areas of the city.

Lili Roubiczek, like Montessori herself, radiated a kind of intelligence, charm, and energy that drew idealistic young people to her and, at twenty-four, she became the center of a little group of educated middle-class Viennese girls, mostly of assimilated Jewish families and most of them socialists, who were equally fascinated by her sense of purpose and the Montessori philosophy and its philanthropic possibilities. They believed they could help build a better society in the new Austrian republic and Montessori seemed to be telling them how to go about it: through education, and by beginning with very young children.

The original group consisted of five young women sixteen to eighteen years old who formed a working commune they called the Arbeitsgemeinschaft. They threw themselves into the challenging but exhilarating business of making preparations for the opening of the school, no easy matter. Life in Vienna was difficult for everyone except the very rich; inflation was rampant, food, clothing, and fuel were scarce and expensive, furniture and equipment hard to come by.

The group worked feverishly to get things ready for the opening of the school. To have the different colors of the spectrum painted on little boards wasn't good enough, said one of them later. "Montessori had said silk was much better, so we sat there in the middle of the night covering the boards with colored silk."[12]

When the doors of the Haus der Kinder were finally opened in the summer of 1922 they admitted twenty-five children aged two to four whose parents were astounded to find that their children had been asked to call the school's directress "Lili." It was the first of many innovations in a school that was from the early twenties to the late thirties to be a model of its kind and the center of a group many of whom would go on to make significant contributions to education, social work, and psychoanalysis.

The children, inadequately dressed and underfed, some surly and rebellious, some just listless and unresponsive, came at six in the morning, half-frozen in the winter, and stayed until six in the evening when their mothers picked them up after the factories they worked in had closed. It was 1906 in San Lorenzo all over again, with the same results. The unprepossessing group of children settled down, began their work/play, learned, became enthusiastic yet orderly, and thrived.

With money from the British backers, and the efforts of the young worker-teachers, who did everything from collecting the necessary equipment to painting the classroom walls, the new school was attractively decorated and furnished, not only with Montessori materials but with child-sized plates and bowls for the children's meals which had been ordered in Dresden and small tables and chairs built by a neighborhood carpenter in his basement shop. Later, additional furnishings would include a special set of drinking mugs from the Bauhaus, the world-famous center of modern design, a gift from the Montessori school in Jena.

The British backers had provided no funds for paying the teachers or for their expenses such as food, for which Roubiczek used the monthly allowance she received from her family in Prague. The pupils' parents paid a small tuition fee which went toward covering part of the daily operating expenses including the children's food. With no money for salaries, the dedicated young teachers worked full-time with the idea that before training as Montessori teachers they would first have a year of practice in some area necessary to the school's maintenance—the kitchen or the garden as well as the classroom.

Emma N. Plank, one of the original members of the Arbeitsgemeinschaft, who was later to become professor of child development at the School of Medicine at Western Reserve University in Cleveland, Ohio, started in the kitchen. She later remembered, "We lived mainly on potatoes and raw cabbage dunked in oil. Lili invented a kind of pressure cooker to save gas, by having a tight-fitting wooden lid built—but we forgot to put a safety valve in. My potatoes landed on the ceiling. We had small rolls baked for us of graham flour, which one of us fetched by streetcar and knapsack from the finest bakery in town. I guess the allowance from Prague paid for them too."[13]

That first year, the young women all lived at the school, sleeping on the children's cots. In the evenings they studied Montessori's books and learned Italian, to prepare themselves to understand her lectures when their turn came to attend one of the international training courses.

Roubiczek kept in close touch with Montessori, informing her about the progress of the school and urging her to come to Vienna to see the Haus der Kinder for herself and meet with the dedicated little group who were running it. By now there were forty pupils, including a small group of elementary-school age in addition to the two- to five-year-olds.

MARIA MONTESSORI: A BIOGRAPHY

It was March 1923 when, at Roubiczek's urging, Montessori first came to Vienna to visit the Haus der Kinder and give a series of lectures for teachers to which parents were also invited. These lectures formed the basis for Montessori's book *Il bambino in famiglia*, which appeared in English in 1936 as *The Child in the Family*. The lectures were conceived of as part of the Arbeitsgemeinschaft's plan for educating the public, of involving the community in the effort of educating its young, a somewhat unorthodox aim in the view of the Austrian educational establishment of the time.

The news that Montessori would come to visit threw the young women into a fever of preparations like the one that had preceded the opening of the school itself. They spent whole nights at the Haus getting things ready; in their few spare moments they practiced their Italian so they would be able to understand her and to answer her in her own language if she should ask them questions about their work.

Montessori observed the activities from a visitors' gallery that had been built overlooking the classroom. When she smiled and expressed her approval, to one of the young teachers, "It was one of the greatest events in my life."

Montessori was less well known in the German-speaking countries than in the other countries of Europe and in the Anglo-Saxon world, and the introduction of the system in Vienna met with initial hostility from the public and especially from teachers in the regular school system who saw in it a threat to the authority of the adult and particularly of the teacher. Soon newspaper and magazine articles began to appear, but while the Viennese press found the experiment noteworthy, in the beginning it greeted it with open skepticism when it was not actually critical. A writer for a liberal parents' magazine of the time, *Die Mutter*, ascribed the lack of official interest in the Montessori school to the fact that the children developed an independence which led them to resist suppression. Unlike their counterparts in the regular school system, they did not act out of fear of punishment.

Despite Montessori's seeming belief that her method was simply a matter of allowing the child to develop spontaneously his innate capacities in the right kind of environment through the right use of the right materials, and thus would work in the same way with any children in any place, there was clearly more involved. There was not only the child and the materials in the classroom, but the adult with his personality, values, and way of relating to the child. And that factor made the system more malleable than Montessori would have liked to admit or perhaps even saw. It made it acceptable in Rome to a dictator who thought he could use it to serve his own ends, and in Vienna to a group of humane liberal intellectuals who saw in it a means to their own educational and social goals.

Slowly, as reports, largely published through Roubiczek's efforts, revealed the academic progress as well as the initiative shown by the well-behaved Montessori children, the tide began to turn, until by the late twenties admiring articles were being published in profusion in Vienna's newspapers and magazines.

It was a period of economic distress and social unrest, of wild inflation in Austria. When the school opened in July 1922 the tuition fee was 300 kronen a day. By December 1924 it had risen to 30,000 kronen a week. In such a time it was no surprise that the government had no initial interest in supporting the Montessori school, especially when the experiment was seen by many of the authorities as a somewhat subversive one.

The Vienna school was always in a precarious financial situation but this seemed to serve as a spur to the efforts of the little group around Lili Roubiczek. At one point when the school seemed in danger of folding they managed to secure the support of a baroness, Luisa Leithner. On other occasions they held public exhibitions of the Montessori materials and furniture produced by the local carpenter to raise funds to keep the school going. Then Roubiczek thought of undertaking to manufacture the materials for export to other countries where the system was being used and she was instrumental in founding the Montessori Verlag, which produced equipment and furniture, mounted exhibitions, and published books and pamphlets. In addition, she wrote a steady stream of articles about the Montessori method and the Haus der Kinder for popular magazines.

Within a couple of years the worker-staff of the Haus der Kinder had increased to fourteen, but the influence their work was having in Vienna was out of all proportion to their numbers, largely because of Lili Roubiczek's efforts. She had stimulated the interest of educators and social workers in the project and a series of seminars had begun for kindergarten teachers working in the day-care centers run by the city. These seminars grew into a two-year training course in the Montessori method the last four months of which were spent studying with Maria Montessori. Among the many students of that course who went on to become distinguished educators and psychoanalysts was Erik Erikson.

There was a growing interest in school reform all over the Continent in the twenties and nowhere was the movement stronger than in Vienna, where the socialist government was also subsidizing new housing for workers. Roubiczek persuaded the socialist mayor and councilmen to include Montessori classrooms for very young children in the plans for some of the new housing projects, to furnish them with the Montessori materials and child-sized furniture, and to support a six-month course for teachers to staff these classes. The local inspector of schools was friendly to these efforts, and little by little various aspects of the method were introduced and absorbed into all public day-care classes.

Roubiczek also became a consultant to the child welfare department of the city of Vienna, adding the Montessori approach to the planning for more than ten thousand of the city's children, and succeeded after two years in getting the municipal welfare department to undertake, through the Jugendamt, to subsidize the operation of the Haus der Kinder, paying teachers' salaries, other operating expenses, and fees for individual children.

In addition to the remarkable degree of support she was able to obtain from public agencies for an institution run by a small group with no official credentials, Roubiczek, through her interest in all aspects of Vienna's lively intellectual life, aroused the interest and gained the collaboration of leaders in such varied fields as the dance, graphic arts and architecture, the biological sciences, and psychoanalysis.

By 1925 she had succeeded in creating a favorable climate of opinion about the Montessori system among the Viennese of the upper middle classes, intellectuals, and businessmen. All of the qualified Montessori teachers in the city—admittedly a small number—were working, seven in private schools, five in preprimary classes in the municipal day-care system. Outside Vienna, there were two Montessori schools in the provinces.

When Montessori visited Vienna again in March 1925 she was received by the president of the city's school board and she found herself better known and her ideas more widely accepted in Vienna than she had ever expected, as a result of Lili Roubiczek's tireless and imaginative efforts. Roubiczek had even offered her services as a consultant in the planning of playrooms in leading department stores as well as a general workers' store where parents could leave their children while shopping. These Montessori waiting rooms with their child-sized furniture and Montessori materials soon became a topic of conversation among a public that might otherwise never have heard of the Montessori system. The idea spread and by 1928 department stores in Berlin and Cologne in Germany as well as in Holland had fitted up Montessori classrooms where the materials were displayed.

Roubiczek also arranged for the Austrian Montessori Society to hold frequent meetings at which teachers and parents discussed their problems with leading experts from among Vienna's medical specialists and psychologists. Among those invited to speak at these gatherings were members of Vienna's psychoanalytic community, the group of Freud's students who were closely involved in the exciting process of breaking new ground in the understanding of child development, particularly in tracing the roots of that development back to the child's earliest experiences.

A number of accidental circumstances explain the vitality and particularly the intellectual ferment of the Vienna Montessori movement in those days. One of these, ironically, may have been the fact that Montessori was not a regular presence but an occasional visitor and that the movement was led by someone who was more than a mere disciple of hers, a spirited and highly intelligent woman in her own right, alert to all of the currents alive in the Vienna intellectual world of the time and both interested in and free to relate Montessori's educational ideas to what was going on in that larger world of artists, writers, academicians, and, in particular, psychoanalysts.

The Viennese group had more latitude, exercised more freedom in adapting Montessori's ideas to their own sense of the needs of their time and place, than other groups of her followers. This was partly because of Lili Roubiczek's personality, hardly that of a sponge, and, at least in the beginning, of Montessori's feeling for her and appreciation of her qualities. According to Emma Plank, "Montessori trusted Lili explicitly—I think she was the only one of her students who could experiment and broaden the system. Lili accompanied her often on her travels, as catalyst and interpreter. Her dedication to Dr. Montessori at that time was limitless."[14]

Eventually, that dedication would lessen as the two women grew farther apart in their thinking about the educational process, and the familiar story of disagreement and estrangement would be repeated, but throughout the 1920s Vienna was, like Amsterdam, a place to which Montessori could return again and again on her travels to find hospitality for both herself and her ideas.

By 1921 the original class directed by Caroline Tromp had expanded into the Amsterdam Montessori School for preprimary and elementary-school children and Montessori accepted Tromp's invitation to visit the school and offer her impressions and suggestions. Accompanied by

Mario and Adelia Pyle, she spent two weeks at the school after her 1921 London training course had ended, visiting classes and conferring with the staff and parents, and while in Amsterdam met with influential citizens,.scientific leaders, and municipal authorities. Montessori was as impressed with the Dutch as they were with her. Here again, as earlier in Spain, seemed to be a ground for experimenting and building, and here the hopes were more realistic. The Dutch society was a stable one, there were no political upheavals to threaten the integrity of the growing movement or its implementation in the schools, and the Amsterdam school steadily developed as the center of a movement that spread throughout Holland. It became a center for disseminating information about Montessori activities, trained teachers, kept up close contact with local educational authorities, and served as a demonstration school where foreign visitors could observe the method in operation at its best.[15]

In 1924 Montessori gave a four-month international training course in Amsterdam. Students were sent by all of the leading Dutch cities and the interest aroused by press reports led to even greater public support among the prominent and the influential. In addition, she gave a series of eight lectures for the public, attended by parents, teachers, and a mixed bag of members of the intellectual community.

The Amsterdam school continued to take the initiative in spreading information and maintaining liaison with officials and regularly sent groups of students to Montessori's international training courses wherever they were held—Barcelona, London, Rome. When they returned, clutching their newly won diplomas and full of inspiration, there were places waiting for them where their enthusiasm could be channeled in the direction of expanding the classes and strengthening the movement.

It was in Holland that the Montessori system became most firmly established in the educational institutions of the country, both public and private, secular as well as parochial. The application of Montessori's methods to older children on the secondary level received its impetus there from interested middle-class parents eager to see the method extended into the continuing educational life of their own children and from the cooperative efforts of interested academics who undertook to investigate the various aspects of the method in university departments of educational and psychological research.

In 1924 a new quarterly journal began publication in Amsterdam. *The Call of Education* was devoted to explaining the Montessori principles, answering criticisms such as those most frequently made that the Montessori system did little to encourage community values or the child's creative imagination, and reporting news of the innumerable schools and societies that by now existed in various parts of Africa, Asia, South America, Australia, and New Zealand, as well as all over Europe and North America. Montessori was editor, a position in which she was assisted by Professors Géza Révész and J. C. L. Godefroy, two members of the faculty of the University of Amsterdam.

19

Throughout the twenties and thirties, until the outbreak of World War II, Montessori continued to give training courses every other year in England. Hundreds of students from most of the countries of Europe as well as from other parts of the world attended.

Over the years her lectures became more general and philosophical, dealing not only with the psychological principles underlying the method, the nature and purpose of the didactic materials, and practical problems in directing a Montessori school, but also with the wider application of her principles in the home and in society, and with such topics as "the cosmic mission of man on earth" and "education as the armament of peace." She continued to maintain that "the real teachers of the Montessori method are the children themselves. They are the last and incontrovertible argument in favor of it."[1]

Her interpreter for many of the English courses, and the one remembered most vividly by former students, was Dorothy Cornish, a bony, colorless caricature of the English schoolmarm, to whom Montessori referred as "my English voice."[2] Montessori was aware that Miss Cornish cut a somewhat ridiculous figure, and joked about her in a gentle way, but appreciated her understanding of her ideas and her skill at translating. Montessori had a sense of humor, and sometimes made gentle fun of some of the silly young—and old—things who surrounded her. "But if they were good teachers," one of her former students said years later, "she'd forgive them anything." That was the most important thing about people—how well they understood and carried out her ideas.

Many of her students retained a vivid image of the short, heavy Dottoressa in black, gesticulating with her beautiful hands as she lectured, and beside her the tall, thin, expressionless Miss Cornish, dressed in dowdy gray. Sometimes Montessori would break off to stamp her foot and say, "No, no!" if she felt Cornish hadn't translated a phrase correctly. Her corrections made it clear that she did understand English very well even though she was shy about speaking it.

During the 1920s Montessori's training courses continued to be reported in the press in some detail, with accounts of what she had said in her lectures and of the endless official receptions and dinners given for her each time she arrived in England to begin a new course. At the time

294

of her 1923 course the reading public was informed that at a dinner in her honor chaired by Sir James Crichton Browne and with Dr. Kimmins as speaker, the toasts to the royal families of England and Italy were followed by Suprême de Sole Chiaravalle accompanied, in addition to pommes nouvelles, by macaroni au gratin. And her name was well enough known to the public for a columnist in the *Daily Sketch,* inveighing against amateur dabbling in child psychology based on only half-understood theories, to express a longing for a return to the days of "the old-fashioned mother who had never heard of Freud or Montessori."

There were accounts of the many honors bestowed on her, such as the honorary doctorate conferred on her by Durham University in 1923 and her reception at Court at Buckingham Palace in 1927. And there were brief reports from time to time of continuing research on children. By 1923 it was reported that she was turning her attention to the observation of newborns and the question of how unnecessary obstacles to their development could be removed, but there were no details of clinical observations of any depth or controlled experiments of any kind, although psychological research had become increasingly sophisticated both in its clinical and experimental aspects.

By the mid-twenties more and more was appearing about the Dalton Plan, which was replacing the Montessori method as the newest focus of interest in education. There were numerous reports of the plan being adopted in various parts of the world, in a replay of the same scenario that had featured the Montessori method a decade earlier. Schools and societies were founded to implement the Laboratory Plan, as it was sometimes called, in which students worked independently on assignments of their choice which they contracted to complete in a given period of time, usually a month. There was a laboratory for each subject in the curriculum and the students moved freely from one laboratory to another. A specialist-teacher was available to consult with them in each subject laboratory, where they were also encouraged to work together collectively, cooperating on their projects. The system was set out in detail in Parkhurst's book *Education on the Dalton Plan,* which appeared in 1922 and which, like *The Montessori Method* before it, went into numerous editions and had been translated into eight languages by 1924. In it, Parkhurst mentions Montessori in passing, but nowhere indicates the extent of her debt to the older woman's thinking. The plan itself was original, and nothing like Montessori's own ideas for secondary education, which stressed less the academic than the life experiences of adolescents in a rural setting. But the principle on which it was based—the pupil's liberty as the basis for developing independence, his freedom to work when and for as long as he wants to on a given task and to progress at his own rate—is pure Montessori, and it was from her former teacher that Parkhurst had learned the attitude toward education which she had adapted in a special way for older pupils.

One wonders what Montessori thought of "Margherita" now.

With the Dalton Plan spreading in both the United States and England, Dr. Kimmins, whose pleas for a widening of the Montessori movement had sparked the split among the English Montessorians, was now chairing meetings of the Dalton Association. Some of the liveliest minds among its members having left it, the Montessori group began to stagnate in a kind of codified orthodoxy. Its remaining members were schoolmarms and schoolmasters whose personalities meshed with the demands of Maria Montessori and the organization dominated by her.

To those outside the movement, the uncommitted, admiration for Montessori was tempered with a more skeptical view of the character the organization had taken on, an attitude expressed in an article entitled "Dr. Montessori's Return" which appeared in the spring of 1923:

> The greatest curiosity, zeal and reverence of old and new disciples could be felt in the YMCA Headquarters Drawing Room on Tuesday evening last, for every seat was occupied by teacher-students expecting to begin that night Dr. Montessori's Eleventh International Training Course. Five per cent of the audience were men, the rest women and young girls. Many familiar faces were there of those who were among the battered remnant of "loyalists" after that disastrous earthquake of disunion which shattered the London Montessori Society well within living memory!
>
> Mr. C. A. Bang, a truly titanic organising secretary, has vanished from the room, to reappear a minute later pushing open the folding doors.
>
> She, Dr. Maria Montessori, herself!
>
> As by a common impulse the roomful of proselytes reverently stand up in silence. Half a minute of almost oppressive silence while Dr. Montessori, accompanied by Mrs. Hutchinson (whose zeal for the cause has won her the honour of acting as chairman in Sir James Crichton-Browne's absence), has reached the speaker's table, seats herself thereat; whereupon, like a church congregation, the company sit down amid a rustle of clothes and sighs. Mrs. Hutchinson delivers a rather long speech of welcome to "the great master" and of exhortation to the audience to honour and obey, which, if one studies faces in the back row, sounds just a shade over-strained, over-dogmatic.
>
> Dr. Montessori rises. That big, kindly, authoritative face is a little tired. The Dottoressa has fought a long intellectual and moral fight for "sweetness and light" in education. She arrived in London from the

Continent only the night before. She will say little this evening, except that "Every time I hear the words of one of my pupils or loyal friends, I feel profoundly touched and also a great wonder." She speaks in musical Italian that sounds slightly sharp-edged with weariness. Her interpreter standing beside her translates at frequent intervals. "There is something in this movement which is so entirely apart from me personally, that whatever I hear about the work always brings me back to that profound origin with which we will come into contact together—the child." A few reminders to her hearers that the way is simple and that the child is the real teacher, "and many of us are often bad pupils" and she sits down again. A burst of enthusiastic applause, and the gathering of pupils from all parts of the world slowly disperses. The Eleventh International Course has been opened.[3]

Montessori and her followers continued to maintain that she was simply protecting her method of educating the young, that since the apparatus she had worked out "scientifically" was perfect to do the job, it should not be changed. In a lecture to the students of her 1925 training course in London she said, "Every Montessori school is a scientific laboratory in which the teacher prepares the conditions of the experiment, and permits the phenomena to take place. We have given her a guide, and a material to be used. This has been studied exactly in every detail, and we should do as scientists do when handling a new instrument, use it exactly in the way intended."[4]

Her critics continued to maintain that it was the principles of auto-education which were primary, not a particular unchanging method for their implementation. The idea of spontaneous activity in a prepared environment was a valid one, but as more was learned about the psychology of child development the exact mechanics of that environment might change. Montessori gave the unfortunate impression that everything that could ever be known on this subject was already known to her, an attitude more compatible with religion than with science.

A Dublin University professor summed up the feeling of many educators when he wrote of Montessori, "Here is a great enthusiast . . . a great reformer . . . a great woman who loves children, of whom she has amazing intuitive knowledge; here too is a great teacher; but she is not a scientist, and does not think or write as one."[5]

As the rift widened, the preoccupations of the Montessorians seemed to grow more precious, more backwater. A lecture at a meeting of the Montessori Society in 1924 was entitled "Nose-breathing and Its Importance to Education."[6]

The Montessori method was still being used, and it still worked, but its

297

results were seen by more and more people as less and less dependent on a specific methodology. It was less and less in the limelight as new ways of achieving the same or similar results were discovered and tried.

During these years the two Montessori training colleges, St. Christopher's in Letchworth and St. George's in Harpenden, offered courses for younger, inexperienced teachers which were preparatory to Montessori's own four-month training course. In an appeal for funds, the chairman of St. George's School described its aim as "providing in England an exact model of the Montessori Method, as progressively developed by Dr. Montessori, whose word was (and is) to be law in the school."[7]

Neither these training colleges nor the one in Rome under the auspices of the Italian government could confer a Montessori diploma until a student had taken Montessori's own course afterward. What would happen, asked critics of the Montessori system of educating educators, when she died?

Despite the arguments over the method and the dwindling public attention given it, those teachers Montessori had trained continued to carry on her work in England.

At the University of Manchester's Fielden Demonstration School the Montessori method was used with notable success. In London, primary schools in the Borough of Acton were run on Montessori lines by teachers trained in Montessori's courses, with the encouragement of Dr. Ewart Smart, Borough Officer for Education in Acton, who was for many years chairman of the English Montessori Society.

Interest in Montessori's method in the British Isles was not confined to England. During the 1920s there was a growing enthusiasm among teachers and school officials in Ireland, much of it stimulated by lectures on her method by Professor Culverwell of Dublin's Trinity College.

Here again the lack of trained teachers and the self-contained character of the Montessori movement discouraged adoption by the ministry of education in the official system, but Montessori's influence was felt in countless local schools through the application of her general principles as they filtered down to classroom teachers who read her books or heard her lecture.

When Montessori visited Waterford, Ireland, where there were three Montessori schools in operation, she was greeted by a band of loyal devotees, whom she received in audience in groups.

She was becoming a grande dame, but no longer a vital figure except to her followers, who were becoming fewer and fewer although at the same time more and more fervid in their devotion. She was treated as a kind of majestic presence and she accepted the role, although she continued to say that it was not herself but her ideals that were import ant.

Those ideals continued to have their supporters among the well known. Bertrand Russell had sent his own little boy of three to a Montessori school and "found that he quickly became a more disciplined human being." Impressed with the method, he wrote about the child's joy in the success achieved by his own efforts and praised Montessori warmly in *Education and the Good Life* in 1926.

And George Bernard Shaw, in a characteristically acerbic attack on the pretensions of unqualified teachers he wrote for *John O'London's Weekly* in 1928, anticipated the way in which the Montessori name—despite all her efforts to prevent its exploitation—would later be abused by some self-proclaimed followers as well as by manufacturers of "educational toys" and "teaching games."

"If you are a distressed gentlewoman, starting to make a living," wrote Shaw, "you can still open a little school; and you can easily buy a second-hand brass plate, inscribed Pestalozzian Institute, and nail it to your door, though you have no more idea who Pestalozzi was and what he advocated, or how he did it, than the manager of a hotel which began as a Hydropathic has of the water cure. Or you can buy a cheaper plate, inscribed Kindergarten, and imagine, or leave others to imagine, that Froebel is the governing genuis of your creche. No doubt the new brass plates are being inscribed Montessori Institute, and will be used when the Dottoressa is no longer with us by all the Mrs. Pipchins and Mrs. Wilfers throughout this unhappy land."

Montessori continued to travel indefatigably, giving courses in Spain, Holland, Germany, France, and Austria, overseeing the establishment of new schools and societies.

She spent the fall of 1926 in South America, giving a series of lectures in Buenos Aires, La Plata, and Córdoba, and by means of her presence stimulating the burgeoning movement in Argentina. She returned to Europe in midwinter for a brief visit to Italy, then stopped in Vienna and Berlin before going on to London for her four-month training course there. The pattern of travel from place to place, training teachers, lecturing, overseeing the activities of local Montessori groups, was typical of her life throughout the twenties and thirties.

In Italy by the end of 1926 there was an experiment under way sponsored by the government in which some sixty teachers trained by her were directing Montessori classes in schools in Milan, Venice, and Ancona.

In 1926 Montessori received official recognition from the Tessera Fascista, the Fascist women's organization, and was made an honorary member of the party. Her method was being established in the nation's schools; in the same way that Paris had been worth a mass to Henry IV, this was worth a party card to Montessori. And if she entertained any doubts about the compatability of her principles of education with those of the government which was implementing them, she still found it possible to quell them and to work under its leader.

There was some common core of intention which these two unlikely partners each felt they could rely on and make use of in the other. The idea of order appealed to each of them in a different way, and Montessori must have felt she could make use of the regime's willingness to support her system in order to somehow ameliorate the effects of that system itself—an idea it is obviously easier for us to see the hopelessness of today than it was for her then—while Mussolini saw in the Montessori method not the aspect that stimulated individual development but the replacement of chaos with order. He saw that, to her, freedom meant freedom to choose from what was made available to the pupil; what he failed to anticipate was that she would never allow anyone but herself to decide what that would be.

After Rome and Milan, on her return from Argentina in November 1926 Montessori came on to Vienna as the guest of the municipality and the Vienna Montessori Association. A group of children carrying flowers to present to her were waiting at the South Station along with a welcoming committee led by Lili Roubiczek. When asked, "Who is Dr. Montessori?" they replied, "She loves us children." Montessori, swathed in black furs and accompanied by Mario—who, now twenty-eight, was still publicly identified as her "nephew and secretary"—was photographed accepting flowers from the delegation of Girl Scouts. Even after all the receptions, all the children's flowers at all the train stations over the years, she was visibly moved.

By this time there were thirty Montessori teachers in Vienna employed by the municipality and there was talk of plans to establish Montessori schools in every district of the city by autumn of 1927.

Montessori's Vienna lecture was a resounding success. It took place in the Hofburg, the palace that had been the imperial residence, and a crowd of more than a thousand without invitations tried to storm the

300

doors and had to be held back by the police. It took over half an hour to convince them there was no more room inside, and only then could the lecture begin.

Her talk on the rights of children met with an enthusiastic response from liberal socialists intent on building a future in what they still hopefully perceived as a postwar era rather than another prewar one. The Montessori system was seen as a system combining day care with meaningful education in a way that would be of unique value for the families of workers.

Montessori schools had begun to multiply in Vienna. Early in 1926 a Jewish Montessori school was opened and by the end of that year interest in and popular support for the Montessori system was increasing. Educators were encouraged to observe the children at work from the visitors' gallery and on Saturdays there were guided tours through the Haus der Kinder directed by Lili Roubiczek, just as there once had been through the Casa dei Bambini directed by Maria Montessori. There was an active movement afoot for reform of the schools, and among other changes being demanded of municipal school officials was the establishment of Montessori schools in more of the city's districts.

From Vienna Montessori went on to Berlin to give a two-month series of lectures before leaving to give her bi-annual training course in London.

In 1926 a group of parents of the Amsterdam Montessori School established a secondary school to continue their children's education along Montessori principles beyond the age of twelve.[8] Montessori was delighted with the idea and made a number of recommendations for the preparatory school, to be known as the Montessori Lyceum of Amsterdam. The parents and the staff felt like pioneers and used their own time, hands, and money to get the experiment going. Soon there were three other secondary schools, at Rotterdam, the Hague, and De Bilt.

That same year, 1926, Montessori was invited to address the League of Nations at Geneva. She spoke on "Education and Peace."

"The crisis we are witnessing," she told the delegates to the League, "is not one of those that mark the passage from one era to another: it can only be compared to the opening of a new biological or geological epoch, when new beings come on the scene, more evolved and more perfect, while on earth are realized conditions of life which have never existed before. If we lose sight of this situation we shall find ourselves enmeshed in a universal catastrophe. . . . If the sidereal forces are used blindly by men who know nothing about them with the aim of destroying one another—the attempt will be speedily successful, because the forces at man's disposal are infinite, and accessible to all at all times and in every place.

"Humanity today resembles an abandoned child who finds himself lost in a wood at night, and is frightened by the shadows and myterious forces that draw them into war, and for that reason they are defenseless against them."[9]

It was a prophetic warning, anticipating by two decades the development of atomic weapons in World War II and identifying the greatest threat to mankind as man himself—the failure of the education of human instincts to keep pace with human technological achievements and their destructive possibilities.

In March 1927 Montessori was received in private audience by Mussolini, who expressed his interest in hearing about her most recent lecture tour in Germany and renewed his promise of continued support for her work.[10] Then she left for England to begin her London training course in April. In one of her lectures during that course, explaining why her technique of teaching drawing emphasized the ability to reproduce given geometric figures and why children should be taught to move properly by walking on a straight line, she said, "There is no need to teach diversity. What we must indicate is something fixed, to which the developing intelligence can attach itself,"[11] and she spoke of the child's instinct for order.

It was this emphasis on order that must have appealed to Mussolini, and Montessori was probably as little aware of what he was really responding to as he was unable to understand what her ultimate aims were. And at this point neither may have been trying too hard to understand the other, each being convinced of being able to win out in the end. She would use the facilities which only the official establishment could make available to her in the hope of accomplishing her ends, while he would make use of two things he thought she brought him in return: one was the emphasis on order he saw as helping him create a docile group of citizens for the Fascist state; the other was the international prestige he felt Montessori's name lent that state.

A month after their meeting, in April 1927, it was announced that the government had requested the mayor of Rome to establish a Montessori training school and that plans were under way for the publication of a monthly periodical of Il Comitato de Milano dell'Opera nazionale Montessori to be called *L'Idéa Montessori*. The minister of education made a public statement describing the kinship between Fascism and the Montessori method. Fascism, he said, was restoring to Italians "the sacred sense of life"; both systems were alike in being essentially "spiritual, not materialistic."[12] Mussolini's dream—his obsession—was to establish Italy once again as a proud imperial nation, culture-giver to the rest of the world. He had as little understanding of culture as he had respect for it; what he was really talking about was power. But in his emphasis on nationalism he overlooked the international character of Montessori's thinking, her aims, and her appeal—just as she seems to have allowed herself for a time to be blind to what he was actually doing and saying. To him, she was a native heroine, and that counted for a great deal—as long as she stayed in line.

The first issue of *L'Idéa Montessori* appeared in June 1927, the official organ of the Opera nazionale Montessori, of which Mussolini was honorary president, the ministers of education and of the colonies joint vice-presidents, and which included officials of the municipal governments of Rome and Milan as well as Gentile and a number of other prominent individuals. The first number contained news of the Montessori movement in eleven countries and seventy-four Montessori schools in Italy, articles on the method, and a foreword by Montessori in which she described the aim of her work as "not so much to invent a teaching method as to establish the right of every child to grow to its full stature, spiritual and physical, helped and not hindered by the adult."[13]

Today we read that statement in that context and ask, "Under a Fascist regime?" How, we wonder, could she have been so blind to what Fascism was all about, to the kind of man Mussolini was, to what was happening to the institutions and in the streets of Italy? The only possible answer is that there are none so blind as those who will not see—that for a time Montessori was able to convince herself that she could accomplish something being in charge of Italian children's education that even a dictator who celebrated power for its own sake, whose political technique was brutality, and who was outspokenly anti-intellectual could not undo. If she did not join the Italian intellectuals who spoke out against Fascism and those who went into voluntary exile she was not alone in taking the position that her presence and activity might make a difference. Italy had still not come to the final disgrace of the racial laws, the Ethiopian atrocities, the complicity with Hitler in the Spanish Civil War and the ensuing disasters that would overtake Europe. She must have seen this government and its leader were at best a bunch of thugs, but allowed herself to believe they might give way to something better and to dream that perhaps she might even be instrumental in that process. And so she stayed, and went on working with them.

In December 1927 Mussolini presented his council of ministers with a draft decree for the establishment of a training college for teachers in the Montessori method;[14] it would be the only such institution outside England. By 1929 government-sponsored Montessori activities in Italy included the training college, the Regia Scuola Magistrale di Metodo Montessori in Rome; the society, active in both Rome and Milan, and its publications; Montessori's training course at Milan; and over seventy infant and elementary classes in schools throughout Italy.

The Montessori training college, which included a model Montessori school for demonstration purposes, was housed in a new building at Via Monte Zebio 35, in the pleasant Monte Mario section of Rome, and was designed and built according to plans suggested by Montessori in consultation with architects and engineers. Facilities were planned so that the institution would be a suitable site at which to hold future international training courses.

Montessori took charge of directing the classes in the Monte Zebio, where the curriculum included "Fascistic Culture" along with the application of the Montessori method and religion. At the opening of the first course there in 1929 she said that she took no interest in politics, that what was important was the child, that the adult must not impose his will on the child.

It's hard to believe that anyone was really listening to her or that, if she was listening to herself, she was looking around her. No one who understood what Mussolini was up to or what Montessori's aims and interests were could have expected them to be able to work together for long. But even outside Italy Mussolini's government still had its apologists. An admiring article published in the *Times* of London in the spring of 1929 on "Fascism and Women" took note of the growth of the movement among Italian women in organizations devoted to "social services," and concluded "A Mme. Montessori will not be born every day, even under the Fascist regime."[15] She was acknowledged to be the best type of woman a country could hope to produce, and the products of the regime were to be measured against her.

20

The year 1929 was an important one for Montessori and the move-ment. A new edition of *The Montessori Method* appeared, for which Montessori wrote a new introduction to the "document which has laid the foundation of schools in all parts of the world." In it she recounted the extraordinary spread of the ideas put forth in *Il Metodo* in the years since the book's first printing in 1909, and restated her view of education as a dynamic process in which children are transformed according to "the in-ner dictates of life" by means of their "voluntary work" when placed in an environment created to meet their needs, an environment she de-scribed as "not prepared in order to *mould* them by the suggestion of the example or the will of teachers but meant to leave them free to express themselves" and which she called "the revealing environment."[1]

To critics who had charged her with being "unscientific," her reply was:

> My experiences, far from being rigid, were logical conclusions corre-sponding to the application of an exact and positive method. The be-havior of the children, being uncontrolled by rigid research, gave new evidence, something living, which issued from my experiments as a spring of water gushes from a rock. In good faith, like the simple Alad-din, I thought that I held in my hand a lamp which at the most could lead me into a place hitherto unexplored, but what I discovered unex-pectedly was the treasure hidden in the depths of a child's soul, and it is this new, surprising revelation, and not what might be called "the im-portance of my contribution to official science," which has spread my method so far over the world, so far from the land of its birth.[2]

In August, at the end of the 1929 English training course, she and Mario, who was still not publicly acknowledged to be her own son but was her constant companion and full-time collaborator in all organiza-tional aspects of her work, founded the Association Montessori Interna-tionale as a parent body to oversee the activities of schools and societies all over the world and supervise the training of teachers. Montessori was president of the AMI, which would be headquartered in Berlin until 1935, when it was moved to Amsterdam. The AMI was founded during a ten-day International Montessori Congress, the first of nine such con-gresses which would be held over the next quarter of a century in various cities of Europe and the British Isles. The 1929 congress was held in connection with the Fifth World Conference of the New Education Fellowship, a prestigious organization of educators from all over the world, at which Montessori had been invited to deliver one of the main addresses before close to two thousand delegates.

Throughout the 1920s meetings of international educators had been spreading the word about philosphies of learning and methods of teaching that their devotees hoped could effect reform that might contribute to international understanding and help maintain the increasingly precarious troubled peace of the world. Montessori had taken part in the first International Congress of New Education in Calais in 1921 and had been a participant at many similar gatherings since. In the late twenties a World Conference on Education was held at Geneva, a World Conference on Adult Education at Cambridge. At the highly publicized Conference on New Education held in Elsinore, Denmark, in the summer of 1929, Maria Montessori was very much in evidence and her method one of the half dozen which were major topics of discussion. Of these, it is interesting to note that of the three European plans under discussion—the Montessori Method, the Decroly Method, and the Cousinet Method— each was known by the name of its inventor, an Italian, a Belgian, and a Frenchman respectively, while the three American systems—the Dalton Plan, the Winnetka Technique, and Purposeful Activity—were impersonally designated.

Many Danish students had taken her course in England and hundreds of teachers attended the Montessori congress held in conjunction with the conference; in addition, Montessori gave a short introductory course in the method to the larger conference, delivered one of its main open lectures, and heard her method described by some of its leading proponents—Claude A. Claremont of the London Montessori Training College, Lili Roubiczek of the Vienna Montessori School, and Caroline W. Tromp and Rosa Joosten-Chotzen of the Amsterdam Montessori Elementary School, each of whom described the work being done at their institutions.

The conference, held under the auspices of the New Education Fellowship, brought together eighteen hundred teachers and school administrators from forty-three countries. They met in the great hall of Kronberg Castle overlooking the sea. Journalists who reported on the conference invariably pointed out that it was on these battlements that Hamlet had confronted the ghost of his father.

The Indian poet Rabindranath Tagore was there to tell about the school he had founded near Calcutta as well as the many other Tagore-

Montessori schools throughout India. There were a number of Indian delegates who shared Tagore's enthusiasm for Montessori's work and who brought the method back with them when they returned to various parts of India, finding it peculiarly adaptable to the all but staggering needs of their huge illiterate, impoverished, agrarian population.

Helen Parkhurst was there too, now an authority in her own right, no longer a follower but a peer of her one-time teacher.

The king must die, the child, if he has any mettle, overtake and supersede his parent, something it was always hard for Montessori to accept about her own followers. But despite the passage of time and the burgeoning of new developments in the field of educational thought, Montessori retained the same ability to impress her audience.

To the reporter for the *Scottish Educational Journal*[3] there was "something wonderfully fascinating in Dr. Montessori as she quietly, simply and affectionately speaks of the *bambino* who should be given the opportunity to develop in a suitable environment with the helpful, not hampering guidance of the adult."

There were those who wondered about the consistency of such a view with the tenets of the Italian government with which she was now officially associated. A correspondent for the London *Teacher's World* wrote that "Mme. Montessori was accompanied by her nephew, and was honored by the presence and greetings of a representative of Sr. Mussolini. In connection with this latter fact I hear that at one of the Montessori meetings a questioner asked how the methods advocated by Mme. Montessori and the freedom implicit in them could be reconciled with the present political regime in Italy. Mme. Montessori's answer was discreet. The child must lead, she said, and its education must be adapted to its nature, its aspirations and needs. That she would apply as the guiding rule. The political implications she did not pursue, and her questioner had to draw his own conclusions."[4]

It is one of the paradoxes of Montessori's personality that, given her dedication to fostering independence in children, she was so little able to tolerate independence in those around her. Her students began by being as children to her; they even called her "Mammolina." When they "grew up" and showed any indication of using what they learned from her to strike out on their own, she perceived it as a betrayal, although she eventually forgave them.

Typical of this pattern was the experience of Elise Herbatschek, one of the young members of the Vienna Arbeitsgemeinschaft who worked with Lili Roubiczek at the Haus der Kinder in the early 1920s. "Lisl," as she was called, was a talented pianist whose unconventional outlook on life was the despair of her proper, cultured, upper-middle-class parents. Like many of the young people who were magnetized by Montessori, she felt herself at loose ends, uncertain how to use herself or her gifts. "I didn't know what I wanted but I didn't want to dress up and go to parties and get married. I was interested in Indian thought, in Theosophy, and at the same time in doing something to make a better world."[5] A friend who was working at the Haus der Kinder invited her to visit, and a new world seemed to open to her. Turning her back on a promising concert career, she threw herself into the social-work project in the slums, where she took charge of the teaching of music in the Haus. When Montessori visited the Haus in 1923 the young woman was thrilled by Montessori's approval and her suggestion that Lisl undertake to extend her repertoire of musical pieces which would stimulate the spontaneous movements of the children.

To the young women working at the school, some of them, like Lisl, barely out of adolescence, Montessori's presence brought new inspiration. "She was a fantastic personality. When she was around there was nothing else in the room. She seemed very motherly, very kind. She had beautiful dark eyes. We loved and respected her. To us she was next to God. She was vain, which amused us, but we loved her for that, too. She had put on weight in middle age; her legs were heavy, and she always wore long dresses and would never go upstairs in front of someone else, or go to the bathroom in any one else's presence. She was an old-fashioned lady. She loved young people, liked to watch them dance and enjoy themselves; it was as if she wanted to be young too, at the same time that she wanted to be recognized for her achievements. She was very human."[6]

The young teachers who didn't speak Italian spoke French to Montessori, who in turn spoke to them in Spanish, a language in which she felt at home, or Italian. Except when she was lecturing, translation never seemed to be necessary.

Montessori was interested in developing the musical aspect of the method and she liked the pretty and irrepressible young girl, whom she liked to call "the Klavier-Lisl with the wine-red cheeks," and she invited Lisl to visit her in Rome and try out some of her musical ideas with Mario's children, Marilena and the little Mario, and some of their friends. Montessori found time to be present when Lisl played for the children and made suggestions Lisl found as stimulating as she found the time she spent with the family enjoyable. When it was time for her to return to Vienna, Montessori told her she thought it would be a good idea for the young woman to take the Montessori training course in order to understand the ideas behind the method more fully and be able to apply them to the field of music. Lisl had no money from her family, who saw her present life as a distinct comedown from their expectations for her, and Montessori offered to arrange for her take the course without paying. Lisl enrolled in the Montessori Department at St. Christopher's College in Letchworth, where the students under Claude Claremont attended Montessori's lectures and observed children in Montessori classes in various London schools.

During the course the Montessoris were living in a house in St. John's Wood, where Lisl was often invited to play her "little marches" for the children. Montessori would stand by the piano urging her to play with "a strong clear rhythm" and "singing" melodic lines, and once she told Lisl that on her numerous train trips she would listen to the sound of the wheels, finding a rhythm to which she could hum the melodies she had heard Lisl play.

The young woman felt herself almost a member of the family, a replacement for the real family temporarily lost to her, like so many of the young people who clustered around Montessori throughout her life. She babysat for the lively little Montessori children, went on outings with the family, and acted as the Dottoressa's assistant during her lectures on musical training for the course, where she demonstrated the use of the bells and tone blocks that formed the materials for learning to read and write music. When Lisl returned to Vienna, it was with Montessori's blessing for a project in which she would put together a collection of musical pieces to be published as part of the Montessori materials.

In 1926 Montessori asked Lisl to come to Milan to assist in the training course she was giving under the auspices of the government there. Montessori introduced each of the classes in music, during which Lisl played and the student-teachers, many of them nuns in traditional habits, skipped, ran, or marched to the music. It was Lisl who on this occasion had to substitute more "suitable" Italian tunes for her original eclectic selection that the Fascist authorities found unacceptable.

One of Lisl's friends in the Vienna Arbeitsgemeinschaft had married B. Shiva Rao, a journalist who later became a member of the Indian parliament, and was living in Benares, where she had started a successful Montessori school. In 1927 Kitty Shiva Rao sent a cable inviting Lisl to come to India for two years to start and be in charge of a Montessori school in Allahabad under the auspices of the Theosophical Society. Lisl was already interested in the ideas of Theosophy and in Indian mysticism, and the idea of combining this interest with her interest in the Montessori method fascinated her. The prospect of going to India, and to do such work, was irresistible. Without thinking of consulting anyone, she accepted the offer.

Montessori and Lili Roubiczek were then working out plans to make the Vienna Haus der Kinder a model demonstration school for Montessori training, and had counted on Lisl's taking charge of the music program. When Lisl informed Montessori of her plans, the Dottoressa was furious. Lisl received a four-page letter, full of reproaches for her ingratitude. Montessori had undertaken to train her, let her take the course "for nothing," and now she was leaving Vienna just when she could be useful to Montessori there.

Lisl was despondent. "The letter," she said, "threw me into a deep well of unhappiness."[7] However, she felt she could not go back on her decision; she had made a commitment. She was just twenty-one at the time, and healthy enough to need to assert her majority, however painful the process. She had never taken to the hangers-on around Montessori. "I loved Montessori," she said later, "but I also had a mother to love. And I was Viennese—I wasn't like the rest of them. At first I felt like committing suicide but then I bought myself some chocolates and life became good again."[8]

Montessori refused to let her come to Milan to say goodbye, and Lisl left for India, where she set about establishing the school at Allahabad. During the two years she spent there she sent regular monthly reports on the progress of her work to Montessori, along with news of the Montessori movement in India, and she repaid the money which the course would have cost.

She had no reply, but after returning to Vienna she decided to attend the Montessori Congress during the New Education Conference in Elsinore in 1929. Of course, the two women met. "No words can describe my relief and joy," the younger one remembered later, "when the Dottoressa took me into her arms. She had forgiven me."[9] Without further ado, Montessori asked her to give a report on Montessori schools in India to the congress.

Lisl described traveling in Denmark with the Montessoris that summer: "We went through all the castles with a carload of children, Montessori's little grandchildren sitting on the hood of the car. She delighted in them."[10]

With Mario at her side as her assistant, the activities of the movement became increasingly organized, particularly after the establishment of the AMI. Both Montessoris were convinced that it was necessary to keep control of the movement in the Dottoressa's hands in order to keep the method from being watered down, that the ideal situation was to have the method accepted by government officials and carried out in the state schools under Montessori's direction by teachers trained by her and supervised by her. She did not want to be employed by and thus responsible to any educational institution except one which she herself would direct and therefore would accept no university teaching position such as she might have been offered in a department of education or child study. She wanted to be free to travel from country to country, giving her lectures and training courses. Both Montessoris were dedicated to the idea of creating a world movement. Inevitably, there was a commercial side to the movement. With no other salary or regular source of income, in order for her to live comparatively well and take care of Mario and his family, Montessori had to retain—a task she increasingly came to delegate to Mario—control of the profits from the sale of the teaching materials she had designed rather than allow them to go into the pockets of imitators and adapters. The AMI was to function not only as organizer of courses and overseer of teacher training, not only as a way of keeping the various worldwide Montessori schools and societies in touch with each other and disseminating information about the movement's ideas and activities, but also as a firm controlling rights to the publication of Montessori's books and the manufacture and sale of the materials as well as recipient of training-course fees.

Among those whom the AMI official letterhead listed as sponsors in its early years were government officials, including presidents, ministers, and ambassadors of numerous countries in Europe and Central and South America, as well as such distinguished private individuals as Sigmund Freud, Giovanni Gentile, Guglielmo Marconi, Jan Masaryk, Jean Piaget, and Rabindranath Tagore.

The years 1929–30 were also the apogee of Montessori's career in Fascist Italy. Plans were announced for a six-month international training course to be held in Rome in the winter of 1930 sponsored by the Opera Montessori under the auspices of the Italian government. Mussolini would honor Montessori by accepting the presidency of the Fifteenth International Theoretical and Practical Training Course on Child Education, the first of Montessori's international training courses to be held in Italy since before World War I. Gentile would be acting president. News reports pointed out that "the importance the Italian government attaches to the course is demonstrated by the fact that the Minister of Foreign Affairs has undertaken to make it known in foreign countries, while the Education Minister has asked that two teachers from each of the larger Italian cities shall be sent to attend the course. It is the first time in

311

history that the Italian government has taken such an interest in a system of education devised by a private individual."[11]

It was now three years since the establishment of the Montessori method on an experimental basis in schools throughout Rome following Montessori's preparation of a first group of teachers in her 1926 training course for Italian teachers at Milan. At first it had been intended to institute the method only in infant and early elementary classes, the authorities being inclined in the beginning to think of the method only in terms of young children, but the first year's results convinced the authorities to extend the experiment to the upper elementary and the secondary levels, and the results were so successful that it was reported that officials and employees of the ministry of education were sending their own children to Montessori classes and asking for admission for their daughters to the training college.

Italy was still talking, along with the great powers, England and the United States, about the reduction of armaments and the establishment of a lasting peace in Europe, bargaining for prestige and power in the community of nations. As part of his propaganda efforts, Mussolini saw the international Montessori course as a showcase for modern Italian culture in general and educational reform in particular.

Newspapers in Italy and those in other countries fed by press releases from Rome pointed out that although Montessori was known all over the civilized world, the Fascist government was the first to recognize Montessori and her methods officially in her own country; that although Montessori schools had existed in Italy for many years the government had now taken up the cause of developing and extending them under its direct patronage. The fifteenth international Montessori training course would be the first ever held under official government auspices.

Montessori was still living in Barcelona, and although she had spent a part of every year in Italy since coming back in 1922 to begin giving training courses and oversee the various developments of the movement under the new government, her "return to Rome" as a national heroine was to be the theme of the press reports on the course.[12] The occasion was described as "a real homecoming, for although, like the Duce, a child of the Marches, her early life was spent in Rome," and as "a landmark in the history of child education." The foreign press saw it as "a triumph for Dr. Montessori that her results have aroused such enthusiasm in the conservative and bureaucratic Ministry of Education and that the head of state should be moved to call students from all over the world to the six-month course."[13]

Three times a week Montessori would lecture to the students—one

312

hundred teachers from twenty-one different nations—and some seventy practical demonstrations of the use of the didactic materials would be held under her direction. Italian citizens and members of religious orders would pay 1,000 lire (then a little over fifty dollars) to take the course; foreigners would pay around three times that sum. Translation for those who did not understand Italian would cost the equivalent of about five dollars a month.

The course was officially opened on January 30, 1930, by the then minister of education Signor Giuliano, other government notables, and various officials of the Opera Montessori, some of whom were ex officio members of that body by virtue of their government positions. The opening ceremonies were held in the Senatorial Palace of the Capitol and pictures recording the event make it unmistakably clear what the real interest of the government in the occasion was. Montessori, ever alert against exploitation by private individuals and commercial enterprises, was being exploited as never before by a government using her name and the prestige of the movement that bore that name to bolster its own credentials in the world of education and culture. In the official photographs of the occasion Montessori stands, dressed as always in black, her middle-aged figure portly and her rounded face serious under a close-fitting black hat, dwarfed before a neoclassical statue of an ancient Roman. They are an odd but significant pair, hardly an accidental one—Mussolini's chosen symbols of the grandeur that was Rome in ancient days and which he liked to think of himself as restoring to Italy, juxtaposed with the glory of Italy's present in the person of a world-famous and ubiquitously admired figure in education whom he could also claim to be restoring to the nation.

As for Montessori, she was not the first to have dreamed of returning to Rome in glory. Now she was back in the city where, in the last decade of the previous century, she had walked from her parents' home to enroll herself at the university from which she would be the first woman to graduate as a doctor of medicine. It would have taken more political acumen than Montessori possessed, whatever her other strengths of understanding, to resist such a homecoming, the realization of the very human dream we all have of coming back where we began our lives to be honored for what we have made of ourselves since. The rest of the world had heaped honors on her; to the child within every man and woman the only honor that counts is the honor of home.

After their reconciliation at Elsinore in 1929, Lisl Herbatschek, who was now Frau Braun, had kept in touch with Montessori and the move-

313

ment in Vienna. In the spring of 1930 Montessori asked her to come to Rome to give some music demonstrations for the international training course. Montessori's former anger by now completely forgotten by both of them, the Dottoressa welcomed the younger woman back into the fold. Her recollections of that time provide some glimpses into the personal side of Montessori in middle age, when a curtain of pious respect was already being closed over her individuality and making her a public figure like that of the marble—or was it plaster?—Roman statue in front of which she was photographed at the opening of the course.

Montessori invited Lisl to a reception at St. Peter's at which the pope would be present. Lisl had no proper clothes to wear in the presence of the pope; all the dresses she had with her were short-skirted and short-sleeved. Montessori delighted in dressing her up for the occasion, wrapping one of her own long black cloaks around her young friend and adding one of her own dark veils to cover her head, re-creating the situation of the little girl dressing up in her mother's clothes, part of the kind of play Montessori had missed out on, having raised no small child of her own.

On another evening she asked Lisl to keep her company in the spacious apartment where she lived during the course. She asked the younger woman to go through the large rooms turning on all the electric switches so all the rooms would be brightly lit. Someone had given Montessori a box of chocolates in the shape of a book, and as they sat together eating the candy, Montessori recited a piece of poetry in her melodious Italian for every piece she took out of the box.

On a warm day when there were no classes, "Mammolina," Mario, Lisl, and two other Montessori teachers drove out to the beach in Ostia for a picnic. Montessori was happiest in the company of the young and she delighted in watching them frolic on the beach, running, shouting, singing, and dancing. "In her presence," said Lisl, "we all felt like children.[14] Over the years, whenever we saw her, it was a lovely time. Wonderfully serious, but with fun."[15]

The Brauns, whose sympathies were strongly anti-Fascist, did not go to a reception where Mussolini was to be present, but they made allowances for Montessori's willingness to work with him at the time. "He helped so much, and that was enough."[16]

One of the young Americans who took Montessori's training course in Rome in 1930 was Catherine Pomeroy (later Collins).[17] She was just seventeen when she came to Rome to visit a married sister living there. Hearing about the course, she applied for admission, only to be told by Mario Montessori that she was too young. "But I'll be eighteen soon!"

she objected, whereupon Mario laughed and agreed to allow her to enroll.

The course enthralled her. Remembering Montessori's teaching years later, she said, "Her lectures were always dramatic. She would use props to demonstrate her points, like having two model skeletons, one of a child and one of an adult, side by side, to illustrate that the child was not just a little man or woman. She'd had the child's skeleton made up to be the same size as the adult one, and of course it looked grotesque. And she would say that the child was just as different psychologically as physiologically, mentally as physically, and if you tried to treat him like a miniature grown-up the result would be as monstrous as the blown-up skeleton." (In retrospect, Montessori's use of the human skeleton for her own teaching purposes inevitably suggests a kind of reassertion of her mastery over once-feared emotions and the objects that aroused them. One remembers the terror and repulsion the young Maria had felt when confronted with a skeleton on her first day in the anatomy hall of the medical school, described in the letter she wrote after passing her exams.)

Young Catherine Pomeroy soon become friendly with both Mario and his mother, and when the course ended she joined them and two young Indian students on a trip to the Dolomites. The Montessoris stayed in an elegant hotel and the students in a simpler one; during the days they drove into the mountains in an Isotta Frascini touring car, picnicked together, and explored the mountain scenery. The Montessoris returned to Rome, to the beautiful apartment they had been given in the Monte Mario section for their stay there, one of the lovely houses or apartments friends made available to Montessori wherever she went to give courses. Except for Barcelona and, later, Holland, she had no permanent home of her own; what was important in life to her was her work, which kept her constantly on the move.

Catherine Pomeroy Collins remembers Montessori as retiring, almost shy, in company. "She would sit quietly; if you came to her she would talk." And she had a sense of Montessori as frustrated by the "politics" of dealing with people, in which capacity Mario had become more or less her "agent," standing between her and the crowd of would-be hangers-on—not her students but those always ready to make some proposition involving her method or her materials—who always seemed to be approaching her. "She liked to eat," recalled Mrs. Collins years later, "had become quite heavy, was self-conscious about her heaviness and always wore long dresses in the fashion of a bygone decade—like my grandmother would have dressed." A large figure in black, she indulged her delicate taste by always wearing a flower or a jewel pinned to her dress.

Now that he was grown up and had joined her in her work, Mario had become her protector. They always seemed to be surrounded by an entourage, to most of whom Montessori was a queen if not a saint. Only those who got closest to her were aware of her human qualities, the tastes and habits of the person behind the public figure presented to the world at large. Mario, too, worshiped her, and made helping her in her work his own life work, second to everything else, even his own family, as he traveled with her and took over more and more of the tasks of organizing and administering the activities of the movement through the AMI. He made it his mission to see that neither the method nor the materials were exploited for the advantage of others but would accrue to the movement itself through the AMI. And there were perquisites of the position that were enjoyable too—traveling in style, staying in wealthy private homes or in the grand hotels of Europe, being honored by the important and the influential on all the unending occasions of arrival and departure in cities all over the world. As time passed, Montessori came to depend more and more on her son—although she could not acknowledge the relationship outside the intimate circle of their closest friends and associates—in the countless organizational details of her work.

And she was always thinking of her work. Wherever she went she observed, made notes, thought, wrote. Mrs. Collins remembers her as "always working on some new idea. If she was left alone for a minute we'd come back and find her working out some new material in geometry or inventing some kind of game that would begin by challenging the child and end by teaching him something—he'd discover the square root of some number or the solution to some equation, see the application of some algebraic principle."

Anna Maccheroni once told of going to the movies with Montessori. Even there, in the dark theater with the action unfolding on the screen and Maccheroni herself "far from thinking about children and mathematics," the younger woman found Montessori turning to her and whispering a thought she had just had about teaching the Pythagorean theorem.[18] (Again, one thinks of Maria Montessori as a young girl—the child Maria studying her math book in the semidarkness of a theater.)

Looking back, Mrs. Collins judged, "She was too anxious to make sure her ideas took hold to make sure of the people doing it. Sometimes this led to bad judgement, such as her suggestion, when I left Italy to come home to college, that I take charge of starting up the movement again in the United States. I was too young, too unprepared, and not even really very good as a teacher of young children. Montessori—we called her Mammolina then—never understood that many of the people she

316

trained didn't have sufficient training before that. They would come to her unprepared by previous education and she would train them in her method and then consider them experts, despite the fact that, like me, they had no previous credentials, were not really equipped to understand the full scope of her intellectual work.

"Her mind was always on the cause. She had to direct things herself. She would tolerate anyone who would carry out her work in her way—the only important thing was getting her message about the child across—but over and over again she broke with those who tried to do things a different way or carry out her ideas on their own in another direction."

As her secretary and protector, Mario laid the political groundwork and represented her to the world. And he too tolerated only those who accepted her word as law, believing it indeed to be so. The last in a series of acolytes, he remained faithful to the end.

As for Montessori's thoughts about Mussolini at the time, Mrs. Collins agreed with many others who knew Montessori that "she couldn't have cared less about politics as long as she could go on with her work, develop her ideas about educating children. When they tried to influence her, when the iron fist began to show in the velvet glove, she got out." It could, and would, happen in a day.

When the Rome course ended late in June 1930 Montessori returned to Barcelona, where she celebrated her sixtieth birthday that August with her family and her close circle of associates. There were messages of congratulation from admirers and followers all over the world.

She returned to Rome again the following year to give the sixteenth international course, from January to June 1931, the regular English course being postponed from summer to autumn that year. Students from Italy were joined in Rome by others from England, Ireland, Sweden, Denmark, Holland, Switzerland, Germany, Austria, Hungary, Portugal, Lithuania, Rumania, India, Argentina, and Chile. And in February the first issue of a new Montessori review, *Revista Montessori*, appeared in Rome.

Later that year she gave an address to the faculty of medicine at the University of Paris. Montessori liked to have a child present whenever she spoke in public. The little girl chosen to present her with flowers on this occasion—Anna Marie Bernard, the daughter of playwright Jean-Jacques Bernard—later became head of the Montessori Association of France.

Several members of the Arbeitsgemeinschaft, including Lisl Braun and her husband, came from Vienna to Rome in 1932. Once again Klavier-Lisl had been asked to assist Montessori by demonstrating the use of the Montessori musical material, which Lisl had enlarged on with the approval of the Dottoressa. Montessori liked her protégée's husband, an engineer with whom she had long discussions about how abstract mathematical problems could be "materialized" and solved. Several times they all dined together in Italian restaurants. On one occasion, disapproving of their technique for eating pasta, Montessori gave them a lesson in how to roll the spaghetti over a spoon onto a fork, demonstrating the same seriousness of purpose about skill and dexterity in the practical little things of life that she had shown to the children in the Casa dei Bambini when she taught them how to blow their noses. To her admiring audience it seemed that "whether lecturing, solving mathematical problems, listening to music, or showing how to eat spaghetti, there was always the same intensity and artistic perfection in the Dottoressa."[19]

21

Throughout the 1920s Montessori's influence continued to be felt in and around Austria's capital. Montessori schools began to crop up outside Vienna, mostly in outlying areas not too far from the metropolis. By 1928 Roubiczek's original school had fifty children aged two and a half to ten. In 1930 a new school was opened on the Rudolfsplatz in the center of town. It included a number of middle-class children and was widely publicized. The school on the Rudolfsplatz had been designed, after two years of planning and revising with the Montessori group, by architect Franz Schuster in the style of the Bauhaus, the German school that was revolutionizing industrial arts and architecture in the West.

By 1930 Vienna was seething with ideas for social welfare programs and new schools were being built at a rapid pace. On the outskirts of the city a new municipal building complex included at its center a unique day-care center where two hundred workers' children spent all day and hundreds more were received for half a day. A special section was run along Montessori lines.

In December 1930 Montessori lectured again in Vienna, with Lili Roubiczek as her translator. Roubiczek's influence in not only implementing the Montessori movement in Vienna but relating it to a larger context of ideas about education informed by the new field of psychoanalysis as well as classroom teaching itself cannot be overemphasized. She was as magnetic a personality as Montessori, the center of a group of young teachers whose devotion to her was combined with their dedication to the ideal of somehow making a better world at a specific historical moment when a sense of social needs was joined with a belief that one's efforts could accomplish something real and worthwhile, useful and significant.

On the occasion of this visit by Montessori, Roubiczek introduced her to members of various groups the younger woman had interested in helping with the organization of new schools and arranged for her to meet and exchange ideas with some of the more important figures in psychology and education, including Anna Freud.

As early as 1917 Montessori was well enough known and highly enough regarded by intellectuals throughout Europe and in particular by those who, like Anna Freud, were interested in early childhood, to have received the following letter from Sigmund Freud:[1]

319

MARIA MONTESSORI: A Biography

Vienna, IX, Bergasse 19
December 20, 1917

My dear Frau Montessori

It gave me great pleasure to receive a letter from you. Since I have been preoccupied for years with the study of the child's psyche, I am in deep sympathy with your humanitarian and understanding endeavors, and my daughter, who is an analytical pedagogue, considers herself one of your disciples.

I would be very pleased to sign my name beside yours on the appeal for the foundation of a little institute as planned by Frau Schaxel.* The resistance my name may arouse among the public will have to be conquered by the brilliance that radiates from yours.

Yours very sincerely,
Freud

In the late twenties Roubiczek's growing interest in the relationship between psychoanalysis and education had led to a series of biweekly seminars with Anna Freud. Several of the Montessori teachers had enrolled in the training program for teachers at the Vienna Psychoanalytic Institute, and Roubiczek was invited to participate in the institute's seminar in which Anna Freud trained the first child analysts.

Roubiczek had hoped to establish some connection deeper than a polite exchange of compliments between the two women, but the younger had already ventured too far into the new field led by her father and its new way of looking at the mind, for Montessori to be able to follow her. Ideas like infant sexuality and the primacy of emotional conflict in determining later development were alien to the older woman. When later most of her early Viennese followers went into psychoanalysis as a profession, one of them remembers, "She didn't like to hear about that."[2]

When Roubiczek's hopes of interesting Montessori in psychoanalysis were disappointed, as indeed they were bound to be, Emma Plank surmised that "this probably was the beginning of the loosening of their bond."[3]

While many of the early pioneers in psychoanalysis came from the field of medicine, a number in the early Viennese group came from the field of education. In particular, many of the early child analysts began as teachers who became interested in psychoanalysis in the years between the two world wars, when the psychoanalytic movement in Vienna was a frontier of intellectual pioneering and new ideas were being generated that would change man's way of understanding himself, radically and forever. "Forever," not because they were formulated definitively

*Later the wife of Willi Hoffer, one of Freud's early followers in Vienna who later practiced psychoanalysis in London.

and would not be subject to revision, but because there could be no going back to a way of thinking before them. On the occasion of Lili Roubiczek's death in 1966, Anna Freud wrote to her colleague Rudolf Ekstein:

> The first meetings of my colleagues and myself with Lili Peller [Roubiczek had married Dr. Sigismund Peller and in her later years was known professionally by her married name] were most exciting ones. This was in Vienna, in the 1930's, i.e., when we were intent on forging links between psychoanalysis and education. At that time Lili Peller had already built up a model nursery school which combined the best elements of the Montessori method with the application of the most important principles of psychoanalytic child-psychology. Her work in that setting was admirable and acted as an inspiration.[4]

By 1932 Roubiczek was publishing papers like one on the theory of play in the *Zeitschrift für Psychoanalytische Pädagogik,* the journal concerned with applying the contributions of psychoanalytic thought to education, particularly in such areas as the development of language and that special language of the child—his play. During the next few years she continued to publish reports from the seminars of the Vienna Montessori school in the psychoanalytic literature, writing on early childhood education from a point of view combining Montessori pedagogy with psychoanalysis. Gradually, she identified more and more with the psychoanalytic point of view, eventually becoming a psychoanalyst herself. Ekstein described her contribution as maintaining "the best of ideas from educational philosophy, as well as the findings of the experimentations of Montessori. She created a synthesis between the most progressive educational thinking and the discoveries of psychoanalysis."[5]

Roubiczek belonged to a group that included such early leaders of the new movement in Vienna that was relating psychoanalysis to education as Anna Freud, Erik Erikson, Robert Waelder, Peter Blos, and Fritz Redl, who when they were forced out of Vienna by Hitler's takeover brought with them to England and the United States a significant residue of Montessori's thinking if not her name, just as exposure to her ideas influenced the work of Piaget in Switzerland and of numerous other less well known but influential figures in fields of child psychology allied to education.

Montessori had lectured in Berlin in the fall of 1922, at which time, despite the spread of Montessori schools and classes all over the world, there was only one Montessori school in Germany, and again at the end of 1926 on her return from Argentina, when she gave a course for teachers in Berlin at the invitation of the German Montessori Society. She did not return until 1931, by which time she was somewhat better known there, partly as a result of ties between the Vienna and Berlin educational circles. In the decade since her 1922 visit the number of Montessori schools in Germany had grown to thirty-four, eighteen of them in Berlin.

She spoke at Berlin University, where she had what was for her a uniquely cool reception. *Der Tag* reported that the academic community criticized her as "hardly a serious lecturer" (one has only to think of the German professorial style and of Montessori's somewhat impressionistic and inspirational tone, her extemporaneous delivery, her expressive gestures, to appreciate the incongruity between the two), that her talk consisted merely of empty phrases and theoretical clichés, and that her view that children were being treated like property, "enslaved by their schools and their families," was ridiculous. The lecture, it was reported, was well attended but there was little applause from the almost two thousand people in the hall.

Even before the event Montessori had anticipated the nature of her reception, remarking that she was not understood in Germany, where her ideas had been misinterpreted and her teaching misapplied by people who were "not qualified." She might have meant that they were not trained by her, but the real reason probably lay deeper in some underlying antithesis between her Latin temperament and the stolid authoritarian German academic community. She might talk about order and discipline, but few had actually read her book. What they did know was gleaned from the popular press, in which she was associated with that other radical and probably dangerous theoretician, Freud. The popular understanding of the ideas of both of them was the distorted one that one must never "repress" a child's impulses, that home and school should allow the child complete freedom to do as he pleased. Of course this could only lead to anarchy and to disruption of social institutions. And of course it was as far from what Montessori meant as it was from what Freud actually said.

Montessori spent little time in Germany and the movement never really spread there beyond a small circle of followers outside the official educational establishment. An American visitor to the model Montessori school in Berlin found it an anomalous institution there, in marked contrast to the idea of Germany he had "so long thought of as a land of regimentation in its lower schools."[6] By 1933 all Montessori schools in Germany were forced to close, and an effigy of Montessori was burned over a pyre of her books in a public square in Berlin.

The Second International Montessori Congress was held at Nice in the summer of 1932, again in conjunction with the conference of the New Education Fellowship. It ended in early August. Tentative plans to hold the Third Montessori Congress in Germany in 1933 had to be canceled because of the political situation and the location was shifted to Amsterdam at the last minute with the help of some of Montessori's many influential Dutch friends and supporters. As always, there were representatives of many different countries present. The lectures and visits to the schools were supplemented by an impressive exposition in which the materials were displayed and the work of children from all over the world was shown, and there were excursions like the one to the Zuiderseewerken—the newly reclaimed land—that were planned to bring together the Montessori emphasis on "building" the future through education and the kind of building that was an expression of the small and well-integrated country's interest in national development.

At the third congress, held under the auspices of the Dutch Montessori Society in the summer of 1933, Montessori gave a series of lectures entitled "The Spiritual Regeneration of Man." In person she remained as down-to-earth, as practical as ever, but her public pronouncements were increasingly taking on the lofty tone and unspecific character that made her seem less and less scientist, more and more prophet.

By the mid-1930s the Netherlands Montessori Society had around a thousand members, an impressive number for a country with a total population of less than eight million. By that time there were over two hundred Montessori schools, both infant and elementary, in twenty-eight communities throughout Holland, with over six thousand children enrolled. Most of these were private schools, but there were public ones in Amsterdam, Rotterdam, and Haarlem.

Of all the Montessori schools throughout the world, the Dutch had the most consistently best. The wealthy middle class adopted the system, seeing in it what they wanted for their children, and the circle of teachers and interested parents remained in constant contact with her. The social milieu was a stable one, and no political upheavals threatened the movement or interfered with its activities.

In January 1930 an English branch of the AMI was inaugurated and the members of the existing London Montessori society transferred to it

323

en bloc. The group was now as "official" as it was possible to be, a branch of a parent body headed by Montessori herself.

Despite the benevolent despotism of her own organization, Montessori continued to preach a revolutionary freedom for the child. In a paper read to the English Montessori group in 1932 she spoke again of the oppression of the child. "Never were slaves more completely the property of their owners, never have laws so forgotten the rights of men, never was laborer so forced to work just as his employer decided, and without possibility of appeal, as the child at home and in school, always subordinate to the grownup, who imposes upon him the length of his work and the length of his sleep."[7] The idea of the child as a social being with rights of his own, she reminded her audience, had yet to be generally accepted. It was an idea she had been urging on the world since her earliest public speeches in the 1890s.

When Montessori gave her nineteenth international training course in London in the fall and winter of 1933 a simultaneous course was held in Dublin for teachers unable to make the journey to London. Her lectures were read there and she personally gave a two-week series of lectures to wind up the Dublin course early in January 1934. As always, her presence on the scene stimulated publicity, new interest and enthusiasm, the formation of committees and of a Montessori Society of Ireland.

By the mid-1930s press reports of her training courses in England became still more cursory, the detailed accounts of her lectures gradually giving way to short paragraphs summarizing the entire course. Montessori was no longer "news," and accounts of her thoughts and activities increasingly took a back seat to discussions of the Dalton Plan and other educational systems. Her quasi-mystical style began to sound more and more old-fashioned as she was quoted in such statements as that education deals with "the secret of the soul of the child—the incarnating of the spirit—the most mysterious and marvelous of creative processes."[8] Few teachers could live happily with a philosophy of education which stated that "in this work adults can take no part except to offer the necessary means for its consummation without let or hindrance."[9]

But the real threat to the Montessori movement in Europe was the deepening political crisis spreading throughout the Continent and affecting all intellectual institutions and social movements. What Churchill called the "gathering storm" had been apparent to many for some time before its nature was made manifestly clear to all by events in Austria.

Postwar Austria was sharply split between the urban working-class socialists and intellectual members of the Austrian Labor Party and the conservative rural Catholics of the Christian Social party, the peasantry and lower middle class who formed a national majority. By the 1930s, the socialists, who controlled the municipal government of Vienna, had developed one of the most advanced social welfare programs, including housing and education, in Europe at the time.

With the deepening crisis brought on by worldwide depression and the growth of the Austrian Nazi party, the country became increasingly paralyzed politically. Something close to a brief civil war broke out in Austria early in 1934 between the militantly atheistic socialists and the conservatives and clericals led by the Christian Social chancellor Engelbert Dollfuss, supported by the Austrian Fascist militia, the Heimwehr. When Dollfuss closed down parliament and began to rule by decree in the name of the new native Fascist movement, the Fatherland Front, the Viennese socialists rebelled and the militia moved in to subdue them. All the socialist organizations were broken up, their hundreds of thousands of followers scattered. In the conflict there was an attack on the model workers' housing that had been admired throughout Europe, bombarded by government forces which succeeded in ending Austrian democracy and replacing it, after the assassination of Dollfuss, with a weak totalitarian government under a new chancellor, Kurt Schuschnigg. Powerless to resist the Nazis within and across the border, the new government prepared the way for Hitler's takeover four years later.

In 1934, when the socialists lost power and many of them had to leave Austria, and with further financial backing uncertain, the Montessori schools seemed doomed, but they were temporarily saved through the efforts of a sympathetic government official.[10] Dr. Ernst Buschbeck, an art historian who had been a curator at the Kunsthistorische Museum before becoming a government commissioner, had taken an interest in the young people involved in the Haus der Kinder experiment. Wearing the Nazi insignia, he visited the classes, talked with the anxious teachers, and promised them his protection. Like so many conservative intellectuals identified with the new government, Buschbeck considered himself not a forerunner of a new barbarism but a preserver of culture.

Buschbeck's efforts enabled the Montessori school to survive for another four years. Eventually the group involved in the Vienna school reform movement, most of whom were liberal socialists, many of whom belonged to the Austrian Labor Party, and a large number of whom were Jewish, had to leave. By 1938, like most of the psychoanalysts, they had become exiles.

Lili Roubiczek Peller left Austria with her physician husband in 1934, first for Jerusalem, and later for the United States, where from 1940 until her death in 1966 she practiced psychoanalysis, taught and wrote on child development and early-childhood education.

With the annexation of Austria by Germany in 1938, Vienna was absorbed into the Third Reich. The Anschluss marked the end of the Montessori movement—as it did the end of all creative intellectual life there—until after World War II.

The last Montessori Congress held in Rome before the closing of the Montessori schools in Italy took place in 1934. Among those attending was Swiss psychologist Jean Piaget, who returned to Switzerland to head the Montessori Society there.

During the 1920s Piaget had made his early observations on how young children learn while watching them at play and in the classes of the Maison des Petits, the modified Montessori school at the Institut Jean-Jacques Rousseau in Geneva, of which he became director. A series of publications on the child's construction of his mental world based on his observations at the Maison des Petits and culminating with *The Language and Thought of the Child* in 1924 had already made him internationally famous by the time he reached the age of thirty.

Piaget, who also began as a biologist, found much to use in Montessori's work, particularly in what Montessori had come to call "sensitive periods," the developmental schedule of the child's mental growth; in the role played by repetitive behavior in that process as it developed from motor to mental abilities; and in the need for the environment to provide the stimulation that nourished the child's mental growth just as food did his physical development.[11]

But although Piaget remained for many years president of the Swiss Montessori Society, his studies of children's thinking eventually led him to formulate a theory of cognitive development that went beyond Montessori into avenues of his own. While Montessori's focus was always the practice of teaching, Piaget was a more rigorous theoretician, and became one of the significant contributors to a systematic science of developmental psychology.

By the time plans were under way for the 1934 congress, friction had begun to develop between Montessori and the leaders of Mussolini's Italy. The government, always on the lookout for ways to capitalize on the occasion and put its best foot forward for the visiting foreigners who would attend, proposed to Montessori that she accept an appointment as "Ambassador of Children." Her answer was that she would do so only as a representative of the AMI, not of the Italian government.

By now the government was no longer willing to let Montessori alone determine what would go on in the schools with which it was providing her. Mussolini had organized the schoolboys of Italy into a Fascist youth organization, the Figli della lupa, and now he decided they were to wear their uniforms to school and be required to give the Fascist salute in class.

Why Montessori drew the line at this particular decision is not clear. After all, she had closed her eyes to so much else. Perhaps the bloom of hope had rubbed off with the accumulation of small frustrations, the daily increment of observable repression and brutality that could no longer be denied. In any case, in a single day Montessori schools ceased to exist in Italy.

When Mussolini first came to power a number of Italian intellectuals, writers and academics among them, had found it possible to support him in their desperate hope that he could get the country out of what was a paralyzing political situation. After all, he came to power legally, by royal appointment and with the approval of the parliament, in which even liberals, socialists and Catholics joined in voting him emergency powers for a year in the expectation that he might extricate them from the postwar morass in which the government was floundering. During that crucial first year it became apparent to many what he was up to and by 1923 the only intellectuals who continued to support the government were those who were able to convince themselves that they could use the power given them by the strong new state for some goal they could not otherwise accomplish. Gentile had undertaken to revamp the entire educational system, changing the rigidly classical curriculum stressing Greek and Latin to a more modern one emphasizing history, geography, science, modern languages. And like him, Montessori felt she could use the power given her by the government to accomplish her long-range educational goals, to reform education through the unique opportunity offered her by this government to implement her system throughout the nation's schools. If it had taken her longer than most others to see the tremendous error she had made in her calculations, it was less the result of moral insensitivity than of the depth of her conviction that her system properly carried out under her own supervision must accomplish good results in individual children and in the long run in all of society.

Margaret Homfray, one of her English students who lived with Montessori while taking the 1931 course in Rome, remembered her as "completely apolitical. She went back to Italy when Mussolini invited her because it was her home—Italy was where she felt she belonged, doing her work for the children there. To the extent to which she thought about it at all, she felt her influence would be a liberating one, for the children and their parents. She stayed as long as they left her alone to do things in her own way. She never talked politics."[12]

By 1926 all political parties other than the Fascists had been banned, and all freedoms of press, of assembly, and of speech were ended. The instrumentalities of the dictatorship had been implemented in full. Italy was now a police state and the stage was set for Mussolini's eventual partnership with Hitler.

Still, until Mussolini's formal alliance with Hitler it was not too difficult to live under Fascism in Italy even if you did not agree with the regime, as long as you did not openly oppose it. The authorities were willing to settle for even modest signs of acquiescence—it was enough to wear a party button in one's lapel or simply to appear in public at a Fascist rally and not say anything. The prestige lent by one's presence would be enough. Mussolini saw Montessori's presence and activity in Italy as a coup for his regime, and probably did not care what her private opinions were as long as she made no public anti-Fascist statements and engaged in no clandestine anti-Fascist activity.

Then too, after 1929 the regime was cloaked in the official respectability given by the approval of the Catholic Church.

Italy had been unified at the expense of the Church by leaders who were philosophical children of the Enlightenment and therefore traditionally anticlerical, creating a cleavage in Italian society which was not even partially healed until well into the twentieth century. Ironically, the modus vivendi which was finally arrived at between church and state in modern Italy was formalized by the Fascist regime. The Church was given official recognition again in 1929 by Mussolini and there is reason to think that Montessori, with her political naïveté, failed to see the action as representing the coming together in common interests of the most reactionary and repressive aspects of both institutions, government and church, and saw it instead as a sign of hope for the restoration of traditional and what she called "spiritual" values to Italian society. She had returned to the religion of her childhood after her mother's death, had been received and blessed by the pope, and found in Catholicism an avenue for the expression of the spiritual force she talked about education releasing in the child. She began to write about the application of her method to religious education. In 1922 she had written *I Bambini viventi nella Chiesa*, an account of the application of her method to the religious education of young children at the school in Barcelona, where a special children's chapel had been designed, like a Montessori schoolroom, to the child's own scale. In 1929 her essays on religious education were collected and edited by E. M. Standing and published in English as *The Child in the Church. The Life in Christ (La Vita di Cristo)*, a study of the liturgical year, appeared in 1931, and *The Mass Explained to Children (La Santa Messa spiegata ai bambini)* was published in England in 1932 and in the United States, where it was titled *The Mass Explained to Boys and Girls,* two years later. In addition, she wrote *The Opened Book*, an unpublished missal for older children.

It is hard to find in these books the Maria Montessori who in the early years of the century had, in what she spoke and published and practiced in the schoolroom, broken through old ways of thinking about society and the learning process through which the child comes to understand and take his place in it. Her approach to religion, like her attitude to politics, had become simplistic. In both, she sidestepped the complexities that characterize the searching mind. Increasingly concerned with the practice of the Montessori method and the preservation of the Montessori movement, she was no longer an innovator. Her sense of mission had overtaken her genius. She had gradually changed from a radical inquirer into a conservative who judged social conditions and political institutions primarily on the basis of whether they seemed hospitable to the practice of the method and the spread of the movement she so firmly believed would ultimately transform both the individual child and human society.

It was not the perquisites of power that had made it a Faustian temptation for her to accept the government's invitation to return to Italy and accomplish her work there but her belief in how she could make use of that power to mitigate the worst aspects of the regime rather than merely to talk in the vacuum of continued exile. In the beginning she may have thought of herself as working for Gentile rather than for Mussolini. By the time she saw the preschoolers she had trained wearing Fascist uniforms as teenagers she could no longer deny the brutal realities of the regime and the hopelessness of combating it from within and she left.

And even aside from the specific political style of the regime—after all, she stayed on even after 1931, when all secondary-school teachers, college and university professors were required to take an oath of loyalty to Fascism—there was the personal element. Montessori had always insisted on being the final arbiter, the sole authority on how her ideas were to be expressed and implemented in practice. Any government which stepped in to tell her how things should be done in her schools—whether the radical Catalonians of Spain or the Fascists of Italy—she would oppose, not necessarily on political grounds but on educational ones, not necessarily because she couldn't live with their way of running the country but because only she could determine the way of running her schools.

Whenever she was asked how she could reconcile her role as a fighter for the social rights of children with the actions of a particular regime Montessori simply answered, as she did to a reporter in Vienna in December 1930, "I do not belong to any existing political party." And, indeed, she always thought of herself as the representative of an idea that transcended politics, perhaps missing the point that an idea can be realized only in the context of a specific reality.

With the ambition that had burned in her for so long to have the opportunity to demonstrate what her system of education could accomplish, and after so many disappointments in other places, when this opportunity presented itself she had found it possible to blink at those aspects of the regime that we, with the perspective of hindsight, would have wanted her to see more clearly and to oppose. The truth is that she did not openly oppose the regime until it began to interfere with her own activities as a teacher and a teacher of teachers. There is no evidence of a direct personal confrontation between Montessori and the government authorities. The sudden closing of the Montessori schools may have been ordered by the minister of education because of reports that many of the teachers employed as Montessori directresses were known to be opposed to the Fascist regime.

In any case, once again it was the end of the method and movement in a European country where it had been flourishing, until after World War II.

Montessori returned to Spain, to carry on her work in Barcelona, writing two short works on further applications of the method, *Psico Aritmética* and *Psico Geométria,* published in Spanish in 1934, as well as the unpublished "Psico Gramática," and continuing to give her training courses in London and to travel and lecture elsewhere throughout what was left of a gradually shrinking Europe. And throughout the 1930s she traveled to peace conferences—in Geneva, Brussels, Copenhagen, Utrecht—giving speeches which were later collected and published in Italian as *Educazione e Pace* and appeared in an English translation as *Education and Peace.*

22

Nowhere were local conditions more volatile in the pre-World War II years than in Spain, where the political crisis deepened and terrorism continued through the spring of 1921 until the Moroccan disaster finally undermined the authority of the king and army and brought down the parliamentary regime.

In the wake of the Moroccan defeat of 1921, in an attempt to save the wobbling monarchy of Alfonso XIII and restore order, the military dictatorship of General Miguel Primo de Rivera was declared in September 1923.

Although the Catalonians had withdrawn official support from the Montessori schools, they had been left to operate privately. In October 1924, a year after coming to power, the government of Primo de Rivera closed the model Montessori school at Barcelona that had been Montessori's pedagogical laboratory for almost ten years. The experiment had been caught in the struggle between the central state governing from Madrid and the movement for cultural autonomy and home rule for Catalonia centered in Barcelona. The Associacio protectora de la Ensenyança Catalana (Association for the Encouragement of Catalan Teaching), a private group which had been supporting and administering the schools, had been teaching in the Catalan language, flying the Catalan flag, performing the traditional songs and dances of the region. The new government stepped in to crush this threat to its authority and, with it, the Montessori schools it had sponsored.

At first, the middle classes, terrorized by the syndicalists' violence and particularly the anarchists' disturbances in Barcelona, did not oppose the dictatorship, which rode its crest through the mid-1920s when, after a period of relative order and prosperity, its effectiveness and popularity began to decline. It was a classic case of a dictatorship winning acceptance with the promise of being a temporary measure until conditions could be stabilized and liberties restored. Disillusionment set in when the new government intensified repression and censorship. The middle classes, particularly the liberals and intellectuals of Catalonia with their aspirations to local government, withdrew their support and revolted when the desired reforms failed to materialize in the face of opposition

331

from the two most reactionary forces in the country—the army and the Church.

With renewed economic crisis deepening day by day, the military regime was ousted in 1930, and by 1931 the monarchy had collapsed and a democratic republic was proclaimed in Spain. With it came the promise of renewal of official support for the Montessori movement in Spain.

The Second Republic was inaugurated in a mood of optimism, and nowhere more so than in Barcelona, its stronghold. One of the first cultural acts of the new government was the announcement that it would sponsor a Montessori international training course to be held from February to June of 1933 in Barcelona.

At the 1933 Barcelona international course, the first to be held in Republican Spain, there were two hundred students from seventeen nations on three continents. The course was held in the historic old Town Hall and present in the fourteenth-century Gothic setting were cabinet ministers and government education officials of the modern state. The students were lodged in the former royal palace with its park, library, swimming pools and tennis courts, now known as the Residencia. The two universities of Barcelona were put at Montessori's disposal, and she held her lectures at one and her demonstrations at the other.

Montessori was photographed in front of the former palace, seated among about one hundred and fifty of her students, some in Western dress, some in saris, others in nuns' habits, a few holding young children. Plump and smiling, her hands folded in front of her over her ample dark cloak, surrounded by young faces, she looks for all the world like a satisfied Old Woman in the Shoe—but one who knows exactly what to do.

Now once again in Barcelona the Catalan language was brought back to the schools where its use had been forbidden by the dictatorship along with the Catalan flag and even the national dance, the *sardana*. The dancing, like Montessori's life in Spain, lasted only until the revolution of 1936 established the dictatorship of General Francisco Franco.

The new republic had inherited both the need for radical labor reforms and the problem of the demands for Catalan and Basque independence. Measures aimed at the separation of church and state aroused the antagonism of the powerful clerical establishment and its traditional conservative supporters in the army, and the large Catholic population responded to the Church's cry of persecution at the hands of the government and bitterly resented the violent anti-church acts of extremists. In Catalonia, stronghold of the republic, local leaders were divided on the question of the degree of socialism—moderate or radical—

the region was ready for. And even in Catalonia the republic had its opponents, supporters of the Falange including right-wing intellectuals, among them the Castilian-speaking students at the university.

With the country's large middle-class population, mainly Catholic and nationalist in sentiment, alienated by the separation of church and state—especially the denial of Catholic education for children—and by the concessions of regional autonomy to Catalonia, rightists and conservatives won in the 1933 elections. Fearing a Fascist dictatorship as a result, leftists launched an insurrection in 1934 in northern Spain. Once again, the cycle of disorder and repression was under way.

In a hopelessly polarized Spain the Popular Front electoral coalition of Republicans and Socialists which won the general election of February 1936, with its strongest support in Catalonia and the Basque provinces, was doomed. The bitter division between left and right culminated in the generals' revolt in July 1936. The Spanish Civil War had begun.

The military revolution was dedicated to "order," the rebellious generals presenting themselves as defenders of Catholic Europe against the Red Menace. While it is not clear that a victory of either side would have threatened Montessori personally—she had credentials both as a spokesman for liberal social reform and an educator devoted to the traditions of religion and the value of order—the confused situation of those desperate days clearly augured the violence and bloodshed to come. Whichever direction the crisis took, the schools would not be left free to educate children in their own way, Montessori's way. And besides, she had a family which now included her young grandchildren.

Friends in England with government connections arranged for Montessori to leave Barcelona on a British battleship, and with only a few hours' notice, leaving behind most of her personal possessions, she quit the country that had been her home for twenty years and the educational laboratory she had dreamed of for so many years before that.

She arrived in England just as the Fifth International Montessori Congress, the first held in England, was to begin at Oxford in early August. Montessori presided as president of the congress, the theme of which was "The Child's Place in Society" and which was attended by two hundred delegates from almost every country in Europe as well as South America and India.

It was now thirty years since the establishment of the first Casa dei Bambini, and the influence Montessori had had on the English primary-school system in the intervening years, despite the separatist character of her movement's organization, had been considerable. The *Times Educa-*

tional Supplement summed it up this way: "Infant teachers who have never read a line of her books may arrange their classrooms as she did, and copy her material. Education authorities, who believe her ideas to be exotic, may plan school buildings on her lines." Still, "the spirit of her work has been less understood than the letter."[1] This was the same point that Montessori had made about the followers of Seguin before the turn of the century.

"The effect of the international short courses which Dr. Montessori has held, and the visits she has paid to many countries," the *TES* article went on to say, "has been that there are people all over the world who have caught something of her inspiration without understanding its applications. . . . Schools have grown up here and there, and vanished again, in which children have been free, above everything else, to be rude and dirty. . . . The Montessori method has come to be connected with precocious literacy: common superstition associates that with poor character and physique, and it is forgotten that the author of the method started as a doctor of medicine, far more concerned with health than with scholarship."[2]

Montessori's latest book, *The Secret of Childhood*, was published while the congress was taking place. A retelling of the story of the founding of the Casa dei Bambini and a restatement of her educational philosophy, it added nothing really new to *The Montessori Method*. Reviewers found themselves "annoyed by the not infrequent outbursts of sentimental hyperbole"[3] and chose charitably to overlook these "rhapsodic lapses" in the light of her practical achievements and the soundness of so much of her teaching.

The criticism of *The Secret of Childhood*—and it was the criticism made of much of what she published in her later years—was not that what Montessori said was not true but that it was not new. It was another restatement of what she had already said in previous decades, embroidering on her early ideas without really adding to them.

It was a book which could not seem new or significant to anyone—professional psychologists or educators, or even sophisticated lay people—aware of what had already been demonstrated about the relationship between children's emotional development and the other aspects of their growth, including learning, by Freud and his followers. The reviewer for the London *Times* wrote: "There is of course an important educational factor that no application of theory and no formal instruction can provide. As Freud has taught us, the human emotional impacts of early childhood have important lifelong results. Unfortunately we cannot by deliberation adapt our emotions or those of others to fit needs or expediencies. It is on the intellectual, physical, and aesthetic planes alone that formal educational planning can help us, and it is a weakness of many enthusiastic educational reformers—including Dr. Montessori—that they do not sufficiently recognize this limitation."[4]

It was no longer possible to consider any aspect of human development without considering the influence of the way in which certain inevitable emotional conflicts arise and are resolved in the early years of life. A system that limited itself to the acquisition of skills—formal education—no longer seemed like a fruitful avenue for reform of education in its broadest sense—the development of more creative individuals and a healthier society. Thus Montessori, who had begun by anticipating the psychoanalysts' discovery of the crucial importance of the earliest life experiences in determining the course of later development, was now being left behind by them. For it was not only the senses and the intellect of the child that required proper early training; there was the matter of those feelings and fantasies whose hidden effects were now being explored in the work of Freud and his followers. There were "secrets of childhood"—the existence of the unconscious, the role of sexuality and fantasy in the child's mental life—which Montessori never confronted, which remained alien to her way of understanding child development and human nature and left her sounding curiously unscientific and mystical to the modern consciousness in her emphasis on a vague "spiritual force" and on the manipulation of external reality.

She talks about the child's "soul" without defining in what it consists, how it comes to be, or how it works. Her ideas about the importance of early experience were not incompatable with the psychology that psychoanalysis was shaping for the twentieth century, it was just that they were limited to formal learning and to a way of seeing character development—and she was always concerned with the development of character as well as cognition—that was beginning to seem increasingly outdated to the world beyond the Montessori movement.

At the 1936 congress in Oxford, the fifth, she spoke about her extension of her ideas to the secondary-school level, the education of adolescents. Since 1920 she had been developing these ideas, which would eventually be published in "The Erdkinder" and other essays. Now she said that the first stage of education, to which she had devoted her earliest efforts, consisted in the child's exploration of his environment and ended with puberty, when the most important need of young people was acquiring a new form of independence—independence as a separate social group. For Montessori, the process of education always has to do with acquiring independence, the nature of that independence changing with the child's stage of development. For the adolescent, the task was to be "born again" as a conscious member of a society beyond the narrow circle of family life, and to accomplish this Montessori suggested a form of communal living in the country away from the dependency on parents and "in contact with nature and on equal terms with his fellows."[5] Academic lessons would be replaced by real work on the land and in the workshop, with the young selling what they were able to produce and thus learning the meaning of economic independence. They would learn the meaning of money not just as a "promise to pay" but as a medium of exchange of the goods produced by their labor, a means of linking the members of society together. This miniature society would thus be a means, like every stage of education as she saw it, toward the reform of society at large.

Another topic discussed at the congress was the growing interest in the Montessori movement in India, where the mystical element in her thought was as much in tune with the culture as it was increasingly out of step with the rationalistic tendencies of the West. Montessori was being urged to come to India by a people who felt she had a message to which they could respond, with the same fervor with which Americans had welcomed her more than twenty years earlier.

During the Oxford congress the AMI announced it was Montessori's intention "to elaborate a social plan to be submitted to the governments of the world for an international league of child psychic welfare." By now an exile from Spain as well as Italy, her schools in Germany and Austria closed down, she was preoccupied less with the specifics of training teachers and classroom methods than with the larger social task of education in preventing the new war that was obviously threatening once again to engulf Europe. To those who were still listening she made the same appeal she had made to Italian teachers almost forty years before. Her experiences in the intervening years had only made her surer of the truth of her message: "If man is to overcome war and his own conflicts and complexes, education must be given a scientific basis, one which places at its center the laws of the child's psychic development, discovery of which will indicate the sensitive periods of growth during which—and only during which—psychic functions can be perfectly acquired."[6]

For the next two years Montessori repeated the message tirelessly, culminating her efforts to influence the world's leaders in a speech she made at the Sorbonne in Paris in 1938, in which she again made her plea for a system of education that would accomplish peace through moral reform. Those who heard her were already convinced; the rest were busy preparing for another war.

When Montessori and her family arrived in England in the summer of 1936 they had no definite plans for the immediate future, no clear idea of where to settle next. Many friends and admirers offered suggestions and hospitality, but the most persuasive was a student of Montessori's English training course named Ada Pierson, a forthright, energetic young woman who was the daughter of a Dutch banker and one of a group of young women who had taken the Montessori training course and who now urged her to come to Holland. Ada Pierson called her parents at their home in Baarn, outside Amsterdam, and asked if she could bring the Montessoris home with her. They agreed to open their home to the Dottoressa and her family, and she and Mario, who had separated from his wife, arrived in Holland with his children to stay with the Piersons for a few weeks until a home of their own could be found.

The following summer, in August 1937, the Sixth International Montessori Congress was held in Copenhagen, its main theme "Education for Peace." When Montessori called the first session to order, looking over baskets of pink and red roses, she saw an audience that included more than two hundred representatives of over twenty nations. The sponsors included France's Edouard Herriot and Czechoslovakia's Thomas Masaryk. There were many supporters of the League of Nations, no representatives of Italy, Germany, or the Soviet Union.

The Danish newspapers referred to Montessori as "the greatest living Italian orator" after she had given her keynote speech in which she declared, "The adult must understand the meaning of the moral defense of humanity, not the armed defense of nations. He must realize that the child will be the creator of the new world peace. In a suitable environment the child reveals unsuspected social characteristics. The qualities he shows will be the salvation of the world, showing us all the road to peace. And the new child has been born! He will tell us what is needed!"[7]

At the closing session of the congress, Montessori proposed the foundation of a ministry of childhood and a social party—Il Partito Sociale del Bambino—to defend the rights of children through official representatives in the parliaments of all nations.

It was a utopian proposal, reminiscent of her plea for the establishment of the White Cross organization at the end of World War I. She was increasingly focused in her public pronouncements on large issues— world peace, the reform of social institutions. She talked about humanity, about society, about "the child," but said little about individual relationships. It was an approach that—like a system of learning emphasizing the child's physical and cognitive activity, his manipulation of things in the outer world, rather than his emotional life, his intimate relationships to nurturing adults—would seem to have had an obvious appeal for Montessori in the light of her own past. Such a way of looking at things would have minimized the sense of loss to her own child and to herself, the feelings of sorrow and even of guilt that must at some time have shadowed the mind of a woman who had not been able to raise her own son, had no close contact with him during his earliest years.

But whatever poignant personal meaning may have lain hidden in her declarations, her listeners heard in them answers to a deeply felt need for hopeful solutions to the problems plaguing Europe and leading the world inexorably toward another era of disaster.

There were honors and expressions of admiration from government officials and private individuals who still believed in the possibility of peace, still hoped that the League of Nations could be made what one of them referred to as "a means of international political hygiene." A cable from the new government in Barcelona announced plans to open one hundred and fifty Montessori schools for sixty thousand children, raising the question of why Montessori had fled the revolution. It is possible that as Standing later wrote, "as a Roman Catholic, and one who had written books on the teaching of religion, her life [was] in danger"[8] but it seems unlikely. Religious teaching was never an essential part of the system, which indeed had proved itself useful to many kinds of governments and societies. It seems more probable that the outbreak of violence in itself and the uncertainty of what would follow had decided her to leave, rather than any specific disagreement with either republican or rebel forces. She had learned by now by bitter experience that in any situation of social upheaval demands would be made from one faction or another for her to choose sides and demonstrate her position in ways that could affect what went on in her classrooms, and that, rather than any particular political regime, was what she would not tolerate.

By the end of 1936, with the help of Dutch friends and supporters, including the Pierson family, a Montessori school was founded not far from Amsterdam in Laren. The plan was for Montessori to teach there during five months of each year, reserving her other time for training courses elsewhere, continuing to travel and lecture, organize congresses and oversee the worldwide Montessori society activities.

Amsterdam was now the headquarters of the Montessori movement with the AMI established there and the small model school and training center at nearby Laren as the latest in a series of institutions planned as laboratories for further experimentation with the method and centers for the training of teachers and the dissemination of information, the work referred to as "propaganda" until the word took on an invidious meaning during the war. There, in surroundings smaller but no less idyllic than those she had enjoyed at Barcelona, Montessori was happiest. No social upheaval, no public resistance or internal struggles beset the Dutch movement, and once again it seemed that Montessori had found the ideal conditions for which she had been yearning since her first conversations with S. S. McClure about an institution in which to carry on her work.

Laren was like a benign little island apart from the bitter struggles of the outside world. While young men all over Europe were putting on uniforms in which to kill each other, Boy Scout leaders and Montessori directresses watched their young charges cooperating in preparing and serving meals to each other—the exercises of practical life—and talked about how to integrate the common aims of the Scout movement and the Montessori movement through sports, games, and handcrafts.

Again, of course, paradise was soon to be ended, this time by the culmination of the events which had already driven her out of Vienna, Rome, and Barcelona and which eventually reached throughout Europe full blown into World War II.

Another Montessori Congress, the seventh, was held in Britain in the summer of 1938, this time in Edinburgh. That same year Montessori held another international training course in Amsterdam, her second there and the last she would conduct in that country until after the war. Returning to England again in the spring of 1939, Montessori spoke at a meeting in a London once again bracing for war. She was still speaking on the topic that had engaged her attention in her native Italy forty years earlier—the education of the child as a key to the reform of society. Of the tyranny of the totalitarian nations, she said, "Something more complex than oppression lies behind their growth. It is the fact, as powerful as armaments, that they understand the power of childhood. When these states arm, they do so not from the age of eighteen but from the age of four." And she urged that the free nations do likewise. "If a changed society is desired a moral rearmament must be preached to the child as well as the adult."[9] She was right about the importance of the early years in determining social attitudes, but perhaps she still attached too much importance to what could be "preached" or even taught to children outside the context of how those most intimately related to them took care of them, establishing how they would feel about themselves and about others.

When Hitler's troops had marched into Vienna in 1938 and all Montessori schools still in existence were transformed into establishments more suitable for the education of a Master Race, the few members of the Arbeitsgemeinschaft who were still in Vienna and were able to get out left Austria. Elise Braun and her family, with the help of her old friend Kitty Shiva Rao in India, had gone to Benares, where Mrs. Braun took charge of a Montessori class again. In December 1938 she received a letter from Mario Montessori in which he spoke of plans for the Dottoressa and himself to come to India within the next few months. The Montessori movement had been gathering momentum there over the years, and the time seemed ripe for its leader to make the long journey to meet with her followers and train as many of them as possible to carry out her work. Indian leaders of the stature of Gandhi and Tagore were friendly to Montessori and believed her methods could be of great use in their country, and leaders of the Theosophical Society had expressed interest in establishing a Montessori training center in India. In the state of international unrest, with Europe close to conflagration, it was a tempting proposition.

23

Montessori left her new home in Holland in October 1939 at the age of sixty-nine to make a journey that would have seemed formidable to most people half her age. With Mario at her side, she was going to give a training course in India, organized by the Theosophical Society on the grounds of the society's headquarters, an estate at Adyar, in Madras.[1] The plan was for the course to last three months and to be followed by a lecture tour and visits to various universities in India. Montessori expected to return to Europe by the summer of 1940 in order to continue her training course at the new school in Laren, but in fact she was not to return to Europe for almost seven years.

Montessori's associations with India and with the leaders of the Theosophical movement had begun many years earlier. Montessori told K. Sankara Menon, who acted as her personal assistant during the years in India and was secretary of the first three courses given there, that she had attended a meeting in London when she was young and not yet famous at which she had heard Annie Besant give a talk in which she spoke with admiration about the then very new Montessori method. It must have been after the establishment of the first Casa dei Bambini in 1907 but before news of the experiment had reached the proportions that made Montessori's name one that would be mentioned as a matter of course by anyone discussing new trends in education.

Dr. Besant, the second president of the Theosophical Society, was a very well known figure in England at the time. A former Fabian socialist reformer, union organizer, and strike leader, a close friend of fellow atheist George Bernard Shaw, she was converted to Theosophy around 1890 when she read Madame Blavatsky's *The Secret Doctrine*. From 1907 until her death in 1933 she was president of the Theosophical Society and a leader of the movement for home rule for India, deeply involved in both the effort to revive traditional Indian culture and to educate the vast masses of the illiterate Indian poor. In 1909 an English student at Montessori's first training course had asked her to help translate Besant's book.

Montessori later said she was overwhelmed that such a famous person was talking about her educational experiment in such glowing terms. Although she did not introduce herself to Dr. Besant on that occasion, she

341

did meet her later and formed a friendly relationship that was renewed whenever Dr. Besant came to Rome in the years before World War I and Montessori's move to Barcelona.

Dr. Besant's successor as head of the Theosophical Society was George Sydney Arundale, who assumed the presidency in 1934. Arundale, a distinguished educator in India for many years, had been principal of the college at Benares, head of the university at Madras, and a government minister of education.

In 1937, when Montessori had left Spain and was living with the Pierson family in Baarn, outside Amsterdam, Dr. Arundale and his wife, Rukmini Devi, visited Holland and the three met for the first time. The Arundales returned to Holland again in 1938 and on that occasion invited Montessori to come to India, where interest in the Montessori movement had been growing for many years.

There was a hunger for practical ideas about how to cope with the overwhelming problem of educating India's impoverished masses. In a country of 300 million people, over 90 percent of whom were illiterate, it was a problem of unprecedented and staggering proportions. The Montessori method seemed to many to provide one possible answer.

Mysore had been the first Indian state to send a student to study with Montessori, at the very first international course in Rome in 1913, and other Indian students had taken her course throughout the 1920s and 1930s in London, Barcelona, and Rome, and had brought her method back with them to many parts of India.

A Montessori conference held in Bhavnagar in 1926 had led to the formation of a Montessori Society in India and to translation of *Il Metodo* into Gujarati there and into Hindi in Bombay the following year. And by the late twenties there were Tagore-Montessori schools scattered throughout India as well as on the island of Java.

A number of wealthy Indians had started private Montessori schools for their own children and those of friends, and the schools run under Theosophical Society auspices had Montessori departments. It was to take charge of the Montessori department in the Theosophical School at Allahabad that Montessori's young Austrian pupil Elise Herbatschek (now Mrs. Braun) had gone, against Montessori's wishes, in 1927.

Montessori and the Theosophists had always found each other's thinking congenial. The core of Theosophy was the Indian doctrines of the union of the human soul with the divine consciousness, of reincarnation as a gradual unfolding of innate powers in successive lives, and of *karma*, the principle of self-realization leading to the liberation of the true self and to ultimate wisdom. There was some affinity between these beliefs and Montessori's view of education as a process of liberating the spirit of the child, the increasingly vague and mystical language in which she spoke of her very practical classroom methods as she grew older. And many of the same people who were drawn to Theosophy were attracted to the Montessori movement.

The Arundales were uncertain about whether Montessori would accept their invitation. After all, she was almost seventy at the time, India was a totally new world to her, with not only a foreign culture but a climate that could be fiercely hot, and the trip there would be arduous, air travel facilities being still in a somewhat primitive state of organization. To their surprise and delight, she accepted their invitation with enthusiasm.

Sankara Menon remembers going with the Arundales to meet the Montessoris at the Madras airport. Despite her age and portliness, Montessori stepped out of the tiny plane with a springy step, alert and full of interest in everything she saw around her. She felt no need for a rest; she was eager to begin at once planning and organizing the course she was to give at the society's headquarters at Adyar.

Since there were no buildings in Olcott Gardens, the section of the Theosophical Society compound where Montessori would live and give her course, which were large enough to accommodate the number of students who had enrolled in the course, a village of palm-leaf huts was built, one of them large enough to serve as a lecture hall. The students sat barefoot on rush mats on the floor of the hut, which Montessori seated in a wicker chair before a table on a flagstone platform, Mario beside her translating her lectures into English.

In India her black gowns were replaced by long, flowing white ones, and she often wore around her neck the traditional garlands of flowers presented by her students. There were always fresh flowers brought by them and placed on the table before her as she lectured.

Three hundred teachers and student-teachers from all over India attended that first course. Montessori was unprepared for the interest roused by her presence in India and the response of the Indian students to her lectures, which they found "eloquent and illuminating." Never in all the long years of travel and fame, of adulation from her students and praise from the great, had she met with such an overwhelming reception of herself and her ideas. Coming to this faraway place, in a way she had come home. The core of her sense of self was her work; it had always mattered more to her than anything else in life—home, family, friends. She had moved wherever her work had taken her, at home wherever it was accepted, for as long as it remained so. Now, toward the end of her life, she had found a place and a people eagerly waiting for her message and asking only to help her implement her ideas. This time it seemed as though she would meet with no obstacles to carrying out her work in the way she wanted to.

The assumption was a realistic one as far as the Indians were concerned, but failed to reckon with the forces operating in the world beyond their borders. Once again, political events upset her plans, this time reaching out from Europe to touch her here.

World War II had already broken out in the fall of 1939 and when Italy entered the war on the side of the Germans in June 1940 the British interned all Italians in the British Isles and in their colonial possessions overseas as enemy aliens.

When word reached England that the Montessoris had been interned in India, efforts were soon under way to have them released. In a letter published in the London *Times,* Claude Claremont wrote: "One hopes the British Raj will be quickly visited, if not by a sense of proportion or duty, at least by a return of humor, and place on Dr. Montessori no restrictions that could impede her never-ending and arduous educational work, in a gesture that will be worthy of England."[2]

In fact, it was only Mario Montessori who was actually interned, in a camp for civilians in Amednagar. Montessori was at first confined to the compound of the Theosophical Society, and then allowed to leave Adyar to spend the summer months in the hill stations of Ooty and Kodaikanal. She felt it a bitter betrayal that the British should have interned Mario. Not only did she feel herself above politics, but had they not left Fascist Italy six years earlier?

The separation caused her great distress. She was used to having him at her side and had come to rely on him more and more, emotionally as well as in practical matters. Nevertheless, she carried on through the summer, comforted and assisted by Indian friends and supporters. Then, on August 31, 1940, she was handed a telegram from the Viceroy of India which read: "We have long thought what to give you for your seventieth birthday. We thought that the best present we could give you was to send you back your son."[3] It was the first recorded public reference to Mario as her son. Perhaps the Viceroy felt that in view of Montessori's age and distinction no one in India would criticize her; perhaps he felt he could make the point of his dramatic gesture no other way. Montessori made no comment; she accepted the gift that was her due. The two were reunited for her birthday, and a few days later Mario was finally released from the camp and they spent the remainder of the war years working together in India.

In addition to the training courses they gave during those years at the Theosophical Society headquarters in Madras and in Kodaikanal, they gave others in Karachi, in Srinagar, under the sponsorship of the Maharajah of Kashmir, and in Ahmedabad, in Gujarat, under the auspices of a wealthy philanthropist, Sarala Devi Sarabhai, an admirer of Montessori's who, with her daughter and daughter-in-law, founded Shreyas, a small school set up for their own children under the guidance of the Montessoris which eventually grew into an educational center for children from infancy through high school. Some of the elements of the elementary-school materials were developed there and Montessori dedicated the English version of *The Secret of Childhood* to Mrs. Sarabhai when it was published in India.

With the aid of G. D. Birla, one of India's leading industrialists, a Montessori society was established in Pilani Rajasthan, and in the Besant School in Kalakshetra, an art and educational center founded in Adyar, near Madras, by Rukmini Devi, a Montessori section was set up in classrooms designed according to plans drawn up with Montessori.

Elise Braun, who saw Montessori while they were both in India during the war years, felt Montessori was happiest there and in Spain. "She liked it where there were friends. She was at home in India. The Indian girls were so lovely and they understood her and loved her and she needed that at the time. She felt she had been rejected in Europe and America, but in India every word of hers was soaked up. She was like a guru."[4]

Musing later about Montessori's ready acceptance and influence in India, another of her former Viennese pupils said, "The Indians were so willing to learn everything from her. She always preferred to associate with those who would accept what she said, whether or not they were her intellectual peers. She was like a queen; the queen elects who she wants to see."[5]

Another of Montessori's students later remembered how, in 1941, hearing that the famous educator was in neighboring India, she had arranged to come from her home in Ceylon to Madras and, in words echoed by so many of Montessori's students from all over the world throughout the years, "the course of my entire life was changed."[6]

Montessori was seventy-one, "with an air of venerable, gracious charm as she welcomed each one of us students as someone precious and dear to her. Here she was in a foreign country so completely alien to any she had previously visited, meeting people so different in their language, dress, customs, and culture. Though at times we were somewhat awed by her intellect and fine oratory, her captivating smile and shining eyes radiating kind humor endeared her to us all. . . . There were times when I saw her depressed and tired out by people who could not understand her ideas, but the vitality of her mind and the intensity with which she believed in those ideas revived and encouraged her constantly. . . .

"On the tropical mountain of Kodaikanal in southern India, in peaceful and beautiful surroundings, we worked together with children of different ages, as they developed from day to day, planning and making new projects and materials under her guidance. Each evening the day's happenings were recounted to Dr. Montessori, who would then comment on the reactions of the children and what they had said. We would then set to work on new illustrations, charts and models, until we found that we had made so many that she decided to give an advanced course for work with children of six to twelve years."

During the years she spent in India Montessori personally trained over one thousand Indian teachers. To pay for the course, some of the students had pawned their family jewelry, others had gone into debt. For many, the difficulties involved in traveling over the vast distances separating their homes from wherever Montessori was giving her course in order to study with her went beyond financial sacrifices. There were cultural traditions and parental prejudices to overcome. The fact that children of Brahmins and untouchables lived harmoniously together during the months they spent in the Montessori course seemed to her to bear out her belief that her system of education was not limited to any country, philosophy, religion, or social conditions and, moreover, that it could serve as a means of breaking down the barriers that separated national and social groups from each other and thus serve as an effective tool for peace. It seems a naïve expectation, based on the experience of a self-selected group, and ignoring the darker complexities of human nature and political reality, but it was a belief and an expectation that enabled her to renew her efforts over and over again throughout her life in new places among new people. And of course it would be shattered again in the bloodshed that was to sweep India after partition. But she would pick it up and go on.

Writing to Montessori from his home in Bengal a few months after her arrival in India, Rabindranath Tagore said, "As you know, I am a great admirer of your work in education and along with my countrymen think it very fortunate indeed that India, at this hour, can get your guidance in creative self-expression. I am confident that education of the young, which must underlie all work of national reconstruction, will find a new and lasting inspiration in your presence."[7]

Montessori knew Gandhi, who had visited Montessori classes in Rome in the early 1930s; in India she met Nehru and Radhakrishnan and heard herself praised in similar terms by each of India's leaders.

During the years in India, Montessori turned her attention to the study of very young infants. She had extended her ideas about the school to elementary-age and secondary-school children throughout the 1920s and 1930s. In the 1940s she began to focus the interest she had always had in small children on infants. She had been interested in babies as early as 1913 when, in her U.S. interviews, she had talked about the responsiveness of the newborn to his handling and to other forms of stimulation. Her interests always began with life observed; in India she was surrounded by babies. They were everywhere. Other cultures kept them at home in crib and cradle; in India extended families lived together in compounds, all generations from oldest to youngest. Observing them, among her students, among local villagers, among the families of the well-to-do, she applied her ideas to their needs, to what conditions from the earliest days of life could best contribute to the optimal development of the child.

Here she had more chance to observe infants in any single day than in a year in any of the European countries where she had lived. She watched them, became fascinated, applied the same intuitive thinking to infancy that she had forty years before to schoolchildren. Watching the early development of babies in the Indian family, where they were stimulated by being in the center of things, seeing, hearing, being touched and handled, she worked out the ideas that she set down in the books written during the Indian years, particularly *The Absorbent Mind.* Inspirational in tone and sometimes rather archaic in style, at the very least they are statements of ideas that would gain general acceptance over the next decades. In 1946 she told her students she thought infants were damaged by the kind of handling they were given routinely at birth in Western countries. Instead of being cleaned, weighed, measured, they should simply be wrapped and placed at their mother's breast, and not separated from her in the first hours of life.

It was not a new point of view with her. Ten years earlier, in the spring of 1936 while Montessori was on a visit to Budapest, Elise Braun had given birth to a daughter in Vienna. On her way back to Barcelona, Montessori had stopped off in Vienna and come to see the new baby. She stood for a long time watching the baby asleep in her cradle. When it was time for the baby to be nursed, "Mammolina" wanted to be present. When she saw Lisl rigidly following the rules of her Viennese pediatrician, weighing the baby before nursing, checking how much it had gotten by weighing it again, and refusing to go on with the feeding after the assigned eighty grams of milk had been consumed, Montessori was horrified.

"Don't you think the child knows when she has had enough?" she scolded the young mother, and told her to throw away the scale and follow the baby's instincts,[8] anticipating the idea of "demand feeding," like so many other child-rearing practices, long before her medical colleagues caught up to her.

Both her longstanding feeling for the needs of babies and the fact that she waited until late in her life to turn her attention in an organized, intentional way to the study of infants seem related to her own life. As a young woman it was an area of emotional conflict for her, a mother deprived of caring for her own infant, of experiencing the mother-child symbiosis. Now she was an old woman, a grandmother, and the passage of time and the resolution of earlier conflicts over the passing years had brought her to a point at which she could look calmly at a matter that must have once been as painful as it was intriguing to her.

In 1944 at Ahmedabad she gave a course of thirty lectures on the first three years of life. That same year she gave a course in Ceylon, officially recognized by the government.

One has to look at a map of India and think of how difficult travel was there in those years to realize what it meant to journey from Madras to Kashmir in the north or across the country to Ahmedabad and to neighboring Ceylon. For a woman of Montessori's age it was an impressive undertaking and a proof of the openness to adventure that she retained throughout her life.

In 1949, in her seventy-fifth year, she wrote to Anna Maccheroni from India, "I am well, but my energy and faith are gradually diminishing. Perhaps it is because all goes well and I have no anxieties: the stimulus of having to struggle is missing."[9]

In late December 1945 the first All India Montessori Conference was held in Jaipur, where Montessori saw in the new year of 1946, the first in a world no longer at war, and began to make plans to return to Europe in the summer and resume in the fall her series of London training courses that had been interrupted by the war and the years in India.

With the war over, Montessori flew back to Europe with Mario. On July 30, 1946, she returned to Holland after almost seven years' absence, a month before her seventy-sixth birthday. In Amsterdam they were reunited with Mario's children, who had remained in the care of the Pierson family in Baarn during their long wartime separation.

After a month spent resting, visiting with old friends, and celebrating her birthday with the family, the Montessoris left for England to take up where they had left off, to give a training course in which she would report on the progress made since the last course given there before the war, the work she had done during the years in India.

Early in September they flew from Amsterdam to London, where they were met at the airport by two of Montessori's former pupils, Phoebe Child and Margaret Homfray.[10]

The two women thought Montessori would want to go straight to the house that had been rented for her stay and rest after her trip, but this was no ordinary old lady, this was Montessori, the same Montessori who stood on the deck of the ship that brought her to New York in 1913 wanting to "see everything." Now she said she wanted to drive around first and see the damage that had been done by the bombs.

"Don't you want to rest first, Mammolina?" they asked her. "Rest?" she said, staring at the two young women. "What for?" They drove through the ruins of London and while she took in everything they passed she never stopped talking, asking questions, trading information about what had happened to this one, to that one, during the years of the war while she had been away. ("She loved gossip," said Miss Homfray later. "Up until the end she was full of life, interested in everything.") The car stopped and Montessori got out and stood looking at the desolation around her, in which only St. Paul's seemed to be left standing. Then she said, "Well, the Quetta earthquake was worse than this."

When they reached home Montessori was still looking around. The young women had wanted to receive her in style, and thinking of the grandeur to which she was accustomed, they had a tea service spread out and waiting. "It was right after the war," said Miss Homfray, "and nobody had anything. So we collected pieces of silver from here and there." Montessori came in and looked at the silverware spread out on a tray and said, "Margherita, your silver needs polishing," and, just taking off her coat and not even bothering to unpack first, she demanded an apron and some rags and polish and sat down to do the job herself. She had always enjoyed the "exercises of practical life," as they were called in the Casa dei Bambini, and on many of the evenings she spent with her English pupils she donned her apron again to cook them dinner. It was always very good and always—she never lost her taste for pasta—very fattening.

From the early 1920s England had been one of Montessori's main bases, a place to which she came back again and again and was listened to with interest and respect, although her method was not as widely or officially institutionalized as in Italy or Spain or Holland.

During the years of the war and her sojourn in India Montessori had been all but forgotten in Europe. When Maria Mills, one of her former pupils from Vienna, heard that Montessori was giving a course after the war, she later remembered thinking, "It can't be, she must be dead by now. So much had happened, and she was so old, almost eighty. I went, along with some others from the old group. I hadn't seen her since 'twenty-eight or 'thirty. The car pulled up and there she was, wearing black, looking like always, only older, with white hair and a tired face but very interested in everyone, taking in everything around her. I went over to the car and she recognized me at once—after all those years."[11]

Back once more in London in that postwar autumn she was welcomed by crowds of teachers and students to whom she had become a symbol of hopefulness for humanity, of the kind of optimism necessary to once again rebuild a ravaged world. She had become even more impressive a presence as she had grown old. With her white hair, dressed in the fashion of an earlier time, she still had the same dignity to her bearing and the same calm smile for public occasions. She had always liked to wear flowers, to ornament herself with some jewel, a ring or brooch, and now she wore a simple string of pearls on her plain dark dress, a single rose pinned to the furs that protected her against the English climate she had grown unused to after the years in India. She spoke about "the miracle of man's growth . . . his potential greatness . . . the problem of peace and mutual understanding."[12] They were the vague, high-flown words of an old woman, but they met a need that was widely felt. She had become the universal grandmother.

To her followers she was a queen, and it is not surprising that she assumed some of the prerogatives of royalty. She was always late, the last to arrive at a lecture where a hundred people had been sitting and waiting for her for a quarter of an hour. They never seemed to mind.

"In 1946," remembered Miss Homfray, "it was almost impossible to find a car. But Montessori never went from place to place on foot. She was very heavy by then, and for her to go anyplace there always had to be a car. We had managed to get one to take her from the house to the lecture hall for the opening of the course, but she wasn't ready on time. We urged her to hurry, but by the time she came down the car had left and we had to spend half an hour on the telephone before we could find someone who could drive her." The story, like all the anecdotes in which her little foibles are remembered by her students, is told with affectionate amusement rather than irritation. They loved her.

Although officially Montessori did not speak English, Miss Homfray remembered her lecturing in English at the 1946 course. When she had trouble occasionally hitting on the right word to say exactly what she had in mind, the whole class would help her find the word she wanted.

"She was always thinking about her work," remembered Miss Homfray. "She would get an idea and tell you clearly exactly how to work it out. She was always willing to help you figure out how to handle a problem with the children. She'd make a suggestion and if that didn't work she'd think of something else and finally, if nothing seemed to work, she'd say, 'The only thing you can do now, Margherita, is pray.'"

Teachers who had been trained by Montessori and remembered her in the classroom—and those I was able to talk with had known her in the late 1920s and early 1930s when she was around sixty—never forgot the effect she had on children. They saw her differently—to some she radiated love, others described her as coming into a room and looking around "like Robespierre"—but all agree that she made an unforgettable impression. Her mere appearance in a room full of unruly children instantly transformed them. They would calm down, go to their places, set to work with complete attention. Whatever it was the children felt, its effect was to make them perfect examples of what she wanted them to be. She was never able to understand why other teachers complained of being unable to cope with undisciplined children, said Maria Mills, who later became a psychotherapist, "because where *she* was there was order."

Even her most devoted and loyal followers recognized a certain imperiousness in Montessori. Mother Isabel Eugenie, a student of hers and an Assumption nun whose life was devoted to implementing Montessori education in Catholic schools, also remembered her as "like a queen. She made royal entrances; she expected to be courted. She always expected to be the center of attention, and she enjoyed it.[13]

"She was witty, often funny, but she could lose her temper too, and got angry when she felt crossed." Mother Isabel remembered years later having taken pains to move Anna Maccheroni out of London to the countryside during World War II to keep her from being interned. Maccheroni was by that time an eccentric little old lady, outspokenly anti-English. Maccheroni wrote to the Montessoris that she had been thrown out on the street in the middle of the night and Montessori seems to have accepted her version of the event and become furious with Mother Isabel, who wrote to her, "You know her and you know me. How could you believe her?" During the war years the two had no further contact but when they met again after the war, when Montessori returned to England, Mother Isabel remembers each of them reproaching the other, "How could you?" "How could *you*?" then starting to laugh, after which they made up and became good friends again.

351

Montessori's followers had a way of finding in her philosophy whatever it was they were looking for. To Mother Isabel the Montessori system taught that "religion is the center of education and the center of religion is Jesus Christ." Montessori might not have put the matter just that way herself, but it is probably true, as Mother Isabel stated, that she had no use for the theory of evolution, just as she had no use for some of the basic theories of psychoanalysis. She preferred to think, in her later years, in terms of some special "spirit" with which human beings had been endowed by God, something beyond the body and the brain dealt with by the materialistic science she herself had begun by championing in her youth.

When the London course ended in December 1946 Montessori went with Ada and Mario to Scotland, where she donned academic robes for the ceremony in which she was made an honorary fellow of the Educational Institute of Scotland in Edinburgh. Someone asked her what nationality she now held. Her answer was, "My country is a star which turns around the sun and is called the Earth."[14]

In London in January 1947 a Montessori Centre was established by Maria and Mario Montessori. Her two former pupils, Phoebe Child and Margaret Homfray, were to represent them in their absence. Eventually a disagreement about the training of teachers arose, and before Montessori's death a statement was issued by her to the effect that "this institution [which became the St. Nicholas Training Centre] is no longer authorized to issue Montessori diplomas or to use the name Montessori."[15]

On January 4, 1947, a group of friends and former pupils gathered in Montessori's house in Amsterdam to celebrate with her the fortieth anniversary of the founding of the first Casa dei Bambini. On that occasion Montessori reminisced about the ecstatic words in which she had been moved to describe the significance of the experiment at the time and the skepticism with which her predictions had been reported by the press. Looking back, it was easy to say that she had been right after all. The Casa dei Bambini had not changed the whole world in the way in which she had hoped, but it had changed the education of young children to an impressive extent in many parts of that world.

After her return from India after the war until the end of her life Montessori was constantly on the move, traveling from one country to another, lecturing and giving training courses, receiving honors and awards. She liked to travel by automobile or airplane, coming to prefer those means of transportation to trains.

She had been a nomad most of her life. In a sense she had no home;

but she was at home anywhere. She retained the ability to the end of her life to take her ideas and go among strangers and start anew. She had come to stand for something. A kind of elder statesman of education, no longer bound by the specificity of rigorous scientific work as in the earliest period of her career, she had become a symbol of generalized aspiration—hope for the world through the education of its children—to a postwar generation hungry for affirmative messages. To many, the view of human nature implicit in the theories of more systematic philosophers—whether they spoke from the vantage point of politics, economics, psychology, or aesthetics—seemed depressingly grim and limiting.

In 1947 she returned to Italy at the invitation of the government to reestablish the Opera Montessori and help reorganize the Montessori schools. She lectured at the University of Rome, half a century after she had first stood up to lecture there to a group of her fellow students. This time there were no lions to tame. She was received with honors and given a standing ovation. An official reception was given by Count Carlo Sforza, the minister of foreign affairs. In May the Constituent Assembly of the Italian parliament received her with more honors. Once again it was a homecoming in which speeches by her countrymen paid tribute to the work she had done throughout her long life.

Reporters who had come to interview her now that she was "back in Rome for the first time since she walked out on Mussolini" found her majestically overflowing a stiff little armchair in her suite at the Grand Hotel, her voluminous form robed in the Indian fashion in beige raw silk from throat to shoe tops. It was a scene reminiscent of the interviews she gave at Holland House in New York on her 1913 American tour: to the reporters it seemed, "despite the steamy dampness of the day she radiated a cool vitality," had "the kind of quiet magnetism that makes commonplaces take on color and enchantment. And this magnificent old woman is anything but commonplace."

Asked about her educational method, she told them, "Mine is not an educational method, but a sort of revelation. You see, I never studied education." About her departure from prewar Fascist Italy: "They abolished my schools because they were based on an international idea, and I refused to teach war. So I left and went to Spain. *Per me c'é sempre libertà.* For me there is always freedom. I do as I like. I don't want to be made out as a furious anti-Fascist. Politics don't interest me. Besides, they are all mistaken. We must make a new world, with new form and new fabric—not today's harlequin mixture of rags and silk."

The new Italian government had invited her back to Rome and she was planning to reopen Montessori schools there and in Florence once teachers could be properly trained. "If they really intend to do something, I'll come back," she commented, laughing, "otherwise I'll stay in India where they are registering infants in the Montessori school from birth the way they do at Oxford."[16]

In 1947 she was offered a chair at the university in Berlin but she chose instead to return to India, where she felt she had been so effective and where so much still remained to be done. Plans were in progress for the establishment of a Montessori university in Madras, and she was scheduled to give another course there at Adyar.

The plan for the university was never realized. Once again political turmoil—this time the partition of India and Pakistan—put an end to one of her dreams.

Now that India had gained independence, there was a greater hunger than ever for what she could bring to the new nation's enormous task of educating its young. Her books were being translated into numerous Indian dialects and she was being urged to give courses in various parts of both India and Pakistan.

In July Mario Montessori married his second wife—Ada Pierson, who had looked after Mario's four children during the years he had spent with his mother in India. The Pierson family had not only given the children a home but had supported Montessori's work in Holland since the Montessoris arrival there in 1936. Now Ada Montessori-Pierson joined her husband as his mother's companion and assistant in her work and on her travels for the remaining years of Montessori's life. A warm, lively woman, she was devoted to her mother-in-law and took an intelligent interest in her affairs without the deadeningly reverential attitude of so many of Montessori's followers. In many ways she was like Montessori herself as a young woman. She had a sense of humor not unlike Montessori's. She could tease her ("Mammolina, you can't wear that hat!") and in moments of discouragement she knew how to make her laugh.

In August 1947, accompanied by Mario, Montessori returned to India, traveling by air from England. She was now in her seventy-eighth year. Ada joined them in October, bringing Mario's youngest daughter, Renilde.

The Adyar course included students from all over India. There were greetings from Gandhi, whose life would soon be ended by an assassin's bullet, and from Tagore. And there were reports from the five states in the new Indian nation that had already officially established Montessori schools.

Still indefatigable, she spent the time she was not involved in the training course lecturing to the South Indian Teachers Union and the Madras Teachers Guild, to women's conferences, Boy Scout groups, Catholic organizations, and the new colleges that were springing up everywhere. When the course at Adyar ended in late February she took off on a lecture tour to Ahmedabad, where she gave another course, and Bombay.

She found time and energy to offer practical help to the government authorities in one of the greatest problems facing the new nation—adult illiteracy—suggesting materials and methods for more effectively and easily teaching reading and writing to grown-ups.

With Mrs. Arundale, she established a Montessori training center at Kalakshetra as a memorial to Dr. Arundale, who had died in 1945.

When she was asked in the fall of 1947 during her course at Adyar whether she was a Theosophist, Montessori replied, "I am a Montessorian." Sitting in the shade of a giant banyan tree in front of the yellow brick and plaster house where she was working, she told an interviewer that she had no thoughts of retiring ("Work is necessary; it can be nothing less than a passion; a person is happy in accomplishment") and spoke of the years before the age of six as the child's "age of formation" and the years from seven to twelve as the time for "cosmic education"—grasping the interdependence of everything in nature.[17]

Another course in Adyar in 1948 was followed by one in Poona and by a visit to Gwalior, where she supervised the establishment of a model Montessori school for children up to the age of twelve.

That same year she went to Ceylon and visited the school attached to the Montessori Training Centre in Colombo, where she looked on benignly as the children presented the flowers they had brought her to her young granddaughter Renilde.

In April 1949 Montessori went to Pakistan at the invitation of the new government there to give a month-long training course in which she was assisted by Mario (described by the newspapers as her nephew) and her former pupil Albert Joosten, whose mother had been instrumental in starting the Montessori movement in Holland. The course was inaugurated by Pakistan's minister of education at the Theosophical Society Hall in Karachi.

During her stay there the Montessori Pakistan Association was founded. Then, at the end of May, she announced that she would leave for Europe with her family (this time the press referred to Mario as her adopted son), to attend the Eighth International Montessori Congress in San Remo, returning first to Amsterdam and then going on to Italy, France, Austria, England, Scotland, and Eire.

When she left Pakistan she was garlanded with flowers by her adoring students, many of whom also pressed into her hand photographs—some of themselves, others of the great Gandhi—and was presented with a large cake in the shape of a book on which was written "The Secret of Childhood—With Gratitude to You Who Discovered It."

A number of works were published under Montessori's name in India in the late 1940s. These include shorter works like *Education for a New World,* published by Kalakshetra at Adyar, Madras, in 1946, a summary of lectures she had given in her advanced training course at Kodaikanal; *The Child* and *Reconstruction in Education,* pamphlets first published in 1941 and 1942 and reissued by the Theosophical Publishing House in 1948; *Child Training,* twelve talks she broadcast on the Madras station of All India Radio in June 1948, published that year by the ministry of information of the government of India; and *What You Should Know About Your Child,* published in Colombo, Ceylon, in 1948; as well as her books *The Discovery of the Child (La Scoperta del bambino),* a revised edition of *The Montessori Method,* and *To Educate the Human Potential (Come educare il potenziale umano),* both published at Adyar in 1948, and *The Absorbent Mind (La Mente del bambino),* published at Adyar in 1949. *The Absorbent Mind* was first published as a summary of her training-course lectures in less than adequate English. She later rewrote it in Italian, and that version was published in an English translation made by Claude A. Claremont.

Montessori's late writings present something of a problem. Her early books, the major works published before 1920 *(The Montessori Method, Pedagogical Anthropology,* and the two volumes of *The Advanced Montessori Method—Spontaneous Activity in Education* and *The Montessori Elementary Material),* were written by her in Italian and translated under her supervision. Much of what appeared under her name late in her life consists of expressions of her ideas as they were developed and evolved in lectures she gave in her various training courses, much of this material surviving only in secondhand form in translations of lecture notes taken down by her students.

A typical example is *What You Should Know About Your Child,* notes of the lectures she gave in her course in Ceylon in 1948. Montessori described this little volume in a letter written to Anna Maccheroni from Adyar in 1949 as "the most recently published book *in my name* [italics mine]: a beautiful synthesis, clear, concise and organized on the ideas I expressed during a course in Ceylon, written by an important person, a lawyer . . . a member of the British Psychological Society. His name is Ghana Prakasam. . ."[18]

Education for a New World restated ideas she had developed in lectures she gave in Italian in Laren between 1936 and 1939, which later appeared in Dutch in the book *Door het Kind naar een nieuwe wereld,* published in Holland in 1941. "The Erdkinder," "The Reform of Education During and After Adolescence," and "The Function of the University," based on lectures given in Italian in Holland and England, were first published in Amsterdam in 1939 and reappeared in 1973 as *From Childhood to Adolescence* in English translation from a French translation that had been published in 1948!

According to those who heard her speak and lecture, Montessori seems to have been one of the great teachers in an oral tradition going back to Socrates; unfortunately, she had no Plato. Many of those who took down her lectures and translated them may have caught her meaning but were something less than literary stylists; often they have been translated into another language from an earlier translation made from the original Italian or French.

What exactly has been lost in the multiple stages of transcription and translation is hard to estimate, but it is possible that some of the vagaries of style and organization and some of what appears to be her deepening mystical tone are the results of this process of multiple translation at the hands of those who may have taken down her words literally but actually obscured what they conveyed in their original context by an absence of literary sensitivity. *The Montessori Method* remains a more satisfactory statement than the later *Discovery of the Child.* The original work is a period piece, but has a kind of authenticity because of, rather than in spite of, that fact. The contents, the style, the expression of her ideas, its very excesses are Montessori's own, belonging to the time in which she wrote it. It is more coherent than the later revision of the work, as all the early works written by her in Italian and translated from her written texts are more coherent and more reliable, because they can be checked against an original text written by her, than the later translations made second- or third-hand of material set down by auditors and interpreters.

As an example, surely "I felt this, intuitively" on page 37 in the original edition of *The Montessori Method* is preferable to "I was possessed by this inspiration" in the corresponding passage on page 28 of the later revision. When *The Discovery of the Child* was retranslated for an American edition published in the 1960s, the phrase became "I felt this instinctively" (page 26). "Intuitively" is still the better word in this context.

357

Similarly, neither "I had thought of taking into account other research work, whilst keeping myself independent of it" on page 64 of the Indian edition of *The Discovery of the Child* nor "My intention was to keep in touch with the research of others, but to preserve my own independence" on page 42 of the American edition is an improvement over Montessori's original "My intention was to keep in touch with the researches of others, but to make myself independent of them, proceeding to my work without preconceptions of any kind" on page 72 of *The Montessori Method*. They both omit "preconceptions," the key word in the passage since it explains what she means by "independent."

These are not isolated examples and may explain in part what has happened between the early writings and the later ones—not only the "deepening mysticism" of Montessori herself but the predilections of her listeners, her transcribers, and her translators may be operating.

The way her ideas were transmitted in her later years is illustrated in this description by Maria Remiddi of how she dealt with the lecture on "Education and Peace" Montessori gave at UNESCO in 1947:

> Maria Montessori never wrote out her lectures or lessons, and spoke without notes. When I went to ask her if I might have a copy of what she had said, she looked surprised and told me she had not got one. So I hurried home and wrote down everything I could remember. She read my notes afterwards and agreed that they were her words. Even so, they gave only a pale reflection of her ideas.[19]

In the atmosphere of uncritical acceptance of every word published under her name by her followers, words which were not really her own have come to represent her later thought. The style of her early works may be old-fashioned in its floridity, but that is a characteristic of their time and place. They were literate, and always intelligible. She may have approved many translations of words she had spoken but never herself committed to paper which are really adaptations of what she actually said and which may do less than justice to the talks which those who heard them were so impressed by. She, with a less than perfect knowledge of English and a desire that her ideas be as widely disseminated as possible, may not have been the best judge of the accuracy of the form in which that dissemination took place.

This may be a factor in explaining why the later works in which she extended her thinking to infants on the one hand and to adolescents on the other have seemed less compelling as well as less systematically reasoned to readers beyond the immediate circle of her followers than the work of her earlier years in which she herself set down her ideas on the three- to six-year-olds and six- to nine-year-olds who were her original subjects.

Then too, to read Montessori in Italian is a different experience from reading her in English translation; the language lends itself to her flowery phrases and the almost musical cadences of her speech which often seem overblown and incongruous in translation into languages in which they are less at home.

24

The Eighth International Montessori Congress was held at San Remo on the Italian Riviera in August 1949. Montessori spoke eloquently of the need for recognition of the interdependence of mankind, for educating children in a way that would bring out the human qualities needed in a changing world. Her listeners included educators from all over the world, Catholic prelates, Quakers, Hindus, Muslims, and Buddhists, lay teachers and psychologists, and Montessori found hope in the fact that they were "speaking from a common platform and working in harmony for a common cause."

The congress was indeed international. Amid the palms and sunshine of the Côte d'Azur, the large contingent from India in their native costumes moved among the exhibitions of children's work from Montessori schools in Holland, Italy, England, and Ceylon. Once again, the needs of the Montessori schoolroom were translated into architectural form. Twenty-five children worked with the Montessori apparatus, including some new materials relating to fundamental concepts in geography, botany, comparative anatomy, and geometry, in two specially constructed octagonal rooms with waist-high walls. The five hundred enrolled congress members could circulate freely about them on the floor of the Villa Ormond pavilion or watch them from a gallery above.

The winter of 1949–50 was a busy one for Montessori in a Europe once again liberated and once again in a mood of renewal, full of hopes and plans for rebuilding a better world.

She had been nominated for the 1949 Nobel Peace Prize, a distinction she would receive again in 1950 and 1951.

In December 1949 she was invited to Paris, where the rector of the Sorbonne presented her with the cross of the Legion of Honor in the name of the French Republic. The rector's speech traced her long career and spoke of the significance to humanity of her work. She responded with a moving improvised speech in which she thanked the French government, *"toujours penché sur la cause de l'enfant, cette part divine de l'homme."* It was less apt a description of the government of France—or of any country in the real world—than it was of herself. At the reception that followed she was greeted with admiration and respect by such notables as the French director of cultural relations, the Italian ambassador, the director-general of UNESCO, and the aging socialist leader Léon Blum, who told her, "I have learned from you the meaning of liberty." She visited the Montessori schools in Paris, where the French Montessori movement had been revived after the war under the leadership of playwright Jean-Jacques Bernard and his wife and daughter.

Early in 1950 she made a lecture tour of the Scandinavian countries, Mario as always at her side as she spoke to enthusiastic audiences in Norway and Sweden.

Montessori was almost eighty now. Plans were made for a small gathering to be held in Holland that spring, but when the time approached there were so many who wanted to join in honoring her that the occasion become an international conference. Some three hundred dedicated followers from thirteen countries, mostly in Western Europe but including India, Ceylon, and Indochina, met in Amsterdam in early April 1950 and heard Mario Montessori give the opening address in honor of his mother. For the first time, press reports referred to him simply as "her son."[1]

Montessori was scheduled to give three lectures. When she arrived to give the first of them, on Mario's arm, the entire audience rose in silence and the storm of applause broke out only after she had taken her seat. She responded with a smile and wordless gestures before beginning her lecture in French. Her lecture summed up the ideas she had developed over half a century—the importance of the early years, the absorbent nature of the child's mind, the need to allow the child to develop his capacities spontaneously rather than by means of the force of adult pressure. The child's plea, she said, is "Help me to do it myself." To see a child absorbed in learning, she felt, is to witness "a miracle."[2]

Despite a bad toothache which made it difficult for her to speak, she insisted on lecturing as planned. She listened intently to the other speakers, who included her old friend Anna Maccheroni, herself a bent old lady now, and received the good wishes of her followers, responding to all of them, a distinguished professor of psychology from the University of Utrecht, a young student from Ceylon, with the same grace.

Although she was living in Amsterdam at the time and preferred to consider herself a citizen of the world rather than of any particular country, she was asked to be a member of the Italian delegation to the UNESCO conference in Florence in June 1950, where Jaime Torres Bodet, UNESCO's director-general, announced at the plenary session, "In our midst we have someone who has become the symbol of our great expectations for education and world peace: Maria Montessori."[3] She was given a standing ovation by the delegates. To the press, she was still a star, and there were echoes of those early rhapsodies accompanied by photographs of her that had appeared in the Italian newspapers of the 1890s in the 1950 newspaper articles that printed her picture alongside that of another delegate to the conference, the American movie actress Myrna Loy.

That summer she returned to Italy, this time to lecture in Perugia at the International Center for Educational Studies which had been established at the University of Perugia. She was made director of the center and an honorary citizen of Perugia in ceremonies attended by the city's mayor and archbishop and the university's prefect. She wrote to her friend and collaborator Mrs. Joosten in Holland, after referring to the announcement that she had been made a Doctor Honoris Causa by the University of Amsterdam and asking for some of the newspaper accounts of the event to be sent to her, "It is the epoch of surprises for me. I was greeted with applause when I entered the General Plenary Session of UNESCO. And here in Italy they have conferred upon me a professorship at the University of Perugia. How shall I be able to keep up with all these things? If only I had enough time—to be able to earn them! It is necessary to work hard, isn't it? [She was now eighty years old.] I met so many interesting people in Florence, especially among the delegates from the East: India, China, Iraq, the Philippines, Lebanon, Pakistan, Egypt, Israel—all were friends, all full of enthusiasm. I was surprised to see how alive the idea is among these faraway populations; we all but embraced when we met." She ended the letter, *"Viva il bambino!!"* and signed it "Mammolina."[4]

When the course at Perugia ended she visited her birthplace, Ancona, where she was also made an honorary citizen, and Milan, which conferred the same honor on her.

On her return to Holland in the fall she was decorated with the Order of Orange-Nassau at the ceremonies in which she appeared in person to receive the honorary degree that had been given her by the University of Amsterdam. She received this honor from the land that was her last adopted home with tears in her eyes, a white-haired old woman in black, her hands pressed together in a gesture that in the West suggested prayer, in India peace. To her it meant both.

The audience of academics who had come expecting to hear the usual speech of acceptance from the recipient of an honorary degree were surprised and touched by her eloquence and by an incident that occurred midway in her speech, which was given in French. She mentioned the Casa dei Bambini and then, oblivious of the change, went on in Italian until her grandson, Mario Jr., called her attention to the fact, when she stopped, excused herself, and continued in French again. Once more, she had won an audience completely..

The Ninth International Montessori Congress organized by the AMI, and the last which Maria Montessori would attend, was held in London in May 1951. Some one hundred and fifty delegates from seventeen countries attended lectures on the theme of "Education as an Aid to the Natural Development of the Psyche of the Child from Birth to University."

During the days Mario, who had become her alter ego in her work—carrier of the message and keeper of the flame—spoke on the method. Teachers she had trained gave examples of its specific application to the teaching of subjects from arithmetic to music.

In the evenings Montessori, now in her eighty-first year, spoke on her philosophy of education. She had no set topics for her talks; she had never read her lectures or even spoken from notes, and she still talked informally in voluble Italian or sometimes now in halting English, seated at a table on which lay flowers presented to her by children on the opening of the congress. Observers commented on her "benevolent domination" of her audience. To all of them she was, in the words of her grandson, "a grand old lady."

Sounding more like the mystic she had gradually become over the years than the positivist she had prided herself on being as a young physician in turn-of-the-century Italy, Montessori spoke of the child as a "psychic embryo" endowed with a capacity to "create himself" spontaneously by means of a mysterious inner psychic force. An educator and teacher, she ended her life by saying that neither teaching nor education brings about the child's development: all educators and teachers can do is refrain from placing obstacles in the child's path by providing him with an environment in which he is "free to create himself."[5]

If her language was vague and mystical, her methods had always been practical, based on the observations of a shrewd common sense. She liked to talk about a mysterious spiritual power within the child; in practice that became a respect for the individual child's personality. She saw that repressive teaching or parenting could stunt a child' growth, but she was somewhat disingenuous in her talk of allowing the child's inner capacities full freedom to develop. The child, after all, has many contradictory impulses. Montessori knew this as well as we do, and she simply assumed that it was only those tendencies of which she approved which were to be provided with the proper soil in which to grow, like the plants she was fond of comparing to children. The Montessori teacher guides the child through a constant process of suggestion in the "right" use of the material in the "right" order. The child is given freedom to develop spontaneously only in a carefully controlled environment. And there is always the implicit value placed on the "practical," of knowledge for use, as in the exercises of daily life performed with such pleasure by the Montessori children—as they were by Montessori herself. The emphasis on independence, on the practical, and on control were at the basis of the Montessori system. If Montessori chose to talk about them in terms of mysterious spiritual forces unfolding without adult direction, it was a paradox of her mind, an unresolved polarity that characterized her thinking more and more as she grew older and older.

She was speaking now not only about the elementary-school child and the adolescent, but about the infant, a subject that had come increasingly to occupy her attention during the years in India toward the end of her long career. And what she advocated in this stage, from birth to three, was avoiding too early a separation of the child from the mother. Here too she used her highly personal vocabulary. Mothers should carry their babies about with them as they went about their normal activities so that the babies might come in contact with the environment from which they need to draw their "spiritual nourishment." Once again, as so many times before, she was on to the right thing intuitively although her reasoning appeared shaky and the basis for her conclusions more rhetorical than scientific. But the scientific community has confirmed what she was saying: infants thrive on a combination of physical security and stimulation. We accept it today as a commonplace. And there is a special poignancy in her sensitivity to the need of the child for closeness to his mother when we remember that she had not been able to mother her own infant.

The edition of the *Times Educational Supplement*[6] which reported on the congress at which Montessori talked about the importance of not separating infants from their mothers reported, in an adjoining column, on the just-published study by Dr. John Bowlby, *Maternal Care and Mental Health*,[7] a landmark work which was to influence the next generation of child-development experts and, through them, child-care practices in families and institutions. A detailed study sponsored by the World Health Organization, it amassed clinical evidence and statistical studies showing clearly that deprivation of maternal care in the first year of life was a direct cause of physical, intellectual, and social retardation and sometimes of mental illness. The Bowlby study established conclusively that the child's optimal development and mental health in later life depended on "the warm, intimate and continuous relationship between the infant and young child and his mother (or mother-substitute), in which both find enjoyment and satisfaction." The formulation and the evidence are certainly more scientific than Montessori's, but the conclusion is the same. The scientist had given the evidence for what the mystic had been saying all along in her own way.

When she spoke of the child as the teacher rather than the taught, Montessori had in mind her own cognitive style as a researcher, which was to make intuitive conclusions from her observations. She once said, "Whenever I reasoned, I was wrong."[8] When asked to sum up her educational philosophy, she did so in two words: *"Attendere, osservando—* watch and wait."[9]

Summing up Montessori's contribution to English education on the occasion of the congress, the *Times Educational Supplement* ran a lead editorial that described it as "a contribution of principles rather than practice. . . .

"It is worth remembering that much of what she advocated in the past is now part and parcel of standard practice. The child moves freely about his school. He learns to help himself. His equipment is suited to his stature. In these things Dr. Montessori was not necessarily original, but hers has been the personality that has carried conviction."[10]

Forty years after the opening of the first Casa dei Bambini there was hardly a school for young children anywhere that had not been influenced to some degree by the ideas of the Montessori movement, even without knowledge or use of the Montessori method. Those elements in Montessori's own character which became the goals she sought in the education of children—independence, ability to exercise control in the world beyond the self—had been both the means and the ends of her efforts and her system. The school was now a far cry from the kind of institution she had attended, had seen as a young physician, and had set out to change—the rigid, repressive structure in which immobilized pupils, "like butterflies mounted on pins," passively received standardized information, motivated by a system of prizes and punishments.

Her critics continued to maintain that her system underestimated the value of play and gave insufficient rein to the free imagination of the child, that her didactic apparatus was costly and restrictive, and that the observations on which she based her conclusions were not really scientific. They claimed that she made use of expedient and called it experiment, of empiricism and called it science. But no one could deny that her attempt to reconcile freedom with order had changed the school for all time.

The question of how her influence would proceed from this point was put this way by an English critic writing in the *Times Educational Supplement* in 1951 at the time of the congress:

> The truth is that Dr. Montessori has deceived herself. No system can be scientific, in any accepted sense of the word, that depends so much on the personality of its advocate. *La Dottoressa* has always attracted followers as much by the dominant force of her personality as by the strength of her arguments. She has an intuitive understanding of children, and her ability to instruct them is such that she taught idiots to read and write and brought them to compete with normal children. She is, in short, a scientist in education by conviction, but an artist in teaching at heart. The danger is that her personal magnetism will create a coterie that ignores criticism, so that what she has to offer of value to teachers in general will be lost in the jealous preserve of a few.[11]

Montessori does not seem to have been aware of the paradox inherent in her system, the inconsistency between the insistence on the principle of "following the child" and the practice of limiting the choice of activities available to him according to the adult's view of what will best serve his developmental needs.

The congress was pervaded by a sense among those who attended that it would be the last such gathering at which Montessori, over eighty and in frail health, would be present. It was also notable for two things that had characterized the movement from its inception—internationalism and a great personal affection for its leader. There were numerous tributes from representatives of many nations, and Montessori's response on this highly emotional occasion suggests that at the end at least she was aware of the dangers to the movement inherent in the establishment of a personal cult. After thanking her followers for the homage they had paid her, ranging from formal statements by high officials to a bouquet from some little children, she asked them to turn their attention from her to what she had been talking about. She was, she said, like a finger pointing to something beyond herself, and she asked them to look not at the outstretched finger but at what it was pointing to—"the child."

Now, not far from her eighty-first birthday, she worked every day from seven-thirty in the morning until one o'clock of the next morning with only a short nap in the afternoon, which she took under protest at the insistence of her doctor. She still loved to eat, enjoying the rich Dutch cuisine and supplementing it with her favorite pastas. She was growing frail with age, but insisted that her health was good and was indignant when she developed a toothache and had to have a molar extracted.

Age had only increased her sense of certitude about her beliefs. She still felt her method of education was the best way of solving the world's problems ("I know—I don't merely believe") and still dismissed political solutions, waving aside "Truman, MacArthur, Churchill and all that" with an imperious amethyst-ringed hand. An observer reported that "devotees kiss her hand, bow low, hang on her every word. She enjoys it all very much."[12]

In the summer of 1951 she accepted an invitation to visit the Tyrol. Back in Austria for the first time since the early 1930s, she gave a training course at Innsbruck which lasted from July to October. It was the last diploma course she would give. When the course ended she stood leaning on a beaming Mario's arm, an indomitable figure amid the storybook mountain scenery, listening intently as a group of students sang their farewells to her. Then she left for Italy, where she gave a series of lectures in Rome before returning to Holland.

Despite the eclectic character of her following, the variety of nations and cultures that had found her educational methods useful, she came to be referred to frequently toward the end of her life as a "Catholic educator." Her last public statement, finished the day before she died, was a message to be read at the first meeting of the Catholic Montessori Guild which had just been formed in England.

On May 6, 1952, a few months before her eighty-second birthday, she was seated in the garden of the house of friends in Noordwijk aan Zee, a little village on the North Sea coast near The Hague where she liked to come from time to time for a brief rest. She had been thinking of making a trip to Africa, but it had been suggested that because of the state of her health she ought not to travel but arrange instead for her lectures to be given by someone else. Mario was with her and she turned to him and said, "Am I no longer of any use then?" An hour later she was dead of a cerebral hemorrhage.

She was buried in the little cemetery of the Roman Catholic church at Noordwijk. She had wanted to be buried wherever she died. A tablet later placed at the graves of her parents in Rome says that Maria Montessori "rests far from her own beloved country, far from her dear ones buried here, at her wish as testimony to the universality of the work which made her a citizen of the world."

Even in death she remained what she had said as a child she would never be and had spent her life becoming—a teacher.

At the time of her death Montessori was virtually forgotten in the United States and, despite many honors heaped on her, little known even in Europe outside the world of her own followers and a somewhat larger circle of international educators. The response of many who read her obituaries and were old enough to remember her was surprise that she was still alive. Thousands of followers scattered around the world considered themselves Montessorians, but to the public at large, if they knew of her at all, she was a relic of another age.

Reporting on her death, the London *Times* said, "The final judgement on the system may well be based not so much on the degree to which it has won integral acceptance in the schools as on the measure wherein its principles have been assimilated into the general consciousness of the race."[13]

By the time she died, the pendulum of educational reform was ready to swing back again, and by the next decade her ideas were rediscovered and used in schools all over the world, including the United States, where the predictions about the effect her ideas would have on early childhood education at the time of her triumphant American tours half a century earlier might finally be said to have been realized.

Montessori's last home was a house in Amsterdam, at 161 Koninginneweg, which after her death was made into a memorial and the headquarters of the AMI. Her study still remains as it was during her lifetime, full of her furniture—graceful setees and ornately carved and inlaid chests and bureaus as well as the desk at which she wrote—and memorabilia—photographs of her parents, herself as a child and young woman, dressed for presentation at the English Court in her late fifties, signed photographs from popes, kings and queens and old friends, an idealized academic oil portrait of her that is barely recognizable and somehow for that reason seems symbolic of the distance from any sense of her as a real person that her public image had taken on in the late years of her life. The shelves are full of early editions of her own books and books by followers and admirers inscribed to her. Drawers are filled with awards, letters from students over the years, beautifully executed scrapbooks made by students of the many international courses. To a visitor, she is more present in her old study than in many of the classrooms where so often the Montessori materials are used, the spirit missed.

Leaving him for the last time, Montessori bequeathed to Mario not only all her possessions and the legacy of her work, but the unequivocal statement that he was her own son. Her last will and testament[14] refers to him quite simply as *il mio figlio*—"my son." It reads in part: "with respect to all my possessions, I declare that they belong to my son materially and spiritually . . . also belonging to him by right are all the fruits of my intellectual and social work, because they were undertaken with him as inspiration and with his constant collaboration from the time he was capable of acting in the world, when he devoted his life entirely to helping me in my work."

Entrusting him with the task of continuing the work she had begun "for the good of mankind," she concludes with the hope that his children will be a comfort to him and "that the world will render him the justice due his merits, which I know to be so great," adding, below her signature, "and that my friends and those who labor in my work should feel their debt to my son—*il mio figlio!*"

Unable to acknowledge him publicly during her lifetime, she was finally able to do so in death.

369

Afterword

Afterword

Montessori's intention had been to create a scientific pedagogy—a science of education. She defined the school as a prepared environment in which the child is able to develop freely at his own pace, unhindered in the spontaneous unfolding of his natural capacities, through the manipulation of a graded series of self-correcting materials designed to stimulate his senses and eventually his thinking, leading from perception to intellectual skills.

Today what seems most impressive is not Montessori's science but her intuition, which led her to invent new methods and materials to implement children's learning. Unfortunately, it was sometimes the specific methods and materials rather than her more general insights which were emphasized by her most enthusiastic followers, for whom the method itself became sacrosanct, the materials ritual objects.

Like her somewhat older contemporary Freud, she was a clinician. She began as a physician, and applied the clinical method of observation to individuals, constructing a theory and a method from her observations of children's behavior rather than beginning with a theory and trying to fit children's learning to the imposed ideal. Like Freud, she began with the study of the pathological—in her case the retarded—and used it as a point of departure for an understanding of normal development. And like both Freud and her other contemporary in education, Dewey, she was often known best for what were really popular distortions of her ideas and misconceptions about her methods. A chaotic classroom was no more a consequence of her ideas correctly interpreted than unbridled self-expression was of Dewey's or total lack of frustration of the impulses was of Freud's, although these caricatures often came to prevail in the public mind.

She passes the test for the real innovator—many of her ideas have become part of our common language of discourse about the subject of educating the young. A random list of ideas, techniques, and objects familiar to everyone in the field of childhood education today, all of which go back to Montessori's work at the start of the century, all of which she either invented or used in a new way, might include:

> —the concept that children learn through play and the ubiquitous "educational" toys and puzzles that stimulate early reading

373

and writing and basic math skills as well as programmed "teaching machines" and child-scaled furniture;

—the "open classroom" of the British infant and primary school model, the "ungraded" class in which children are grouped by interest and ability rather than age and in which there is individually paced instruction, the child given the freedom to proceed at his own rate—grading the material the children have access to but not arbitrarily grading the children;

—the idea of the child as different from, not just a smaller edition of the adult;

—the observation that infants are learning from birth on, that age six is late to start thinking of the child's education and three is not too early to begin schooling of the right kind;

—the importance of the environment in which learning is to take place;

—the significance of early stimulation for later learning and its implications for the education of the culturally impoverished child;

—the observation that children take a natural pleasure in learning to master their environment and that this mastery, beginning with the manipulation of objects, is the basis of the sense of competence necessary for independence;

—the judgment that real learning involves the ability to do things for one's self, not the passive reception of a body of knowledge;

—that the things that teach—the child's learning materials— should be intrinsically interesting and self-correcting, should train the senses in the perception of and therefore in the ability to deal with reality;

—that imposing immobility and silence hampers children's learning and that given interesting work to do children will establish their own order and quiet;

—the concept of "sensitive periods," phases of development appropriate to the learning of specific motor and cognitive skills such as "reading readiness";

—the right of every child to develop his own fullest potential and the idea that the school exists to implement that right;

—the idea that the school must be part of the community and involve the parents if education is to be effective.

If the objects sound old hat and the ideas like truisms, that in itself is proof of how right Montessori was about how many things. Her contemporaries in the field of education did not find them so natural or so obvious.

As a young woman, Montessori was passionately concerned with humanizing society and was a spokeswoman in Italy for the new child-saving institutions—special schools, settlement houses, juvenile courts— that people like Jane Addams were developing in the United States.

Afterword

There is no doubt that when she first arrived on the American scene just before World War I she was out of step with the psychological and educational movements which were then emerging as dominant academic and professional influences—on the one hand the behaviorists and intelligence testers and on the other the psychoanalytically oriented psychiatrists.

Intelligence was still thought to be determined by heredity. The notion that intellectual development could be affected by experience—by appropriate stimulation or the lack of it in early life—was not part of the thinking of the psychological establishment of the time. Schooling—and therefore the taxpayer's money—would be wasted on three-year-olds. Spencer and other post-Darwinian thinkers emphasized inherited factors in mind as well as body. The race might evolve; the individuals's course was predetermined and not subject to significant influence during his lifetime. The testing movement was reinforcing the idea of fixed intelligence. Montessori's view that mental retardation could be affected by pedagogical means seemed absurd to the followers of Cattell with their belief in the "constant I.Q."

At the same time, psychoanalysis was beginning to reveal the role of instinctual drives and unconscious conflicts as determinants of behavior, and the way in which identification with nurturing adults was related to the child's view of himself and the world—to the learning process seen as an aspect of personality development. These were concepts Montessori never reconciled with her emphasis on the child's "spontaneous interest in learning." Although she had anticipated the psychoanalysts by being concerned with cognitive development before they were, she never really integrated the cognitive with the emotional aspects of development. The result was to leave her ideas seeming, in the light of later psychoanalytic ego psychology, not so much incorrect as incomplete.

When Montessori came to America the dominant voice in psychology was still that of G. Stanley Hall, whose developmental theories stressed the view that ontogeny recapitulates phylogeny, with its implication that certain skills could be learned with profit only at certain stages in life. Although there was no disagreement in principle—after all, the idea of "sensitive periods" for learning of various kinds was one of the basic ideas of Montessori's system—the timetables did not agree. Most psychologists held that attempts to teach too early were a waste of time. Hall's students included Arnold Gesell, who later taught American parents what to expect of their children at any given age. His developmental schedules did not include reading and writing at three or four.

Among academic psychologists, stimulus-response theory was just

375

coming into its own, replacing the "faculty psychology" of Montessori's background in which the sharpening of one kind of perception—that of the senses—would affect other kinds of perceptions—the "higher" ones of the mind. The dominant belief now was that "transfer of training" was not possible, You could not, as Montessori held, eventually educate the intellect by first training the senses. The one set of stimuli were not directly related to the other; sense perception was not related to cognition. It was in this context that Kilpatrick had described Montessori's theory as "some fifty years behind the present development of educational theory."

Critics also charged that her "scientific pedagogy" was not really good science, that she did not provide adequate evidence or proof of her findings, had no control groups, did not provide detailed accounts of her experiments in such a way that they could be replicated by other investigators. While this is perfectly true, we now know that she was right about much of what she said about how children learn. Although she insisted on the scientific basis for her statements, they were largely the result of remarkably intuitive observations integrated with creative genius into a body of thinking about education which came down from Itard and Seguin. Which is not at all the same thing as laboratory science subject to statistical analysis, but is no less valuable for that failure to be something other than what it so brilliantly was. And there is a sense in which she was more scientific than any of her contemporary critics. She based her methods on empirical data, testing and reworking them on the basis of further observations, whereas the ideas of such educators as Kilpatrick were in the main theoretical.

Today, her science may seem sloppy, her language romantic and mystical, her style sometimes embarrassingly florid. But modern science has proven her right about many things.

Animal experiments, observations of stimulus-starved children in institutions, and cognitive studies of infants have all established the crucial influence of early experience on later development. Other studies have shown that while intellectual capacity may be genetically determined, interaction with the environment—early stimulation—has a great deal to do with whether an individual will realize his full potential or not. Enriched environments in the preschool years are now seen as possible antidotes to cultural deprivation—just what Montessori was providing in her work with the children in San Lorenzo in 1907.

Even the belief in the child's spontaneous interest in learning has found a contemporary foundation in the work of psychologists like Jerome Bruner and J. McV. Hunt, who have shown experimentally that young children have an intrinsic interest in novelty and tend to seek out new sights and sounds and pay attention to them, to approach their enviroment like explorers, but that each new experience has to have just the right degree of novelty and complexity—what Montessori was providing in the graded series of didactic materials she developed and the reason why she insisted they be used in the "correct" order.

She began with a program—and what could sound more contemporary, more relevant?—for counteracting cultural deprivation by enriching early experience. It was a radical, even revolutionary, concept at the time. She went on to apply what she learned from working with deficient children to a way of educating normal children—all children—based on certain insights we take for granted today, but which she was the first to articulate and apply: that true learning has to take into account the nature of the learner, that education must be child-centered, must engage the child's interests and proceed through his spontaneous activity, freed from the threat of punishment or the promise of reward—in short, that the child must be self-motivated in order to become an active learner, one who does not merely receive a given body of knowledge as inert ideas to be memorized and repeated but who discovers for himself and is able to apply what he learns to new situations. Montessori believed that an education which could do that, by forming healthier individuals would help create a better world. She shared these insights with others in the child-study movement and among social reformers, but it was her contribution to show how they could be applied and made to work in the context of the school.

In time, her insights tended to become enshrined in a movement. Clashes of culture, personal jealousies all played a part in turning what had been innovative into a closed system, defensive of orthodoxy rather than open to the change that all ideas must undergo with the passage of time.

The estrangement between Montessori and so many of her brightest followers, such as Lili Roubiczek, is significant for the light it sheds on the fate of the Montessori movement. For despite Montessori's continuing following among large groups of ardent supporters, and the tribute paid her as a symbolic figure in the late years of her life, and even though so many of her ideas were to find their way into schoolrooms all over the world, the movement became isolated from the newly developing currents of thought that were influencing the most creative European psychologists and educators just as in America it had become cut off from the mainstream of development in those fields and remained drifting in the backwaters of a few private schools.

Just as Montessori identified herself totally with her work, she identified the work itself—the ideas on which it was based and the practice and teaching by which those ideas were carried out—with the movement bearing her name. Her sense of the dangers threatening what she considered to be the ideal implementation of her ideas from contact with other systems based on other insights was stronger than her sense of what might be gained from intellectual cross-pollination. She chose to gather her followers aroud her and make them the nucleus of an organization which became a universe of its own. The frequent eruptions of internecine warfare between those followers, as in the United States and again in England, could only result in further schisms and separations that increased the isolation of the "true believers," and the movement, although nominally dedicated to research and discussion, became limited in what was tried and what was said to what came from within. Nothing is as inimical to the pursuit of truth as the conviction that one has already found it.

It is difficult to gauge the extent to which the institutionalization of Montessori's following served to promote her ideas and the extent to which it served to retard their further development. The retrograde influence institutionalization has on thought of all kinds is one of the clearest lessons of intellectual history. Where the Montessori movement was isolated from those pursuing related ideas in allied fields such as psychology and even—as in the United States—in education itself, the separation tended to limit the intellectual growth of the movement, although not its spread. The Montessori movement continued to have an influence among numerous dedicated followers, but one can only wonder what that influence would have been if it had not been isolated from the best that was being thought and tried by others outside the movement, especially in Vienna among the "analytic pedagogues" and in the United States in the universities, the traditional places of research and teaching.

The preservative intention of the movement could not but create a conservative spirit which continued to characterize those who remained within it. They went forward as proselytizers but not as discoverers. And a revolutionary new way of seeing the relationship between the child and his school and the process of education itself stopped short of whatever it might have become if allowed to interpenetrate and encouraged to mix freely with the rest of what was going on in the larger world of those who were thinking about the nature of learning, practicing and teaching what they in turn found interesting and workable.

The earlier part of Montessori's life is more interesting to read, as it

378

was to write, because it is a story of discovery, with all the elements of risk-taking and suspense such a story implies. Then, like her books, it becomes repetitious, and somewhat duller, no longer involving new adventures in ideas but only the safeguarding of earlier ones. The movement had become a fortress. It protected those within from external dangers but left them with a rather impoverished set of experiences, seldom seeing new faces, hearing other voices than their own.

Nothing is as corrupting as worship—unless it is being worshiped. It was Maria Montessori's fate that she reached a point at which she stopped growing intellectually and instead retreated into the church her disciples had built around her in the later years of her life. She never really confronted the challenges of new ideas in fields as close to her own as psychoanalysis, anthropology, and linguistics.

That is a truth that has to be stated in any attempt to understand her life and evaluate her work. It is a postscript, however; it is not meant to obscure the reach of her early vision, the range of her early accomplishments. She belongs on any list of those whose existence shaped our century, and the fact that she was a woman, born in Italy thirty years before the end of the last century, makes that fact even more remarkable.

She began her professional life as an innovator, breaking a traditional barrier. It was no small thing for a woman to force her way into medical school against the weight of social custom and professional reaction, and then to graduate with the high honors that meant she was not just good "for a woman," but as good as any of her male colleagues. In her work with abnormal children, then in the Casa dei Bambini, and later in the extension of her methods for the education of normal children to the elementary-school years, she continued to be a pioneer, and to note that she did not remain one all of her life is not to make light of her genius or the significance of her work but to understand something more about both the life and the work, and about the moment in intellectual history to which they belong.

Notes

Notes

Introduction
1. The details of Montessori's arrival are taken from articles which appeared in the *Brooklyn Daily Eagle* and *The Evening Post* (New York) on December 3, 1913.

Chapter 1
1. For much of the material about Montessori's background and childhood I am indebted to Mario Montessori and Ada Montessori-Pierson, who generously provided a chronology of events in the lives of Alessandro and Renilde Montessori and of Maria Montessori's early school years based on documents in the possession of the Montessori family and in the files of the Association Montessori Internationale (personal communications, April 3, 1974, *et seq.*).
2. Both remarks are quoted in Helen Zimmern, *The Italy of the Italians* (New York, 1906), p. 23.
3. The anecdotal material on Montessori's childhood in this chapter appears in Anna Maria Maccheroni, *A True Romance: Dr. Maria Montessori as I Knew Her* (Edinburgh, 1947) and E. M. Standing, *Maria Montessori: Her Life and Work* (London, 1957).
4. Standing, *Maria Montessori*, p. 23. The original edition of this work is out of print; page numbers refer to the reprint published by New American Library (Mentor Books, New York, 1962).
5. Bolton King and Thomas Okey, *Italy Today* (London, 1901), p. 233.
6. *Ibid.*
7. Some of the material on Montessori's childhood is taken from an article by her grandson, Mario M. Montessori, Jr., "A Grand Old Lady," published in *Around the Child* (Calcutta), vol. 10 (1965–66), pp. 12ff.
8. A. Gallenga, *Italy, Present and Future* (London, 1887), vol. 2, p. 29.
9. George B. Taylor, *Italy and the Italians* (Philadelphia, 1898), p. 301.
10. Gallenga, *Italy, Present and Future*, p. 152.
11. The Hon. Margaret Collier (Mme. Galletti di Cadilhac), *Our Home by the Adriatic* (London, 1886), p. 41
12. Luigi Villari, *Italian Life in Town and Country* (New York and London, 1902), pp. 254–255.
13. Maccheroni, *A True Romance*, p. 12.
14. *The Globe* (New York), December 3, 1913.
15. *The Evening Mail* (New York), December 3, 1913.
16. *The New York Herald*, December 4, 1913.

Chapter 2
1. Federico Garlanda, *The New Italy* (New York and London, 1911), p. 153.
2. *Ibid.*, p. 154.
3. Villari, *Italian Life*, p. 249.
4. *Ibid.*, p. 253
5. Gallenga, *Italy, Present and Future*, vol. 2., pp. 34–35.

6. Maria Montessori, Letter to Clara, 1896, from the personal papers of Maria Montessori in the possession of Mario Montessori, to whom I am indebted for permission to quote from it.
7. Anna Maria Maccheroni, "Maria Montessori," *AMI Communications*, 1966, no. 3, p. 40.
8. Standing, *Maria Montessori*, p. 26.
9. Maccheroni, *A True Romance*, pp. 12–13.
10. Standing, *Maria Montessori*, p. 26.
11. *Ibid.*, p. 25.
12. The events in Montessori's medical-school years and early career (1892–1900) described in chapters 2, 3, and 4 are taken in large part from newspaper reports and magazine and journal articles in "Memorie," a souvenir album of clippings assembled by Alessandro Montessori in 1900, now in the possession of Mario Montessori, to whom I am grateful for the opportunity to peruse its contents and to have photocopies made of many of its pages. Alessandro Montessori was clearly a scholar manqué. To him I am indebted for the painstaking recording of dates and sources illuminating these otherwise unrecorded chapters of Maria Montessori's life.
13. Standing, *Maria Montessori*, p. 27.
14. Maria Montessori, Letter to Clara.
15. Villari, *Italian Life*, p. 255.
16. "Sul significato dei cristalli del Leyden nell'asma bronchiale," *Bollettino della Società Lancisiana degli Ospedali di Roma*, vol. 15, no. 2, Rome, 1896.

Chapter 3
1. Julia Maria, "Le Feminisme Italien: entrevue avec Mlle. Montessori," *L'Italie*, Rome, August 16, 1896.
2. Maria Montessori, Letter to Alessandro and Renilde Montessori from Berlin, September 29, 1896, reprinted in "Maria Montessori: A Centenary Anthology," Association Montessori Internationale, Amsterdam, 1970, p. 14.
3. *Il Corriere della Sera*, Milan, September 25/26, 1896.
4. Quoted in *Don Chisciotte di Roma*, October 6, 1896.
5. Ugo Sogliani, "La Settimana delle Donne," *L'Illustrazione Italiana*, Milan, October 4, 1896.
6. Maria Montessori, Letter to Alessandro and Renilde Montessori, "Centenary Anthology," p. 14.
7. Standing, *Maria Montessori*, p. 34.
8. *Idiocy and Its Treatment by the Physiological Method* (New York, 1866), p. 33.
9. Maria Montessori, *The Montessori Method* (New York, 1912), p. 31.
10. Jean Jacques Rousseau, *Émile* (New York, Everyman's Library, 1911), p. 31.
11. Quoted in Ellwood P. Cubberley, *History of Education* (Boston, 1920), p. 539
12. Giuseppe Sergi, "Il Movimento femminista," *Revista politica e letteraria*, Rome, April 1898.

Chapter 4
1. Maria Montessori, "Miserie Sociali e nuovi ritrovati della scienza," *Il Risveglio Educativo*, Milan, December 7 and December 17, 1898.
2. The speech as quoted here is taken from the version that appeared in *Risveglio Educativo*.

Notes

3. The material in this chapter on Montessori's lectures is based on numerous newspaper accounts from various cities in Alessandro Montessori's book of clippings, "Memorie."
4. *The Montessori Method*, p. 35.
5. *Ibid.*, p. 36.

Chapter 5
1. *The Montessori Method*, p. 32.
2. *Ibid.*
3. *Ibid.*, p. 36.
4. *Ibid.*, p. 261.
5. *Ibid.*
6. *Ibid.*, p. 266.
7. *Ibid.*, pp. 38–39.
8. *Ibid.*, p. 37.
9. *Ibid.*, p. 37–38.
10. *Ibid.*, p. 33.
11. *Ibid.*, p. 14.
12. *Ibid.*, p. 41.
13. *Ibid.*, pp. 32–33.
14. Milan, 1910.
15. Maccheroni, *A True Romance*, pp. 1–4.
16. Maria Montessori, *Pedagogical Anthropology*, (New York, 1913), p. 17.
17. *Ibid.*
18. *Ibid.*, p. 341.
19. *Ibid.*, p. 443.
20. *Ibid.*, pp. 414–415.
21. *Ibid.*
22. *Ibid.*, p. 453.
23. *Ibid.*
24. *Ibid.*, pp. 302–303.
25. *Ibid.*, p. 125.
26. *Ibid.*, p. 126.
27. *Ibid.*, pp. 266–267.
28. *Ibid.*, pp. 474–475.
29. *Ibid.*, p. 473.
30. *Ibid.*, p. 475.
31. *Ibid.*, p. 449.
32. *Ibid.*, pp. 449–450.
33. *Ibid.*, p. 360.
34. "Ricerche batteriologiche sul liquido cefalo-rachidiano dei dementi paralitici," Rome, 1897. "Sui caratteri antropometrici in relazione alle gerarchie intellettuali dei fanciulli nelle scuole," Florence, 1904. "Influenza della condizioni di famiglia sul livello intellettuale degli scolari," Bologna, 1904. "Caratteri fisici delle giovani donne del Lazio," Rome, 1905. "L'importanza dell'etnologia regionale nell'antropologia pedagogica," Milan, 1906.

Chapter 6
1. René Bazin, *The Italians of Today* (New York, 1897), p. 5.
2. *Ibid.*, pp. 97ff.
3. Dorothy Canfield Fisher, *A Montessori Mother* (New York, 1912), p. 221.
4. Sheila Radice, *The New Children* (New York, 1920), pp. 140–141.
5. *The Montessori Method*, p. 43.

6. "'How It All Happened': Dr. Montessori Speaks," *AMI Communications,* 1970, no. 2/3, p. 4.
7. *Ibid.*
8. Maria Montessori, *The Secret of Childhood,* p. 117. Since the original editions of *The Secret of Childhood* (London, 1936; New York, 1939) are long out of print, page numbers for this title refer to the reprint published by Ballantine Books (New York, 1972).
9. "How It All Happened," p. 5.
10. *Ibid.*
11. *Secret of Childhood,* p. 119. (Bracketed words are my translation.—Au.)
12. "How It All Happened," p. 5.
13. *Secret of Childhood,* pp. 123–124.
14. *Ibid.,* p. 126.
15. *Ibid.,* pp. 126–127.
16. *The Montessori Method,* p. 82.
17. *Ibid.,* p. 93.
18. *Ibid.,* p. 88.
19. *Ibid.,* pp. 92–93.
20. *Ibid.,* p. 93.
21. *Ibid.,* pp. 70–71.
22. *Ibid.,* p. 95.
23. *Ibid.,* pp.96–97.
24. *Ibid.,* p. 98.
25. *Ibid.,* p. 102.
26. *Ibid.,* p. 141.
27. *Ibid.,* p. 172.
28. *Ibid.,* p. 173.
29. *Ibid.,* pp. 61–62.

Chapter 7
1. The quotations are taken from the inaugural address as it appears in Chapter II of *The Montessori Method;* the passages quoted are from the section between pages 55 and 69. Where I felt that the original translation did not serve to render Montessori's real meaning to the modern reader, I have changed a specific word ("house" to "home"; "collectivity" to "community," etc.). These words appear in brackets.
2. *Secret of Childhood,* p. 128.
3. *The Montessori Method,* p. 267.
4. *Ibid.,* p. 287.
5. *Ibid.,* p. 288. (Bracketed words are my translation.-Au.)
6. *Ibid.,* pp. 288–289.
7. *Ibid.,* p. 270.
8. *Ibid.,* p. 298.
9. *Ibid.,* p. 300.
10. *Ibid.*

Chapter 8
1. Maccheroni, *A True Romance,* p. 3.
2. *Ibid.,* p. 5.
3. *Ibid.,* p. 6.
4. *Ibid.,* p. 7.
5. *Ibid.*
6. *Ibid.,* p. 9.

7. Fisher, *Montessori Mother,* p. 223.
8. Maria Montessori, *The Discovery of the Child* (Madras, 1948), p. 59.
9. The story of Montessori's relations with Umanitaria is told in Marziola Pignatari, *Maria Montessori e la sua riforma educativa* (Florence, 1970), pp. 31ff.
10. Maccheroni, *A True Romance,* p. 28.
11. *Ibid.*
12. *The Montessori Method,* p. 28.
13. *Ibid.,* pp. 29–30.
14. *Ibid.,* p. 356.
15. *Ibid.,* p. 358.
16. Quoted in Radice, *New Children,* p. 74.
17. *The Montessori Method,* p. 365.
18. *Ibid.,* pp. 366–367.
19. *Ibid.,* pp. 22–23.
20. *Ibid.,* p. 8.
21. *Ibid.,* p. 10.
22. *Ibid.,* p. 24.
23. *Ibid.,* p. 87.
24. *Ibid.,* p. 106.
25. *Ibid.,* p. 376.
26. *Ibid.,* pp. 126–131.
27. *Ibid.,* p. 154.
28. *Ibid.,* p. 299.
29. *Ibid.,* p. 191.
30. *Ibid.,* p. 221.
31. *Ibid.,* p. 110.
32. *Ibid.,* p. 326.
33. *Ibid.,* p. 45.
34. *Ibid.*
35. Radice, *New Children,* p. 137.
36. *The Montessori Method,* p. 46.

Chapter 9
1. Fisher, *Montessori Mother,* p. 229.
2. These quotes are from an interview which appeared in an English-language newspaper in 1947, a copy of which is among the clippings in the offices of the AMI but without the name of the newspaper or the date.
3. Anna Maccheroni, "Maria Montessori," *AMI Communications,* 1966, no. 3, p. 39.
4. Josephine Tozier, "The Montessori Schools in Rome," *McClure's Magazine,* Vol. 38, No. 2 (December 1911), p. 133.
5. *Ibid.,* p. 137.
6. Quoted in Tozier, "The Montessori Schools in Rome," pp. 135–136.
7. Florence Elizabeth Ward, *The Montessori Method and the American School* (New York, 1913), p. 11.
8. The quotations from Merrill are taken from her series of articles which appeared in *The Kindergarten-Primary Magazine,* vol. 23, nos. 4–10 (December 1909–June 1910).
9. Standing, *Maria Montessori,* pp. 61–62.

Chapter 10
1. Josephine Tozier, "An Educational Wonder-Worker: The Methods of

Maria Montessori," *McClure's Magazine*, vol. 37, no. 1 (May 1911), p. 21.

2. S. S. McClure, *My Autobiography* (New York, 1914), pp. 252–253.
3. *McClure's Magazine*, vol. 37, no. 6 (October 1911), p. 702.
4. *Ibid.*
5. Josephine Tozier, "The Montessori Schools in Rome," pp. 122–137.
6. Josephine Tozier, "The Montessori Apparatus," *McClure's Magazine*, vol. 38, no. 3 (January 1912), pp. 289ff.
7. Vol. 39, No. 1, pp. 95ff.
8. Vol. 38, No. 2, p. 123
9. Anne E. George, "Dr. Maria Montessori," *Good Housekeeping*, vol. 55 (July 1912), p. 25.
10. *Ibid.*
11. Anne E. George, "The First Montessori School in America," *McClure's Magazine*, vol. 39, no. 2 (June 1912), p. 178.
12. Anne E. George, "The Montessori Movement America," *Report of the U.S. Commissioner of Education*, Washington, D.C., 1914, vol. 1, ch. 15, pp. 355ff.
13. *Ibid.*, p. 356.
14. George, "Dr. Maria Montessori," p. 26.
15. George, "The First Montessori School in America," p. 178.
16. "A School Without Desks, or Classes, or Recitations," *The New York Times*, December 24, 1911.
17. Vol. 40, No. 1, pp. 77ff.
18. The Bells' involvement with the Montessori movement is discussed in Robert V. Bruce, *Bell: Alexander Graham Bell and the Conquest of Solitude* (Boston, 1973), which provided much of the material in the following pages.
19. McClure, *Autobiography*, p. 253.
20. William Boyd, *From Locke to Montessori* (New York, 1914), p. 14.
21. *Ibid.*
22. Alice Payne Hackett, *Seventy Years of Best Sellers* (New York, 1967), pp. 108–109.
23. The sales figure is from a letter to Montessori from Frederick Stokes, her New York publisher, January 1913, quoted in "Centenary Anthology," p. 24.
24. Mary Antin, *The Promised Land* (Boston, 1912), p. 353.
25. "Preface to the American Edition," *The Montessori Method* (New York, 1912), pp. vii–viii.
26. All of the quotations from Professor Henry W. Holmes are taken from his "Introduction" to the 1912 American edition of *The Montessori Method*, pp. xvii–xxxvii.
27. Ward, *Montessori Method and the American School*, pp. xi–xii.
28. I am indebted for many details having to do with the vicissitudes of the Montessori movement in America to the authors of two unpublished doctoral dissertations: Phyllis Appelbaum, "The Growth of the Montessori Movement in the United States, 1909–1970," New York University, 1971; and Mary L. K. Wills, "Conditions Associated with the Rise and Decline of the Montessori Method of Kindergarten-Nursery Education in the United States from 1911–1921," Illinois University, 1966. Appelbaum's work was particularly helpful in citing the documents relating to Montessori in the McClure Collection at Indiana University and the Bell Collection at the National Geographic Society.
29. Maria Montessori, Telegram to S. S. McClure, June 5, 1912, McClure

Notes

Manuscripts, Personal Correspondence and Documents: Lilly Library, Indiana University, Bloomington.

30. Fisher, *Montessori Mother*, pp. 52–53.
31. *Ibid.*, p. 65.
32. *Ibid.*, p. 64.
33. *Ibid.*, p. 131
34. *Ibid.*, p. 105.
35. Maria Montessori, Letter to the Editors, *Times Educational Supplement* (London), September 1, 1914.
36. Fisher, *Montessori Mother*, pp. 222; 224–226.
37. W. A. Baldwin, "The Conflicting Pedagogy of Madame Montessori," *Journal of Education*, February 1913.

Chapter 11

1. Maccheroni, *A True Romance*, p. 39.
2. *Ibid.*, p. 40.
3. The 1913 course is described in a memoir by one of the Americans who attended it: Leocadia Casademont, "The Italian Past and the American Present," *American Montessori Society News*, vol. 2 (1971), no. 3.
4. Quoted in personal communication to the author from Helen Parkhurst, September 1972.
5. Radice, *New Children*, p. 35.
6. *Ibid.*, p. 34.
7. *The New York Times*, July 13, 1913.
8. Myron T. Scudder, Letter to S. S. McClure, October 3, 1912. McClure Manuscripts.
9. *The New York Times*, August 10, 1913.
10. *The New York Times*, July 24, 1913.
11. *The New York Times*, August 1, 1913.
12. S. S. McClure, Letter to Harriet Hurd McClure, November 15, 1913. McClure Manuscripts.
13. S. S. McClure, Letter to Harriet Hurd McClure, November 7, 1913. McClure Manuscripts.
14. S. S. McClure, Letter to Harriet Hurd McClure, November 11, 1913. McClure Manuscripts.
15. "Memoranda of Agreements entered into between the Dottoressa Maria Montessori of 5 Via Principessa Clotilde, Roma, and S. S. McClure of 126 E. 24th Street, New York City on the 14th of November 1913." McClure Manuscripts.
16. *The New York Times*, November 20 and 21, 1913.
17. McClure Manuscripts.

Chapter 12

1. *New York Tribune*, December 3, 1913.
2. *Brooklyn Daily Eagle*, December 3, 1913.
3. *The Times* (London), December 5, 1913.
4. *The New York Times*, December 7, 1913.
5. Margaret Naumburg, "Maria Montessori, Friend of Children," *Outlook*, December 13, 1913, p. 796.
6. *Brooklyn Daily Eagle*, December 3, 1913.
7. The quotations that follow are from "Dr. Montessori Talks of Her Mode of 'Auto-education,'" *The New York Times*, December 7, 1913.
8. *The New York Herald*, December 4, 1913.

9. *New York Tribune,* December 4, 1913.
10. *The New York Herald,* December 7, 1913.
11. *Ibid.*
12. *Brooklyn Daily Eagle,* December 7, 1913.
13. *Ibid.*
14. *The Sun* (New York), December 9, 1913.
15. Quoted in the *New York Tribune,* December 9, 1913.
16. Quoted in *The New York Times,* December 9, 1913.
17. The occasion is described in "When Helen Keller Met Montessori," *Literary Digest,* vol. 48, January 17, 1914, pp. 134ff.
18. *The New York Times,* December 12, 1913.
19. Quoted in the *Brooklyn Daily Eagle,* December 12, 1913.
20. *Ibid.*
21. *New York Tribune,* December 14, 1913.
22. Quoted in *The New York Times,* December 16, 1913.
23. *Ibid.*
24. Quoted in the *New York Tribune,* December 16, 1913.
25. *Ibid.*
26. *New York Tribune,* December 15, 1913. The quotations that follow are from the same source.
27. Quoted in *The New York Times,* December 24, 1913.
28. *The Times* (London), January 28, 1914.
29. Peter Lyon, *Success Story: The Life and Times of S. S. McClure* (New York, 1913), p. 351.
30. McClure Manuscripts.
31. Lyon, *Success Story,* p. 351.
32. The clippings (undated) were enclosed in a letter from McClure to Montessori dated March 12, 1914, in the collection of the AMI.
33. Maccheroni, *A True Romance,* p. 46.
34. Robert McClure, Letter to S. S. McClure, April 5, 1914. McClure Manuscripts.
35. *Ibid.*
36. McClure, *Autobiography,* pp. 251–253.
37. Gilbert H. Grosvenor, Letter to Mabel Bell, December 4, 1914. Bell Collection: Personal Correspondence and Documents. National Geographic Society, Washington, D.C.
38. Maria Montessori, *Dr. Montessori's Own Handbook,* (New York, 1914), p. 17.
39. *Ibid.,* p. 77.

Chapter 13
1. *West Side News* (New York), April 25, 1915.
2. *San Francisco Chronicle,* April 27, 1915.
3. Helen Parkhurst, "The Legacy of Maria Montessori," tape recording of a talk delivered in June 1965 at a seminar held by the American Montessori Society at the New York Hilton Hotel. From the files of the AMS.
4. *Ibid.* The anecdotes and quotations throughout this chapter are taken from the AMS tape and from a tape-recorded interview with Parkhurst also made in 1965, now in the library of the Whitby School, Greenwich, Connecticut.
5. *San Francisco Chronicle,* September 11, 1915.
6. *Ibid.*
7. *Ibid.,* August 18, 1915.
8. (Cambridge, 1965), p. xxv.

Notes

9. The letter is in Mario Montessori's collection of personal papers of Maria Montessori, Amsterdam.
10. "Education in Relation to the Imagination of the Little Child." See Note 13.
11. "My System of Education." See Note 13.
12. *Ibid.*
13. Montessori's four lectures at the NEA meetings—"My System of Education," "Education in Relation to the Imagination of the Little Child," "The Organization of Intellectual Work in the School," and "The Mother and the Child"—appeared in the *Journal of Proceedings and Addresses of the National Education Association* (vol. 53, 1915, pp. 64ff., 661ff., 717ff., and 1121ff.) and were reprinted as separate pamphlets by the House of Childhood for the National Montessori Promotion Fund in 1915.
14. Letter from Bailey Willis, n.d. Bell Collection.
15. Bell Collection.
16. "Home Notes," September 29, 1915, pp. 19ff. Bell Collection.
17. Mario Montessori, "A Long Letter to Montessorians in America, In Answer to Some of the Many Questions I Receive," pamphlet distributed to members of the American Montessori Society, May 1963, unpaged.
18. Whitby tapes.

Chapter 14
1. *Current Opinion,* vol. 56 (February 1914), p. 127.
2. William Heard Kilpatrick, *The Montessori System Examined* (Boston, 1914), pp. 27–29.
3. *Ibid.,* p. 52.
4. *Ibid.,* pp. 63–64.
5. *Ibid.,* pp. 63 and 66.
6. Elizabeth Harrison, "The Montessori Method and the Kindergarten," U.S. Bureau of Education, *Bulletin,* 1914, No. 28.
7. Kilpatrick, "Montessori and Froebel," *Kindergarten Review,* vol. 23 (April 1913), pp. 491ff.
8. "Dr. Maria Montessori and the Montessori Movement: A General Bibliography of Materials in the English Language, 1909–1961," compiled by Gilbert E. Donahue, appears in Nancy McCormick Rambusch, *Learning How to Learn: An American Approach to Montessori* (Baltimore and Dublin, 1962), pp. 139ff.

Chapter 15
1. Edmond Gore A. Holmes, *The Montessori System of Education,* Great Britain Board of Education, Educational Pamphlets, No. 24. London, 1912.
2. *Times Educational Supplement* [hereafter abbreviated as *TES*] (London), November 5, 1912.
3. *Ibid.*
4. Quoted in "Centenary Anthology," p. 17.
5. Theodate L. Smith, *The Montessori System in Theory and Practice* (New York, 1912).
6. *TES,* November 5, 1912
7. London, 1914.
8. London, 1913; New York, 1914.
9. *TES,* November 4, 1913.
10. Quotations from *The Times* (London), November 18, 1912.

11. *The Times* (London), December 3, 1912.
12. *Ibid.*
13. *Parents' Review* (London), December 1912.
14. *TES,* January 7, 1913.
15. *TES,* December 3, 1912.
16. *The Times* (London), January 3, 1913.
17. *TES,* January 7, 1913.
18. *The Times* (London), January 11, 1913.
19. *Ibid.*
20. *TES,* May 6, 1913.
21. *TES,* March 4, 1913.
22. *The Times* (London), January 20, 21, 23, 26, 28, 1914.
23. Quoted in *The Times* (London), January 7, 1914.
24. Quoted in *The Times* (London), January 5, 1917.
25. London, 1913.
26. *TES,* February 3, 1914.
27. *Ibid.*
28. Quoted in *The Times* (London), February 26, 1914.
29. *Ibid.*
30. *The Times* (London), January 9, 1914.
31. *TES,* June 2, 1914.
32. *TES,* August 4, 1914.
33. *Ibid.*
34. *TES,* May 10, 1916.
35. *TES,* January 5, 1915.
36. Quoted in *TES,* March 2, 1915.
37. *The Times* (London), January 6, 1916.
38. Quoted in *The Times* (London), May 22, 1915.

Chapter 16
1. Articles on Montessori schools and societies in various European countries appeared in the *TES,* March 3 and April 7, 1914, and the *Westminster Gazette,* January 20, 1923, as well as in various other newspaper articles in the collection of the AMI, Amsterdam.
2. *The Times* (London), November 11, 1920.
3. Palau's activities are recorded by Eladio Homs in "Maria Montessori 'Barcelonina,'" in *Maria Montessori: cittadina del Mondo,* Marziola Pignatari, ed. (Rome, 1967), pp. 257ff. Reprinted from *Vita dell'Infanzia,* Rome, vol. 1, no. 5/6/7 (May/June/July, 1952).
4. Helen Parkhurst in *AMI Communications,* 1966, no. 3. p. 15.
5. From a letter to C. A. Bang written by a student at the Barcelona course in the spring of 1916, in the collection of the AMI.
6. A number of articles describing the 1916 course and the Montessori school at Barcelona appeared in the *TES* throughout March, April, and May of 1916.
7. Letter to C. A. Bang. Note 5, above.
8. The school at Barcelona was described in an article in the *TES,* May 1, 1919.
9. Homs, "Maria Montessori 'Barcelonina,'" pp. 260–261. Note 3, above.
10. Jerome S. Bruner, *Toward a Theory of Instruction* (Cambridge, Mass., 1966), p. 34
11. Montessori's proposal for the White Cross and its influence in the establishment of schools in France are discussed in articles which appeared in

The *Times* (London), September 24, 1917, and in the *TES*, January 16, 1919.

12. *TES*, January 10, 1918.
13. Reprinted in the *TES*, January 31, 1918.
14. Maccheroni, *A True Romance*, p. 63.
15. Montessori's arrival was described in *The Times* (London), September 1, 1919.
16. Quoted in *TES*, September 4, 1919.
17. Radice, *New Children*, pp. 33–34.
18. *TES*, October 23, 1919.
19. *Ibid.*
20. Radice, *New Children*, p. 46.
21. *Ibid.*, p. 47.
22. *Ibid.*, p. 60.
23. Sigmund Freud, *An Autobiographical Study* (London, 1935), p. 22.
24. Radice, *New Children*, p. 60.
25. *Ibid.*, p. 30.
26. *Ibid.*, p. 105.
27. *Ibid.*, p. 65.
28. *Ibid.*, p. 21.
29. *Ibid.*, pp. 28–29.
30. *TES*, July 10, 1919.
31. *Nursery World* (London), September 18, 1929.
32. Radice, *New Children*, p. 49.
33. *TES*, October 2, 1919.
34. Radice, *New Children*, p. 101.
35. *Ibid.*, p. 106.
36. Maccheroni, Letter to the Editors, *TES*, November 20, 1919.
37. Radice, *New Children*, pp. 141–142.
38. *TES*, December 4, 1919.
39. Sir Percy Nunn, quoted in *TES*, December 4, 1919.
40. Dr. Crichton Miller, quoted in Radice, *New Children*, p. 139.
41. Dr. Wildon Carr, quoted in *TES*, December 18, 1919.
42. *TES*, December 18, 1919.
43. Quoted in *TES*, December 18, 1919.
44. Quoted in *TES*, January 29, 1920.

Chapter 17
1. Maria Montessori, "The 'Erdkinder' and the Functions of the University: The Reform of Education During and After Adolescence," Association Montessori Internationale, Amsterdam, 1939. Reprinted as *From Childhood to Adolescence* (New York, 1973).
2. Maria Montessori, Letter to the Editors, *TES*, February 12, 1920.
3. Much of this material is based on newspaper clippings of articles about and interviews with Montessori in scrapbooks and in the files of the AMI in Amsterdam. Many of the articles are undated, and sometimes the name of the periodical is missing as well.
4. *TES*, December 30, 1920.
5. *TES*, December 23, 1920.
6. *TES*, January 13, 1921.
7. *TES*, January 20, 1921.
8. *TES*, July 2, 1921.
9. Quoted in *TES*, October 1, 1921.

10. *TES*, October 22, 1921.
11. *Ibid.*
12. *Ibid.*
13. *TES*, December 17, 1921.
14. *TES*, January 21, 1922.
15. *TES*, December 10, 1921.
16. *TES*, December 17, 1921.
17. *Ibid.*
18. *Ibid.*
19. *Punch* (London), December 14, 1921.
20. *TES*, October 22, 1921.
21. *Ibid.*
22. *Ibid.*
23. *TES*, January 21, 1922.
24. Quoted in *TES*, June 3, 1922.

Chapter 18
1. Quoted in *TES*, June 24, 1922.
2. *TES*, November 4, 1922.
3. *TES*, December 23, 1922.
4. Mario Montessori's letter and Maria Montessori's subsequent meeting with Mussolini, as well as many other details in this chapter, were reported in the Italian press in articles and interviews preserved in the files of the AMI in Amsterdam.
5. Quoted in *TES*, May 17, 1924. Further details concerning the society appeared in *TES*, November 29, 1924.
6. *TES*, April 4, 1925.
7. *TES*, March 13, 1926.
8. *TES*, June 16, 1926.
9. Elise Braun Barnett, "My Personal Contacts with Dottoressa Maria Montessori," unpublished manuscript.
10. The account of the activities of the Arbeitsgemeinschaft and the Vienna Montessori School as well as much of the material on the development of the Montessori movement in Vienna is based on "In Memory of Lili Peller," unpublished manuscript of a talk given by Emma N. Plank at a memorial meeting of Peller's friends and colleagues at the Waldorf Astoria Hotel in New York City on December 17, 1966, and on conversations with Mrs. Plank in New York in May of 1975, as well as on Elise Braun Barnett's unpublished memoir cited above, an interview by the author with Mrs. Barnett in New York on December 5, 1972, and an interview by the author with Maria H. Mills in New York on May 23, 1973.
11. *TES*, July 23, 1921.
12. Maria Mills, interview.
13. Plank, "In Memory of Lili Peller," pp. 3–4.
14. *Ibid.*, p. 4.
15. Much of the material on the Dutch Montessori activities in this and following chapters is based on Rosa Joosten-Chotzen, untitled article dealing with the history of the Montessori movement in Holland, *AMI Communications*, 1966, no. 3, pp. 17ff., on an unpublished manuscript by Mrs. Joosten on the history of the Amsterdam Montessori Society in the files of the AMI, and on various publications of the Dutch Montessori Society also in the AMI files in Amsterdam.

Notes

Chapter 19

1. *TES,* January 20, 1919.
2. *TES,* January 25, 1936.
3. *Teacher's World* (London), April 18, 1923.
4. Reported in *TES,* July 25, 1925.
5. R. J. Fynne, *Montessori and Her Inspirers* (London, 1924).
6. Reported in *TES,* February 16, 1924.
7. *TES,* February 7, 1925.
8. See Note 15, chapter 18.
9. Quoted in Standing, *Maria Montessori,* pp. 80–81.
10. *The Times* (London), March 30, 1927.
11. Quoted in *TES,* May 27, 1927.
12. See note 4, chapter 18.
13. Quoted in *TES,* June 11, 1927.
14. *The New York Times,* December 19, 1927.
15. *The Times* (London), May 18, 1929.

Chapter 20

1. Maria Montessori, *The Discovery of the Child* (Madras, 1948), p. ix.
2. *Ibid.,* p. viii.
3. Edinburgh, November 1929.
4. *Teacher's World* (London), August 28, 1929.
5. Elise Braun Barnett, Interview.
6. *Ibid.*
7. Barnett, "My Personal Contacts with Dottoressa Maria Montessori," p. 4.
8. Barnett, Interview.
9. Barnett, "My Personal Contacts," p. 4.
10. Barnett, Interview.
11. *New York Herald* (Paris edition), October 25, 1929.
12. See Note 4, chapter 18.
13. *Glasgow Herald,* October 14, 1929.
14. Barnett, "My Personal Contacts," p. 4.
15. Barnett, Interview.
16. *Ibid.*
17. The material in the following pages is based on an interview with Catherine Pomeroy Collins in New York in May 1973.
18. Maccheroni, *A True Romance,* p. 102.
19. Barnett, "My Personal Contacts," p. 5.

Chapter 21

1. Ernst L. Freud, ed., *The Letters of Sigmund Freud* (New York, 1960), pp. 319–320.
2. Maria Mills, Interview.
3. Plank, "In Memory of Lili Peller," p. 7.
4. Quoted in Rudolf Ekstein, "Lili E. Peller's Psychoanalytic Contributions to Teaching," *Reiss-Davis Clinic Bulletin,* vol. 4, no. 1 (Spring 1967), pp. 6ff.
5. *Ibid.,* p. 7.
6. *The New York Times,* March 15, 1931.
7. Quoted in *TES,* January 16, 1932.
8. Quoted in *TES,* September 7, 1935.
9. *Ibid.*
10. I am indebted to Emma N. Plank for the information about the fate of the Montessori schools in Austria.

11. David Elkind discusses "Piaget and Montessori" in the *Harvard Educational Review* (Cambridge, Mass.), Fall 1967.

12. I interviewed Margaret Homfray in New York in July 1973.

Chapter 22

1. *TES*, August 8, 1936.
2. *Ibid.*
3. *The Times* (London), August 14, 1936.
4. *Ibid.*
5. Quoted in *TES*, August 22, 1936.
6. Quoted in *The New York Times,* July 26, 1936.
7. Quoted in *Time* Magazine, August 16, 1937.
8. Standing, *Maria Montessori*, p. 85.
9. Quoted in *The Times* (London), March 13, 1939.

Chapter 23

1. Much of the material on Montessori's activities in India was provided by K. Sankara Menon, Co-director of Kalakshetra in Madras, in a personal communication to the author, May 19, 1973. Another source of information about the years in India was Mario Montessori, "Impressions of India," *A-MI Communications*, 1968, no. 1/2 (January/February), pp. 12ff. In addition, clippings of articles from the Anglo-Indian press (in many cases without title of publication or date) preserved in scrapbooks in the AMI offices in Amsterdam also described various events during those years.
2. *The Times* (London), June 15, 1940.
3. "Centenary Anthology," p. 47.
4. Barnett, Interview.
5. Mills, Interview.
6. Lena Wickramaratne, "The Maria Montessori I Knew," *AMI Communications*, 1970, no. 2/3, pp. 7–9.
7. "Centenary Anthology," p. 49.
8. Barnett, Interview.
9. "Centenary Anthology," p. 19.
10. The material that follows is based on an interview with Margaret Homfray in New York in July 1973.
11. Mills, Interview.
12. Quoted in *The Times* (London), September 4, 1946.
13. Interview with Mother Isabel Eugenie, R.S., in Germantown, Pennsylvania, in May 1973.
14. "Centenary Anthology," p. 50.
15. Interview with Mario Montessori, Amsterdam, August 1973.
16. See Note 2, chapter 9.
17. *Time* Magazine, October 20, 1947.
18. "Centenary Anthology," p. 20 (my translation).
19. Maria Remiddi, "Vision of Mankind Transformed: Maria Montessori and Education for Peace," *The UNESCO Courier*, April 1964, p. 16.

Chapter 24

1. *TES*, April 21, 1950.
2. *Ibid.*
3. "Centenary Anthology," p. 57.
4. *Ibid.*, p. 56 (my translation).
5. Quotations from *TES*, May 11, 1951.

Notes

6. *Ibid.*
7. Geneva, 1951.
8. Quoted in a letter from Claude A. Clarement in *TES*, May 30, 1952.
9. Quoted in *TES*, June 9, 1923; also in Maccheroni, *A True Romance*, p. 42.
10. *TES*, May 18, 1951.
11. *Ibid.*
12. *The Evening Standard* (London), December 5, 1951.
13. *The Times* (London), May 7, 1952.
14. Extracts from the will left by Maria Montessori appeared in *AMI Communications*, 1953, no. 1/2 (January/February) [my translation].

INDEX

Index